09

)0

Strategies for Sustainable Architecture

First published 2006
by Taylor & Francis

2 Park Square, Milton Park, Abingdon,
Oxon OX14 4RN

Simultaneously published in the USA and Canada
by Taylor & Francis Inc
270 Madison Avenue, New York, NY10016

Taylor & Francis is an imprint of the
Taylor & Francis Group, an informa business

© 2006 Paola Sassi

Typeset in Univers and Bembo

Designed and typeset by Gavin Ambrose

Printed and bound in Great Britain by
the Alden Press, Oxford

British Library Cataloguing in Publication Data
A catalogue record for this book is available from the
British Library

Library of Congress Cataloging in Publication Data
A catalog record for this book has been requested

ISBN10: 0-415-34142-6 (pbk)
ISBN10: 0-203-48010-4 (ebk)

ISBN13: 978-0-415-34142-4 (pbk)
ISBN13: 978-0-203-48010-6 (ebk)

Contents

Introduction

Introduction

0.1 Sustainability

Sustainable development is development that meets the needs of the present without compromising the ability of future generations to meet their own needs.
Our Common Future
Brundtland *et al.* 1987

Conditions for society to meet in order to achieve sustainability:

– *Its rates of use of renewable resources do not exceed their rates of regeneration.*

– *Its rates of use of non-renewable resources do not exceed the rate at which sustainable substitutes are developed.*

– *Its rates of pollution emissions do not exceed the assimilative capacity of the environment.*
Steady State Economics
Daly,1991

The North has to understand that sustainable development worldwide simply will not happen unless and until the North itself learns to live with far smaller per capita rates of resource consumption. This is why we see Factor Four (in the North) as a target for and a prerequisite of sustainable development.
Factor Four
Von Weizsacker *et al.* 1998

Sustainable development is about ensuring a better quality of life for everyone, now and for generations to come. This requires meeting four key objectives at the same time in the UK and the world as a whole:

– *social progress which recognises the needs of everyone;*

– *effective protection of the environment;*

– *prudent use of natural resources; and*

– *maintenance of high and stable levels of economic growth and employment.*
Achieving a Better Quality of Life
DEFRA 2002

Anyone involved in building design, procurement or maintenance in recent years will have been confronted in one way or another by the term *sustainability*. The term remains elusive to many, and while a number of definitions exist, they give little indication of how to apply principles of sustainability in practice. Moreover, these definitions differ slightly, one from another, and in any attempt to implement sustainable development it is essential that the meaning of sustainability be understood. It is generally agreed that sustainability fundamentally affects the way we live; consequently, personal ethics will influence the way an individual interprets its aims. Like architecture as a whole, sustainability involves addressing a wide spectrum of issues, sometimes, seemingly, conflicting ones. Acquiring a basic knowledge of these issues is the first step towards establishing or clarifying personal values and moving towards a more sustainable future. *Strategies for Sustainable Architecture* aims to contribute to this process.

This book illustrates many different approaches adopted by building designers and developers that all achieve some level of sustainability. The case studies examined focus on different issues within the wide spectrum of sustainable design. Perhaps one common ingredient in all the different approaches taken is the wish to provide better buildings, buildings that are better for the environment, the users and the community.

This publication is designed to provide basic theoretical and practical information about sustainable design to help the reader formulate a personal approach to sustainability, and make more informed decisions with respect to sustainable architectural design. The case studies show how sustainable design principles have been implemented, offer practical support and provide confidence to those who would like to replicate particular design strategies. Clearly, not all existing technical solutions can be described here, nor can more than basic details be included; therefore, each section includes references, which point the reader to further sources of useful and relevant information.

This book demonstrates that sustainable design is feasible and that much has already been done. Thousands of completed buildings have addressed sustainability in one way or other and many more are on the drawing boards, despite the fact that sustainable designers are still struggling with issues of lack of awareness among clients, authorities and the public; the potential for higher costs; and difficulties in complying with legislation and standards. The challenge for the future is to address sustainability in a holistic rather than a piecemeal fashion. In many of the case studies included here, a holistic approach was hampered by the barriers mentioned above, yet in a few cases a comprehensive approach was possible: large-scale issues, including land use, local ecology and community issues, were addressed simultaneously with issues relating to the building's inhabitants and the use of resources.

This book advocates such a comprehensive approach and is structured to cover six main areas relating to sustainable design. Chapter 1 introduces large-scale issues of land use and the ecology of the building site and its surroundings. It considers the effects of architecture on the immediate physical and social environment, as well as its connections to the broader urban, rural and global context. Chapter 2 considers the social implications of architecture and how buildings can help to create viable communities and enhance people's quality of life. Chapter 3 addresses both physical and mental human well-being, and considers issues of comfort, indoor air pollution and other health-related building design issues. Chapters 4, 5 and 6 deal with the use of resources to build and operate buildings, covering materials, energy and water. Appendix 1 lists the case study buildings and their sustainable design features. Appendices 2 and 3 also include weather data and location maps of the case study buildings.

Sustainability, why bother?

Species of plants and animals are disappearing a hundred or more times faster than before the coming of humanity, and as many as half may be gone by the end of this century. An Armageddon is approaching at the beginning of the third millennium. But it is not the cosmic war and fiery collapse of mankind foretold in sacred scripture. It is the wreckage of the planet by an exuberantly plentiful and ingenious humanity.

(Wilson 2002)

In his book *The Future of Life*, Edward O. Wilson describes the state of our planet and the pressures imposed by human activity on the environment: human-induced global warming, pollution, deforestation, habitat destruction and resource depletion are contributing to an environmental crisis which is threatening the survival of many species, including the human species. Wilson warns against a human attitude that considers itself separate from its environment. He points out that humans are not aliens that colonised the Earth, but have evolved on Earth as one of millions of species. Importantly, '[the] natural environment we treat with such unnecessary ignorance and recklessness was our cradle and nursery, our school, and remains our one and only home' (ibid.).

It is not only the nature of human activities that threatens the environment, but also their increasing occurrence. Currently up to two billion humans, without reliable access to safe food, urgently require resources to cover their basic needs, while several billions more are rapidly increasing their resource use to improve their living standards. Compounding this, the global population is growing: currently at 6.2 billion, it is expected to stabilise at around 9 billion by the end of the century (Whitaker 2004). Ninety per cent of this population growth is expected to take place in developing countries. Population growth and the raising of low living standards will require more resources, produce more waste and increase the impact on the natural environment.

The principles of sustainability aim to address the problems of environmental degradation and lack of human equality and quality of life, by supporting development that is sustainable in economic and social terms and is capable of retaining the benefits of a healthy stable environment in the long term.

0.2 Main environmental issues

Global warming Global warming describes the process by which greenhouse gases accumulate in the atmosphere in abnormally high amounts, trapping the Earth's radiation and causing its temperature to rise significantly. This is linked to environmental problems such as changes in rainfall patterns, rising sea levels and expansion of deserts.

Pollution Pollution of air, water and land, resulting from burning of fossil fuels, industrial processes, agriculture, and other human activities, is endangering human health, biodiversity and the built environment.

Ozone depletion Ozone shields the Earth from ultraviolet (UV) radiation and its depletion is caused by emissions of chlorofluorocarbons (CFCs) and other ozone-depleting substances into the atmosphere. Increases in UV radiation are thought to be linked to a rise in skin cancers, damage to the human immune system, and altered crop yields.

Water A third of the world population is still without access to safe water and, as the global population grows, the need for water will grow, as will waste and pollution which will increasingly threaten the quality of groundwater and rivers.

Resources Some non-renewable resources, including natural gas and petroleum resources, will eventually be depleted. The economically viable extraction of some abundant mineral ores may also be limited. Renewable resources, such as timber, are also at risk of over-exploitation.

Deforestation Deforestation through commercial logging, conversion of forest land to agricultural use, and other activities causes the destruction of natural habitats and extinction of plant and animal species and exacerbates the effects of global warming and pollution.

Soil degradation Urbanisation, construction, mining, war, agriculture and deforestation can cause soil degradation. Soil erosion, increased salination, altered soil structure, drainage capacity and fertilisation can diminish crop yields, increase the risk of flooding and destroy natural habitats.

Waste Increasing amounts of waste add pressure for more landfill sites, which pollute air, soil and groundwater and for more incineration, which pollutes the air and produces generally toxic residue.

Extinction of flora and fauna The current mass extinction rates of plant and animal species are the culmination of the environmental damage to our planet.

Population Global population growth is associated with increases in the human-induced environmental impacts mentioned above.

However, thinking about and applying sustainable principles are not easily done. Sustainable thinking goes against our primitive instinct of putting ourselves before others in the fight for survival. It rationally prioritises globally favourable long-term solutions over short-term individual gains; it is, therefore, in contrast to the most primitive survival instincts, which remain powerful despite no longer having a rational basis in today's developed countries. Sustainable thinking, which is altruistic and long term, requires reasoned and sophisticated thought processes that involve high levels of abstraction and are underpinned by an understanding of complex interconnecting networks.

Sustainability, therefore, necessitates a contemporary way of thinking. It requires the scrutiny of traditional values and economic measures and a definition or perhaps a redefinition of *quality of life*. Questioning values that are often culturally determined is challenging, and perhaps for this reason definitions of sustainability remain open to interpretation. As part of the process of reviewing values and ethics with respect to sustainability, it is essential to consider their development.

The roots of sustainability, as currently defined, lie in the environmental movement of the 1960s and 1970s, which built upon an increasing consciousness of the link between living beings and their environment dating back to the 1800s. From the 1960s to the present, a growing number of scientific publications have supported the notion that current (and historic) human activities are affecting the environment. Furthermore, changes to the environment are affecting all species on the planet, including humans.

Why should human-generated changes to the environment matter? Do humans need the environment to survive? Does the environment have 'rights'? The responses to these questions range from the technocratic anthropocentric to the non-anthropocentric, reflecting opposing views of the place of humans within the environment. The anthropocentric view believes that nature exists for the benefit of humans and that when a choice has to be made between human and environmental interests, human interests should always be put first. The non-anthropocentric views put sentient beings, living beings and nature as a whole on equal standing, deserving equal priority. Somewhere in between these two extremes are many shades of green, including the mixed theorists, who put human life, but not other human benefits before environmental welfare (Shrader-Frechette 2003)

At the technocratic anthropocentric extreme lies the belief that technology will resolve any environmental challenges and problems, whether they result from human activities or not (many sceptics still deny any human responsibility for the current environmental crises, such as global warming). Pre-emptive action to protect the environment is not only unnecessary, but detrimental to current economies and, consequently, to human well-being.

An anthropocentric view with less confidence in technology reacts in a similar way to the technocrat, but adopts a slightly more cautious approach. An anthropocentric approach may include wanting to know if the destruction of the environment will affect humans and, if so, how. If nature does provide humans with benefits, it may be important to control changes that can affect nature's ability to contribute to humans' well-being. Nature does in fact provide humans with physical and psychological life support. The 'goods and services' provided by nature include:

- Provision of food, fuel and fibre
- Provision of shelter and building material
- Purification of air and water
- Detoxification and decomposition of wastes
- Stabilisation and moderation of the Earth's climate
- Moderation of floods, droughts, temperature extremes and wind forces
- Generation and renewal of soil fertility, including nutrient cycles
- Pollination of plants, including many crops
- Control of pests and diseases
- Maintenance of genetic resources as key inputs to crop varieties and livestock breeds, medicines and other products
- Cultural and aesthetic benefits
- Ability to adapt and change
 (Convention on Biological Diversity 1992)

In monetary terms, nature is thought to contribute globally the equivalent of $33 trillion or more each year, nearly twice the world's gross national product of $18 trillion (Girardet 2004). Ecological economists believe that it would be physically impossible for humans to replace all the services nature provides, even if they wanted to, as the rise in value (and therefore cost) of nature's services rises sharply as their availability decreases. Consequently, a cautious anthropocentric viewpoint may aim to protect the environment so that humans can continue to benefit from it.

In opposition to a view that values nature only for its ability to satisfy human needs, is the non-anthropocentric view, which perceives the value of nature as intrinsic to all life on Earth. This approach sees humans as part of nature and dependent upon nature; their intelligence does not give them rights, but rather the responsibility of stewardship. The non-anthropocentric view is becoming more prominent, manifesting itself in a growing membership of and political power exerted by pressure groups ranging from animal rights to forest preservation organisations. While believing a flower has the same rights as a human may seem radical, it simply represents one extreme of a sliding scale of values that is constantly shifting. Historically, the Western world accepted the view that slaves were inferior beings; now, this is unthinkable. Today, we know that dolphins communicate with one another, we know that animals suffer stress, we know of numerous animals that use tools and others that mate for life. In future, as we understand more about animal behaviour, we may all come to accept some or all animals as being equal to humans and deserving of equal rights. The non-anthropocentric view, driven by the belief that nature has intrinsic value, therefore, not only advocates taking action to

1995 The Intergovernmental Panel on Climate Change concludes that 'The balance of evidence suggests that there is a discernible human influence on global climate.'

1996 The Habitat II Conference focuses on sustainability in the city in view of the increasing urban population and trends towards a predominantly urban population.

1997 *Factor Four,* a report by Von Weizsacker *et al.* for the Club of Rome, illustrates how current technology can produce four times the efficiencies typical at the time and advocates environmental taxing.

1997 Kyoto Summit for Climate Change – terms for an international legally binding protocol to reduce greenhouse gas emissions are negotiated.

1999 *Natural Capitalism* by Paul Hawken puts forward and illustrates the concept of nature's value.

1999 The world population exceeds 6 billion, half live in cities, 2.8 billion live below the poverty line.

1999 The Worldwatch Institute reports that 7 out of 10 scientists believe the world is undergoing the greatest mass extinction of species in history.

2001 The EU's Sustainable Development Strategy is agreed in Gothenburg.

2001 The Bonn Agreement – 189 countries adopt the Kyoto Protocol. Despite scientific advice for a reduction of 60–80 per cent of greenhouse gases by the 37 more developed countries, the 189 signatory nations agree to reduce greenhouse gases by 8 per cent of 1990 levels by 2010, whereby industrialised countries will set higher targets to allow developing countries to develop. Annually £350 million is to be provided by developed countries to developing ones. Nations can claim credits by increasing CO_2 sinks, such as woodlands which absorb CO_2.

2002 The World Summit on Sustainable Development in Johannesburg is regarded as unsatisfactory by environmentalists, but does set a number of goals including that for reducing by half the number (2.4 billion) of people without sanitation, and halting the decline of fish stocks by 2015.

2002 Monterrey Conference on Financing for Development – international agreement to increase the volume and effectiveness of international aid.

2004 Russia ratifies the Kyoto Protocol.

2004 Scientists warn that global warming is happening at a faster rate than previously believed.

2005 The Kyoto Protocol comes into force, but the US (the biggest CO_2 polluter in the world) and Australia think it is too expensive and have not signed up.

0.4 The value of nature

Services in water supply and drainage
In 1997, the city of New York faced the fact that the water from the Catskill Mountains, which they had been drinking for generations and which used to be exceptionally clean, was now polluted. The pollution had come about as a result of the reduction of watershed forest to make room for farms, houses and resorts for the increasing population in the area and the increase in sewage and agricultural run-off. To clean the water the city had two choices: reinstate the watershed area or build a new filtration plant. The new filtration plant would have cost between $6 and $8 billion to build and $300 million to maintain yearly. Reinstating the watershed forest cost $1 billion and had minimal subsequent running costs. The city upgraded septic tanks in the Catskill area and purchased and maintained forest area, which helped filter the water and at the same time provided a leisure area for the local population.
(Wilson 2002)

Services in provision of medicine
Three thousand plants are known to have some medicinal properties and 75 per cent are in the tropical rainforests. Only 4 per cent of tropical plants have been analysed for their medicinal properties.
(Bush 1997)

address environmental problems, but accepts the possible need to compromise human quality of life to prevent environmental degradation.

A truly non-anthropocentric approach is, in practice, rare. Perhaps nature conservation organisations that invest time and money towards saving and protecting natural environments are the closest examples of a non-anthropocentric approach. In reality, most humans would put human survival before that of nature, and many would put human well-being before nature's survival.

As mentioned earlier, addressing sustainability requires in the first instance the formulation of a personal position regarding the relation of humans to the natural environment. Only then can one attempt to turn principles into actions. However, while establishing a position on the issue may be difficult enough, implementing one's theoretical views in practice is even more difficult. Whether adopting a person-, quality-of-life- or nature-focused approach, the translation of a personal philosophy into practice comes up against practical issues that can be difficult to consolidate.

It is unrealistic, for instance, to expect loggers struggling to feed their families in the central African rainforest to see the advantage of conserving the forest, even if the environmental facts are made clear. Faced with starvation, most individuals would instinctively place their survival before nature's, even if unwittingly they may be compromising their own distant future.

As mentioned earlier, sustainability thinking goes against our primitive instinct for immediate survival. A significant problem the world faces today is that too many people are still struggling to survive and do not have the education or financial means to consider environmental issues at all. There is immense inequality between developed and developing countries: developed countries, on the whole, enjoy provision for health, employment, education and an average gross national product hundreds of times greater than that of some developing countries, while elsewhere in the world 1.1 billion people lack access to clean water and 2.4 billion lack adequate sanitation (Worldwatch 2003). While the media brings us news of the launch of Richard Branson's Virgin space travel service for individuals with £100,000 to spend for a few hours of entertainment, over 800 million people globally are chronically malnourished. Addressing such deprivation and inequality must be a priority for the global community if individuals in developing nations are to be able to consider environmental issues. Developed countries have a major role to play in this respect, particularly since the high debt repayments they require of developing nations divert funds from basic services. In Zambia, for example, 30 per cent of the yearly budget in the 1990s was used for debt repayments while only 10 per cent went to social services (ibid.).

Given their advantageous economic position, developed countries must lead the drive for sustainability and substitute a single-minded focus on economic growth with a balanced concern for sustainable growth and environmental stability. Such an approach, however, is hampered by pressure groups lobbying against environmental improvements for fear that they will affect company profits. For example, house-builders in the United

Strategies for Sustainable Architecture

Paola Sassi

Taylor & Francis

Taylor & Francis Group

Acknowledgements

I would like to thank all the architects, building occupants, and owners who showed me around their buildings, helped me compile the information for the case studies and kept my enthusiasm alive throughout the project. I am very grateful to Alessandra Cavalli, Paul Chamberlain, Allison Dutoit, Julie Gwilliam and Enrico Sassi for taking the time to review chapters and provide technical guidance. Special thanks to Adam Sharr and my sister, Egle Sassi, who read the whole manuscript commenting from the point of view of an architect and lay person respectively. Thanks also to Caroline Mallinder for her excellent advice and enthusiasm and Katherine Morton for all her help and patience.

Kingdom, concerned with safeguarding their interests, have lobbied for years against increases in the required thermal properties of houses, obstructing attempts to reduce carbon dioxide emissions from buildings. The reality is that even educated people, who enjoy comfortable lives, will address immediate and personal interests before long-term communal or environmental interests. This has led to a complex approach to addressing environmental issues. Today the UK government recognises the need for 'reconciling aspirations for social progress, economic development, protection of the environment and conservation of natural resources, and the integration of these into decision-making, so that progress in one does not adversely affect another' (DEFRA 2004a).

The current government approach to sustainability, while reflecting an understanding that both environmental health and social inequalities need to be addressed, pragmatically accepts the reality of human behaviour, which makes a socially stable and economically prosperous environment a prerequisite to environmental improvements. The concept of sustainability now embraces a triple bottom line that addresses social, economic and environmental sustainability concurrently. Social and economic issues are considered of equal importance to environmental issues, despite the fact that many perceive any further deterioration of the environment ultimately as negatively affecting the social and economic well-being of the global population. The current approach and the most used definition of sustainable development – 'development that meets the needs of the present without compromising the ability of future generations to meet their own needs' (Brundtland 1987) – reflect a deeply anthropocentric position, and while purporting to consider long-term impacts, the focus on human interests may, in fact, prove short-sighted.

For most individuals, embracing principles of sustainability, whether adopting an anthropocentric or non-anthropocentric approach, requires a major ethical shift. One of the key concepts of sustainability is equity: equity between all people around the world living today, and also equity between people living today and people living in the future. In addition, a non-anthropocentric approach extends the concept of equity to all species and nature. Embracing the concept of equity requires refocusing away from personal benefits onto the needs and interests of others. Achieving the ambitious goals of sustainability requires a realism that recognises the limitations of humans, but also recognises the urgent need to embrace a different life philosophy. 'If sustainability is to be achieved, the ethics and values that support it will be just as important as scientific and technological advance' (Parkin et al. 2004).

Society has to recognise that, in developed countries, economic growth is no longer inextricably linked to increased well-being (Daly and Cobb 1989; Max-Neef 1995; Layard 2005). This is in contrast to developing countries where an increase in economic wealth is still essential to provide a basic standard of living to nearly a third of the world population. Once a basic quality of life is achieved, the benefits of economic growth begin to decline: quality of life and happiness are not perceived to increase with rising economic wealth. In developed countries, economic wealth, often perceived as a

0.5 Environmental impacts associated with the construction, use and disposal of buildings in the UK

- Buildings are responsible for 50 per cent of primary energy consumption
- Buildings account for 25 per cent of sulphur and nitrogen oxide emissions and 10 per cent of methane emissions
- In 1997, the construction industry was responsible for 16 per cent of the water pollution incidents in England and Wales
- Construction work on site is responsible for 4.7 per cent of noise complaints
- 6 tonnes of materials per person are used for construction
- 30 million tonnes per year of excavated soil/clay waste are estimated to arise from construction site preparation
- 30 million tonnes of waste arise from demolition work each year
  (Howard 2000)

0.6 Action for the construction industry

The Department of Trade and Industry's *Sustainable Construction Brief* suggests the following themes for action for the construction industry:

- design for minimum waste
- lean construction and minimise waste
- minimise energy in construction and use
- do not pollute
- preserve and enhance biodiversity
- conserve water resources
- respect people and local environment
- monitor and report
  (DTI 2004)

0.7 Addressing sustainable design

Issues to consider taken from the Royal Institute of British Architects' Key Indicators for Sustainability Design and the RIBA Environmental Checklist for Development and grouped according to the structure of this book.

Issues to be recommended for consideration:

Land and ecology
- use of brownfield sites
- reuse of existing buildings
- appropriate density
- investment in landscaping
- public transport
- new pedestrian routes
- effects on micro-climates

Community
- consultation with the local community
- mixed development
- contribution to the economic and social well-being of the community
- amenity of the wider area
- visual amenity space
- aesthetic excellence
- collaborative enterprise involving all the design professions

Health
- comfort for building inhabitants
- maximum use of natural light

Materials
- conservation of natural resources
- use of recycled materials
- low embodied energy materials
- renewable materials from a verifiable source
- no ozone-depleting chemicals
- no volatile organic compound materials

Energy
- highest standards of energy efficiency
- renewable energy sources
- use of natural ventilation
- use of passive solar energy
- user-friendly building management systems
- exploiting the constant ground temperature
- use of planting for shading and cooling

Water
- efficient use of water
- harvesting rainwater and greywater
- minimising rainwater run-off

measure of personal success, has failed to provide increased happiness: individuals, particularly in the US, are no happier now than they were in the 1950s, despite relative wealth having greatly increased (Layard 2005). It can be argued that concepts of progress and quality of life urgently need to be redefined; indeed, the consumerist society needs to reinvent itself. Non-materialistic, socially- and nature-oriented values of sustainability could form the basis for a new ethics.

Given the above, working towards sustainability may appear to be an overwhelmingly daunting task and individuals may be tempted to question their own potential for contributing to the goal. To answer such concerns, one must look at environmental history. Change has been slow and fraught with compromise. Sometimes it has been driven by unrealistic idealism that pushed the agenda of sustainability well beyond its pragmatic possibilities. Nevertheless, change has taken place, and it is primarily because of individuals deciding to go it alone or at least go against the tide that today we have a wealth of examples of sustainable ways of life and sustainable buildings. Many individual small steps have together created big changes. No matter how seemingly isolated a contribution may appear, it can add to a growing mass that will eventually become large enough to alter mainstream thinking and practice.

Sustainable building design

As suggested above, sustainability is not an academic pursuit or even a professional activity: it is a way of life affecting everything an individual does. Knowing what kind of a relationship we want to have with the global and local environment is the first consideration. Then we should address how to achieve this relationship. To move from theory into practice it is necessary to understand the impacts associated with our work- and life-related activities.

Buildings, their construction, use and disposal, have a significant impact on the natural environment and social fabric of our society. Sustainable architecture can help put into practice and even encourage a sustainable way of life. But how can buildings be designed and built to contribute positively to the sustainability agenda, to achieve economically strong, socially inclusive, stable communities while minimising the impact on the environment? There are perhaps two main aims for sustainable architectural design.

- First, sustainable buildings should metaphorically 'tread lightly on the Earth' by minimising the environmental impacts associated with their construction, their life in use and at the end of their life. Sustainable buildings should have small ecological footprints (discussed in Chapter 1).

– Second, buildings should make a positive and appropriate contribution to the social environment they inhabit, by addressing people's practical needs while enhancing their surrounding environment and their psychological and physical well-being.

The above are neither optional nor mutually exclusive. It is not a question of addressing one or the other point, but both. No matter how energy- and water-efficient a building might be, it becomes a waste of resources and a potential detriment to the community if no one wants to occupy it. Also, making a positive contribution to the community environment means addressing more than just practical requirements, it means addressing the aesthetic and psychological needs of people. Buildings that are loved become part of the community's own culture, have long lives and are economically sustainable. The concept of economic sustainability is well understood among architects: successful buildings make money, sell quickly, command more rent, have long lives or help induce the regeneration of an area. Sustainable buildings are those that can be an asset for many years to come.

Buildings have potential lives spanning hundreds of years. What is being built now could affect the next ten generations. Not to build for maximum energy, water, materials and waste efficiency is to place an unacceptable burden on future generations.

Sustainable technologies are available, sustainable design strategies have been implemented, and studies have proved that these approaches can contribute positively to reducing the ecological footprint of a society. There aren't any practical or ethical reasons for not designing and building sustainable buildings. The case studies in this book show that it is feasible to create architecture that is socially responsible and desirable, economically viable in the long term, and that respects and protects the environment.

0.8 Further reading

The Ethics of the Global Environment
Attfield, R. (1999) Edinburgh University Press, Edinburgh

The Human Impact on the Natural Environment
Goudie, A. (2000) Blackwell Publishers, Oxford

Happiness: Lessons from a New Science
Layard, R. (2005) Penguin Books Ltd, London

The Sixth Extinction
Leakey, R. (1996) Phoenix Press, London

Our Changing Planet
Mackenzie, F. (1998) Prentice-Hall, Upper Saddle River, NJ

The Future of Life
Wilson, E. (2002) Abacus, London

Worldwatch Institute publications including:

Vital Signs
Worldwatch Institute W. W. Norton and Co, New York

Chapter 1
Site and Land Use

1.0 Introduction

1.0.1 A sustainable site and land use

Select the development site with care

- Select sites with public transport facilities
- Select sites with existing or potential links for pedestrians and cyclists
- Select sites with low ecological value
- Select sites, the development of which would benefit the community

Use land efficiently

- Consider the needs of the community
- Create viable and attractive developments
- Consider mixed use developments
- Design to appropriately high densities
- Build on previously used and derelict land

Minimise impact of development

- Protect local natural habitats
- Enhance existing and introduce new planting
- Enhance potential for pedestrians and cyclists
- Include food production opportunities where possible

Land is one of the Earth's most precious resources, not only because it provides space for human inhabitation, but because it provides many of the resources required to enable human activities and to absorb the waste from these activities. Land is also essential to support the life of plant and animal species other than humans. While some plant and animal species can live together with humans in an environment structured to suit human requirements, many cannot.

Historically, humans have had significant impact on the nature of the land and the flora and fauna supported by it. Activities such as agriculture, mining, forestry and urbanisation have changed the landscape from, for example, grassland to desert, or forest to agricultural land. Such changes can be catastrophic for the flora and fauna dependent on these habitats. Moreover, as illustrated in the previous chapter, changes to the land can compromise its ability to provide useful services that benefit humans. As human impacts on the land increase, the land suitable to support species of flora and fauna, to absorb pollution and waste, to support farming, and to provide humans with material resources and natural environments for leisure steadily decreases.

This chapter focuses on the local impacts of the handling of development sites and considers the associated global impacts. It illustrates ways to use land efficiently, ways to minimise the encroachment onto natural ecosystems, and ways to develop new and enhance existing ecosystems.

The 'ecological footprint'

Considering the impact of buildings beyond their outline is the first step towards a sustainable architecture. The selection and use of a development site affect a number of sustainability issues, including land use, the conservation of natural ecologies, flora and fauna, and the provision of natural spaces to enhance human well-being.

Land is a limited resource used in a variety of ways: it may be built on, covered by roads, forests or other plants, it may remain barren or be used for agriculture. Land uses vary from country to country. While globally 11 per cent of the land is used for agriculture, in the US it is approximately 20 per cent, in the UK 25 per cent, in Australia 7 per cent, in Germany 35 per cent, in Austria 18 per cent and in Switzerland 11 per cent (FAO 2005). In agricultural-based economies the percentage is far higher. In India, for example, approximately 50 per cent of the land is used for agriculture. Land uses depend on the nature of the land, the economy and culture of the country and the population. In environmental terms, what counts is how much land is required to sustain life, including that of humans and of other species.

The ecological footprint is a way to address this question. This concept, developed by William Rees and Mathis Wackernagel, is a measure of the amount of land required to sustain human activities, in the long term, by providing food, water, energy and materials and by assimilating waste. The ecological footprint can be used to calculate the land requirements of a population, building or activity.

For example, using this system, it was calculated that to sustain the average US lifestyle an area of 9.6 hectare is required. The typical European's ecological footprint ranges between 3–6 hectare and that of the average Indian is 1 hectare. The ecological footprint of the total population of the US is well in excess of the country's total land area. Even considering populations with low ecological footprints, such as that of India, the mere number of inhabitants means that the ecological footprint for that whole country is 50 per cent larger than the country's productive land area. Today most cities and several countries have ecological footprints that are larger than the land available to them, including the UK, with an ecological footprint three times its surface area (Chambers *et al.* 2000; Girardet 1999a).

The global ecological footprint is affected by the nature and the quantity of human activities. If the current world population of 6 billion were to adopt a lifestyle associated with a high ecological footprint of 5 hectare per person, three more Earth-like planets would be required. Population increases are equally detrimental as they are associated with a greater quantity of human activities. Ninety per cent of population increases are expected in developing countries, but this does not mean that population increases in developed countries are insignificant. The population of the US grows by 3 million per year and that of India by 16 million per year; however, as a result of the far higher consumption rates of the US, the 3 million Americans will be responsible for an additional 15.7 million tons of CO_2 emissions, while the 16 million Indians will be responsible for only 4.9 million tons of CO_2 emissions (Worldwatch 2004).

Current thinking is that the world is living beyond its means, using resources faster than they can regenerate and producing waste in larger amounts faster than can be assimilated naturally and without danger to the environment or to humans (Meadows *et al.* 1992).

If the global population, projected to rise to 9 billion by the end of the century, is to share a total global landmass of 14.9 billion hectare, of which 11.5 billion hectare is vegetated (excluding ice, rock and deserts), the average available vegetated land per person would be 1.3 hectare. Of the 11.5 billion hectare of vegetated land 1.9 billion have been degraded by human activities such as overgrazing and deforestation, thus leaving less than 1.1 hectare per person. Living within the limits of a sustainable and just global society would imply all world inhabitants adopting a lifestyle associated with an ecological footprint of a maximum of 1.1 hectare per person. This would necessitate a reduction in ecological footprints of 85-90 per cent for the average person in the US and 60-85 per cent for the average European. This ambitious goal is, however, necessary, as the Worldwatch research team concludes in their *State of the World 2004* publication: moving to a less consumptive society is fundamental to achieving a sustainable society.

Such a huge reduction is only, if at all, possible by addressing all aspects of human activity concurrently with the aim of reducing resource use and waste production. Methods for reducing resource use associated with architecture are discussed in Chapters 4, 5 and 6. While efforts to reduce resource use now benefit from new technologies,

1.0.2 Human impact on biodiversity

The rate of species extinction is considered to be catastrophically high. It is estimated to be between one thousand and ten thousand times the rate before the impact of humans on the environment became significant (Wilson 2002).

This high level of extinction represents what scientists believe to be the sixth period of mass extinction in the Earth's history. Previous extinctions, including the most recent Cretaceous extinction 65 million years ago, are thought to have been caused by cataclysmic occurrences such as the collision with an asteroid. This time the destruction is triggered by human activity (Leakey 1996).

The extinction of plants and animals as a result of human activities has a long history. Some 10,000 years before, present in America, 1,000 years ago in New Zealand and Madagascar, and similarly in Australia, the arrival of humans coincided with a steep decline and eventual extinction of large mammals and birds (Wilson 1994). These changes in the ecosystem would also have had repercussions on the survival of other species. An example of the interdependence of different species, including humans, can be seen on Easter Island. Settled by the Polynesians in 400 AD, over-harvesting of the palm trees on the island left the Polynesians without palms as a source of food or a means to build boats and hunt. Suffering from famine and war the Polynesians and the biodiversity of Easter Island failed to recover and by 1500 AD the Polynesians had died out (Bush 1997).

Today the threat to biodiversity comes from human activities involving the conversion of natural habitats into urban areas or areas for infrastructure, agriculture or mining; pollution that renders natural habitats inhospitable to native plants and animals; and directly through over-harvesting and poaching.

1.0.3 Assessing the level of environmental impacts

IPAT is a formula to assess environmental impact that considers factors that negatively affect the overall impacts as well as those that positively affect the impact.

Impact = population x affluence x technology

Where:

– the higher the population, the higher the impacts

– the higher the affluence, the higher the resource consumption and therefore the impacts

– the more developed the technology, the higher the efficiencies and the lower the environmental impacts (Phillips 2003)

1.0.4 Protecting the environment by reducing urban sprawl

The UK Department of the Environment, Trade and the Regions recognises the importance of protecting the natural environment from over-development. The publication *Our Towns and Cities: The Future. Delivering an Urban Renaissance* (DETR 2000a) sets out a recommended approach to the design and development of urban areas which:

– makes efficient use of the available land and buildings and reduces the demand for greenfield development

– provides homes that are attractive and environmentally friendly

– encourages well-laid out urban areas with good quality buildings, well-designed streets, and good quality public open spaces

– allows people to get to work easily and to the services they need like local shops, post offices, schools and health and leisure facilities

– makes good public transport viable and makes walking and cycling attractive options

which increase efficiencies and make use of alternative energy and water sources, assimilating waste still relies largely on natural land-based processes. The purification of water and the assimilation of carbon dioxide are two examples. Water is purified by the filtering mechanism of the earth, a mechanism that is compromised when the extent of natural landscapes is reduced and pollution increases. Carbon dioxide, the most significant greenhouse gas associated with global warming (see Chapter 5), is absorbed by growing plant matter. The continuing reduction of global forest cover is rapidly reducing the Earth's natural ability to counteract global warming. Reliance on dwindling land resources to assimilate an increasing amount of waste produced by a growing population is one of the reasons why waste production is seen by some researchers as more serious than resource depletion (Edwards and Du Plessis 2001).

In terms of land use, there is therefore a need to increase the area of land able to assimilate waste and pollution including areas to filter water, biodegrade waste and absorb carbon dioxide. Not only are natural systems for waste assimilation cost-effective in providing these services, but the same systems can also provide habitats for flora and fauna and natural environments for people to enjoy.

Despite the advantages of retaining natural environments, the trend is still one of increasing encroachment resulting from expanding urban developments and transport links. In the UK, 6,300 hectare, equivalent to an area of a small city, is urbanised each year (CPRE 2003). Such encroachment not only destroys the land's potential for providing useful services, but it also endangers biodiversity. While concerns regarding biodiversity often focus on equatorial regions with the highest numbers of different species, habitat loss occurs world-wide. In the UK since 1945, 97 per cent of wildflower meadows, 98 per cent of peatland raised bogs and 50 per cent of ancient woodlands, heaths, farm ponds, fenland and coastal marshes have been cleared. There are 1,666 wild species in the UK that are of environmental concern and 3,612 are endangered or rare (FOE 1997).

To counteract this trend it is vital to concentrate new developments in previously developed areas and avoid further encroachment on greenfield land. The UK government recommends making efficient use of land and encourages high density developments as part of its sustainable urban agenda. Chapter 1.1 discusses issues relevant to high density compact cities and the link between high density developments and reduced car dependence. Compact developments not only reduce land use by virtue of their more intense use of land, they also reduce the need for land for roads connecting developments. Research in the US has shown that, based on the same house sizes, dispersed low density developments can require twice as much road area as compact development and four times as much development land (Maurer 1998). Car use impacts on land use directly in terms of tarmacked areas, but also indirectly through the emissions of carbon dioxide and pollution that need to be assimilated by natural waste sinks. To reduce these impacts, sustainable development aims to reduce car dependence and offers a framework for a car-free existence with a high standard of living (see Chapter 1.2).

Avoiding encroachment on greenfield sites is fundamental to retaining natural ecosystems and the flora and fauna they support. Equally there is a need to reinstate lost habitats and generally increase the amount of land supporting natural ecosystems to counteract the rate of species extinction. Natural landscapes should not be restricted to rural areas and should be extended into urban environments. People need contact with nature and studies have shown that even individuals who are not interested in nature benefit physically from contact with it (see Chapter 4). As cities become home for the majority of people in the world, more natural environments need to be introduced into cities and existing landscaped areas must be enhanced and enlarged. Parks, planted corridors and landscaped streets as well as landscaping within individual developments can contribute to creating a green network in the city. Chapter 1.3 illustrates a number of developments that protect existing natural environments, enhancing and enlarging them or introducing new ones into an urban context. These planted areas need not only be decorative and absorb carbon dioxide; they can be designed as productive planted areas. Growing food within development sites combines the advantages of natural environments with a reduction in energy use for the preparation and transport of food. This is particularly relevant for cities, which are normally reliant on large land areas outside their own boundary for food production. Chapter 1.4 completes this chapter on land use with two examples where food production is integrated within building development.

1.0.5 Further reading

Green Urbanism
Beatley, T. (2000) Island Press, Washington DC

Sustainable Urban Design
Brophy *et al.* (2000) Energy Research Group, Dublin

Sharing Nature's Interest: Ecological Footprints as an Indicator of Sustainability
Chambers *et al.* (2000) Earthscan Publications Ltd, London

Planting Green Roofs and Living Walls
Dunnett, N., Kingsbury, N. (2004) Timber Press, Oregon

Sustainable Housing: Principles and Practice
Edwards, B., Turrent, D. (2000) E & FN Spon, London

Creating Sustainable Cities
Girardet, H. (1999) Green Books, Totnes

Building Green: A Guide to Using Plants on Roofs, Walls and Pavements
Johnston, J., Newton, J. (1997) London Ecology Unit, London

Sustainable Cities
Satterthwaite, D. ed. (1999) Earthscan, London

Our Ecological Footprint: Reducing Human Impact on Earth
Wackernagel, M., Rees, W. (1996) New Society Publishers, Gabriola Island, BC

1.1 Compact Cities

1.1.1 Characteristics of sustainable cities

– compact living

– mixed land uses

– public transport-oriented designs

– pedestrian-friendly streets

– well-defined public spaces

– integration of nature in developments

– developments based on walking and cycling distances (Lock 2000)

1.1.2 High density developments

Potential advantages

– efficient use of land

– protection of the natural landscape

– access to culture and leisure facilities

– access to commercial facilities

– employment opportunities

– access to transport

– potential for district heating

– efficient recycling

Potential disadvantages

– less space availability

– predominance of flats versus houses

– no parking and smaller roads

– small or no gardens

– reduced potential for food production

– loss of privacy

– higher levels of noise and pollution

– higher levels of crime

– higher levels of deprivation

At the end of the twentieth century nearly half of the global population was living in cities, and this figure is expected to rise to 60 per cent by 2030 (Girardet 2004). In many developed countries already more than two-thirds live in cities (Australia: 91 per cent; the UK: 90 per cent; Germany: 88 per cent; the US: 78 per cent; Austria: 68 per cent; Switzerland: 67 per cent) (World Bank 2004). Urban growth and economic growth are linked and research shows that city dwellers currently have higher consumption rates than rural dwellers, linked to their higher spending power. The high consumption levels and concentration of people in cities mean that the ecological footprint of many cities is often many times their own areas; that of London has been calculated to be 125 times its area of 159,000 hectare at nearly 20 million hectare (Girardet 1999a). As the current urbanisation trend persists, considering how to reduce the environmental and social impacts of cities is becoming ever more urgent. The compact city is believed to offer many opportunities to reduce some of these impacts and develop sustainable communities.

High population densities make services such as public transport, recycling and district heating more viable. Compact cities supported by the provision of public transport effectively reduce car dependence and research shows a link between urban density and transport fuel consumption. A comparison of European, Australian and US cities shows the five main Australian cities with average densities of up to 30 persons per hectare consume 30,000–45,000 MJ (MegaJoules) of transport fuel per year; US cities, which generally have similar low densities, consuming between 40,000 and 80,000 MJ of fuel per year; while European cities with densities varying from 50–125 persons per hectare consuming between 10,000 and 22,000 MJ of fuel per year (Newman and Kenworthy 1989). Overall energy use per capita is also reduced in compact cities where energy-efficient building forms, such as terraces or flats, predominate. A comparison of per capita carbon dioxide emissions from US and European cities, which on average proved to be 12,7 tonnes and 8.4 tonnes respectively, supports this view (Torrie 1993). The proximity of buildings not only reduces the amount of energy used, but also the extent and consequently the cost of infrastructure. District heating, for instance, becomes viable above densities of 40 dwellings per hectare. Other services such as recycling and community composting are also more economically viable at higher development densities.

Compact cites not only can provide efficient living and working settlement configurations, but can also offer a high standard of living. Cities, with their access to culture, leisure facilities, and employment, attract many people aspiring to a high quality of life. The prospect of employment also attracts people hoping for work, but who may fail to fulfil their aspirations. Unemployment is a cause of deprivation, stress and unhappiness, and statistics show cities to have higher levels of unemployment, poverty, graffiti, crime and, ultimately, a higher death rate compared to rural areas (DETR 2000a). While city living can prove very attractive, especially to those with sufficient financial means to enjoy what cities can offer, others are priced out of affluent areas or feel threatened by the potential of antisocial behaviour, no matter how low the risk of it occurring might be, and retreat to the suburbs or to the countryside. In the UK more people are moving out of cities than moving into cities. In depressed city neighbourhoods, buildings are abandoned, businesses fail and communities disintegrate.

To create sustainable cities, life has to be brought back into the city, not only to a privileged few, but to all social groups. Employment, housing, education, culture and leisure facilities should be available to all. Architecture can contribute to creating a framework for people to realise their ambitions within a viable community.

Appropriately high development densities help to create economically viable communities. However, developing to high densities without considering the social infrastructure is not enough. The outdated principle of zoning uses has been overtaken by the concept of mixed use, where working, leisure and living are as close as possible. The city becomes a configuration of small self-sufficient neighbourhoods linked by public transport, with the advantages of low car dependency, more leisure time, strong community feeling and a high quality of life. Such neighbourhoods can be sized to human scale and, as opposed to suburban sprawl, can provide many of the facilities required by residents within the neighbourhood, including shops, schools, transport and leisure facilities. The ultimate aim is to create communities where people will want to live in the longer term.

In countries with an already large urban population, sustainable development aims to increase the viability and improve the sustainability of existing cities. There is a need to repair the urban fabric and regenerate depressed areas, and create quality public spaces and more green areas that enhance people's health and quality of life. The first step should be to regenerate abandoned and derelict parts of the city. In England alone there are currently 58,000 hectare of brownfield land (see 1.1.3), that is not in use and which could be built on (DETR 2000a). This is enough to accommodate the 3.8 million new dwellings required in the UK by 2021 at a density of approximately 65 dwellings per hectare. By building on brownfield sites, which often add to an atmosphere of desolation, poverty and insecurity in a city, land is used efficiently, development densities are increased and whole neighbourhoods benefit.

The challenge for compact cities is to make the advantages of energy efficiency, independence from cars, access to employment, culture, leisure and green spaces outweigh potential disadvantages and dispel the prejudices many people still have. Compact cities do not need to compromise quality of life. On the contrary, they can provide a multitude of opportunities only available in agglomerations of people and activities.

1.1.3 Building on brownfield sites and contaminated land

Brownfield sites

Brownfield sites are previously used sites. Previous uses can include any type of built structure, including industrial uses associated with contamination (see below).

The UK government has set a target of 60 per cent of the new housing to be built on brownfield sites or provided by conversions by 2008. Despite these targets pressure groups such as the Council for the Protection of Rural England (CPRE) continue to express their concerns that too much urban sprawl is still taking place. Should the 3.8 million new dwellings be built at current average densities of 25 dwellings per hectare, an area larger than that of Greater London would be required. In 2003, a CPRE survey identified proposals for greenfield housing development which would cover an area of 35,000 hectare, the equivalent of Birmingham and Coventry combined. Consequently CPRE supports a higher target of 75 per cent of housing to be built on brownfield sites.

Using brownfield land is considered to have the following advantages:

– It reduces pressure on undeveloped land including greenfield sites.

– It raises densities, making better use of infrastructure and improving the viability of public transport.

– It assists social and economic regeneration.

– It enhances the appearance of towns.
  (DETR 1997)

Contaminated land

Contaminated land is defined as land representing a potential hazard to human health or the environment. Contaminated land arises as a result of past industrial and other polluting uses of a site. Contaminants that may have been left behind include oils, tars, heavy metals, organic compounds and soluble salts. Much of the contaminated land is located in urban areas, but rural mining, agricultural or waste disposal areas may also be contaminated.

As more brownfield sites are developed, the issue of contamination needs to be addressed. Brownfield sites that are contaminated require remediation before development can commence. Past examples of developments on contaminated land, that had not been suitably remediated, resulted in the residents suffering serious ill-health.

Case study: Appropriate high densities

The Point
Bristol, UK

Client: Crosby Special Projects
Architect: Feilden Clegg Bradley
Consultation: BDOR
Town planning: Chapman Warren
Services engineers: BME Partnership
Structural engineers: Clarke Bond Partnership
Landscape architect: Cooper Partnership
Quantity surveyor: Cyril Sweett
Main contractor: Skanska
Completed: 2002

The Point includes three-, four-, five- and six-storey blocks of flats.

The town houses and the top floor flats of the four-storey blocks have roof terraces with views over the river.

The Point is a city centre speculative housing development on the south side of the Bristol Harbourside regeneration area. It is an energy-efficient, high density development that addresses many of the prejudices against high density living, while also taking advantage of the benefits of its city centre location (see Chapter 1.2). The development includes 105 apartments and nine houses. The location on the River Avon provides residents with an attractive and quiet environment benefiting from relatively good air quality, which easily competes with the typical suburban environment. The development addresses the availability of indoor and outdoor space. The units have floor areas 25 per cent larger than typical developments in the UK. Each unit has an outdoor space: flats benefit from generous balconies or terraces and the houses have both a small garden and a roof terrace. Secure parking is provided in an underground car park and in overground garages. Unlike the typical car-oriented suburb, The Point has also succeeded in creating car-free outdoor areas where children can play safely and which everyone can enjoy.

The mix of dwelling types addresses the current need in the UK for single-person dwellings. By 2016, nearly 2.7 million new dwellings for single-person households are expected to be needed, representing 70 per cent of the total 3.8 million houses required. These single-person dwellings are expected to be a mixture of one-bedroom flats and larger units for those with higher disposable income, such as two- or even three-bedroom dwellings with a garden or alternative outdoor spaces. The Point's mixture of one-, two- and three-bedroom flats, all with generous terraces, responds to this demand.

In the UK development density can be measured in dwellings per hectare (dph), persons per hectare or habitable rooms per hectare (hrh) and can be gross or nett. Gross development densities relate to whole communities or cities and take into account the infrastructure, while nett densities relate to individual developments. Using dph as a measure does not necessarily give a clear indication of the nature of the development, as the size of a dwelling, which could be a one-bedroom flat or a five-bedroom house, is not taken into account; hrh gives a better idea of the massing of the development. However, as discussed in relation to single person households, it does not necessarily reflect the occupancy levels. In other countries different measures are used. In Germany and Austria, development densities can be defined as the ratio of built area to total development area. Recent housing schemes in Germany and Austria used a development density ratio of between 0.6 and 0.7 (see following case study).

	Density in dph	Density in people per hectare	Density in hrh	Comments
Broad acre, typical in areas of USA	2.5			
Garden City	15			
Average densities in rural England	22			
Average densities in UK 1997–2001 (4)	27	50-60		Supports a school/post office
Minimum density in areas designated for development in the Netherlands	33			
Minimum target for development in England set by UK government Planning Policy Guidance note 3 (Housing)	30			
Older UK suburbs (3)	35-40			Supports combined heat and power and bus services/ 50 dph is maximum density to ensure good solar access in the UK (2)
solarCity Linz, including infrastructure	40	100		
Higher development densities encouraged by UK government	40-50	100		
New development in Harlow, East London	45-80			
Victorian terraces, Hertfordshire (3)	80			
9% of UK population live in densities of 85+ dph	85			
London Bloomsbury and Regent's Park	100			
Greenwich Millennium Village with infrastructure	106			
The Point development in Bristol	114		400	500 persons per hectare is the maximum recommended density, 1000 persons per hectare is possible, but not advisable
Areas of San Francisco (3-storey houses with gardens and integrated garages) (3)	118	237-474		
Edinburgh centre	250		500	

1.1.5 Comparison of development densities – Newman 1999/Barton 2000 (2)/Hall 2001 (3)/ CPRE (4)

The Point has a density of 114 dwellings and 400 habitable rooms per hectare. This is substantially higher than current average development densities in the UK (27 dph), than older suburbs (30-40 dph) and higher than the UK government targets (30-50 dph). Similar densities of around 100 dph can be found in many city centres including some of the most desirable areas of San Francisco or London. The Point's development density is very high, yet appears appropriate in an environment with so much to offer. The character of the development is not one of crammed or impersonal housing, often associated with high density. The dwellings are grouped in apartment blocks, between four and six storeys high, and the treatment of the blocks gives each one an individual and human character.

Had the whole site been occupied by flats, such as those developed at The Point, a density of at least 130 dph could have been achieved, while if the site had been designed as terraced housing, a density of 40-50 dph could still easily have been achieved. The Point successfully illustrates how UK government targets can be achieved and surpassed with a variety of housing types, without compromising quality of living and creating a framework to support a sustainable lifestyle.

1.1.4 Sustainable design features

Site and ecology
The development was built on a brownfield site and forms part of a city regeneration programme in Bristol.

Community and culture
The local community was consulted during the design stage. Community facilities such as communal children's play area, shop and communal garden are included.

Health
The dwellings benefit from ample natural light and are easily heated.

Energy
The dwellings are well insulated, relatively airtight and heated efficiently. Perhaps the biggest problem to overcome on the project was the conflict between orienting the development towards the south for solar access and towards the north for views to the river.

All dwellings benefit from good natural light and views of the river and the surrounding city.

A children's play area is situated on the south side of the housing development.

See also: desirable city centre living **Chapter 1.2**

Case study: Comprehensive planning

solarCity
Pichling, Linz, Austria

Masterplan: Prof. Roland Rainer
Architects: Richard Rogers, Norman Foster,
Herzog+Partner, Martin Treberspurg, Schimek, Loudon,
Auer+Weber+Partner
Energy consultant: Norbert Kaiser
Landscape architect: Atelier Dreiseitl
Construction began: 2001
Completion: due 2005

The community and commercial centre, where the future
tram stop will be located, forms the heart of the new
neighbourhood. (Architects Auer+Weber+Partner)

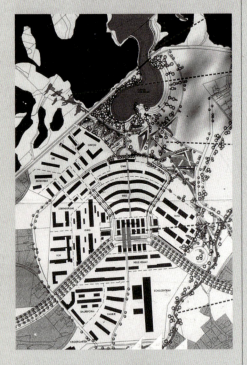

The commercial/community centre in the centre is
surrounded by housing. Green spaces and a lake are to the
north and the school is in the south-east section of the site.
A tree-lined boulevard connects to the development centre
from the southwest and southeast.

Designing for high density has to be part of a comprehensive approach to sustainable
design. A high density development should not be isolated from the services that people
need, including access to transport, work, and essential facilities such as grocery shops,
schools, leisure facilities and green spaces. Essential needs have to be accommodated in a
coordinated manner. Such a holistic approach was adopted by the planners for the
solarCity in Linz.

The idea for the solarCity came about in 1990 in response to a housing shortage in
the Linz region. In 1992, the city of Linz commissioned Professor Roland Rainer to
prepare a masterplan for the area of Pichling, located south of the city centre. The
development was to have a potential to accommodate 5,000–6,000 dwellings, and by
1995 the city of Linz had the commitment of 12 non-profit housing developers to
develop a first phase of 1317 mixed tenure dwellings on 32.5 hectare of land. The
development density is 40 dph, equivalent to 100 persons per hectare or 0.65 ratio of
built footprint to overall area. Construction began in 2001 and completion is due in
2005. Over a third of the construction cost (190 million euro) is associated with
development infrastructure including community facilities, transport network and
landscaping.

The solarCity is intended as a model of sustainable city development, the name
referring to the all-encompassing use of the sun, which ranges from providing passive
and active heating and electrical needs to contributing to human comfort and plant
growth. All buildings are low energy and the development addresses issues of occupant
health, women's needs (which focus on security and safety), sustainable water use and
drainage, community building and restoration of natural environments.

The houses are of mixed tenure with approximately half shared ownership, 40 per
cent for rent and the rest for purchase. Half of the dwellings are generously sized three-
bedroom flats or terraces, a quarter are two-bedroom and a quarter four-bedroom
dwellings. By 2005, fourteen fully accessible flats will be available for disabled individuals
together with a ten-person shared and supervised accommodation. Car parking is
underground, creating landscaped car-free spaces between terraces and children's play
areas with sandboxes, climbing frames and other games.

The development has been designed as a self-sufficient neighbourhood. At its centre
is a commercial and community centre, which includes general facilities (grocery shop,
bakery, medical centre, pharmacy, bank, citizens' advice office, hairdresser, bookshop,
tanning studio) as well as facilities for leisure activities (library, children's club, seniors'
club, adult college, café, restaurant). The centre building consists of timber- and glass-clad
blocks joined by glazed roofs, forming attractive all-weather covered streets.

A new school and nursery, which is already oversubscribed, are located on the south
side of the development and on the north side is a landscaped park that connects to a
nature reserve with a lake. A tram line is under construction that will link the solarCity
to the centre of Linz by the end of 2005. In the interim, bus and taxi services are in
operation. The tram stop at the commercial and community centre is designed to be no

more than approximately 300 metres from any of the houses, thus encouraging people to walk and use public transport rather than cars.

The holistic approach adopted on this project considered people's needs beyond the basic housing requirements and consequently provides a framework for a healthy and sustainable life with a high standard of living. Feedback was sought from new residents, who reported to be very satisfied with the development. Whether young or old, with or without family, the development seems to have universal appeal. The combination of low energy and healthy homes, the facilities and infrastructure that make cars dispensable, and the access to nature is clearly a successful solution to achieving a sustainable neighbourhood with a potential for a very long sustainable life.

1.1.6 Sustainable design features

Site and ecology
See Chapter 1.3.

Community and culture
The design involved a community consultation and provides help for people newly moved into the area. The community and commercial centre provides most facilities required by individuals.

Health
The scheme focuses on providing healthy indoor and outdoor environments through the use of healthy materials and access to natural sunlight as well as providing an accessible environment for disadvantaged people. See also Chapter 3.

Materials
A document listing preferred material specification is part of the building contract agreement (e.g. avoidance of polyvinylchloride (PVC), chlorofluorocarbons (CFCs) and preference for natural and local materials).

Energy
Levels of energy efficiency vary. Solar thermal collectors have to make up a minimum of 34 per cent of the roof area. District heating provides the rest of the heating requirements.

Water
See Chapter 6.3.

A play area is located near each housing block.

The seating in the internal street of the community and commercial centre.

The restaurant entrance in the centre.

The centre forms a square that accommodates a seating area for the café and restaurant. Facilities on the first floor are accessible via a lift.

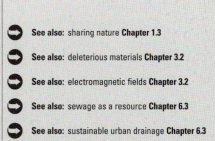

See also: sharing nature **Chapter 1.3**

See also: deleterious materials **Chapter 3.2**

See also: electromagnetic fields **Chapter 3.2**

See also: sewage as a resource **Chapter 6.3**

See also: sustainable urban drainage **Chapter 6.3**

1.2 Reducing Transport Impacts

1.2.1 The environmental impact of cars and other motorised transport

– Cars currently consume half the world's oil and create nearly one-fifth of its greenhouse gases.

(*Ethical Consumer*, Feb/March 1997)

– Motorised transport is responsible for a fourth of total greenhouse gases.

(Metz *et al.* 2001)

– Over 40 per cent of vehicle mileage is in built-up areas.

– Nearly half of airborne particle emissions arise in urban areas.

– 3,400 people die on the roads in the UK each year.

(DETR 2000a)

– More than 20 million people are severely injured or killed on the roads each year world-wide.

– 3,000 people die each day on the roads world-wide.

– In certain countries, such as Austria, France and Switzerland, pollution from vehicles causes twice the number of deaths than those caused by road accidents.

– Noise from traffic causes annoyance.

– The global economic cost of road crashes has been estimated at about $518 billion annually, of which the developing world shares $65 billion.
(WHO 2003a)

1.2.2 Reducing pollution by using alternative car technologies

Since 1950, annual car production has grown by 500 per cent. In 2002, there were 531 million cars in the world, of which one-quarter were in the US. However, while global annual car production is growing at approximately 2 per cent, in China the number of cars increased by 60 per cent in 2002 and by 80 per cent in 2003. Car use is not abating and a realistic approach to minimising the impacts of car use has to include the use of alternative, less-polluting technologies. Alternatives to fossil fuel-burning cars are commercially available and include:

– electric cars and electric hybrids

– liquid petroleum gas and natural gas cars

– biodiesel cars

– fuel cell cars

The impact of road-based transport is manifold, ranging from global warming to fragmentation of communities. The most urgent issue is currently global warming. Most vehicles run on fossil fuels, the burning of which is associated with global warming. Transport is responsible for approximately 26 per cent of CO_2 emissions in the UK (Howard 1995). In the US, road transportation accounts for half the oil consumption and one-third of CO_2 emissions (Hoffman 2001).

Vehicles are also responsible for environmental problems other than those concerned with global warming. Vehicle emissions pollute the local environment and are linked to increases in respiratory illnesses, particularly in cities. Transportation accounts for 77 per cent of CO emissions, 57 per cent of all NO emissions, 40 per cent of all volatile organic compound emissions, 73 per cent of atmospheric lead emissions, 51 per cent of black smoke and 28 per cent of particulate (PM10) emissions in the UK (Howard 2000). Vehicles are also smelly, noisy, dangerous and cause congestion. Road accidents cause more deaths than wars: in 2002, nearly seven times as many people were killed on the roads than as a result of armed conflict (WHO 2003a). Vehicle use is also associated with substantial land use. World-wide a third of urban land is allocated to car use (Southworth and BenJoseph 1997).

The dominance of cars has changed the way people live, reducing the extent to which people walk and have opportunities to meet neighbours, interact and develop closer communities. The convenience of the car has reduced the physical exercise people used to enjoy by walking to local facilities and to work; and the lack of exercise, combined with current eating habits, is contributing to high levels of cardiovascular disease, which is the cause of nearly 30 per cent of deaths globally (WHO 2003a). Developments built around the use of the car are also discriminatory against those who are too old, too young or unable to drive and those without access to a car.

A historic look at travel shows a trend for travelling more, faster and further than before and consuming increasing amounts of energy and space (Marshall 2001). This trend is not sustainable and changing it requires that alternative lifestyles, which are not dependent on car use, be made attractive and easily adopted.

At a strategic city level, reducing car dependency requires the provision of affordable and efficient public transport, including buses, trams, trains or underground; sufficiently high development densities that can support different types of public transport; and the integration of pleasant, sheltered and safe cycle and pedestrian ways in the streetscape (Newman 1999). Other effective methods to reduce car use within a city include making car ownership more problematic, for example, by reducing public and private parking places (Caborn 2002; CPRE 2003); and measures to encourage walking and cycling, such as the Copenhagen Free Bicycle Scheme for the city centre. The scheme makes 2500 bicycles available between April and December. They can be taken at specific racks by leaving a returnable deposit and can be used within the centre for an unlimited time (Brophy *et al.* 2000).

Building developments can also contribute to reducing car dependence as well as reducing the impacts of the car on the quality of life of building users. When selecting a site for development, proximity to public transport should be considered. Four hundred metres, which can be walked in five minutes, is a suitable distance for locating transport facilities from homes and encouraging walking. To achieve a sustainable urban transport system, it is recommended that these transport nodes should include other facilities such as shops and links to larger nodes, including train stations, work and leisure areas. The highest density of development should focus around a train station, with slightly lower density near the tram and bus nodes and decreasing density further away. This would make different housing options available and create a varied city landscape, while maximising the number of people with good access to public transport (Lock 2000).

For developments with no easily accessible public transport, it may be possible to persuade local bus service providers to extend their routes to a development site. Wessex Water, near Bath in England, built a new headquarters building and commissioned a bus stop just outside its main entrance, where employees can catch a bus direct to the local train station and travel with a bicycle if desired.

Within the development site itself, cycling can be encouraged by providing accessible, secure and covered bicycle storage; the need for travel can be reduced by including both work and living facilities in the same development; a facility for housing car clubs can help reduce car ownership, which in turn reduces car use. Commercial organisations can make environmentally friendly transport options, including bicycles or electric cars, available to their employees to use for errands. Car pools can be encouraged by providing an organisational framework and facilities to search for carpooling partners. Larger organisations such as the Presidio Trust in San Francisco encourage carpooling by offering a Guaranteed Ride Home programme that makes alternative transport available for emergency situations when carpool members are unable to travel at their standard time. The Presidio Trust also provides free shuttle buses within the Presidio area and cars, including electrical ones, which can be borrowed to travel for work or other purposes.

In order to reclaim social space lost to cars, as well as to reduce noise and air pollution and the risk of accidents, motorised traffic can be segregated from areas of the city and individual developments. Car-free pedestrian zones in cities have become very popular and have proved economically successful. Similarly, cars can be excluded from sections of developments, handing space over for individuals to enjoy, for children to play in safely or for communities to use. Perimeter parking and underground parking are solutions that reduce the impact of cars. In dense developments close to public transport, car ownership may not be necessary and parking spaces can be reduced, freeing up more space for other uses, including planting. The less that motor vehicles dominate the urban landscape, the more likely it is that individuals will spend time outside their home, sharing public spaces and strengthening community links.

Electrical vehicles use an electric motor and a battery that needs recharging every 60 kilometres or less and have a lower than average maximum speed. They have no emissions during use and are quiet. However, to reduce overall emissions the energy used to charge the battery has to come from a renewable source.

Electric hybrids run on petrol, but also use a battery that is charged through the braking action of the car and are therefore very fuel efficient at over 55 miles per gallon. Honda and Toyota have models available on the market.

As with buildings, an efficient operating system alone may not result in the desired environmental improvements if the base structure is not designed for efficiency. Ford is bringing out a new hybrid four-wheel drive SUV, but as SUV are inherently inefficient, this model is only rated at 36–33 gallons per mile, which is no better than a well-designed standard petrol engine car.

LPG (liquid petroleum gas) motors emit 10–15 per cent less CO_2 than petrol engines, but slightly more nitrogen oxides. Compared to diesel engines, LPG emits 10–15 per cent more carbon dioxide, but 75–85 per cent fewer nitrogen oxides.

Methanol (CH_3OH) is a natural gas alternative fuel that produces 20–30 per cent fewer CO_2 emissions and 95 per cent fewer particulates than petrol engines. Natural gas engines are quiet and in the UK there is an extensive pipeline in place. In Brazil, 90 per cent of new cars run on methanol using conventional internal combustion engines.

Biodiesel can be produced from the oil of crops like rape, sunflower and soybean as well as waste cooking oil. It can be used mixed with standard diesel fuel, typically 5–95 per cent. As biodiesel crops absorb CO_2 while growing, biodiesel can be considered a renewable fuel.

Hydrogen fuel cell car technology is attracting much attention and a small number of fuel cell cars running on hydrogen are now on the roads. The fuel cells are electrochemical engines that, by electrochemically combining hydrogen and oxygen in a flameless process (cold combustion), produce electricity, heat and pure distilled water. This is the mirror image of electrolysis where water is split into hydrogen and oxygen by passing an electric current through it. If the hydrogen is produced with electricity from renewable sources, a fuel cell vehicle can be considered 'zero CO_2 emission'. With this potential in mind, fuel cell technology is perhaps the most sustainable option. This technology is being pushed forward by numerous companies.

By the end of 2004 Daimler Chrysler will have over 100 fuel cell vehicles on the road, including 30 buses already active in cities in Europe, approximately 10 mopeds and 60 cars.

(Hoffman 2002/ EC 2000 / EST 2004 / DaimlerChrysler 2004 / Ford 2004)

Case study: Live-work

London Fields Housing Co-operative
London Fields Road, London, UK

Project details, Chapter 2.2, p.68

The Victorian houses were renovated, extended and reconfigured to provide maisonettes and flats with integrated work facilities.

To the rear are the extensions clad in cedar, metal stairs to access the flats and communal gardens for growing foods and ornamental plants.

Reducing the distance between home and work is one way to reduce the need to travel and, in particular, the need to use the car. Mixed use developments which combine work, retail, leisure and living accommodation can achieve this aim. Another way to reduce the need to travel is to incorporate working areas in the home. Increasingly people are working from home, either running a business from home or working a number of days per week from home, while maintaining an office base. A home office can easily be integrated within a standard home, whilst purpose-built live-work units are designed to accommodate a wider variety of work activities.

Working from home can improve people's quality of life by providing the flexibility that many people, in particular, parents, want, as well as freeing up time normally needed to travel to work. Improvements in information technology have facilitated the move to home-working, while a trend towards sub-contracting work, as opposed to undertaking it in-house, creates opportunities for small consultancies and home-working individuals. With increasing evidence that home-working can be as productive, if not more productive, than working in an office, companies are more inclined to allow employees to work from home, in particular, if overheads can be reduced by doing so. In 1993, 21 per cent of the working population in Australia worked from home (Barton *et al.* 2002) and the numbers are increasing.

As well as reducing car dependence, home-working can help create a cohesive and vibrant community. Grouping live-work facilities together can provide the critical mass required for support facilities, such as cafés, libraries or local meeting facilities that attract people and encourage social interaction. Such facilities can also help counteract the isolation sometimes experienced by home-workers.

The London Fields Housing Co-operative is a successful example of live-work units located in East London. The development is of particular interest as it involved the introduction of live-work facilities in existing buildings. Existing Victorian terraced houses were extended and refurbished to provide a variety of different-sized live-work units. By addressing the needs of home-workers at the project design stage, issues such as building loadings, building accessibility, noise transmission, provision of natural light and other practical building issues could be addressed at an early design stage and included in the construction tender to keep costs under control.

At London Fields other sustainability issues were also high on the agenda. The houses were renovated to be energy efficient and achieved a Standard Assessment Procedure (SAP) rating of 80-90. The development also created terraces and a shared garden space, which together with the communal stairs, provides opportunities for residents to meet their neighbours. This not only helps guard against potential isolation of home-workers, but also creates a quality living environment and helps develop a community feeling.

See also: self-build **Chapter 2.2**

Case study: Desirable city centre living

'One could say that housing is not sustainable unless it can be served by non-car modes' (Lock 2000). Reducing car dependence is key to achieving sustainable communities and city centre developments can contribute to this aim. Both commercial and residential developments in city centres are often close enough to public transport to rely on it for all travel needs. In respect of residential developments, the ability to walk to work, shops, transport facilities and leisure facilities makes the everyday use of the car redundant. However, in the UK, as in other countries, there has been a tendency for people to move away from city centres to the suburbs to find more affordable, larger, quieter and perhaps safer housing. Addressing the real or perceived disadvantages of city centre living is the challenge for new housing designs.

The Point housing development has many of the characteristics that make a development an attractive and desirable place to live. The city centre location on the bank of the River Avon has much to offer. The site is between two daytime tourist attractions, the Bristol Industrial Museum and Brunel's SS *Great Britain*, and there is no through traffic, resulting in a generally quiet location free from road traffic noise and noise from the sometimes problematic city centre night life. The environment on the edge of the river is attractive and soothing. Virtually all dwellings have good views of the river and many also overlook a semi-private planted communal area. The design is contemporary, comprising flat roofs and terraces and making use of metal and rendered finishes. The dwellings have large windows and are light and larger than the average in the UK.

Bristol's Old City, with its restaurants, theatres and art centres is a ten-minute walk away and The Harbourside, which includes an Imax and the Science Centre, is a similar distance. Shopping centres and the main train station are approximately a mile away and accessible by bus. Away from the city centre is the Avon River Walk, which leads into the countryside.

Despite easy access to most facilities, The Point does include car parking, which was seen by its speculative developers as an essential selling point. However, owing to its location, cars should not be required for day-to-day activities. A study of the development showed that The Point offered the potential to reduce carbon dioxide emissions associated with transport to 56 per cent of those associated with similar typical suburban developments (Rickaby 2002). Much of the car parking is in an underground car park located below an elevated and car-free communal area with planting and seating. Other communal facilities include a small children's play area on the south side of the housing and one commercial premise. All dwellings in The Point have private external areas in the form of balconies, gardens, patios or roof terraces.

Through its convenient and attractive location and spacious and well-designed dwellings, The Point makes it easy for residents to adopt and enjoy a healthy and car-free way of life.

Facility	Distance
Toddler's play area	100 m
Allotment	200 m
Community garden	
Bus stop	300 m
Playground	400 m
Primary school	
Pub	
Local shops	
Railway station	600 m
Playing fields	800 m
Park/open green space	
Health centre	
Secondary school	1000 m
District centre	1500 m
Leisure centre	
Technical college	2000 m
Major green space	
Cultural/entertainment facilities	5000 m
Major commercial centre	
General hospital	

Figure 1.2.3 Maximum recommended distances from homes to local facilities (Burton 1995).

The Point viewed from across the River Avon.

See also: appropriate high densities **Chapter 1.1**

Case study: Car-free development

Slateford green
Edinburgh, UK

Client: Canmore Housing Association
Architect: Hackland Dore Architects
Landscape architects: RPS Cairns
Services and structural engineers:
Harley Haddow Partnership
Quantity surveyor: Summers and Partners
Main contractor: Hart Builders
Completed: 2000

The site between Slateford Green Road and Gorgie Road, located a couple of miles south-west of Edinburgh city centre, had been considered for development by a number of organisations before Canmore Housing Association acquired it in 1996. Two previous proposals, one for a retail development and one for private housing, had been put forward to Edinburgh Council, which had requested the construction of a new road linking Slateford Green Road to Gorgie Road. The cost of road construction made the developments financially unattractive and it was only by creating a car-free development that the construction of the road could be avoided.

Canmore Housing Association's proposal for car-free housing on the 6.2-hectare former goods yard site supported Edinburgh Council's strategy to reduce congestion and pollution caused by road traffic and became one of seven potential car-free development sites in Edinburgh. The initial proposal included one car space per ten dwellings rather than the traditional 1.5 car spaces per dwelling.

The timber-framed development creates a secure inner courtyard with a perimeter service access road surrounding the dwellings.

Canmore Housing Association had ambitious plans and the car-free aspect of the development was just one of a list of environmental design targets set out in their brief for a competition run in 1996. The winning architects developed a sustainable and car-free strategy for the housing. Car ownership is not banned, but a Section 75 agreement means that the local authority can ban cars from the site. Limited car parking is available in the neighbourhood. The road at the perimeter of the site surrounding the housing is for pedestrian, bicycle and emergency vehicle use only. Freed from the requirements for parking spaces, the courtyard enclosed by the housing block was landscaped and is used

See also: accessible homes **Chapter 3.3**

by residents as a communal external area as well as a secure play area for the children.

The success of Slateford Green as a car-free housing development relies on two substitutes for car ownership. First, the site is in close proximity to public transport on Slateford Road and Gorgie Road only a couple of hundred metres away. Second, the Edinburgh City Car Club located four of their cars on a designated car parking bay at the entrance to the housing, making joining and using the car club convenient and attractive for residents. The Edinburgh City Car Club (www.smartmoves.co.uk) is the largest car club in the UK, with 22 cars available to over 400 members. The car club offers members the use of a car at any time. The cars can be booked over the phone or internet, up to six months in advance or at the last minute. Members gain access to the club's cars using a card and pin. The on-board computer logs the use of the car and the members receive a monthly bill based on the hours of use and mileage driven.

Each car shared by Car Club members replaces on average five privately owned cars. Manufacturing fewer cars reduces material consumption and energy use since the embodied energy of a car makes up on average 10 per cent of the total carbon dioxide emissions associated with cars.

1.2.4 Sustainable design features

Site and ecology
The development made use of a disused goods yard. The courtyard is planted with native species and copper beech hedges around the gardens benefit wildlife. Adjacent to the development are allotment gardens for the residents.

Community and culture
The design is inspired by Skara Brae in Orkney, and draws on Edinburgh tenement blocks. A protected landscaped courtyard provides a space to meet and a secure play area for children. A 166-square metre community hall is available free to residents, and is used for activities ranging from internet courses to dancing lessons.

Health
The courtyard and allotments provide residents with the opportunity to be outside within nature.

Materials
The timber-framed construction is clad externally with untreated cedar cladding and acrylic render.

Energy
The walls are timber breather wall construction with 170-millimetre solid timber studs and cellulose fibre insulation. Masonry stair cores provide thermal mass. The dwellings have opening windows with trickle vents and continuous passive stack ventilation in the kitchens and bathrooms. Heating for hot water and space heating is provided by means of a district heating boiler using low tariff gas. Heating bills are as low as £10 per month.

Water
An artificial wetland in the courtyard is used to filter the roof and road run-off and acts as a water retention pond delaying run-off.

Four car bays are reserved for cars of the Edinburgh City Car Club.

See also: accessible homes **Chapter 3.3**

Case study: Efficient and reduced vehicle use

Phillip Merrill Environmental Center
Annapolis, Maryland, US

Project details, Chapter 6.2, p.268

The car parking under the building is reserved for car-pooling spaces.

A gas/electric hybrid car is used by employees to run errands.

Providing opportunities for sustainable transport should be part of every organisation's environmental plan. With the development of the new Phillip Merrill Environmental Center, the Chesapeake Bay Foundation took the opportunity to consider transport as part of their holistic strategy to developing a sustainable building. The Merrill Center is not the only foundation building to incorporate environmental thinking, but it is the foundation's first building to address such a broad spectrum of issues ranging from local site issues to global environmental issues. Consideration of issues of transport was in line with their holistic approach to reducing resource use and pollution.

The 12.5-hectare site is relatively remote, approximately 7 kilometres from Annapolis. In order to minimise CO_2 emissions associated with travelling to and from work by the 100 employees based at Chesapeake, the Foundation has taken a number of steps. Walking is encouraged and bike storage, showers and lockers facilitate cycling to work. Storage for kayaks is also provided, making this more unusual commuting option available. Carpooling is encouraged, as is video conferencing. Lunch is provided to staff every day, avoiding the need to drive to outside facilities, and a bright and comfortable staff room with views of the bay provides a high quality environment in which to relax.

In addition to the travel requirements to and from work, The Foundation also considered travel requirements for work. It owns a hybrid car and a gas-powered car to be used for errands and to attend off-site meetings.

View of the Phillip Merrill Environmental Center from the sea. The undercroft is used to store kayaks and bicycles as well as cars.

See also: fine-tuning buildings **Chapter 5.2**

See also: rainwater for general needs **Chapter 6.2**

Case study: Segregating traffic 1

An increasing number of housing developments are excluding cars from parts of the development or only allowing reduced car use in specific areas. The aim is that the development should provide pleasant spaces that are quiet and not affected by car fumes; and safe for everyone and especially for children; and to increase community interaction.

However, to change the current status and give priority to pedestrians, making car use subordinate, requires careful planning and consideration. Realistically, car ownership is unlikely to drop drastically, even though car use may drop as alternative means of transport become sufficiently inexpensive, attractive, reliable and convenient. Therefore, car parking is still required and the issue is where to locate it. Furthermore, there is the question of how far to allow car access into a development and how to address worries about safe parking.

The district of Vauban in Freiburg, Germany, was once used by the French military. When the French left, the town decided to redevelop the area and actively to encourage sustainability. One aim was to reduce the use of cars in residential streets. The solution was to build car parks on the main road, while housing development off the main road remained free of car parking. Access to the houses by car is possible for deliveries and other needs, but the cars are parked at the end of the residential road. The result is that the residential roads are used by cars far less than normal and pedestrian traffic increases chance encounters between residents, which in turn fosters a healthy community. Having situated the car park where public transport is also available makes it easier to select public transport as a means to travel.

The car park in Vauban is not only an element of the city's strategy to reduce car dependence and the impact of cars, but also part of the city's photovoltaic (PV) network. The roof of the car park houses a PV installation with a peak capacity of 90 kW, adding to the 3.4 MW of PVs installed on the city's roofs.

Vauban
Freiburg, Baden-Württemberg, Germany

Completed: construction ongoing

1.2.5 Freiburg's public transport system

The city of Freiburg prides itself on being a progressive and green city. Following the successful protests in 1975 against the construction of a new nuclear power station, Freiburg City Council began increasingly to consider ecological aspects of their policies. Today Freiburg is striving to win the title of Solar City for a second time after its success in 2000.

The approach taken by the city is a comprehensive one that addresses energy production and use. The city has an impressive total PV installation capacity of 3.4 MW. It also benefits from hydro power, biofuel and wind power as well as encouraging energy-saving measures.

To reduce the city's transport energy use and pollution, the city decided as early as the 1970s to expand its existing tram service. Since then, trams have become the backbone of the public transport system, supported by improved cycle ways, pedestrian areas, and city perimeter park-and-ride facilities, interlinking bus and train services. The system now provides most people with access to means of public transport within 500 metres.

The tram corridors have been greened, an increasing number of trams have low level access for wheelchairs and pushchairs, and trams have precedence over other traffic, making them a comfortable and quick means of transport.

The city residents benefit from travel cards that give them access to the whole of the transport infrastructure in the Freiburg Region for a fixed price, which is lower than using a car. Visitors are given free travel cards at their hotels.

The transport system not only has reduced car use, but has also enhanced the mobility for the elderly and the young and improved the quality of life for the whole city.

The roof-mounted PV panels are clearly visible from the neighbouring hills.

The car park seen from the Vauban neighbourhood and from the main road. A food market is also housed in the same building.

Case study: Segregating traffic 2

Petuelring
Munich, Germany

Client: City of Munich
Completed: 2004

Many cities have ring roads and other major thoroughfares cutting through highly populated areas of the city. Occupants of the homes adjacent to these roads suffer from reduced quality of air, high levels of noise, visually unattractive environments and a general inability to use external areas. In some cases, such as with the Petuelring in Munich, these problems can be addressed as part of an overall city strategy of greening the city environment. Munich's inner ringroad was partially sunk underground and a new park was built above it, creating a quiet and healthy leisure area.

The new park links to other green spaces, provides cycle paths, a playground for small children, skateboarding facilities, secluded corners, seating, a reinstated stream and a number of installations with planting, fountains and a viewing box which gives a glimpse of what is happening underground in the car tunnel. A café is being built and will provide a focal point and a very desirable facility.

This new park improves the quality of life of those surrounding and using it, enhances the city's flora and fauna, and contributes to the overall attraction of the city as a whole.

The entrance to the tunnel. The road drops underground and the park is elevated over the road.

Blocks of flats overlook the new park, with walkways, cycle paths and planting.

The car tunnel exit is covered with a glazed roof to protect the surrounding area from traffic noise.

A bridge crosses the reinstated stream which runs on the edge of the park parallel to the road.

Right next to the apartment houses is an area for relaxation with chairs under planted trellises.

A video transfers an image of the inside of the car tunnel to a screen in a box in the park reminding viewers of what used to be on the site.

A water playground is a major attraction.

A dragon sprays water on the children.

Curved seating differentiates uses in the park.

The level differences on site are used to form secluded seating areas.

1.3 In Harmony with Nature

1.3.1 UK action plan for biodiversity

Overall aim: To enhance and protect biological diversity in the UK and contribute to the conservation of the global biodiversity.

Underlying principles:

– where biological resources should be used, such use should be sustainable

– wise use should be ensured for non-renewable resources

– the conservation of biodiversity requires the care and involvement of individuals and communities as well as governmental processes

– conservation of biodiversity should be an integral part of government programmes, policy and action

– conservation practice and policy should be based upon a sound knowledge base

– the precautionary principle should guide decisions

Mile End Park in London created new natural habitats for wildlife in an otherwise urban environment.

As the pressure on land grows globally, it is important to recognise the value of natural environments. Nature contributes towards satisfying basic human needs and improving human quality of life in many ways, as discussed in the Introduction. Architectural and urban design can benefit from nature's services for minimising the use of water and energy resources, reducing pollution and improving human health. Natural elements such as planting and water features can help moderate water and energy use and water disposal in individual buildings and urban and rural developments (see Chapters 6 and 5 respectively). Nature plays a part in purifying our water and air, and helps moderate global and local climate by providing cooling, shading and shelter from winds. Natural environments affect people at a psychological and physical level. Studies have shown that contact with nature positively affects people's mental health, while many leisure activities in nature, ranging from ball games in a park to trekking up mountains, are directly beneficial to people's physical health (see Chapter 3). Considering how nature can be employed to provide such benefits to an architectural development is clearly important, but equally important is to consider how such developments might impact on natural ecosystems.

The description of landscapes as being natural may give an impression of areas unaffected by humans. In fact, most land in developed countries has in some way or other been altered by human activities, ranging from farming and the introduction of plant and animal species to changes to the physical structure of the land. Even though many natural environments are therefore a direct result of human interventions, they can be of high environmental interest, harbouring a unique variety of flora and fauna. In the UK, the Fens and the Yorkshire Moors are examples of rare ecosystems that developed as a result of human activities. Protecting such ecosystems and the biodiversity they support is as important as protecting truly natural landscapes unaffected by humans. In both cases, the loss of an ecosystem would mean the extinction of specific plant and animal species and a reduction in biodiversity. A reduction in genetic diversity decreases the resilience of natural ecosystems to the stresses of disasters such as flooding, drought, pollution and climate change.

In the current post-industrial era in developed countries, the biggest threat to natural environments is the expansion of urban environments and transport routes. As little as 12 per cent of the world's surface is occupied by nature reserves and protected areas but to be successful, wildlife conservation needs far larger areas that also have to be inter-connected. Forests, wetlands, meadows and even agricultural land can, if farmed organically, provide suitable natural environment for wildlife. However, in the UK 6,300 hectare of countryside are converted into urban developments each year (CPRE 2003), and this increasing encroachment into the countryside reduces the size of natural ecosystems and increases their fragmentation and vulnerability. As natural environments shrink in size, it becomes more difficult for wildlife to reproduce, and the increasing isolation means that movement from one natural habitat to another is more difficult, if not impossible. The isolation not only hampers the reproduction of wildlife, but as climate change causes the environmental conditions for particular habitats to shift towards the poles, it will become necessary for both fauna and flora to move with the changing climate (see 1.3.3).

Designing for nature conservation

Avoiding the destruction of natural habitats is as much a priority for architectural developments as the enhancement of existing natural environments, the development of links between them and the introduction of new habitats. The selection of a development site is the first and most critical factor in terms of designing to protect nature. While the use of brownfield sites is preferable to that of greenfield sites, even brownfield sites may have an ecological value that needs to be protected. To establish the ecological value of a site, it may be necessary to undertake an ecological survey.

The aim of such surveys is to establish what the existing ecosystems are and the potential for developing new natural environments. To begin with, the survey records existing natural features including topography, microclimate and landscaping, as well as the wildlife present on the site. An assessment can then be made of what should and can be integrated in the new development. In general, the retention of natural ecosystems should be a priority and where sites are of little ecological value, the survey can help establish how to improve the ecological value of the site.

Improving the natural environment may be achieved by minor interventions such as the introduction of nesting places for birds and bats, or more involved initiatives such as introducing native planting or developing new ponds. The removal of invasive non-native plants, such as the Japanese Knotweed that is plaguing the English countryside, can encourage the return of native plants and the wildlife they support.

The links between a development site and other natural environments should also be considered. The importance of creating natural landscape links for wildlife is now clearly recognised and considered valuable for sites in cities as well as rural environments. Planted corridors and natural networks based on canal ways, rivers and railways, as well as city parks and private gardens, form links for wildlife to travel.

In addition to creating havens for flora and fauna, natural environments provide leisure and relaxation spaces for humans. In progressively dense cities, access to nature for people is especially important for human health and a balance has to be found between making spaces accessible to people and those dedicated to flora and fauna. Considering the increasing pressure from a growing population, only by providing access to nature for people in a way that does not compromise the natural environment can biodiversity be protected.

1.3.2 Benefits of trees and forests

– Trees absorb carbon dioxide from the air and store it as carbon.

– Trees help clean the atmosphere.

– Trees help prevent soil erosion.

– Trees reduce water pollution.

– Trees help recharge groundwater.

– Tree can help reduce traffic noise.

– Trees can help provide privacy.

– Trees are a source of material for manufacturing.

– Some trees are a source of food.

– Tropical rainforests as well as trees from temperate areas are a source of pharmaceutical products.

– Trees are psychologically, and consequently physically beneficial, reducing stress and speeding up recovery.

– For many people, trees have a cultural significance.

– Trees can contribute aesthetically to urban and rural environments.

– Trees can provide shade to buildings, reducing heat gains, thus improving the interior environment and reducing the need for artificial cooling.

– Trees help counteract the city heat island effect by providing shading and evaporative cooling.

– Trees can protect buildings from wind.

– Trees can protect crops from wind and help increase crop yields.

– Trees can help protect livestock.

– Trees are a habitat for wildlife.

1.3.3 The mobility of plants

After the last Ice Age, migrations of plants and animals followed the retreating ice sheets moving, at approximately 190 kilometres per century. The changes in temperature currently experienced as a result of climate change are expected to be faster than those experienced 9,000 years ago, and the migration of plants seems unlikely.

Case study: Enabling the natural ecology to flourish

Lyola Pavilions
Maleny, Queensland, Australia

Client: John and Lesia
Architect: Gomango Architects
Structural engineer: Josh Neil
Hydraulic consultant: Peter Taylor & Associates
Main contractor: Barrett Constructions
Completed: 2000

1.3.4 Sustainable design features

Site and ecology
The buildings minimise the disruption to the natural environment and allow its regeneration.

Community and culture
One of the pavilions is fully wheelchair accessible, allowing less mobile individuals to experience the rainforest and the peaceful and relaxing surroundings.

Health
The close contact with nature has a restorative effect on visitors. The materials used are mainly natural and non-toxic.

Materials
Renewable materials such as timber were used.

Energy
The pavilions are designed to enable cross-ventilation. Minimal heating is required in winter and provided by a wood-burning stove.

Water
Dual flush WCs are installed.

The Lyola Pavilions are two small holiday buildings perched on the hillside of the rainforest above Maleny, north of Brisbane in the Sunshine Coast hinterland. They were commissioned as part of an overall strategy to re-establish primary rainforest and provide natural habitats for local flora and fauna, including the local koala population. The development of the area was also linked to a research project for the native bush turkey.

The pavilions were designed to disrupt the landscape as little as possible and allow space for the natural environment to re-establish itself after the construction period. They are supported on timber posts high above the ground that allow vegetation to grow below them. The two timber structures are modest in size and appear to fit within the gaps between the trees.

The pavilions allow plants to grow under and closely around them, and they invite the visitor to experience and appreciate the rainforest environment. They are oriented to view the Connondale Ranges opposite, and, by opening the sliding corner windows, sounds and smells are allowed into the pavilion, thus accentuating the feeling of being in the rainforest. The elevated nature of the pavilions also enables one of the two pavilions to have level wheelchair access from the gravel-covered car park, making the experience accessible to all.

The timber structure and windows, and the corrugated metal cladding, are simple and in tune with the surroundings. The tree canopy shades the buildings, and the large windows, protected by fly screens, allow cross-ventilation through the rooms, creating a comfortably cool environment. A fire and an electrical fan allow minor temperature adjustments when needed.

By respecting and enhancing the natural environment, these pavilions have become virtually invisible, sitting comfortably in between trees, birds and other animals.

The pavilions are supported on slender timber posts placed on small foundations.

The pavilions are barely visible as one approaches them from the gravel road.

The corner window opens up to become an open balcony among the trees.

From outside the pavilion it is possible to see right through it and view the mountains on the other side.

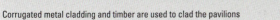

Corrugated metal cladding and timber are used to clad the pavilions

Case study: Sharing nature

solarCity
Pichling, Linz, Austria

Landscape architect: Atelier Dreiseitl
Completion: planned for 2005

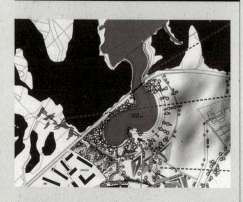

A visitors' sign shows the main landscaping intervention. A path separates the leisure area from the nature reserve. The only leisure area to the north of the path is a nature trail to the west of the forest.

At the edge of the park are seating areas with planted screens providing some privacy.

Contact with nature is beneficial to the wellbeing of humans. Integrating an easily accessible natural environment within a housing development is, therefore, highly desirable. The solarCity development, which addresses sustainable development in a comprehensive way (see Chapter 1.1), also addressed this issue. The solarCity benefits from its proximity to the Kleiner Weikerlsee lake and the Traun–Danube riverside, an area designated Natura 2000 (a network of protected natural sites in Europe) and to become a nature reserve. Making these natural environments accessible to the inhabitants of the 1,317 housing units was one of the development's aims; however, it was also clear that these same environments needed protection from excessive human presence, use and potential abuse.

A balance had to be achieved between natural environments for use by people and natural environments as safe havens for plant and animal species. Residents would be encouraged to enjoy the natural environments, thus improving their physical and psychological health, but the areas designed for frequent use would be limited. A mechanism was needed to restrict the use of the safe haven areas without resorting to regulations.

With these aims in mind solarCity held a landscaping design competition in 1997 that was won by Atelier Dreiseitl. The winning entry, which is currently being implemented, involves creating three main areas: a sculptural landscaped strip separating the housing development from the park; a park for the use of the residents; and the new nature reserve of the Traun–Danube riverside and the lake.

The sculptural landscaped strip consists mainly of planted mounds made from the development spoil, creating a visual barrier between the houses and the park. Framed views are formed when walking between the mounds. The landscape can be enjoyed at low level in secluded areas with benches and at high level from the top of the mounds.

View of the bridge over the Kleiner Weikerlsee and the nature reserve from the housing side of the park area, and view towards the housing from the bridge over the lake.

Beyond the sculptural landscape is the main recreation area for the residents. The existing lake, Kleiner Weikerlsee, was extended to form a bathing area and a beach. Around the extended portion of the lake is a grassed area for sunbathing, relaxing and playing, as well as newly planted wildflower meadows and trees. A cycle- and footpath crosses the lake on a timber and steel bridge and delineates the boundary between the area allocated for leisure use and the natural reserve. People are expected to remain primarily on the south side of the path in the park and around the bathing area of the lake. However, the nature reserve is also an attractive destination and to prevent it being overwhelmed by visitors, a nature trail is currently being developed. The thinking is that most people wanting to visit the reserve will go to the nature trail and only a small number of people will venture into the heart of the nature reserve. Unrestricted access to the reserve is therefore given, but the structured 'walk in the wild' is expected to serve most people's needs, leaving the nature reserve primarily to the flora and fauna.

Other landscaping interventions adopt the same approach of providing a natural environment for the enjoyment and health of the residents, and at the same time reinstating and protecting nature for its own sake. Besides integrating planting wherever possible around the housing, the Aumühlbach stream is being ecologically reinstated and integrated within the park. Residents have reported improved health since moving to the solarCity, supporting the thesis that contact with nature promotes good health (Ulrich *et al*. 1991; Harting and Evans 1993). The way the development respects nature for its intrinsic value reflects an unusually high ethical commitment to addressing sustainability issues beyond immediate human interests.

A planted trellis will shield the housing on the north side of the commercial centre from the gazes of passers-by.

The extended lake with the new bridge.

Planted mounds form a visual separation between the houses and the park.

The concrete wall to the undercroft of a housing block is designed to be covered with climbers.

The extended portion of the lake is surrounded by a bathing area, newly planted trees and a wild meadow area.

See also: comprehensive planning **Chapter 1.1**

See also: deleterious materials **Chapter 3.2**

See also: electromagnetic fields **Chapter 3.2**

See also: sewage as a resource **Chapter 6.3**

See also: sustainable urban drainage **Chapter 6.3**

Case study: Enhancing native flora and fauna

Loudon EcoVillage
Taylorstown, Virginia, US

Project details, Chapter 3.4, p.140

EcoVillage is a co-housing development designed to offer an ecologically sound and community-oriented alternative to typical impersonal suburban housing. Located in the rolling hills of the Northern Virginia countryside, a key concern for the EcoVillage founding group was to respect and restore the native biodiversity of the site. It was decided that only 15 per cent of the 73-hectare site would be built on and the rest would be landscaped or farmed. The housing is divided into two clusters, which, while being about one-tenth of the development densities recommended in European cities, are compact enough to create a communal feel as well as reducing the area of roads required and leaving more of the site to be planted. The previous organic agricultural use of the site was reduced to approximately 8 hectare and, when farmed again, the produce will be used by the residents. The organic certification is maintained throughout the site and enforced through covenants, which also apply to individual gardens. Woodland, which would naturally cover the whole of the region, had shrunk to one-third of the site many years previously. The benefits of woodlands are many (see 1.3.2) and reforestation was therefore a priority. Over 11,000 trees have already been planted and the aim is for three-quarters of the site to be woodland. An area of meadow will be retained for its ecological value, as well as providing an area for outdoor activities. Trails connecting the two clusters and neighbouring areas are being established through use.

The existing forest is rich in biodiversity, including approximately 30 species of trees, over 40 species of birds, plus animals and insects, including white-tailed deer, red foxes, toads and turtles. The group wanted to ensure that the process of reforestation would return native species to the forest, increasing the habitat for native wildlife. Historically, non-native plants have regularly been introduced into natural environments for practical reasons, as in the case of food and other crops, and for their decorative or curiosity value. Plants have also been introduced accidentally, as a result of seeds being transported on people or vehicles and by animals. The introduction of non-native plants can have destructive effects, as with the introduction in England of the Dutch elm disease fungus which devastated the elm population in the 1970s, or the introduction of the chestnut blight fungus in the US in the 1890s, which was responsible for the demise of the American chestnut over a period of less than 50 years. Non-native plants can prove invasive, reducing the habitat of native plants by changing the soil chemistry, water levels or the fire regime, and in severe cases have caused native species to become extinct. Invasive plants that successfully reduce native plants also indirectly affect animal biodiversity.

In the EcoVillage, invasive species such as the Tree of Heaven and the Multi-Flora Rose are being removed and replaced with native plants. Exotic plants are also excluded in individual gardens and residents are encouraged to plant gardens for wildlife. As the native ecosystem grows, so does the potential for other wildlife species moving into the area. Controlled access to the forests will allow people to enjoy nature while limiting human disruption and protecting the native flora and fauna.

See also: health and nature **Chapter 3.4**

A butterfly benefiting from the wildflower meadows.

One house with a newly planted garden with native species. The access road is covered with a layer of chippings rather than tarmac to maintain porosity of the surface and minimise rainwater run-off.

Case study: Creating planted corridors

Mile End Park
London, UK

Client: Mile End Park Partnership (Tower Hamlet Council, the Environment Trust, East London Partnership)
Masterplan/architect (south and north park, ecology centre, art building, children's building): Gardner Stewart Architects (formerly Tibbalds TM2)
Architect (bridge): Pier Gough
Mechanical engineering: Fulcrum Consulting
Main contractor: Fitzpatrick
Completed: 1999 (bridge), 2001 (park)

Retail units and restaurant below the bridge.

An ecology centre and an art centre have been built within Mile End Park. The bermed buildings are energy efficient – they have a seasonal heat storage and make use of wind power.

As the natural environment becomes increasingly fragmented due to construction developments in urban and rural areas, it is necessary to maintain existing and create new planted links between natural habitats. City parks, waterways, private gardens and other green spaces can form planted corridors facilitating the movement of wildlife within and in and out of urban areas. Greater London includes over 1,000 square kilometres of built-up area and is surrounded by smaller towns and villages. London boasts a large number of parks and is also surrounded by many green spaces. However, these tend to be separate from one another, and linking them would create a network of natural habitats that can benefit wildlife.

One way to link green spaces was implemented at Mile End Park in East London. The main aim of the Mile End Park development was to reinstate a bomb-damaged, neglected and notorious strip of wasteland and turn it into a community-oriented park triggering a regeneration of the area, but what it also achieved was the creation of a planted corridor. The 36-hectare city park links Victoria Park to the north and Limehouse Cut to the south along a mile-long stretch of the Regent's Canal. The park, which includes an art centre, an ecology centre and a children's building and was conceived through a consultative process with the local community, adds a new element to an existing chain of green spaces stretching virtually from the River Thames to Epping Forest to the north of Greater London. This chain of natural environments is not currently continuous: the existing green spaces are often separated by roads and buildings. Mile End Park is also divided into two sections split by the Mile End Road, a major road linking East London to the city centre, and could have resulted merely in the addition of further isolated green spaces to the existing chain. This was successfully avoided by joining the two separate sections with a 25-metre planted bridge. The resulting corridor demonstrates how to effectively bridge gaps between natural environments and help form a fully connected network of green spaces.

Building a bridge to join two planted parks may seem an extravagance, and the environmental benefits may be difficult to quantify. However, in this case, retail facilities were included at the base of the bridge and are a source of income to maintain the park. The retail spaces have proved popular, and in the enhanced environment resulting from the redevelopment of the neighbourhood they command well-above-average rent rates. The restaurant and shops situated under the bridge create a vibrant atmosphere and also prevent the area from becoming neglected. By bringing life to a neglected environment, the bridge and the park have proved to be environmentally, socially and economically sustainable.

White lavender attracts bees to the park.

View of the bridge from Mile End Road.

View from the bridge of the south park.

Case study: Green roofs

What appears to be a walkway with benches overlooking an artificial lake on a grassed area is in fact an intensive green roof over the restaurant for the employees of the RWE in Essen. In Germany and Austria subsidies for the installation of green roofs are sometimes available (see case study).

View of the glazed front to the restaurant.

The Pishwanton gridshell in the woods west of Edinburgh has an extensive green roof. Its natural shape makes the building look almost like part of the landscape (see case study).

To many people green roofs are seen as a symbol of a sustainable building and while green roofs alone do not make a building sustainable, they can help to reduce its environmental impact in a number of ways.

There are essentially three types of green roof: intensive and extensive planted roofs (with variations of these) and brown roofs. Intensive green roofs are fully accessible roof gardens where shrubs and even trees can be grown. Extensive green roofs are much lighter than intensive roofs, suitable for sloped roofs, and require as little as 50 millimetres of planting medium. They are accessible for maintenance only and are usually planted with sedum, grasses or other low-growing planting. Brown roofs are not planted roofs, and are designed to take advantage of self-seeding local vegetation. Excavated ground from the construction process is laid on top of a waterproof membrane and planting develops from seeds in the excavated ground and those transported through the air and by wildlife.

At a conceptual level, planted roofs can be seen to replace planting at ground level with planting on an elevated surface. At a practical level, all three different types of green roof provide, to a greater or lesser degree, various environmental benefits. Green roofs can provide additional insulation against the cold and the heat, although the insulating effect of the earth is diminished if it becomes saturated with water. The insulating effect of the earth also protects the waterproofing membrane from excessive thermal movement, extending its life. Green roofs reduce stormwater run-off up to 90 per cent: again the more soil and planting on the roof, the more water will be absorbed and released slowly through evaporation and drainage. Other improvements to the physical environment associated with planted roofs include the reduction of smog and dust particles, the reduction of noise and the cooling effect of evaporation. Reducing the ambient temperature can help counteract the urban heat island effect, which occurs in densely built-up areas with high internal heat gains and dense and absorbing materials.

Green roofs can also visually improve the environment. Planting roofs that are visible from above can enrich the onlooker's experience. Even from ground level, green roofs may be visible and can prove aesthetically pleasing. In rural environments green roofs may help reduce the development's visual impact and facilitate building permission (see Hockerton Housing case study, p.46).

Green roofs can also benefit wildlife. In urban sites devoid of planting, green roofs are one way to introduce a natural habitat to the site and extend a city network of natural spaces sustaining wildlife. As a means of increasing or introducing wildlife habitats to a site, green roofs can be designed to attract and support particular wildlife. In their excellent book *Building Green: A Guide to Using Plants on Roofs, Walls and Pavements* (1997), Johnston and Newton list different plants suitable for green roofs and identify the wildlife each plant supports. For example, many sedum species attract bees, valerian and lavender attract butterflies and Russian vine and forsythia are beneficial for nesting birds. By carefully planting green roofs, the habitat for the local wildlife can be expanded and its survival potential increased.

Case study: Building in character with nature

Respecting nature goes beyond practical methods of protecting biodiversity. A regard for nature can manifest itself through building aesthetics. The Great Sandy Information Centre is a building that acknowledges nature as the inspiration for its design and reflects the character of the environment surrounding it.

Situated on the edge of the Great Sandy National Park, also known as the Cooloola, in Australia, the visitors' centre acts as a welcoming building for visitors to the national park. It provides information on the camping and picnic facilities, walking and other activities possible in the park as well as information on the natural environment. It sets the scene for visitors and the design of the buildings, explicitly reflecting sensitivity towards nature, suggests how to enjoy the fragile natural ecosystems without threatening them.

The visitors' centre, the toilet block and the walkways connecting the car park to the buildings are supported on timber posts and float above the ground among the paperbark trees and mangrove swamp. The timber posts could be mistaken for tree trunks and the layered building cladding relates to the layered effect of the mangrove and melaleuca swamps. The architect claims to have been inspired by the mudskipper fish that lives in the banks of the mangrove. Like the fish, the building sits unobtrusively in the landscape, the message expressed by its design vital to the survival of the ecosystem it inhabits.

Great Sandy Information Centre
Great Sandy National Park, Queensland, Australia

Client: Queensland Parks and Wildlife Service
Architect: John Mainwaring and Associates
Main contractor: Gympie Building Company
Completed: 2001

View of the visitors' centre discreetly positioned between the trees.

The toilet block is situated between the car park and the visitors' centre.

The visitors' centre and the toilet block float over the mangrove swamp.

1.4 Local Food Production

1.4.1 Designing to minimise impacts associated with food

- Include opportunities and space for growing food on buildings or in gardens.
- Allocate a portion of communal space for the production of food in the form of allotments or community gardens.
- Consider planting fruit trees where possible.
- Encourage city farms, and other local food growing facilities.
- Provide opportunities for farmers markets.
- At an urban level, ensure that land adjacent to the city is retained as agricultural.

1.4.2 Advantages of organic farming

- Organic matter is higher in organically managed soil, providing higher fertility and water retention and lower risk of erosion.
- Organic soils have a higher biological activity resulting in improved soil structure and rapid nutrient recycling.
- Organic farming does not pollute water courses with synthetic pesticides and fertilisers.
- Organic farming is more energy efficient per hectare than non-organic farming.
- Wild flora and fauna, including insects and micro-organisms, are more diverse and abundant around organic farms than around non-organic farms.
- Organic farming provides habitats for pollinators and beneficial, pest-controlling birds and arthropods.
- Organic farming constitutes a diverse landscape which contributes to functional and aesthetic diversity. (Hattam and El-Hage Scialabba 2002)

The production of food may not appear to be related to architectural design. However, building developments can play a role in helping to reduce the impacts associated with food production and distribution. Food production and distribution practices can cause pollution; affect land use; affect the health and social and economic well-being of communities; and can be at risk of a volatile distribution network subject to disruption from strikes and rising fuel prices.

Although today there is no scarcity of food in the world, world-wide over 815 million people are chronically hungry, primarily because they are too poor to buy food. In recent years global grain yield has dropped, and so have government and private stocks. The scarcity of grain, which makes up 48 per cent of the calories consumed by humans, drives up prices, thus exacerbating the hunger problem (Worldwatch 2003). As the populations of the poorest countries grow, so do their difficulties in accessing food. Considering that the drop in grain yield in 2002 was caused by drought and other weather conditions, which are likely to increase in frequency with global warming, a scarcity of food world-wide could become a possibility.

In addition to weather conditions affecting farming yields, another issue impacting on the ability of the land to feed people is the change in diet experienced throughout the world. Meat consumption is growing, having increased fivefold since 1950. Meat production requires large amounts of grain for animal feed, reducing the amount available for direct human consumption. Animal feed can also include fish, which is therefore diverted from being used as a high-protein food source by billions in the developing world. A meat-based diet requires about two to four times the land required for a vegetarian diet (UNDP 1998). Land availability is limited and the drive towards a rich, meat-based diet is not sustainable. The land required to produce the food consumed by the average Londoner's diet is 1.2 hectare per person (Girardet 1999b). If the projected world population of 9 billion were to adopt the same diet, 10.8 billion hectare would be required to feed them. However, crop land is unlikely to grow beyond the present 1.5 billion hectare and the total global vegetated area on the planet is only 11.5 billion hectare.

Not only is the type of food consumed a potential risk to global food availability, so is the over-consumption of food. Some 7.6 million deaths in industrialised countries occur from stroke, heart disease, cancer and diabetes, caused primarily by an over-consumption of salt, sugar, fat and calories, often contained in processed food, causing obesity, high cholesterol and high blood pressure (WHO 2002).

Land use is not the only problem: food production and transportation use vast amounts of energy and food is travelling increasing distances to get to the table. In Germany research shows how the ingredients of one of the typical 3 billion pots of yoghurt consumed annually in Germany, will have travelled approximately 3,500 kilometres to the factory (Von Weisacker *et al.* 1997). Research from the US shows that a glass of orange juice requires two glasses of oil to get to it to the breakfast table (Edwards and Turrent 2000). Most food in the US now travels 2,500–4000 kilometres. In the UK, a comparison of a locally produced and an imported meal showed how the imported meal was associated with 650 times the carbon dioxide emission of the locally produced meal.

Farming practices are also a cause for concern, affecting food quality and human health as well as the environment. Pesticides are endocrine disruptors and farmers exposed to pesticides are found to be more at risk of cancer, immune system malfunction, mental illness and other conditions. Pesticides are thought to reduce the levels of antioxidants in the food that can contribute to good health, they pollute ground-water and reduce biodiversity. Chemical fertilisers also pollute water courses (Worldwatch 2004).

Sustainable food production

Reducing the environmental problems associated with food consumption involves changing the current food culture. Apart from consuming in moderation and reducing meat consumption, preference should be given to locally produced food to reduce carbon dioxide emissions from transport and to strengthen the local agricultural economy. In addition, organic production should be encouraged and supported. Compared to non-organic agriculture, organic production drastically reduces pesticide levels in the environment and therefore indirectly supports more wildlife. Moreover, pesticide damage can be costly to clean up. Water companies in Munich, Germany, responsible for purifying groundwater polluted by pesticides, found it more cost-effective to support farmers in changing to organic production than to clean the polluted water (Worldwatch 2004). A change to organic farming need not reduce production levels, which have proved to be as high as from those farms using pesticides and chemical fertilisers. The number of organic farms, while still small, is growing.

Individuals can support local organic farming by buying at organic farmers markets or supporting organisations such as Community-Supported Agriculture (CSA) groups, which operate in the UK, the US and Europe to create partnerships between farmers and consumers who agree to buy a set amount of food from a specific farm.

Within built developments, opportunities for food growing can also be introduced. Whether in the city or in the country, around housing or as a community garden or allotment, food production can bring healthy and fresh food to the table. Even on a small scale, gardens, rooftops or balconies can be used to grow food.

Growing organic food near to where it is consumed benefits the physical and economic health of the consumers and the producers and reduces environmental damage. It also provides opportunities for communities to meet and interact; it is an inclusive activity accessible to those disadvantaged by age or health; and provides health-promoting contact with nature. Growing one's own food is also invaluable in educating people about the links between humans and their natural environment.

1.4.3 Benefits of local food networks (vegetable box schemes, farmers' markets, farmer–user cooperatives)

– greater access to fresh, seasonal produce, leading to healthier diets
– increased employment and recycling of money in the local economy
– closer links between farmers and consumers, increased community involvement in production and greater self-sufficiency
– reduced pollution and congestion
– encouragement of sustainable land management systems
– reduced risk from BSE, foot-and-mouth, 'chicken-flu' and other food-related crises (*Ethical Consumer* 2004)

1.4.4 Urban farming

– Cities like Shanghai are built on only 20 per cent of their land. 80 per cent of the land, mainly in the suburbs, is used to grow crops, making the city self-sufficient in vegetables and growing much of its rice, pork and chicken (Girardet 1999a).
– Singapore is still very agriculturally productive. 30 per cent of its vegetables, 30 per cent of its fish and 90 per cent of its chicken are produced in the city.
– Village Homes, Davies, California, is a suburb surrounded by a ring of orchards and individual orchards in each neighbourhood. Private food gardens and community allotments are also included.
– The city of Göteburg, Sweden, owns 60 city farms on 2,700 hectare of land used for food production as well as for recreational and educational purposes.

1.4.5 Benefits of allotments

– provide access to cheap food
– provide opportunities for growing less usual plants and expand the biodiversity
– give ethnic groups the possibility to grow foods of cultural significance and strengthen their cultural identity
– provide access to nature
– provide a social network
– relieve stress
– encourage greater self-determination
– promote sustainability, reducing dependence on external food
– provide opportunities for exercise in fresh air

Case study: Producing food on site

Hockerton Housing Project
Southwell, UK

Client: Hockerton Housing Project Ltd.
Architect: Brenda and Robert Vale
Reed bed design: David Leigh Landscapes
Main contractor: Self-built
Completed: 1998

View from standing on the bermed side of the roof of the houses. A PV array and the conservatory both harness the sun's energy for use in the houses.

The terraces face south onto the lake, which is used to promote wildlife, for leisure and fishing purposes.

Hockerton Housing Project is one of a few developments in the UK aiming to achieve the maximum self-sufficiency possible in a comprehensive way. The development of five houses located near the village of Hockerton two miles from Southwell, a historic town in the East Midlands of England, aimed to provide a non-polluting way of life and work in harmony with nature.

The project addresses resource use and waste production, aims to enhance the local natural environment, and has created employment and educational facilities on site. The houses are designed to use minimal amounts of energy through a passive solar strategy of combining a highly insulated building envelope with thermal mass. The substantially reduced energy requirements can be covered by energy generated on site from alternatives to fossil fuel. The houses are also designed to be self-sufficient in terms of use and disposal of water by collecting rainwater for all requirements and treating waste water on site. In addition to living in a virtually self-sufficient manner, the Hockerton Housing Project also shares its experience with others, through educational activities, such as school visits and professional consultancies, through a comprehensive selection of publications and fact sheets, available for purchase, and through its website (www.hockerton.demon.co.uk).

The project was also originally envisaged to become self-sufficient in food production by adopting organic permaculture principles on the site. The 10-hectare site was previously used as agricultural land and over 90 per cent of the site was retained as a vegetated or water-covered area. Some of the vegetated area was enhanced to promote biodiversity by planting over 4,000 trees to create visual screens, wind buffers, and protected natural environments for animals. The lake successfully increased the biodiversity and is now harbouring six species of breeding wildfowl, including the little grebe and the endangered water vole. Dragonflies and other pond edge species have naturally colonised the area, while fish were artificially introduced into the lake.

Some of the remaining land was allocated for food production and, as time passes, more is being used for this purpose. The tenancy agreement for the Hockerton Housing Project ensures that the residents actively pursue a sustainable way of life and requires each adult to contribute 8 hours of work per week, half for food production and site maintenance and half for promotional activities. A system of exchange of services among residents allows the necessary flexibility and the result is a healthy-looking and productive food provision system.

A large vegetable garden provides seasonal vegetables and polytunnels extend the choice of food that can be planted. Potatoes, runner beans, cabbage, tomatoes and lettuces are just a few of the vegetables grown. The families are two-thirds self-sufficient in vegetable production and could extend the production if they wished and had the time to care for additional vegetable patches. The children are predictably less tolerant than adults to the limitations in variety of food that eating one's own seasonal vegetables brings with it, but as the food is organic and fresh, there is a bonus in terms of taste. Excess produce is stored in an external larder made with an earth-bermed tube.

The main fruit crop consists of berries from bushes which already existed on the site. Fruit trees have been planted on the north side of the houses and will require several years to produce a first crop, but when they do, the families will be substantially self-sufficient in fruit production.

A few chicken and sheep are kept and contribute a nominal amount to the families' needs for eggs and meat, while the beehives produce more honey than the group can consume. The lake is also proving to be good source of food, particularly carp. Additional food required is bought locally where possible to reduce food miles.

Within developed countries complete self-sufficiency in food would probably require too radical a change in diet and use of time. However, Hockerton suggests that for a small group of individuals supported by a work structure and sufficient land, self-sufficiency in fruit and vegetables can be achieved with time.

The vegetable garden.

The chicken house can be seen behind the polytunnel used to grow tomatoes and other frost-intolerant vegetables.

Young fruit trees planted on the earth-covered roof of the houses.

Globe artichokes in the vegetable patch. Recycled materials such as tyres are used for gardening.

1.4.6 Sustainable design features

Site and ecology
See main text.

Community and culture
The households share childcare arrangements and vehicles, they meet regularly to attend the community's matters and on social occasions. The community is successful and growing with two new units having recently been built on adjacent land. Also a new community building is now used as a venue for occasional village meetings. The lake area is also used by the locals as a place to walk and enjoy nature.

Health
No toxic materials. The contact with nature was maximised.

Materials
The criteria for materials selection included: minimum embodied energy, contribution to reducing running energy, local supply where possible, technologies understood by typical builders, low maintenance, requirement for environmental policy of supplier, low toxicity, no CFCs and HCFCs. Waste is either composted on site or recycled, the remaining waste is collected regularly by the local authority.

Energy
The single-storey houses are built as a compact terrace with high levels of thermal mass and insulation.

Fabric U-values:
   Walls, roof and floor – 0.11 W/m²K (R50)
   Windows – 1.1 W/m²K (0.19 Btu/ft²h°F)

They are passive solar buildings with the south-facing elevations comprising a glazed conservatory along the full length of the building as a preheating and buffer zone. The north elevation is earth bermed with a minimum of 400 millimetres of earth cover. The heating of the homes relies primarily on the solar gains through the south-facing elevation being stored in the concrete thermal mass. Mechanical ventilation with heat recovery provides fresh air and recycles 80 per cent of the heat from the stale air. An air to water heat pump located in the entrance and drawing air from the conservatory provides hot water, which is stored in a 1500-litre cylinder with a back-up immersion heater.

Two 6-kW wind turbines and a 7.6-kW PV array, producing about 20,000 kWhr per year of energy provide most of the energy to run the homes, an on-site office/community building, and an electric car. The average energy demand is 21-32 kWh/yr/m².

Water
See Chapter 6.3. In the new community building composting toilets and a waterless urinal were installed.

 See also: wind energy 1, 2 **Chapter 5.3**

See also: secondary treatment with reedbeds **Chapter 6.3**

Case study: Community food gardens

Argonne Child Development Center
Sixteenth Avenue,
San Francisco, US

Client: San Francisco School District
Architect: 450 Architects
Landscape architect: Cliff Lowe Associates
Structural engineer: Acres Engineering
Mechanical engineer: Hawk Engineers
Completed: 2002

The Argonne Child Development Center is an environmentally sensitively designed pre-school facility that addressed the social as well as the environmental aspects of the building design.

In response to San Francisco School District's proposal to close the existing one-classroom Argonne Children's Center set within a community garden, and sell the 3,500-square metre parcel of land, the local community became actively involved and succeeded in changing the course of events. To be financially viable the pre-school facility needed to be bigger, but at the same time the community wanted to keep their 100 planting plots in the community garden.

With the help of the architects, the community was able to formulate its priorities, which included the wish for a sustainable building that addressed the needs of the community while minimising the development's environmental impacts. Subsequently, with the support of the local community, the architects were able to deliver a low-energy building that improved the quality of life of the neighbourhood.

The classroom bay window faces the garden and the children have a view of the plants.

The classrooms face onto the play area as well as the gardens. PV panels are integrated within the rooflight over the toilets.

The south-facing classroom windows are protected by an ample overhang.

The community had experience in the 1970s of the use of solar thermal panels on the old classroom and wanted the new building to employ passive solar techniques. The new four-classroom building protects against excessive solar gains in summer while taking advantage of the sun's heat in winter, and therefore requires no air-conditioning and only minimal heating. It also makes use of PV panels that convert solar radiation into electricity. The development creates a large play area for the children with a number of different play facilities. It also satisfies the neighbouring community needs by retaining the 100 community garden plots and improving the surrounding environment.

The community involvement was crucial and the determination of the group was evident on a number of occasions. The omission of the PV panels was counteracted by a fundraising effort that raised $5,000 and later the community also secured a grant for acquiring native plant species and organised a community planting event.

See also: educating the community **Chapter 2.5**

The design of the building ensured that none of the existing trees had to be cut down. In addition to edible plants, the perimeter of the children's play area is planted with native species. In an area such as San Francisco where the vegetation has been largely altered by humans, the community wanted to increase the number of native plants. This not only expands native habitats supporting biodiversity and wildlife, but native plants also tend to be more drought resistant, which obviates the need for irrigation.

The rewards for the community were worth all their efforts. The community garden contributes significantly to the quality of life of the neighbourhood and creates a green oasis in what is otherwise a very densely populated city.

1.4.7 Sustainable design features

Site and ecology
The development was built on a brownfield site in a densely populated part of the city. The location close to excellent bus connections avoids the need for driving and therefore car parking.

Community and culture
The centre contributes to the quality of life in the neighbourhood, creating spaces for children to play safely and for adults to relax from the stresses of an intense city life.

Health
The passive and active contact with nature provides the opportunity for relaxation. The building makes use of low VOC materials and all spaces have good natural daylight.

Materials
Low VOC materials were selected for their reduced impact on health, and recycled materials (e.g. soy bean panels) were selected to reduce the use of primary materials.

Energy
The building is naturally ventilated, is well insulated and requires minimal heating.

PVs are integrated in the rooflight glazing over the toilets and produce 10 per cent of the overall electrical needs. When the school district threatened to cut the PVs from the scheme, the community raised $5,000 for the PV installation, which was sufficient to push the school district to fund the rest.

Natural light is available everywhere and is controllable, by means of window blinds, to suit external light levels and the need for privacy. The classrooms are very well lit and do not need artificial light for most of the year.

Water
Low flush WCs and aerated taps were installed. The minimal driveway and paved areas and the predominance of planted surfaces on the site minimise rainwater run-off.

View of the communal garden from the west.

View of the communal garden from the east.

The children look out on the gardens.

A typical 1.5 x 3-metre gardening plot.

A geodesic greenhouse is used by all the gardening community to grow seedlings.

Chapter 2
Community

2.0 Introduction

2.0.1 Aims of sustainable communities

– Minimise resource use and waste.

– Limit pollution to levels which natural systems can cope with without degradation.

– Meet local needs locally if possible.

– Enable everyone to have affordable access to safe food and water, shelter and fuel.

– Enable everyone to have opportunities for rewarding work. Unpaid work should be recognised. Payment for all work should be fair and fairly distributed.

– Protect everyone's health by providing clean, safe and pleasant environments as well as preventative measures and cures for the ill.

– Provide access to facilities, services, goods and other people without reliance on the car and not to the environment's detriment.

– Ensure people can live without fear of crime and personal violence because of personal beliefs, race, gender or sexuality.

– Provide access to skills, knowledge and information for everyone to contribute to society.

– Ensure community participation in decision-making.

– Make opportunities for culture, leisure and recreation available to all.

– Provide places, spaces and objects which are meaningful, beautiful and useful. Provide settlements that are human in scale. Ensure diversity and local culture are valued and protected.
(Phillips 2003)

Sustainability is not only about architectural strategies and building solutions; it is not only about environmental processes and management systems, or even about taxes and legislative systems. Sustainability is about the way people live. Everything individuals do in their lives has an impact on the environment. The choices of food, housing, entertainment, work and mobility all directly or indirectly affect the environment. Such choices are based on personal interests and values which today are often driven by aspirations to acquire material wealth and are associated with high environmental impacts. The Worldwatch team suggests that these consumerist values fill a void in people's lives left by the loss of the belief in the value of religion, the community and the family, and even displaces these beliefs where still intact. A shift away from these consumerist values is, however, essential, as a less consumptive society is the only way of achieving a sustainable global community (Worldwatch 2004).

This view, which suggests that changes in ethics and values are a prerequisite for achieving sustainability, is shared by many, including Parkin as quoted in the Introduction. Societies need to be re-educated in the importance of what is non-material. Basic material wealth is of course desirable, as health and the availability of education, employment, housing and time to spend with the family and community. However, there is no evidence that excessive material wealth increases human wellbeing and, indeed, certain forms of excess can be detrimental. The World Health Organisation has reported that among the causes of the increased levels of cardiovascular disease and cancer ill-health, which are responsible for approximately 40 per cent of deaths globally, are the excessive consumption of inappropriate food and tobacco, combined with inactivity (WHO 2003a).

The difficulty in seeing beyond what one is accustomed to and moving away from the highly advertised consumerist lifestyle are the biggest obstacles to achieving a change of attitudes and values. To overcome these hurdles, individuals have to be presented with a lifestyle that is equally satisfying, if perhaps in different ways, to the one they are used to. Life within an active and safe community, offering access to culture, education, work, leisure and time for friends and family, presents a possible alternative with potential for lower environmental impacts. Vibrant communities can substitute material interactions with human interactions. Community interaction can offer a deep satisfaction derived from the realisation of having developed as a person, having been able to help others, or simply having enjoyed the company or the contributions of other individuals.

At a theoretical level, many people already recognise that a quality of life that creates happiness is more valuable than growth in economic terms alone. As part of a questionnaire on housing densities undertaken in the UK, 74 per cent of respondents agreed that 'Quality of life is more important than economic development.' Only 6 per cent disagreed (Platt 2004 *et al.*). The number of people 'opting out' from a material-oriented lifestyle suggests there is a growing appreciation of the benefits of a lifestyle focused more on people and less on material possessions; and there is also a willingness to put into practice these different priorities.

For changes to a less consumptive and more people-focused life to take effect in a society on a large scale, it is necessary to have supportive frameworks in place. Architecture can contribute to creating environments that help those who are keen to change and persuade others to consider change. 'Lifestyle change cannot be imposed, but it can be encouraged by good design' (Edwards and Turrent 2000).

So what should a sustainable community provide and how can the built environment contribute to realising sustainable communities?

What constitutes a sustainable community?

Sustainable communities offer people the opportunity to enjoy a high standard of living, while having a minimal negative impact on the environment and the economic and social structure. Sustainable communities should be highly desirable places to live, as only that which is desirable has the potential for a long life, longevity being a prerequisite for sustainability. What a sustainable community means in practice may be interpreted in different ways, but common threads seem to exist. Most people associate a desirable sustainable community with a place that engenders a feeling of belonging, an attractive and healthy place within a convivial community, a safe place that is pollution-free, uncongested, planted, less frenetic and offers a more locally based life with a balance of privacy and community interaction (Barton 2000). To create such an environment, the focus has to be on the needs and desires of community residents. This fundamental principle is now recognised by the UK government and its guidance for creating sustainable communities states the need to put people's interests first (DETR 2000a).

Sustainable communities should develop sustainable solutions to meet the basic needs for homes, health, education, employment, an attractive and safe environment, a prosperous economy, good public services and open space. Sustainable communities should aim to be resource-efficient and preferably resource-autonomous, sourcing water, energy and materials as much as possible from the local environment, as well as sourcing services from the local community. They should also aim to be inclusive, addressing the needs of all people, regardless of background.

Sustainable communities have the additional dimension of being able to offer people networks of mutual support and association. A community is a group of people connected through shared experiences. In the case of cities, these experiences relate to the built environment and the facilities contained therein. The character of a place is of importance as people often define themselves by the place they live in. A place is affected by sights, sounds, smells, attention to detail, activities, cultural history and built environment. The character of a place affects how people feel and can engender feelings of civic pride, communal identity, security or, conversely, feelings of indifference or disrespect. This character is affected by the built environment as much as it is affected by how people act within this environment.

2.0.2 Designing for sustainable communities

Recognising and enhancing the social capital

- Respect individuality and diversity.
- Identify and know the stakeholders.
- Encourage community intellectual ownership.
- Encourage and value community involvement.
- Support and facilitate community-driven initiatives.
- Encourage and enhance cultural identity.

Providing basic needs

- Provide decent housing for all.
- Consider opportunities for local training and employment.
- Ensure all environments are healthy, accessible and safe.

Enhancing the quality of life

- Recognise the impact of the built environment on community activities and relationships.
- Consider provision of accessible cultural and leisure facilities.
- Ensure a quality public environment.
- Provide public and private natural environments for people and wildlife.
- Encourage community interaction by providing attractive, comfortable, safe public environments of human scale.

Promoting sustainability

- Educate, discuss, agree and set targets for sustainable design with all stakeholders.
- Design buildings as educational tools with explicit explanations or demonstrations of systems used.

Community networks can significantly affect attitudes of community residents and, consequently, their shared experiences. The relationships between members of a community can range from superficial acquaintances to closer working co-operations. These may not be as close between family and friends, but can be as significant. Informal relationships can be undemanding and casual and can develop through daily activities such as shopping, taking a walk or having a drink in a café or pub. More formal relationships may develop within community groups and voluntary organisations working purposefully towards shared goals, which often benefit the community as a whole. These links engender trust and can develop into friendships, they strengthen the bonds of a community and at a personal level can give meaning to people's lives. These cooperative networks, defined as social capital, as opposed to economic capital, are considered key to the existence of strong communities.

Coherent and strong community can benefit from advantages ranging from lower crime levels, increased sense of security and improved health, to economic advantages resulting from sharing facilities and equipment and exchanging advice and experience with people from other paths of life. Sustainable communities can form a basis for enjoying a high quality of life.

Inclusive communities

A sustainable community should provide a high quality of life for everyone. Eliminating inequalities is a key part of the sustainability agenda. Globally this means ensuring all people have access to sufficient safe food and water to survive, effective shelter from environmental pressures, education, healthcare and an income to support a basic quality of life. The over-consumption of developed countries is jeopardising the ability of developing countries to satisfy even these basic needs (Worldwatch 2004), consequently creating sustainable communities in developed countries indirectly also helps create more sustainable societies globally.

However, even in developed countries inequalities are increasing as the difference in wealth between the top earners and the poorest grows. The US has the most unequal distribution of wealth among high income countries, with 30 per cent of the income belonging to the top earning 10 per cent of the population and only 1.8 per cent of the wealth in the hands of the 10 per cent poorest. Financial remuneration of individuals at the top of the pay scale in the US is 350 times that of those at the bottom of the scale (Worldwatch 2003). Differences in resource use and waste production follow suit. Wackernagel and Rees (1996) calculated the ecological footprint of the poorest 20 per cent of Canada's population to be a quarter of that of the wealthiest 20 per cent. Similarly, inequalities in terms of benefiting from health and education are also related to wealth.

Developing desirable and sustainable communities requires eliminating poverty and social exclusion and redressing inequalities. Everyone's basic requirements for decent housing, education, employment opportunities should be satisfied, but beyond that everyone should have the opportunity to develop their individual potential as well as enjoying a high quality of life. Particular consideration has to be given to groups that have difficulty in expressing their own interests, such as children, the elderly, low income groups and minorities.

The built environment can contribute to creating strong and cohesive communities that can offer residents a high quality of life, benefiting from more democratic and open governance, higher educational levels and lower crime rates. Involving all the community in the planning, realisation and upholding of its developments ensures that changes to the community are in line with its needs and therefore sustainable. By designing and developing the built environment, whether private or public, to be of human scale and of quality, to include pedestrian-friendly environments and community spaces that encourage human interactions; by satisfying basic housing needs with quality building solutions and integrating opportunities for work and education in urban and rural developments; by generally considering the effects of developments on the community, the built environment can help create communities with a sense of identity and belonging that over time will strengthen through a communal memory of place.

2.0.3 Further reading

Consensus Design, Socially Inclusive Process
Day, C. (2003) Architectural Press, Oxford

Building the 21st-Century Home: The Sustainable Urban Neighbourhood
Rudlin, D. and Falk, N. (1999) Architectural Press, Oxford

Community Participation Methods in Design and Planning
Sanoff, H. (2000) John Wiley and Sons, Chichester

Communities and Sustainable Development: Participation in the Future
Warburton, D. ed. (1998) Earthscan Publications, London

The Community Planning Handbook
Wates, N. (2000) Earthscan Publications, London

2.1 Community Participation

Vibrant and successful communities will be created:

- where people shape the future of their own communities
- where people can live in attractive spaces and buildings
- spaces which are more environmentally sustainable with less noise, pollution and traffic congestion
- spaces which are prosperous and enable people to develop their full potential
- spaces which offer good quality services including health, education, housing, transport, finance, shopping, leisure and protection from crime
(DETR 2000a)

Community participation, in all its different guises, aims to involve the people who will be affected by a development in the decision-making relating to its implementation and management. 'Sustainable development at the local level must be implemented in a holistic process which inspires city people and which gives them a sense of ownership and direct involvement.' (Girardet 1999a). Community involvement has to go beyond the process of informing the community or even basic consultation: it should aim to partially or totally hand over control of the project development and management to the local community.

The experience of the past 30 years has revealed the need for community participation. Past regeneration activities have shown that appropriate and lasting change can take place only if driven by those affected by change: the community residents. The UK government paper *Opportunities for Change*, published in 1998, advocates engendering a feeling of ownership among building users when designing new developments, particularly with respect to housing. It suggests that building designers and developers should put the community first, not the cost. This is an approach that may reflect the experience of costly reinstatements of failed community interventions, which did not involve the people affected by them in the development.

Projects may fail because the development feels like an imposition and is resented by residents, or it may simply not be what was required in the area. Community residents are the best people to identify issues and set priorities for their own communities, and future building occupants are the best people to ask about what to include in their buildings. Local knowledge is invaluable as it highlights the community stakeholders, their needs and priorities and the problems and mechanisms unique to a community.

Community participation has many practical advantages that help to make a development successful and therefore sustainable. It also aspires to creating a more just society. Mutual understanding, often developed through community participation, helps dispel prejudices between groups instigating the development and those affected by it. The resulting working relationships are often more collaborative and productive. Even friendships can develop. Recognising and acknowledging the contributions of individuals or groups, in particular disadvantaged ones, creates a more balanced and inclusive relationship, based on mutual respect. For certain individuals, the experience of being able to contribute to improve the community environment has personal benefits, raising their confidence, aspirations and general well-being. Sustainable communities developed through community participation can therefore help to reduce social inequality and exclusion and provide a high quality of life to individuals often marginalised from community life.

Community participation should not stop with the development and completion of the building project. The community should not only psychologically gain ownership of the project, but also in practice take over some responsibility for its upkeep. The sense of ownership and the practical responsibility for a development can change the attitude of residents towards it from one of indifference to one of guardianship. The experience of managing a project can prove enlightening and enhance the understanding of systems that previously had been seen as obstructive. Community participation makes developments feel like personal investments for those who have contributed to their realisation.

Inclusive communities

Equity is a fundamental principle of sustainability and has to be addressed at a local community level as well as on a global scale. Community participation has to include all community members, regardless of age, gender, ability, culture, religion, race, income group and educational background. Sustainable communities have to eliminate inequalities, including circumstances that favour certain groups. Community participation has to consider groups who have difficulty in voicing their own interests and minorities who may consider themselves too insignificant, while not taking for granted more eloquent groups. Achieving a balance between diverging views and perspectives through an open discussion can help enhance mutual understanding and collaboration between interest groups.

Cultural diversity has a particularly valuable contribution to make towards sustainable local and global communities. Diversity is enriching. However, different cultures can also prove obscure and consequently sometimes be threatening. Increased community interaction can enhance the understanding of different cultures, and this increased understanding can help to increase tolerance and cooperation and help avoid conflict between cultures globally.

Participation in practice

The advantages of community involvement outweigh the additional time and cost required to organise and run the consultation process. Before the design and development, the community will want to know what is being planned and where, who is involved and what the budget is, what are the alternatives and the constraints, who will decide and when, who is going to benefit and who is going to lose. The community will also want to be assured that their input will be considered. Voluntary groups can help in accessing more introverted parts of the community as well as helping to organise more time-intensive consultative activities. Throughout the development, the community will want to be kept informed and be offered opportunities to continue contributing views.

If, as recommended, the community is involved in managing the completed development, support has to be made available. Support in terms of expertise is often provided through training, experienced staff or links to like-minded networks. With adequate support, community-run projects can have a long, successful life, proving the wealth of ability and dedication that exists in even the most deprived communities.

2.1.2 Methods for involving the community

– Newsletters and the press provide general information and increase awareness about plans for development.

– Open days and exhibitions provide information and increase awareness, but also provide an opportunity for residents to ask questions, as well as for developers or designers to gather a range of views.

– Informal discussions with community organisations make it possible to gather information about the needs, priorities and differences of the local people.

– Questionnaires can be used to gather basic information from a large number of people.

– Focus groups provide opportunities to discuss specific issues in detail.

– Public meetings are a good way to present information to large groups, but tend to be too large for in-depth discussions.

– Planning workshops can be used to work through different development options in detail as well as discussing different points of view. These workshops are also successful in generating enthusiasm.

– 'Planning for Real'® – involves developing an action plan for an area or a particular development from suggestions made and prioritised by the local community. The extent of the consultation depends on the project.

– Consensus design – a method of community participation developed by the architect Christopher Day (see case study on p.60). It involves group in-depth analysis of the project and site which results in a design proposal derived through consensus.

– The size of meeting will be a factor that determines whether or not people attend. While some prefer intimate meetings and are unlikely to attend public meetings, others may prefer large groups. A variety of consultation options should be made available. The location is also crucial in ensuring attendance and the choice of location should be made in discussion with local residents.

Case study: Community consultation

Fairfield Housing Co-operative
Perth, Scotland, UK

Client: Scottish Development Agency,
Scottish Homes, Perth and Kinross Council and Fairfield
Housing Co-operative
Architect: Gaia Architects
Landscape architects: Turnbull Jeffrey and Gaia Architects
Structural engineer: Allen Gordon & Partners
Mechanical engineer: Gaia Architects
Contractor and developer for the masterplan:
Hall and Tawse
Completed: 2003

The existing blocks were refurbished.

New landscaped pedestrian routes and landscaped
children's play areas enhance the surroundings.

The Fairfield housing estate, dating back to 1935, is located a mile from the city centre
of Perth. What makes Fairfield special is the way it was transformed from a crime-ridden
estate contributing 2 per cent of the crime in Tayside with nearly a quarter of the 450
homes boarded up, to a highly desirable development with a waiting list of 300 families.

The estate had not always been a problem. Up to the mid-1960s it thrived with a
strong community feeling, but by the end of that decade its decline had begun and, in
1974, the local authority paved over the gardens as a desperate measure to 'improve' the
environment. By 1985, when Gaia Architects were appointed, only 500 of the original
1,500 residents were still living on the estate and 75 per cent of these wanted to leave.
However, 15 years later, the estate was again a popular place to live.

The key to the success of the transformation was tenant participation. With the
appointment of the architects, an intense period of consultation began. The community
was invited to a number of meetings and workshops. These were designed to identify the
needs and wishes of the community and relate them to the interests and potential for
implementation of the other organisations involved.

The architects developed a matrix dividing key issues into three groups: work, folk
and place. These groupings, derived from the work of Scottish urban designer Geddes,
were developed into economy (work), to include questions of employment, economics,
affordability and waste and recycling; community (folk), to include issues of social
inclusion, amenity, health and safety and nutrition and fitness; and environment (place),
to include issues of global and local pollution, biodiversity, ecology and resources. Using
these headings the community identified several problems, such as crime levels, poor
street lighting, vandalism, litter, the lack of any facility for meeting with other residents,
lack of confidence by the elderly residents to leave their homes and lack of work for
young residents. At the same time suggestions for what could be funded came from the
funding organisations involved and the local authority considered how to address its
Local Agenda 21 obligations. Through a series of agency workshops a matrix was
developed, which identified where aspirations and the means to achieve them coincided,
and this helped to formulate a feasible programme that addressed the wishes of the
community.

The resulting development included eight phases of work. By the completion of the
first four phases in 1993, most existing dwellings had been refurbished. Further phases
included adapting units for physical and sensory disabilities and 32 new-build energy-
efficient dwellings. In addition, a new activity centre, one of the first items on the
community's wish list, and 56 private homes for sale were built. The redevelopment also
included reinstating front and back gardens, large areas of communal landscaping and
children's play areas.

One of the aims of the consultation process was to identify a way of ensuring the
sustainability of the project after development work was completed. This was achieved
by handing control of the management of the estate to its residents. In 1988, the
Fairfield Housing Co-operative was set up with help from the Scottish Homes and
Perth and Kinross Council. Run by a management committee of volunteer tenants,

Fairfield initially appointed three staff members and bought the first 56 refurbished flats for a nominal sum of £1 at the end of Phase 1 of the redevelopment. Today Fairfield Housing Co-operative employs 13 administrative, maintenance and cleaning staff to manage and maintain their more than 300 dwellings, and is due to expand its remit to another site managing an additional 80 dwellings.

The redevelopment changed the physical nature of the estate and the construction work created opportunities for training and work during the construction period. But the long-term security of the scheme is in the hands of the tenants themselves through the tenant cooperative, which continues to encourage local participation, and offers employment and learning opportunities that help to maximise social inclusion. The tenants are kept informed of the cooperative's activities through an annual report, a quarterly newsletter, *Five News*, and, most recently, through a website. Feedback from tenants is regularly sought, both through interviews and informally. During the most recent kitchen replacement programme, as with the first three phases where the tenants were known, the tenants were involved in selecting kitchen fittings. The co-operative also provides a maintenance service collecting unwanted bulk items, cleaning shared stairs and caring for the communal gardens. This ensures the estate remains clean and pleasant. A subsidised grass-cutting service is provided for elderly and disabled tenants and a garden competition, organised each year and very popular with the tenants, emphasises the importance of the external environment. Increased security has also improved the feeling of safety for the residents and the community centre's IT facilities are contributing to raising education levels among the residents. The average school-leaving age is rising and more young people from the estate are going on to further education.

The feeling of belonging, that had never deserted tenants who had lived on the estate for many years, has now extended to new residents, and a new feeling of pride in the housing and its surroundings has developed.

One of the architects' aims is to make sustainable architecture that is affordable to all, not only those with wealth. The design solutions implemented at Fairfield have succeeded in providing a quality environment within the cost limits of social housing. These physical solutions have the prospect of a long life, not only because they were developed with the residents, but because the community now has the ownership and responsibility for caring and managing their environment.

The achievement of the Fairfield development was recognised in August 2003 when the Building and Social Housing Foundation shortlisted Fairfield for the World Habitat Award. But the popularity of the estate also speaks volumes for its success. In 2002/3 over 200 housing applications were received and the more than 40 houses that became free were re-let within seven days.

2.1.3 Sustainable design features

Site and ecology
Many of the existing buildings were retained and refurbished. The new buildings are constructed on previously built land.

The site is generally well served with shops and other facilities, including bus connections.

The landscaping was enhanced and newly planted areas now house a variety of wildlife.

Community and culture
Refer to text.

Health
The Toll House Gardens houses are suitable for asthma sufferers. See Chapter 3.2.

Materials
The Leslie Court and Toll House Gardens housing makes use of timber treated with borax rather than copper, chrome and arsenic (CCA). Timber sections were screwed rather than nailed to enable their dismantling. The walls are breather walls with recycled cellulose insulation.

Energy
The Leslie Court and Toll House Gardens housing is designed as passive solar with high levels of insulation.

Water
Low flush WCs are installed in the latest developments. A sustainable urban drainage system was implemented.

Passive solar houses at Leslie Court.

See also: appropriate ventilation **Chapter 3.2**

Case study: Community self-build

Goethean Science Centre Craft Workshop
Pishwanton, Scotland, UK

Client: Life Science Trust
Architect: Christopher Day
Structural engineer: David Tasker
Completed: 2002

The craft workshop is nestled among the trees with the turf roof blending in with the surroundings.

A composting toilet is located at the car park and accessible by a ramp. The barn is visible in the distance.

Self-build can be undertaken by individuals or groups. It can refer to commissioning a building from an architect or builder to avoid developers; it can refer to physically constructing some or all of a building; and it can include both designing and physically building. The Life Science Trust adopted the latter approach. Led by architect Christopher Day and Margaret Colquhoun, the founder of the Life Science Trust, the Trust communally designed and built a new craft workshop for their Goethean Science and Art Centre in East Lothian, Scotland. The centre is dedicated to developing the work of Goethean science and art and the education arising out of this. It has a number of buildings, including a stable, a barn, a shed housing a brick kiln, a composting toilet, and the new craft workshop; and is planning to build more new buildings, including some providing living accommodation.

The craft workshop, perhaps the most complex of the buildings currently on the site, is testimony to an exceptional communal effort. With limited funds of £60,000, the project took two years to build, following an equally long period of gestation. The design of the site and buildings came about through an analytical and design process referred to by Day as consensus design (see Chapter 3.4). This combined Day's building-related and Colquhoun's landscape-related methods for analysis, which are complementary. The process involves 'listening to the land' and learning through observation and is in line with the Goethean principles that guide the Trust's activities. The design process builds on a similar process of discovery, where Day, as the technically experienced architect, 'leads quietly from the rear' and, by asking questions rather than giving solutions, solicits informed considerations by those involved in the design, who, through this process, acquire an understanding of their building. Listening is key to understanding the site, the people and creating a design that is appropriate to the site and users' needs.

This process results in a communal understanding of the character of the site and how the building can respond to it, but also gives ownership of the project to all involved. This created a community commitment strong enough to sustain the project throughout its inception and its construction. In the case of the gridshell, the community participation extended to the construction process which was undertaken to a large extent by volunteers.

This building was not simple for unskilled workers to build, in fact the roof over the main workshop area is a double curvature timber gridshell spanning nine metres. Yet guided by Malcolm Lemmon, Pishwanton's carpenter, the gridshell and virtually all the woodwork in the building were hand-crafted by volunteers. The gridshell is made of two layers of 25 x 35 four-metre-long green larch laths, scarf-jointed on site to produce longer sections. These were simply bolted together at 600-millimetre centres in one day by over 20 volunteers, including many disabled adults from the Steiner Camphill community in Edinburgh. Under the direction of David Tasker, the project engineer, the grid was moved from a flat position on the ground next to the building up a ramp to its final location. The corners of the structure were pulled in and the dome temporarily supported until the stone walls were built up to it from below. The gridshell remained unstable until the three layers of 12 x 100-millimetre pine decking were screw-fixed to the top of the gridshell laths, with a fourth layer at the perimeter. The structure was then covered with 150-millimetre cork insulation and a rubber waterproofing membrane. Turf and grass were used to cover the roof and provide a growing medium for the grass and moss, which is now thriving. The gridshell structure was tested to gain building regulation approval by placing more than 13 tonnes of sandbags on the structure, a weight equivalent to the snow loads expected, which resulted in a 25-millimetre deflection. The testing was again a communal effort, with the volunteers adding to the weight by standing on the roof.

Some of the work, such as the stonework for the walls, was contracted out to specialists, but where possible, even demanding elements were handcrafted by volunteers, such as the earth walls made with puddle clay, cow dung, straw and sand, and the cow dung 'paint' on the outside.

The experience of designing and building as a group proved enriching for all. Seeing what one has built with one's own hands is always a rewarding experience, but when the building is as ambitious as this one, the satisfaction in such an achievement must be even greater. The completed building sits comfortably in its surroundings. Its softness, created by the curved roof, the non-rectangular plan form and the chamfered windows, is harmonious with the surrounding natural landscape.

Now occupied, the building continues to be a focus for the community. The centre is a meeting place for Goethean groups and the workshop is used for pottery and woodcarving as well as by disabled adults who make woven mats. The centre has also gained funding from the local authority to run activities for excluded youths, exposing them to a way of thinking they may never have encountered before.

Affection towards the centre is not limited to those interested in its activities: the local community seems to be proud of the quiet development that has engendered such a strong community commitment and created a delightful place.

2.1.4 Sustainable design features

Site and ecology
The 24-hectare site is a mixture of grassland, marsh and forest. The landscape has been designed by using Colquhoun's Goethean principles, respecting the land's character and retaining and enhancing its natural beauty.

Community and culture
See main text.

Health
The spaces have ample natural light. Only healthy low VOC paints and non-toxic natural materials were used.

Materials
The building makes use of reused materials such as whinstone from a collapsed wall nearby and local materials such as the clay on site. Sheep wool insulation was used as well as mineral wool. Portuguese cork was used on the roof. Foundations are in limecrete. Larch was bought from a redundant project in Perthshire, Highland Douglas fir was used for the windows, and larch for the gridshell is from thinnings from a wood 20 miles from the site.

Energy
The building is well insulated and heated by means of a Kacheloven small stove, which burns wood waste.

Water
Rainwater is collected in old barrels for low grade uses.

The gridshell roof forms a rounded and soft structure resembling a natural feature. On one side of the main space are storage facilities and on the other are offices.

The workshop is used for meetings and a variety of craft activities.

See also: place of the spirit **Chapter 3.4**

Case study: Sharing culture

Uluru Kata Tjuta National Park Cultural Centre
Uluru Kata Tjuta National Park, Northern Territory, Australia

Client: Mufifjulu Community and Park Australia – Environment Australia
Architects: Gregory Burgess Architects
Landscape Architects: Taylor Cullity
Structural Engineers: P.J. YHrup and Associates
Services Engineers: W. O. Ross and Associates
Main Contractor: Sitzler Brothers, Alice Springs
Completed: 1995

The centre, hidden among the trees, is located at the junction where the sand dunes meet the landscape of umbrella bush, bloodwood trees and bearded grass.

Timber and copper shingles on the roof.

The curved roof is reminiscent of a rock outcrop or sand dunes,

Cultural diversity enriches the global community and should be protected and preserved. This can only be achieved through reciprocal respect between different cultures. Mutual cultural understanding between groups of people is the first step towards creating relationships of trust and respect and dispelling prejudices, often embedded in ignorance. Learning about different beliefs and values can also deepen the understanding of one's own cultural heritage.

The process of learning and appreciating different cultures can be slow and sometimes difficult. Museums and cultural centres can illustrate the history, bring alive the customs and explain the beliefs of a culture. But listening to people talk about their priorities and interests and interacting with them can develop a deeper understanding of their culture. The visitor centre for the Uluru Kata Tjuta National Park contributes to creating a better understanding of culture of the Anangu, the Aboriginal people of central Australia, by providing information through traditional museum-like methods. However, for those involved in it, the process of designing and building the cultural centre provided a much deeper understanding of the Anangu.

In the 1960s, 1970s and 1980s, the interests of increasing numbers of visitors going to see Uluru and wanting accommodation, food, unhindered access to the land and souvenirs seemed incompatible with the interests of the Anangu people. The Anangu wanted to continue living and working on their traditional lands, caring for the land as required by their culture, protecting important and sacred sites. They wanted their knowledge, expertise and ownership to be acknowledged.

The Anangu have always regarded the area, which is now the Uluru Kata Tjuta National Park, as a place that honours their culture and preserves the ecosystem of their ancestors, their knowledge, history, religion, morality and law. In other words, it preserves their way of life. So, despite informal attempts to relocate the Anangu, for 30 years they persisted in protecting their sacred and important sites against desecration by growing tourist numbers. Their concerns put pressure on the regional and national governments and, progressively, the Anangu's rights to Uluru and Kata Tjuta became recognised. In 1985, the Handback took place: the title deeds for the land were presented to a group of Anangu individuals who, six years earlier, had been formally identified and had become known as the Traditional Owners of the site.

Less than a year after the Handback, discussions began over the provision of a cultural centre. The centre would inform visitors about Anangu culture and landscape and help counteract the negative impact of tourism by providing physical protection to the landscape and promoting the proper interpretation of its cultural significance. The centre would also display and sell Aboriginal art and crafts, providing the Anangu with business opportunities. It was intended that the building should reflect Anangu culture and, importantly, also express the community's successful collaboration with Parks Australia in managing the National Park. Parks Australia, who lease the park back from the Anangu, agree to protect the Anangu sacred sites and maximise Anangu involvement in activities associated with the park. The Anangu pass on their knowledge of the local flora and fauna and their traditional skills to the park rangers and scientists, combining traditional culture with modern science. The success of this multicultural collaboration in respect of the land management was recognised in 1995 with a UNESCO Picasso Gold Medal.

In 1990, the architect Gregory Burgess was appointed to prepare a design brief for the visitor centre. The architects started working in a studio in Mutitjulu, an Anangu community of approximately 250 adults, to the east of Uluru. The design developed through a consultative process that involved the design team and the local community. The building should cause minimal disruption to the site, which was studied by walking the land. The brief for the centre was developed from initial sand drawings through to a consultation with the whole community. The consultation used paintings by Anangu of the stories of Uluru, the ideas of the men and women, and the Tjukurpa. The Tjukurpa, which is the foundation of Anangu society and includes its law, became part of the design considerations, bringing a deeper significance to the building as well as a greater understanding of the Anangu culture to non-Aboriginal participants.

The benefits of the consultation process and the improved understanding of the Anangu can be seen in the building design that reflects the culture of the Anangu. Like the Anangu, the visitor centre respects the land and the environment. The building includes a main exhibition gallery, a shop, a multipurpose hall currently used as a second shop, a café and an external exhibition and dance area, all linked by shaded verandas. It is located where the sand dunes meet the desert and is smaller than the surrounding trees and shielded by bushes. Local materials were used, such as the desert sand to make the floors and the bricks for the walls. The curved roofs and footprint appear organic and the timber shingles are reminiscent of animal scales. Its subtle form and the use of appropriate natural materials make it appear like a living creature adapted to the climate and landscape.

The Uluru Kata Tjuta National Park is listed as a World Heritage Cultural Landscape, a classification that relates not only to the landscape, flora and fauna, but also to the living culture it contains. The visitor centre also celebrates the interrelatedness of the Anangu culture and the landscape shaped by their traditions.

Through education and cooperation the relation between the Anangu and non-Aboriginal people may have reached a state of balance. The management board of the Uluru Kata Tjuta National Park has a majority of six members nominated by the Aboriginal Traditional Owners plus five other members. The Anangu accept that non-Aboriginal people are now sharing the land with them and have had to adapt some of aspects of their traditional law. On the other hand, they have also used non-Aboriginal law to protect the Tjukurpa. As for the visitors, the fact that an increasing number of visitors choose not to climb Uluru, as requested by the Anangu and set out in their law, seems to reflect a maturity of their relationship to other cultures.

2.1.5 Sustainable design features

Site and ecology
Through the provision of information the cultural centre helps protect the landscape.

Community and culture
Refer to text.

Health
The natural materials selected help to provide a healthy indoor environment.

Materials
The foundations are made of compacted earth. The building is made with timber poles and infilled with 90,000 earthbricks made with local soil with less than 2 per cent of bitumen added for strength. The bricks are covered with a slurry of soil and water. Panelling and cladding are made of radially sawn timber to maximise efficient use of material. The copper-tiled roof and bloodwood shingles are installed over plywood sheeting and rubber membrane, mixing traditional with contemporary technologies.

Energy
The building was designed to be naturally ventilated, with mechanical ventilation to the kitchen. Thermal mass is provided by the wall and floor construction.

Water
Water is collected in tanks and available for drinking. Sewage is treated locally with a Diston 'clearwater'.

The timber post construction is filled in with earth bricks covered with earth plaster.

2.2 Housing for All

2.2.1 Decent homes

A decent home, as defined by the UK government, should meet the following criteria:

It should

– be above the current statutory minimum standard for housing;

– be in a reasonable state of repair;

– have reasonably modern facilities and services; and

– provide a reasonable degree of thermal comfort. (DEFRA 2003)

2.2.2 Practical aspects of good housing

– sound separation from other houses and the neighbourhood and traffic

– visual privacy from neighbours and the street

– sufficient internal separation to allow each household member enough private space

– sufficient storage space

– adequate living space standards e.g. Parker Morris

1-person	32.5–33 m²
2-person	47.5–48.5 m²
3-person	60–61 m²
4-person	71.5–79 m²
5-person	80–89.5 m²
6-person	88.5–102.5 m²

Shelter, together with access to safe water and food, is one of life's basic requirements. However, even in developed countries this basic need is sometimes denied people. In the UK, homelessness and the existence of housing of below decent standards are still significant problems. In 2004, over 30,000 households were homeless and seeking housing with local authorities. Over 100,000 households were in temporary accommodation, of which over 30,000, including families with children, were in bed and breakfast accommodation or hostels. In England alone there are also an estimated 500 individuals sleeping rough on the street each night (ODPM 2004a).

Not only should everyone have access to a home, but all homes should be of a decent standard (see 2.2.1). The Sustainable Development Indicators published in 2004 by the UK government reported that in 2001, 33 per cent of homes in the UK were still considered to be below standard (DEFRA 2004a). While this represents an improvement from previous years, it is still a worryingly high percentage. In the UK, 3.1 million households that need heating still do not have central heating. This aggravates the level of fuel poverty which is linked to over 20,000 unseasonal deaths in the UK each winter (Thakrar 2002, 2003a). Defined as having to spend more than 10 per cent of total outgoings to heat a home adequately, fuel poverty particularly affects the elderly, of whom 50 per cent were suffering from fuel poverty in 1998 (DEFRA 2003).

Sustainable housing goes beyond providing decent housing. Sustainable housing should be resource-efficient and provide a healthy, comfortable and uplifting environment for the users. Sustainable homes should address the needs of all community members: those with sensory or physical disabilities, the elderly, children, young families and home-workers; and ensure, by making houses easily adaptable, that these needs continue to be addressed for a long time.

Sustainable housing is effectively high quality housing. This does not necessarily imply large. In line with Schumacher's philosophy of small is beautiful, while a quality home should provide sufficient quality space for the residents to undertake their day-to-day activities, excessive space will not necessarily improve their life. The popularity of traditional cottages, with small rooms and low ceilings, reflects the human need for more than just practicalities. How the space is designed outweighs its size.

The UK government lists a number of contributions that good quality housing can make towards a community. It is thought to 'give people a stronger sense of security and identity; strengthen communities; protect health; and provide a better setting in which people can raise families and promote educational achievements' (DETR 2000a). Good quality housing can help create a sense of place and improve the urban environment as well as making people's life easier to cope with and more enjoyable. Living in a quality environment is a key element in improving people's lives.

Different housing development types can achieve various aspects of sustainability. Co-housing, for example, aims to create a miniature community of mutual support that benefits from the advantages listed above (see Pinakarri case study, p.72). Another approach is mixed tenure housing, where social, rented and privately owned housing is mixed. This addresses aspects of sustainable living ranging from social equity and inclusion to practical resource efficiency. Social housing situated within such mixed developments is less likely to be stigmatised and those living in it less likely to be seen as separate or even inferior. By ensuring that developments contain a variety of housing types, people from all social and income groups should be able to find a place to live anywhere within a particular city, allowing them to live near their place of work or near other members of their family. Mixed developments also help to create a continuous demand for local facilities of different types, ensuring their long-term viability. The sustainable provision of services within any part of a city reduces the need to travel, which has environmental advantages and increases accessibility for those without personal transport. In addition, local services enhance the provision of work opportunities for those living locally, and unable to travel far for work.

Housing developments should offer a variety of different living options: small and large dwellings, houses and flats, with and without gardens. This provides appropriate living options for individuals with diverse needs and ensures a mix of people of different ages and backgrounds within one area. Housing to accommodate special needs and sheltered housing should also be included. Mixed housing developments provide opportunities to accommodate changes in personal circumstances without needing to relocate to other parts of a city away from an accustomed community or family.

While building good quality housing generally depends on sufficient funding, there are a number of ways to overcome the limitations imposed by budgets. One of the most problematic issues facing the UK government today is a lack of affordable housing particularly in certain property hot spots. To create affordable housing, building costs have to be reduced as much as possible. New methods of construction, such as prefabrication, are thought to have potential in this respect. At the other end of the scale, unsophisticated methods of buildings can allow unskilled future residents to self-build the whole or some parts of their home. Self-build schemes organised by housing associations allow future tenants to contribute time in lieu of payments towards their home. In certain cases, the use of unusual low cost materials, such as recycled tyres or straw bales, has further reduced the construction cost.

In addition to lowering construction costs, housing can be made more affordable by reducing running costs. Designing housing to be energy- and water-efficient reduces utility bills for the residents. Developments located within a city centre and accessible by public transport can make the ownership of a car unnecessary. The cost of owning and running a car, without counting depreciation and considering low usage, is equivalent to annual loan repayments on £20,000-30,000. This comparison underlines the importance, when addressing sustainability, of considering all aspects of life, including those not directly related to buildings.

2.2.3 Housing needs

Overall in the UK 3.8 million houses are thought to be needed by 2016. Of these, between 67,000 and 80,000 affordable units are estimated to be required annually and there is currently a deficit of 30-45,000 units.

Affordable housing

In the UK, for individuals with lower incomes there are a number of affordable housing options provided by local authorities and housing associations (otherwise known as Social Registered Landlords):

- social rented homes – The rent is reduced in comparison to market rents, usually by 20–40 per cent.

- shared ownership – The resident buys part of the dwelling and pays reduced rent for the remaining part which remains in the ownership of the SRL. The percentage owned by the resident varies, but is usually between 30 and 60 per cent.

- low cost home ownership – These homes are restricted in size to make them affordable. This option is not viable in property hot spots where the cost of even these small dwellings would prove unaffordable for many.

- discounted open market value (DOMV) – these homes are majority owned (usually 80 per cent) by the resident, with the rest owned by the landlord, who retains control in terms of future sales.

Case study: Affordable housing

Barling Court housing
Stockwell, London, UK

Client: Hyde Housing
Architect: PCKO
Main manufacturer: Buma
Completed: 2004

The flats are accessed through a small car parking area to the side of the block.

The metal and balcony structure forms a bright external space for each flat.

In the UK there is a deficit of between 30,000 and 45,000 affordable housing units being built each year (Crook *et al.* 2002). In the past 20 years the cost of property has risen faster than incomes and currently many people on low to middle incomes cannot afford suitable properties. This is forcing some of the people priced out of the market to move around the country to more affordable areas. Key workers, such as nurses and policemen, living and working in areas with high property values, such as London and the South East, are particularly affected.

The average rent for social rented sector tenants should be between 25 per cent and 30 per cent of their average nett earnings. Affordable rents are typically 30-40 per cent lower than market rents (ODPM 2004b). However, as market prices rise, even these discounted affordable rents become out of reach for an increasing number of people. While housing benefits can make up shortfalls for some low earners, there is simply a need for more affordable housing units to address everyone's needs.

Different approaches to increase the affordable housing stock are being investigated and prefabrication of the whole or parts of buildings is one possible way forward. Off-site fabrication can manufacture housing quickly and more efficiently, and can offer a healthier working environment for the building team. Prefabrication offers a good potential for creating energy-efficient housing by integrating higher levels of insulation in new construction systems. Off-site fabrication helps reduce manufacturing waste and factory construction is also thought to address the skills shortage experienced for decades in the UK construction industry.

Off-site housing fabrication still needs to improve its cost-effectiveness if it is to increase its market share. Currently costing on average 10 per cent more than traditional build, owing to its relatively low uptake, the prospect of increasing off-site fabrication methods is limited by the fact that 50-60 per cent of construction in the housing sector is remedial work (Hyde 2004). Despite possible drawbacks, a number of housing associations in the UK, such as Hyde Housing, continue to investigate the options available including, most recently, systems of relocatable housing that can be installed on underused sites or temporarily available sites. Recently Hyde Housing with architects PCKO have developed designs using a steel frame, demountable, volumetric system, and the first housing association relocatable housing in the United Kingdom was completed in 2004 at Barling Court in London.

The development at Barling Court has eight flats for key workers within a four-storey block located near local facilities. The 50-square metre one-bedroom flats and the 65-square metre two-bedroom flats are larger than those in standard private housing and are finished to a high quality. Each flat has a balcony. This external space is shaded by movable timber solar screens which also provide privacy.

The volumetric system used is manufactured by Buma in Poland. It was developed from a prefabricated panel system and then adapted for high density housing. The modules, designed to have a 60-year life span, have a robust steel frame structure and are clad externally with steel and rendered panels. Each flat is made of two modules and the central stair core is made of one module. All internal finishes and fittings, including kitchen and bathroom fittings, were installed in the factory. The only building elements not part of the volumetric modules are the steel and timber balconies, which were installed on site.

The key feature of the system is its demountability, making it possible to move the housing if required. The individual modules are bolted together and can easily be unbolted, transported to another site and re-erected. The process of dismantling and re-erecting the system was tested by the manufacturers using a model house that was moved to eight different exhibition sites.

Using volumetric construction significantly reduced the construction programme compared to traditional build. From ground work preparation to commissioning the project took four months rather than the typical 14. The installation of the modules took only four days. At £1260 per square metre, equivalent to a 12 per cent reduction on traditional construction methods and a 20-30 per cent reduction on other prefabricated methods, the development disproves the general trend that volumetric housing is not cost-effective. The quality of the finishes also speaks in favour of prefabrication, with minimal defects at the end of the project.

The quality of the project in terms of space provision, quality of space and finishes, combined with the advantages in terms of cost and flexibility and the potential for maximising energy efficiency, confirms the system's potential for addressing the urgent need for more affordable housing.

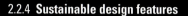

2.2.4 Sustainable design features

Site and ecology
The housing is currently located on a wasteland site in central London, close to public transport and local facilities. The housing can be repositioned if required.

Community and culture
The use of derelict sites helps to improve the local environment. In addition, the sound insulation levels exceed current standards and ensure privacy for the residents. See also main text.

Health
The housing has good natural light and provides external spaces for the residents.

Materials
The main structural materials used are recyclable. The volumetric units are reusable.

Energy
The housing achieved a 'good' Eco Homes rating. The units are heated with small electrical heaters, appropriate for the levels of fabric insulation, which exceed current standards.

Water
Water use is minimised through the installation of low flush WCs and aerated taps.

The external materials include rendered panels, metal cladding and timber louvres.

All finishes are of a high quality.

Case study: Self-build

London Fields Housing Co-operative
London Fields Road, London UK

Client: SOLON Co-operative Housing Services
Architect: Constructive Individuals
Quantity surveyor: R.J. Batley
Main contractor: TRAK construction
Completed: 2002

A converted bay window leads through a ground floor lobby to a rear courtyard and an external access stair, which provide access to the flats.

In the late 1990s, a group of 60 people were living in a number of dilapidated Victorian terraces in the London Fields area of East London. The houses were in desperate need of renovation and there was a risk that the residents would be evicted from their homes. In response to this threat the group formed a housing cooperative that would allow the group to raise funds to renovate their houses. The London Fields Solutions Housing Coop was set up and private funding as well as funding from the European Union Single Regeneration Budget was gained and the design for the conversions began.

The development involved the conversion of six two-storey and twelve three-storey houses in a mix of flats, maisonettes and shared houses, which corresponded to the needs of the existing residents. To reduce construction costs and make the housing more affordable, it was decided that a portion of the building work would be undertaken by the future inhabitants. The concept of 'sweat-equity' is well understood and allows future tenants or owners to pay 'in kind' for a part of their future home.

At London Fields, most of the building work involved the restructuring and upgrading of the existing buildings, but there were some new extensions to be erected as well. The complex building work was undertaken by a construction company, while less demanding work was undertaken by the future occupants. This included second fix joinery, plumbing, kitchens, and decorations. Many of the future occupants had no construction knowledge and had to learn on the job. Experiences were shared and self-builders with building skills taught others. However, the project lacked an overall coordinator and some self-builders contributed more than others. The lack of building experience and the housing association's lack of experience of such projects also meant that the construction period took longer than planned, and in the end minor defects were left unfinished after completion.

Despite these difficulties, the project was felt to be successful and has enhanced the community feeling. In terms of affordability, the additional effort was also worth it. The generously sized flats cost the residents half the going rate in rent. Utility bills are very low. Unexpected benefits also materialise: while the future residents were supplied with materials and fittings, there was some freedom for them to design the space and personalise it as they wished.

Having discovered the freedom of building for themselves, two years on, the residents, now fully settled in and preoccupied with their day-to-day life, are still improving their homes, changing to suit new needs and refining existing work.

The rear courtyard is quiet, private and secure.

2.2.5 Sustainable design features

Site and ecology
The existing buildings were refurbished. This makes good use of previously used resources including land and materials. The roofs were converted into roof terraces providing the flats with external areas.

Community and culture
Refurbishing the existing buildings helped retain the existing architectural character of the area. By allowing the group of people who were already living in the area to remain in the houses, the community was not disrupted. The process of self-building also enhanced the local community feeling.

Health
Access to external space provides an amenity area and somewhere to grow food.

Materials
Timber-framed extensions are insulated with recycled cellulose insulation and clad with cedar cladding.

Energy
The building fabric has been upgraded in terms of insulation and energy-efficient boilers were installed. A £25,000 grant allowed additional investment in insulated plasterboard to line the existing walls, boilers and dedicated energy-efficient lighting. Bulk-buying of high insulation timber sash windows helped reduce costs, while installing good quality products. By reusing the existing buildings, the embodied energy of the resulting dwellings is lower than if they had been newly built.

See also: live-work **Chapter 1.2**

Case study: Opportunities for all

York Road Housing
York Road, Cheam, UK

Client: Threshold Housing Association
Architect: ECD Architects
Main contractor: Benson
Completed: 1998

2.2.6 Sustainable design features

Site and ecology
The site had previously been developed.

Community and culture
See main text.

Health
Good natural light is provided. Sunlight is also allowed to enter the homes.

Materials
The development is clad in untreated cedar cladding, and requires minimal maintenance. The copper roofing includes recycled content and can be recycled, and it also patinates naturally without additional treatments.

Energy
The walls and windows are well insulated. Gas condensing boilers and low energy lighting make efficient use of energy.

Building fabric U-values:
   Walls – 0.3 W/m² C (R19)
   Roof – 0. 25 W/m² C (R23)

The development achieved an 'Excellent' Environmental Standard (precursor of ECO Homes) rating.

Water
Low flush WCs were installed.

A community needs to address the needs of all its members. This includes vulnerable individuals, such as those with learning disabilities and other impairments (see also Chapter 3.3). Building design solutions can address the spatial requirements and the accessibility of housing, but support from the community or health organisations may also be necessary. The needs of people with learning disabilities range widely: some can and want to live independently, an approach that is generally supported, while others need regular support. This support may be provided by carers visiting an individual at regular intervals at home, or it may be provided by live-in carers. While many people with learning disabilities want to live in self-contained housing, others prefer shared accommodation.

The York Road housing development provides such accommodation in two five-person houses, part of a mixed housing development. The housing is accessible through a courtyard behind a block of nine shared ownership flats. The incorporation of the special needs housing within a small general housing development helps to integrate the residents within the community, where they have the possibility of forming a support network. The houses are set back from the street and benefit from a quiet location. On the ground floors are communal living, cooking and dining areas which open onto a rear private garden. One wheelchair-accessible bedroom is also located at ground level, while further bedrooms are on the first floor.

In England there are 1.4 million individuals who require specially adapted accommodation; 74 per cent of them have found suitable solutions, but there is still a need to address outstanding needs (ODPM 2004b). The York Road housing development contributes towards closing that gap with a contemporary design which is also energy-efficient and ecological.

The entrance to the shared houses.

The second floor terraces of the flats provide private outdoor spaces for the tenants.

The shared ownership flats face the quiet, tree-lined residential road.

Case study: Cohousing

Pinakarri Cohousing
Hamilton Hill, Perth, Western Australia

Client: Pinakarri Community
Architect: Hammond and Green
Completed: 1999

The bungalow unit facing the communal garden is fully accessible.

The cars are located at the perimeter of the development.

The passive solar houses face north onto the planted areas where the use of native plant species keeps watering needs to a minimum.

Cohousing offers an alternative lifestyle to the impersonal and isolated life often experienced in modern cities today. It creates a framework for a mutually supportive environment, both at a practical level and at a psychological level.

Cohousing originated in Denmark in the 1960s when, among others, Danish architect Jan Gudmand-Hoyer wanted to create a housing development that resembled a village more than the typical suburb. In the 1970s, the idea spread and has now reached as far as the US and Australia. Its distinctive characteristic is a democratically determined structure, which generally calls for a sharing and supportive attitude between members. Physically, cohousing developments often comprise connected housing around a courtyard or other pedestrian area and a common house with communal eating and other facilities. In respect of sustainability, cohousing has a number of advantages, including more efficient use of land, potential for reduced car ownership and use, reduced requirements for material goods and improved social cohesion and personal well-being. Many cohousing schemes are also developed with resource efficiency and ecology in mind and therefore the buildings tend to be designed to be healthy and have reduced environmental impacts. The combination of environmentally sound building and the community-oriented characteristics of cohousing makes it an exemplar for sustainable living.

The community house has a communal kitchen and dining space, office and guest room.

Pinakarri cohousing was modelled on these principles. Started by a group of like-minded individuals with similar goals in 1991, the Pinakarri community set out to build a sustainable housing community. The main aims, dictated by the initial prevalence of single parents, was to create a safe and supportive environment, managed by the community members, which would be a model of affordable sustainable living in the suburban setting of Perth. Initially the group developed a framework and guidelines to run their community. Group members adopted different responsibilities, such as finances or public relations and developed skills throughout the process of procuring, building and managing the housing.

In 1995, Pinakarri community received $1m from the State Housing Commission charged with providing public housing in Western Australia. A year later two sites were acquired: a 2,000-square metre site for eight houses for rent plus a common house, and an adjacent 1,000-square metre site for four privately owned houses. The resulting development, completed in 1999, is of medium to high density, equivalent to 40 dph. The houses are energy-efficient and the site layout is designed to create opportunities for interaction while ensuring each home has sufficient privacy and its own external space.

Housing approximately 20 adults and 15 children, the community benefits from shared facilities primarily located in the communal house, which comprises a kitchen and dining area, bathroom, guest room, meeting room and communal office. One of the bungalows has been purpose-designed for the particular needs of a severely intellectually and physically disabled resident who requires 24-hour care.

The community interacts and collaborates in various ways. Monthly meetings give people the opportunity to share concerns and discuss community issues. Pinakarri is a Nyangamarta Aboriginal word which means 'deep listening' and the ability to listen to each other is a key factor in the harmonious running of the community. Each individual's view contributes to the common knowledge and is used in the decision-making process. The use of the Internet to discuss issues prior to the meeting adds thinking time to consider other people's points of view. Additional fortnightly meetings are used to address operational issues.

The community shares meals three times a week in the common house; these are prepared in turn by members and are a social event as well as a way to save energy. Once a month meals are extended to neighbours and friends. The Pinakarri members actively promote social and environmental issues through workshops and the monthly dinners help by giving visitors a taste of what communal life can be. Childcare is offered by one of the residents and the children enjoy the social events and the generally caring environment. Especially beneficial for them is the extended play community and the space to play in a safe environment.

Since occupation some residents have left and others have moved in. The community has proved extremely successful and has spread beyond its physical limits; some neighbours are now members. The environmentally benign and socially supportive approach has proved a recipe for a fulfilling and high quality life.

A sandbox in the planted courtyard is used by the toddlers in the community.

2.2.7 Sustainable design features

Site and ecology
The site was previously occupied by four houses. Cars are kept to the edge of the development and car-pooling is organised where possible, for example, to take children to school.

Vegetable gardens are located on the roadside just outside the courtyard enclosure. Organic food is purchased by the group from a local farmer.

Community and culture
The houses are affordable, having been built for less than the housing authority budget. The construction design and even some of the energy-efficient measures provided costs savings, for example, the insulated roof panels saved on average $12,000 per house. This enabled money to be spent on high quality internal finishes, such as the terracotta floor tiles, and financed the construction of the common house. The energy-efficient features resulted in reduced operating costs and the collaborative nature of cohousing also helped reduce the overall living costs.

See also main text.

Health
All the houses have good natural light and provide good private space. One unit is fully accessible. The passive solar design approaches taken make the houses warmer and healthier places than other typical alternatives.

Materials
The houses were built with traditional technologies that enabled them to be affordable. Some reclaimed building elements, such as sinks, were used. Composting and recycling facilities are available.

Equipment, such as gardening and computer equipment, is shared.

Energy
All houses are passive solar designs making use of solar gains in winter, creating comfortable environments without need for space heating. The houses have insulated roofs, helping to reduce heat losses and heat gains in summer. The light-coloured roofs also help reflect solar radiation and prevent overheating in summer. The terracotta-tiled concrete ground floors provide thermal mass. The homes are naturally ventilated (see Chapter 5.1)

Energy-efficient boilers are used to heat water.

Water
Water use is reduced through low flush WCs. Rainwater tanks are planned for the future.

See also: acquiring life skills Chapter 2.3

See also: building orientation Chapter 5.1

2.3 Training and Employment

2.3.1 Considerations regarding the impacts of buildings on employment and education

How will the development affect the local economy in terms of numbers and diversity of new business and jobs created and lost?

How will the development enhance the viability of local businesses?

How will the development provide new opportunities for training and developing the skills of local people?

How will the development make use of local companies and suppliers throughout the design and construction process, e.g. through using local supply chains?
(Bristol City Council)

Education and employment are essential for individuals to achieve independence. They also provide tools for people to fulfil their interests and aspirations. Lack of education and unemployment are two of the main causes of social exclusion, others being issues associated with age and mental and physical health. Their absence can cause alienation and poverty, which in turn exclude individuals from participating in society and can drive them to anti-social behaviour. This link can be seen in the UK, where high levels of burglary committed by 10-17-year-olds correlated with the number of 16-year-olds not in full-time education (Howard 2000). Anti-social behaviour affects individuals and communities as a whole and, in addition to high levels of crime, neighbourhoods with high levels of social exclusion also often suffer from unattractive and even threatening public environments. Often the average income is too low to support anything other than very basic facilities and all these factors combined contribute to lowering the quality of life for the entire community. As a result, people who are able to move, transfer elsewhere, further exacerbating the situation. Providing opportunities for education and employment therefore helps both individuals and the community as a whole.

Building developments can bring employment and opportunities for training to a community in a number of ways. Commercial buildings attract new businesses and jobs to an area and new educational facilities provide opportunities for training. However, depending on its nature, a new facility may have negative as well as positive repercussions. For example, a new retail facility may provide new jobs to an area, but may also jeopardise the livelihood of existing local businesses. High street chains forcing small retail outlets to close down is such an example. To address these issues, some businesses define their scope of activity by respecting existing community facilities and also apply proactive employment policies encouraging the employment of local people.

The provision of affordable work premises can also contribute to increasing employment opportunities by indirectly supporting businesses financially, in particular, small or start-up businesses. Creating affordable premises in an area can attract workers with similar aims and interests and create a lively and mutually supportive work community.

A development can also contribute to reducing social exclusion through its construction activities. Any building project can help increase local employment by purchasing or specifying locally manufactured building products and employing local companies or offering them opportunities to tender for work. This not only has social benefits, but also reduces the environmental impact of the development by reducing the energy required for construction (see Chapter 4).

A building project can also help to address the lack of training opportunities. In addition to encouraging builders from all trades to employ trainees and support them throughout their training period, the construction process itself can be structured as a construction training course.

There are a number of construction companies, such as Gusto (see 6.2.4), which have taken seriously their responsibilities as trainers as well as employers and have a policy of regularly employing trainees. This creates opportunities for young people and strengthens the local community by ensuring that local youngsters find employment locally. Other companies link up with local training colleges and offer practical experience to students. This also helps to address the still growing deficit of construction trainees in the UK, recognised by the industry and the government as a significant problem. In the past 30 years the construction industry has suffered from devastating economic recessions, forcing skilled workers to find work elsewhere. The industry was then unable to attract them back after it had recovered. During periods of recession very few trainees join construction companies and the result is a shortage of skilled workers. Immigration has alleviated the problems, but a skills shortage still exists.

In the UK, 15 per cent of working-age people have no qualification (DEFRA 2003). For some of these individuals a short building course can appear less daunting than a two- or three-year formal apprenticeship or training programme. A number of successful construction projects have trained young or unemployed people on the job and proved an effective vehicle for re-entering the work market.

When a building is complete, there continue to be opportunities for building-related training and employment, whether involved in the building management, as in Pinakarri Cohousing (see p.72), or in maintenance and management, as in the Fairfield Housing Estate (see p.58).

Importantly, providing people with training and employment often has far-reaching impacts on their lives that affect not only their ability to earn a livelihood, but also their psychological well-being. People from deprived backgrounds may simply not have had the opportunity to develop a technical or other skill, or they may not have been in a position where they could make a positive contribution to their community and gain respect from other community members. Being involved in a self-build project and seeing the fruits of one's efforts or gaining employment for the first time can radically change a person's self-perception. It can boost self-confidence and help people become more self-sufficient, balanced and happy individuals.

2.3.2 The building industry and training

- 70,000 trainees are needed in the construction industry to maintain a healthy skills base.

- In many trades, fewer people are completing their training.

- The trades for which there are sufficient trainees are carpentry and bricklaying.

- The main trades where there is the largest deficiency are roofing, scaffolding, glazing, flooring and plant operation.

- Particular areas in the UK, such as the Midlands and Scotland, have a higher number of trainees than construction work output, while other areas such as the South East have a high deficit of trainees compared to work output.
(Howard 2000)

2.3.3 Creating employment opportunities in the built environment

The Wise Group, established in 1983, is a charity based in Glasgow, involved in providing training and employment opportunities for the long-term unemployed as well as installing energy conservation measures in homes. The Wise Group has 1,600 trainees and employs 370 permanent staff. Since it was set up, it has insulated over 150,000 houses, planted over a million trees, improved the external environment around 3,000 houses and made 40,000 houses more secure.
(Sustainability works 2004)

Case study: Training through building

View from the south-west tree-lined pedestrian walk. On the north and west side are the precinct and the housing.

The timber structure was screwed and bolted together by trainees, while the grass roof was installed by specialist contractors.

The Robin Hood Chase Centre is a community centre at the heart of St Ann's, a deprived inner city area of Nottingham. What makes this project exceptional is its social inclusion agenda, whereby the project was intended as a vehicle to train unemployed people. They would learn construction skills on the job during the construction process and it was hoped that they would gain qualifications that would allow them subsequently to find employment in the construction industry.

The project was funded with regeneration money and the new building, which was to be energy-efficient and ecological, was to be built by a group of skilled crafts people and trainees. The Chase Action Group, who had secured the funding and were organising the project, advertised for both skilled and trainee posts. The trainee posts had to be filled by members of the local community. The initial idea was to have a construction team of 13 with nine semi-skilled crafts people and four new-entrant trainees. In practice, there were generally six trainees, four semi-skilled crafts people and a site foreman.

Overall the construction process went well, with only one minor site accident when a barrow slipped off an inclined plank and only two cases of vandalism during the 18-month construction period. There was a higher than expected turnover of trainees and in total about 30 trainees were involved throughout the construction.

The issues that the project coordinator, Jo Brown of TANC, dealt with were not all of a technical nature. Some of the trainees had to learn about the meaning of a full-time job, the importance of turning up when expected and on time, and contributing adequately. Other trainees had more complex personal problems of motivation or substance abuse. The significance for some of the trainees of learning about a typical working life cannot be understated. In deprived communities individuals may simply never have the opportunity of seeing and, even less, personally experiencing, regular work. The Chase project gave many individuals a chance to learn and live through a very exciting project. Even for those with complex personal problems, the interaction with others, the experience of other people's drive and dedication, opened their eyes to different values and ways of life.

At the opening of the project, only two trainees had worked throughout the project and only one had achieved a National Vocational Qualification level 3 (NVQ3), but about 80 per cent of the 30 people who had at one time or other worked as trainees on the project had found employment or other training posts. Some had left the construction industry and found work elsewhere; one trainee, for example, became a full-time carer.

Now that the centre is complete and has been operating, it continues to play a role in educating the local community by running IT courses and other adult classes. There are also more employment opportunities in the centre itself, which includes a café and, in the complex around the centre, a newly opened community laundrette. For a group of local people, building the Chase not only gave them a new facility, but also a new start in life.

See also: focal spaces communities **Chapter 2.4**

Case study: Acquiring life skills

The Pinakarri cohousing development took eight years from the initial idea to the completion of the buildings. In this period of time, the community of determined individuals had to keep their ideal in mind and work as a team, addressing complex administrative and legal issues to realise their goal.

Pinakarri community is a mixed equity (mixed tenure) housing cooperative with privately owned and rented housing. It was the first housing cooperative in Western Australia built as a cohousing scheme. Funding came from the Federal Community Housing Programme, a government scheme which no longer exists, but at the time allowed the group to set up as a non-profit association and work closely with Homeswest, the State Housing Commission, to achieve their goal. The group was primarily made up of single mothers and the scheme addressed the needs of people on low incomes. As a cooperative, while benefiting from guidance from Homeswest, they were self-managed. The process of design consultation, building and managing the completed scheme was the responsibility of the future residents, most of whom had no experience of such activities, so every stage of the process was of personal development value.

The initial design consultation process, which involved discussing the architect's initial plans and customising them, helped individuals gain confidence in the process and its future success. Once construction had begun, the community members had to agree the detail design and learn to compromise in practice. The procedure of discussion and decision-making, followed by seeing the physical results of one's thoughts and work, is deeply rewarding, and at Pinakarri was invaluable in terms of highlighting personal achievements.

Personal development did not stop there. Once occupied, the houses had to be managed. Individual community members took up various responsibilities: treasurer, rental issues, community liaison, community secretary, spokesperson, and maintenance. A maintenance trust fund supported by rental income was set up for all cooperatives in the state and a structure was implemented to manage the community through consensus decision-making.

Whilst some community members thrived with the development, it became too claustrophobic for others, the democratic framework required by the cohousing structure proving too difficult to cope with. Nonetheless, even these individuals gained from the demanding process. As the community settled down in its ways, the members deepened their understanding of their own achievements and beliefs, having learnt from each other and from their own experience. Most individuals enjoy their new way of life, which they consider to be worth all those years of hard work.

Pinakarri Cohousing
Hamilton Hill, Perth, Western Australia

Project details, Chapter 2.2, p.72

Each house has a private garden in addition to the communal space.

North elevation of a typical housing unit.

See also: cohousing **Chapter 2.2**

See also: building orientation **Chapter 5.1**

Case study: Affordable work space

Buoys Wharf
East London

Client: Urban Space Management
Completed: 2003

The front and rear blocks are connected to a stair tower made with an upturned container.

The rear block is made by stacking the containers one on top of the other in a regular manner.

For a business, the cost of renting work space can be one of the largest expenses after employees' salaries. For a self-employed person, they can constitute the largest cost of running a business. Reducing the cost of work premises can increase the chances of success in setting up and remaining in business. Working from home is not possible for everyone. In particular, craft, artistic or other work associated with noise, fumes or large spaces is generally incompatible with the requirements of home life, and a separate work space is essential. But it is also these businesses that often struggle to make ends meet and that can really benefit from low-cost work premises.

These are the issues that Urban Space Management addressed with their container buildings. These buildings are made of 'recycled' containers, which were used to ship products from China to the UK and generally disposed of after one trip. The principle used to achieve a low-cost building is simplicity and the use of standard container systems in steel has proved very effective. Other systems used in the past by Urban Space Management include concrete garage structures and timber frames.

At Buoy Wharf in East London, Urban Space Management has installed a low-cost work and live complex on the bank of the River Thames. Set among partially converted brick warehouses, the orange, white, yellow and burgundy containers appear somewhat surreal. Two blocks have been erected and joined together by a stair element linking them with bridges.

The rear block is made by stacking five rows of containers four storeys high neatly one on top of the other. The corners of each container, which constitute the main structural support points, rest on top of the corners of the container below. The block has a footprint of five 2.4 x 12m containers and measures 12 x 12m overall. A number of the container ends have been opened up to create windows and balconies.

The front block is very different. Each of the five storeys of containers is installed at 90 degrees to the one below. The corners of the containers do not necessarily meet and some of the units protrude beyond the line of the containers below. To support this irregular structure additional framing was needed outside and within the units. Internal finishes are bolted onto a sub-frame in timber and insulation is installed in the thickness of the sub-frame. Circular windows are cut into the profiled steel 'skin', whereby the

The brick contrasts with the brightly-coloured containers of the front block.

circular shapes maintain the structural strength of the profiled steel. The resulting aesthetic is unusual and slightly nautical.

All connections are in steel creating a basic structure in one material that can easily be recycled. The containers can be dismantled and repositioned elsewhere. Urban Space Management has had experience of repositioning a number of units several times without damage to the external or internal structure. This system has proved effective in providing housing, shops and workshops at very low cost.

At Buoy Wharf the system addresses the needs of local creative people with low incomes who need workshop space as well as living space. Cost–effective solutions are a priority and the unconventional aesthetic only makes the buildings more attractive to this community. With imagination such blocks could be placed comfortably along rivers, in green spaces or nestled among converted industrial units in city centres.

2.3.4 Sustainable design features

Site and ecology
The site is not being disrupted and can easily be reused in future due to the minimal disruption to the ground and surroundings.

Community and culture
The development has brought to life an underused part of East London. See also main text.

Materials
The containers are second-hand containers that would otherwise be recycled rather than reused. The structure can be reused and recycled at the end of the building's useful life.

The containers overhang each other, creating a space below the units for vehicles to pass through.

The upturned container is used as a stair core. Planting is being introduced at ground level to soften the environment.

Circular windows and balconies are cut into the standard containers.

2.4 Enhancing the Quality of Life

A small public garden acts as focal point for the local community at Fairfield Housing in Perth.

The community centre in the middle of the Fairfield housing estate of approximately 350 dwellings offers activities for all ages.

Creating strong and cohesive communities is as much about addressing quality of life as about providing basic necessities. Living in a particular community becomes desirable, therefore ensuring a long life for the community, if it offers a comfortable lifestyle with easy access to all necessities and leisure facilities. Increasing prosperity and life spans have brought more free time to many people, increasing the need for leisure facilities ranging from sports, cultural entertainment and enjoyment of green spaces to further education and voluntary work.

A sustainable community should provide leisure activities for all groups of society: elderly people, young people, families, couples and individuals. Facilities are needed for everyday activities, such as meeting at a café or visiting a library, as well as spaces for special occasions, such as wedding or graduation ceremonies. Large and multi-purpose facilities are important, but in terms of creating sustainable communities, small interventions are equally vital. For example, a small public garden can become as much of a focal point as a major cultural centre.

The facilities should address the particular preferences of different groups. While many elderly people are increasingly active, contributing through voluntary groups and pursuing further education courses, others prefer more relaxing occupations, such as gardening in allotments, walking in the park or enjoying meeting with friends at a community centre. Young families are concerned about entertaining their children: playgrounds, youth clubs and cultural centres that cater for the young are essential.

The Glashaus library in Herten has a large section for children, including a performance area where they can attend plays and reading events, while their parents enjoy the other facilities in the building.

There is a toddler play area directly behind the houses at The Point.

The importance of such facilities goes beyond providing opportunities to spend time in an enjoyable way; it can also help avoid anti-social behaviour or behaviour perceived as such. For groups of young people, the lack of after-school facilities can result in them spending time in the street, potentially creating a nuisance, but often simply making others, particularly elderly people, feel uncomfortable and even threatened by their presence. Youth clubs or sports fields are essential in offering young people entertainment, while community education centres offering training in, for example, information technology can be enjoyable as well as educational.

Within a sustainable community, leisure facilities should be accessible without the use of a car. Chapter 1.2 sets out the maximum recommended distances between community facilities and housing accommodation to encourage car-free access. Facilities for small children should be as close as possible. Play facilities for toddlers should be virtually on the doorstep (100 metres is recommended). Like nurseries and other childcare facilities, playgrounds should be not more than a couple of streets or blocks away (400 metres), preferably accessible through safe pedestrian ways that allow children independent access.

Community spaces house the activities that enhance people's lives, but as shown by the following case studies, they can also become symbols through which residents identify with their community. They can help to enhance the feeling of belonging to a community worth living in.

The play equipment need not be extravagant to entertain toddlers effectively (The Point).

In the SolarCity each housing block has a play area with different equipment. Children can easily visit other housing blocks and use different equipment without having to cross busy roads.

Beauford Court housing development in London by Feilden Clegg Bradley Architects for Peabody Trust Housing Association includes a hardtop playground in the centre of the courtyard development above the car parking. This is an ideal facility for the whole neighbourhood and in particular the Rough Sleepers Initiative housing on the site, which provides accommodation for those in transition between sleeping on the street and renting accommodation.

Beddington Zed (BedZED) housing is planning a playing field adjacent to the housing development for use by the whole community.

Case study: Focal spaces for communities

Robin Hood Chase Centre
Nottingham, UK

Client: Community Action Group
Architect: Carnell Green
Completed: 1997

Simple building methods were used to enable the trainees to contribute substantially to the building.

The curved grass roof incorporates a number of roof lights which provide good light levels throughout.

The Robin Hood Chase Centre was developed as part of Nottingham's City Challenge development activities, aimed at improving some of the most deprived areas of Nottingham. In St Ann's the city intended renovating local housing and building a community centre. Suggestions to demolish some of the existing facilities, which include a post office, chemist and health centre, were rejected by the local community, who wanted to keep the centre and build an additional facility next to it.

The local community group, the Chase Action Group (CAG), took the lead. The Technical Aid for Nottingham Communities (TANC) assisted the CAG who successfully bid for £450,000 of the Nottingham City Challenge funding. With the funding in place and with continuous guidance from TANC, the brief for the building started taking shape: it was to be an energy-efficient and ecological building, such as the group had seen on a fact-finding tour at the Centre for Alternative Technology (CAT) in Wales, and the local community should benefit in more ways than just from the built facility. Additional benefits for the community would result from a training programme for the local unemployed integrated within the construction process (see Chapter 2.3).

The site for the new building is within a 1960s precinct along the Robin Hood Chase, a pedestrian walk lined with mature trees. On the right-hand side of the centre is a passage to the 1960s shops and housing.

The requirements for potential architects included attending a Walter Segal course at the CAT, which introduced them to the techniques of timber self-build construction. Consequently the building was planned following self-build construction principles using simple dry-building methods and, where possible, standard size components. The post and beam timber frame is on a 3.6-metre structural grid to allow full-sized infill boards to be used. The demanding elements, such as the erection of the large laminated timber frame or the installation of the grass roof, were undertaken by specialists or skilled crafts people, while the rest of the work was carried out by a team of trainees guided by skilled crafts people.

The community was involved throughout the design and building process in different ways. Before and during the design phase, approximately 2,000 households took part in a consultation process run by CAG, while later newspaper was collected to manufacture the recycled paper insulation in the walls. People were kept informed, and the resentment exhibited by some individuals during the construction phase disappeared

See also: training and employment **Chapter 2.3**

once the building was complete. Vandalism was and remains minimal, an unusual situation for a still highly deprived area, illustrating the positive effects of a community-driven project.

The north wall has been painted by the local residents.

The 630-square metre centre is very popular and well used. On the ground floor is an entrance area with a small office linked to an IT centre which runs classes for the local neighbourhood. There are also a hall, a community café and kitchen, toilets and meeting room. Offices for three community groups, including one for TANC, are situated on a smaller first floor. The centre is a hub, with the community café also acting as an informal meeting place and a place for relaxation.

Originally a canvas roof covered the external passage on the north side of the building, adjacent to the shops in the precinct. This was later removed, letting in more light to the space between the buildings, which is now used as a meeting area outside the shops. The north wall of the centre has been given a local identity; painted with images of a multicultural community it includes a slogan: 'Life is a challenge… meet it, a dream… realise it, a game… play it, life is love… share it.'

The security grilles on the windows suggest it may never be possible to fully eradicate anti-social behaviour until all individuals are offered a real chance to fulfil their potential. Nonetheless, the building remains a symbol of reconciliation. The whole area has benefited from the development and, several years after its completion, the centre remains a focal point for the local community who, on the whole, use it with respect and pride.

2.4.1 Sustainable design features

Site and ecology
The site was an open hard landscaped area within the 1960s precinct, which was improved by forming a courtyard-type space more of human scale on the side of the centre.

Community and culture
See main text and Chapter 2.3.

Health
All the decorative finishes are low toxicity and organic.

Materials
Structural timber, except the Scandinavian glulam, is Welsh larch from sustainable woodland. The glulam beams were competitively priced, having been ordered during the manufacturing plant's off-season period. The flooring timber in the hall is reclaimed from a factory in Warrington and the oak floor in the entrance area is also reclaimed.

The walls are insulated with cellulose fibre insulation. The reception desk is made with boards of recycled drinks cartons.

Energy
The building is well insulated and the south-facing windows make use of passive solar heat gains. A night cooling system was planned but not activated.

Water
Rainwater is collected and used to irrigate the grass roof.

The café is at the centre of the building and the activities that take place within it.

Case study: Cultural centres

Glashaus
Herten, Germany

Client: Herten city
Architect: LOG ID
Completed: 1994

The Glashaus is prominent in the main pedestrian street otherwise dominated by subdued architecture.

In the Rotunde, balconies are used like quasi-open air meeting spaces.

In 1984 the industrialist Karl-Ludwig Schweisfurth offered the city of Herten a million Deutschmarks to build a cultural centre made of glass on a site in the city centre. Schweisfurth, who was born in Herten, but no longer lived there, wanted to give the city a facility that would benefit its population and enhance the city. However, it became clear that the offer was not sufficient to realise the project and it took another seven years before the building could begin. During this period of uncertainty, when the project was almost abandoned a couple of times, funding of 20 million Deutschmarks was secured from the region of Düsseldorf and the design of the centre was rationalised to achieve a total contract sum of 25.7 million Deutschmarks.

The initial vision of a cultural centre in glass developed into a building to include a public library, conference facilities, a bistro and a large multifunctional space, which finally opened in 1994. The architectural practice appointed to design the centre was LogID, a practice renowned for its environmental designs, who won the commission as a result of an invited competition. The design concept was underpinned by the practice's belief that buildings are for people and should be comfortable, relaxing and healthy places to be in as well as being environmentally sustainable. To achieve this holistic approach to design, Dieter Schempp, LogID's principal, enlisted the collaboration of planting, energy and other specialists. The result is an energy-efficient, versatile and extremely popular building that has contributed to the city and the life of its nearly 120,000 inhabitants in many ways.

At a practical level, the new library, consisting of 2,000 square metres spread over four floors, is used by local schools, including nearly 20 primary and secondary schools and 30 kindergartens. Schools from other towns make up a third of all school users. In collaboration with local services the library has set up information stands to which doctors and employment consultants can refer their patients and customers respectively. More than 10,000 regular users have access to over 110,000 books, CDs and videos,

View of the Rotunda, the glazed multi-function hall used for special events.

The café is a popular lunch venue and hosts special events in conjunction with the library.

Tables for reading are located in a brightly lit area overlooking the restaurant courtyard.

2.4.2 Sustainable design features

Site and ecology
The building was built on a brownfield site previously occupied by a car park and outdated police station. The development reinforces pedestrian links and creates pleasant and successful community spaces.

Community and culture
See main text.

Health
See Chapter 3.2.

Energy
The glazed hall is integral with the airhandling system. Exhaust air from all spaces except kitchen and toilets is transferred to the glazed hall where it is conditioned by the plants, minimising the need for external fresh air. During the heating season, the heated air from the glazed hall and the space above the glazed hall ceiling and below the glazed roof is transferred to the spaces needing heat. When heating is not required, a BMS systems diverts the air flow to outside.

Low energy lighting is used throughout.

PVs and solar shading had to be omitted as part of a cost-saving exercise.

Water
Low flush WCs are used throughout.

which are available for borrowing. In 2001, 200,000 visits to the facility were recorded.

The complex is much more than a library. The seminar and conference rooms are used by local organisations including adult college, slimming groups and lunch-time exercise groups. Children's plays are staged in a circular section of the children's library which has built-in raked seating. The 'Rotunde', a 429-square metre, four-storey glazed multifunction space, houses public events such as concerts, readings and exhibitions. In collaboration with the bistro, themed evenings are run, combining music, literature and food. The Rotunde can also be hired and has been used for activities as varied as weddings, dance parties, graduation ceremonies, billiard tournaments and hairdressing fairs. In 2003, nearly 600 events took place in the Glashaus.

The quality of the internal spaces, the programme of the building and the efficiency and enthusiasm with which the staff manage the facilities have all contributed to creating a popular cultural venue open to people of all ages and backgrounds. Making cultural activities conveniently available to the whole community can also help counteract social exclusion by increasing individuals' opportunities to further their education, providing the means to improve their health and providing activities for residents from other cultures.

A measure of the impact this facility has had on the people of Herten is the generosity with which they have responded to the recent request by the library for donations of new books on the occasion of its tenth anniversary, and the selection of donated art works in the entrance lobby. However it is expressed, there is a feeling among the people of Herten that they have a centre they can enjoy, want to support, and are proud of.

The recessed entrance to the library and the Glashaus is used to house stands and other activities.

See also: purifying air with plants **Chapter 3.2**

Case study: Green leisure spaces

Winter Garden
Sheffield, UK

Client: Sheffield City
Architect: Pringle Richards Sharratt
Engineers: Buro Happold
Landscape consultant: Weddle Landscape Design
Completed: 2002

The Winter Garden entrance is off Tudor Square facing the Crucible Theatre.

The plant shop and café are further attractions.

The fans induce air movement and avoid temperature stratification.

The Winter Garden is part of the Sheffield city centre regeneration and is located within a cultural area which includes the Crucible Theatre, the Lyceum Theatre, the Central Library and City Hall. It is linked to the recently completed Millennium Galleries and is part of a network of pedestrian routes within the city centre, linking the university quarter and the main train station.

The city centre has a number of public squares, including the imposing Peace Gardens, but the Winter Garden offers Sheffield's residents a landscaped public place protected from the weather. It creates a complementary space to the open Peace Gardens with its fountain, hard landscaping and surroundings of historic buildings by providing a contemporary space dominated by over 150 different species of exotic plants, mainly from the southern hemisphere.

The dramatic space is 70 metres long, 22 metres wide and at the centre nearly 22 metres high, providing sufficient height for a few taller plants. The envelope consists of over 1,400 single-glazed roof panels, of which 128 open for ventilation, supported on inverted catenary laminated larch sections up to 900 millimetres thick. The larch sections, sourced from sustainable sources, required no preservative and need only minimal maintenance. The embodied energy (see Chapter 4) of the larch structure was shown to be only 5 per cent that of alternative structures in concrete or steel and weighs only 15 per cent and 65 per cent of the concrete or steel options respectively. The timber structure sits on a concrete substructure that forms an underground garage and loading bay for the adjacent Millennium Galleries.

The Winter Garden provides a green space for residents to enjoy any time of the day or night. Background heating, from Sheffield city district heating mains, maintains the appropriate temperature for a cool temperate plant environment and ensures comfort levels suitable for use all year around. The garden has proved a popular place for festive occasions such as marriages, for meetings and for quiet relaxation. A small water feature creates a point of interest for children, while shops and a café are further attractions. Overall, the Winter Garden contributes to the liveliness of the city centre and to the quality of life of the residents. The success of the garden is a testimony to the enlightened thinking of the city of Sheffield which was bold enough to commission a venue with limited potential for commercial return in order to provide its residents with a public space of high quality.

View from Peace Gardens.

Internal view.

Case study: Long-term planning

The creation of new public spaces, such as parks, can be expensive and sometimes difficult for a city to justify. However, considering the long-term opportunities associated with any development may help identify cost-effective ways of providing facilities that benefit the community as a whole.

The flower displays attract bees and butterflies.

A beer garden near a boules area, with a play area to entertain the children.

A restaurant on the edge of the lake.

Westpark
Munich, Germany

Client: City of Munich

The lake is tree-lined and creates a beautiful and healthy environment in which to relax.

Some of the exhibition gardens have been retained and are still an attraction.

Seating surrounded by roses makes a good spot to enjoy lunch and a relaxing read.

The International Garden Exhibition took place in Munich 20 years ago. The foresight of the city organisers made them consider the future development of the city when selecting the site for the exhibition and its programme. The chosen site is near the city ringroad and at the time was partially derelict land. Rather than considering the exhibition as a short-term event, to be dismantled afterwards, the city took this opportunity to plan long-term. The exhibition would be integrated within the existing city network of the green spaces.

The long-term thinking paid off and today a beautiful park, the Westpark, is enjoyed by the local community. The park still has some of the original exhibits, such as the oriental garden displays, a mountain chalet and some of the exotic and not so exotic original plants. It also has cafés, beer gardens, restaurants and areas with benches along artificial lakes. There are places for children to play as well as spaces to sit and enjoy a quiet moment. The park is used by cyclists to ride through, people enjoying a day out, workers on their lunch break and groups of children. Overall, it contributes to the quality of life of many of the city's residents.

2.5 Promoting Sustainability

At the main entrance and the corridors of the Chesapeake Center framed sketches illustrate the principles used in the building and give the relevant environmental background information.

One of the Chesapeake Center artist's sketches illustrates the use of rainwater in the building.

To people involved or interested in sustainability it appears unlikely that anyone could avoid coming across the term. However, in the same way that many people are uninterested in politics and are ignorant of political personalities, there are still many people oblivious of environmental and social sustainability issues.

Buildings can help to promote awareness of sustainability and some sustainable designers use their developments as educational vehicles. Clients, local authorities, consultants, builders, building users and the general public can learn about sustainability from completed buildings and through the building process.

Learning about how sustainable buildings work not only raises awareness, but also ensures a more efficient operation of the building. The success of a sustainable design strategy depends to a large extent on the way inhabitants use their building. Certain aspects of sustainable design are susceptible to misuse, whereby their benefits are lost. Even a very well-insulated building will use up substantial amounts of heating energy if windows are constantly kept open. Unless building occupants are informed and educated about the operation of the building and the rationale behind the design, performance is likely to be compromised.

An overall sustainable building design strategy should include raising awareness about sustainability in general, educating the client and the project team about sustainable design approaches and informing users about the operation of the building. Furthermore, sustainable buildings should be monitored and their design strategy and building performance assessed. This can help to promote sustainable design by improving communal knowledge and understanding of the operation of sustainable buildings and avoiding the replication of unsuccessful designs.

In certain cases, the building itself is used as an educational or demonstration tool, showing how effective sustainable design systems can be and how easily they can be integrated within a building. Sometimes information on environmental issues and the building design is included in the building for visitors and users to see.

Setting targets for sustainable buildings

For all projects, opportunities for promoting sustainability begin by setting appropriate targets to achieve a sustainable building. Clients, the people who ultimately commission and fund construction projects, are key figures. The first step is to make sure that they are aware of the importance of sustainability and of the potential of their development in this respect. The benefits of sustainable buildings are increasingly being recognised and quantified and there are many completed developments that can help demonstrate the advantages to prospective clients.

Setting targets for a development encourages a more structured approach to achieving a sustainable design and helps to monitor the design process, which otherwise may involve a slow erosion of the sustainable design initiatives. Targets can be set by using one of the established environmental and sustainable design assessment systems, addressing design and construction issues, or by using project-specific targets or minimum design requirements.

Minimum design requirements were set for the SolarCity project in Linz (see p.20) and for the Ellenbrook development in Western Australia (see p.92). In both cases a masterplan established the basic site layouts and the number and sizes of homes, but the building procurement systems were different. The SolarCity was built by housing associations developing groups of houses for subsequent sale or rent, while in Ellenbrook individual lots were sold to the future users or builders for speculative development.

In both cases minimum design requirements were set out at the beginning of the project, although goals were very different. The SolarCity minimum requirements were supported by an ambitious city plan to develop a truly compact sustainable neighbourhood linked to public transport, and the ecological and energy ambitions had to match the urban and community structures implemented. Therefore, materials containing polyvinylchloride, formaldehyde and ozone-depleting substances were excluded, energy efficiency was maximised and 34 per cent of the roof space had to be covered with solar hot water panels, the remaining energy supplied through district heating. At Ellenbrook a careful balance had to be struck between commercial viability and environmental objectives. Softer targets were used, whereby only eight of 14 mainly energy-efficiency criteria had to be achieved (see p.92).

While targets and minimum requirements have to adapt to the context they operate in, and any activity promoting sustainability has to consider its audience, they are effective ways of promoting sustainability. In addition, the construction process itself and living in or using sustainable buildings can also effectively promote sustainability. Just as students involved in hands-on construction projects learn far more quickly about construction than those learning from books, builders and building users learn about new technologies, materials and processes of sustainable building by using them or experiencing them in operation. Promoting sustainable buildings is as much about dispelling prejudices and gaining confidence as providing solutions; and first-hand experience is an exceptionally effective way to develop a true understanding and gain confidence in new systems.

2.5.1 Promoting sustainability

Selecting and educating the project team The design and construction team, including the client, should have the awareness, knowledge and expertise to deliver a sustainable building.

Setting targets Appropriate targets should be set, depending on the context of the project. This can be done with the help of consultants and/or by using one of the existing sustainability and environmental checklists or assessment methods:

– **Sustainable briefs** Design briefs and tender documents have to include the aims and targets for the project's sustainability. The aims can be determined with the help of systems developed to give guidance on setting priorities and aims appropriate to each development. Systems include the UK Housing Corporation's Toolkit of Sustainability Indicators, Sustainability Works, a web-based system, and Foundations for the Future, developed by Sustainable Homes.

– **Planning sustainability checklists** Many local authorities in the UK have checklists for sustainable development. While generally not enforceable, the checklists can be used to set voluntary project targets and monitor the design progress.

– **BREEAM, ECOHOMES, LEEDS, ENVEST** Environmental assessment systems can be used to set targets, raise awareness among the project team, guide the design process and monitor progress throughout the project. See 5.2.7

Sustainable construction During construction, sustainability can be promoted at a neighbourhood level and by educating construction participants:

– **Environmental supply chain** Suppliers can be selected on the basis of their environmental credentials, assessed by evaluating their products and manufacturing methods or by relying on environmental management systems such as EMAS and ISO14001. If sustainability awareness is low, it may be necessary to provide training for sub-contractors and suppliers.

– **Minimising on-site impacts** The Considerate Contractor Scheme sets out standards for site management, to ensure minimal impact on the neighbouring area.

Educating users Highlighting a building's sustainability approach can be educational for the users as well as ensuring the building is operated in the most efficient way.

Post-occupancy assessments All buildings, and in particular those with experimental designs, should be monitored to assess the effectiveness of the design strategies. Results should be made public for other designers to learn from. See Chapter 5.2.

Teaching by doing. Bridge built by students at the Cranbrook Academy of Art, in Michigan, US, under the supervision of Dan Hoffman.

Case study: Educating the community

Argonne Child Development Center

Sixteenth Avenue, San Francisco, US

Project details, Chapter 1.4, p.48

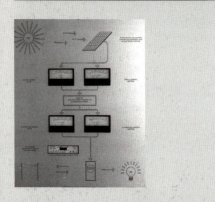

An information panel shows the amount of electricity being produced.

The south-facing classroom windows look out on the play area. The rooflights with PVs are visible from the communal garden around the school.

Internal view of a classroom.

See also: community food gardens **Chapter 1.4**

A recurring barrier to achieving a sustainable way of life is the general ignorance of global environmental and social problems. In addition to a lack of awareness of the problems, many also lack knowledge of the solutions available to reduce the environmental impacts of our lifestyles and improve the social sustainability of communities. Educating children as well as adults about sustainability and about how problems can be tackled is key to changing attitudes and encouraging action. If the education can be practical, if adults and children can be directly involved in sustainable solutions, their understanding will be enhanced and their prejudices dispelled.

The Argonne Child Development Center actively promotes sustainability by demonstrating sustainable building solutions to the users and visitors to the centre. The project, including the goal of creating a sustainable building, was driven by the community and the end result reflects their dedication to educating the public in sustainability.

The modest but elegant, energy-efficient and socially inclusive facility for pre-school children is situated within a substantial community garden. The L-shaped building wraps around the children's playground and is surrounded on two sides by garden plots. The classrooms face south onto the playground and are shaded from the summer sun by a veranda, while the north-facing windows look out onto the gardens. The rooms are naturally ventilated; passive stack ventilation (see Chapter 5.1) draws cool air from north-facing low level inlets and exhausts hot air at high level on the south side. The space remains comfortably cool in summer and needs minimal heating in winter. PV panels, which produce electricity from solar radiation, are integrated in the toilet rooflight and a display panel in the entrance lobby shows real-time and accumulative electricity production. The children experience the bright, airy and comfortable spaces and can see the electricity produced by their building. Whether they feel proud or take it for granted, they will grow up to be confident about such design solutions.

Children from other schools and many members of the public have visited the centre and seen the potential of sustainable design. The success of the building design is as instructive as its success in uniting teaching and recreational uses with the gardening facilities on the same site. From their classroom windows, children can see gardeners working their patch and growing food. The understanding of where food comes from can easily elude children growing up in cities. At the Argonne Center the children can see how to grow food and can even help. During the project building phase, a group planting event was organised. Native species were planted around the grounds. Everyone, from the children to elderly citizens, was involved and the children experienced at first hand a fun and yet constructive and enriching community event. These are the memories that will last and shape the thinking of those individuals who will lead the way in future.

Case study: Demonstration buildings

Piney Lakes Environment Centre is a venue for learning about environmental issues as well as a demonstration of selected technical solutions to sustainable design problems. Located within the 68-hectare Piney Lakes Reserve, the centre is part of an initiative by the City of Melville, which involved restoring the bushland reserve and providing a building for the local community. The Piney Lakes Reserve is the only natural part remaining of a 2,000-hectare pine plantation once owned by the University of Western Australia and then gradually developed to provide housing.

The building's main aim is to educate visitors about environmental issues. The two-storey building has two multifunction rooms on the top entrance level which are rented out and used for seminars, workshops and other educational activities. A kitchen provides catering facilities if required. On the lower level are laboratory facilities used by schools, a waste water treatment room and a battery store. Visitors can wander around the building and a number of information panels explain the operation of the systems installed.

Schools can book excursions to visit the reserve, with its bushland and wetland habitats, and visit the building at the same time. The building is designed as a prototype for an autonomous school building and is not connected to any services. It uses independent systems for water collection and sewage treatment (see Chapter 6.3) and for energy generation. Designed as a passive solar building, it demonstrates the use of solar hot water and hot air panels, PVs, a 5-kW wind turbine and vegetable oil power generation. This eclectic mix of technologies, together with the use of rammed lime and recycled light poles, provides an introduction to environmental building techniques.

Piney Lakes Environment Centre
Melville, Western Australia

Project details, Chapter 6.3, p.280

Solar hot water panels can be seen on the left-hand side of the roof, while on the right of the roof is a hot air panel and in front of the building a free-standing PV installation.

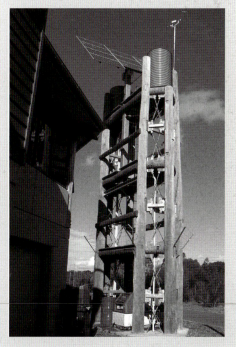

A tower houses the vegetable oil generator and a PV which tracks the sun throughout the day to maximise exposure.

Outside, the amphitheatre is used for demonstrations and activities.

The building applies passive solar design principles, protecting the building from high level sun.

A 5- kW wind turbine.

Car park and street lighting are powered by integrated PV panels.

See also: hybrid toilets **Chapter 6.3**

Case study: Educating buyers

Ellenbrook
Perth, Western Australia

Client: Ellenbrook Joint Venture
Project manager: LWP Property Group Pty Ltd
Development period: 1992-2015

The metal roofs are mostly insulated and light coloured to reflect the solar radiation. Verandas and other shading devices also protect the building from excessive solar gains.

A typical landscaped cycle- and walkway.

Ellenbrook is a new town currently under construction approximately 25 kilometres north-east of Perth in Western Australia. Started in 1992 with a masterplan for the 1,200-hectare site, seven themed neighbourhoods or villages, as they are referred to, are progressively being built around what will become the town centre. Construction began in 1994 and in 1995 the first residents moved in. The fifth village was officially opened in 2004 and work on the town centre has now begun.

The design philosophy adopted is one that promotes a human-scale environment with a village atmosphere. One of the essential elements of Ellenbrook philosophy is to live in harmony with nature and enhance and protect the local natural flora and fauna. The development provides residents with opportunities to enjoy new landscaped gardens, waterways, extensively landscaped streets and pathways as well as the adjacent Whiteman Park nature reserve and other local parks and natural attractions.

Each village is themed – older villages were Mediterranean and Federation style, and different sized plots, from those appropriate for families to those suitable for retirement homes, are available. The third and fifth villages, Coolamon and Charlotte's Vineyard, have been planned to maximise passive solar design opportunities though plot layouts and building orientation, and the sales contracts oblige buyers to consider the integration of energy-efficient features in the buildings they develop.

In Coolamon, builders were encouraged to include four or six of a selection of energy-efficiency measures, depending on the plot type. These would provide estimated savings in energy bills of $400 per year. By the time design guidelines for Charlotte's Vineyard were developed, buyers were contractually bound to integrate eight of a selection of 14 energy-efficient, water conservation or waste minimisation measures, including: orientation of living accommodation on the north side of the building (in the southern hemisphere maximum solar access is north, while in the northern hemisphere it is south); provision of thermal mass; provision of solar shading to the north, east and west sides of the house; minimising west-facing windows; installing openable windows to provide natural ventilation; installing reflective roof finishes and insulating the roof; draught exclusion; roof space ventilation; water-saving devices; waste minimisation; and installing a garden designed to minimise water use.

Coolamon and Charlotte's Vineyard represent an increasing emphasis on, but not radical approaches to, sustainability. With a gross development density of 9 dph and a nett development density of less than 24 dph, Ellenbrook is not breaking the mould of the land-hungry suburban model; and with the closest existing train connection 20 minutes drive away (a new connection is envisaged in the future), it is still highly car-dependent. However, the parameters for the development, and in particular its scale and the culture within which it is set, dictate a cautious approach towards improving its sustainability. Considering that it is envisaged that, by 2015, there will be 10,500 homes and 30,000 people living in Ellenbrook, the strategy to encourage and educate rather than impose will have reached a significant number of people and will have had quite an impact.

One of the educational approaches adopted at Ellenbrook is in respect of water use

One of the lakes at the centre of each village.

A group of Mediterranean and other low water plants.

2.5.2 Sustainable design features

Site and ecology
Ellenbrook is a member of the 'Flora and Fauna' initiative run by the nursery and garden industry. The initiative aims to protect and increase the biodiversity in public and private environments. Ellenbrook garden advisers provide residents with guidance on how to create animal-friendly gardens.

Community and culture
The village and building designs respect and borrow from the local vernacular. Community consultations have helped create a sense of community and belonging and have continued throughout the development process.

The development includes all essential community facilities, including shops, schools, post office, medical centre, library, community centre, sports hall and churches. There is increasing community activity, including a variety of community groups for different ages and interests.

The development commissioned the artist Philippa O'Brien to produce artwork, reminiscent of the history of the land, for 18 locations on the site.

The development includes affordable units for first-time buyers.

Health
The extensive natural environment encourages residents to spend time outside, including walking or doing sports.

Materials
The development operates a recycling initiative which involves all waste materials from construction sites being collected and brought to a recycling depot maintained by Ellenbrook. On site or at the depot the waste is sorted and bricks, mortar and plaster are crushed and used in the construction of paths and roads on the site; timber is made available to the community for a small fee; brick straps and other metals are sent off for recycling. The initiative aims to recycle at least 70 per cent of all construction waste.

Energy and water
Energy and water efficiency is promoted through the design guidelines for each village. These include increasing insulation, appropriate orientation and low water use gardens.

in gardens. Taking into account the significant plot sizes and gardens and the fact that water is the most precious resource in the area, promoting water-efficient gardening was seen as an effective way to reduce the development's environmental impact. Ellenbrook commissioned five demonstration gardens, each with different design styles, to make up the Waterwise garden display. Located near one of the sales offices the display is easily accessible by all and is used as a model for residents who want to design water-efficient gardens. The Waterwise gardens, endorsed by the Water Corporation of Western Australia, also help to increase the general awareness of environmental issues. In addition, Ellenbrook's contractors offer advice on all garden design issues including soil, fertiliser, plant types, hard landscaping and maintenance. Hydro-zoning, where plants with similar watering requirements are grouped to enable effective watering and avoid over-watering, is also promoted.

Unless legislative or financial pressure is applied, people need time to change their practices. By first raising awareness, then educating people about the technical implications of sustainable design and its advantages and, finally, by convincing them that they will gain and not lose, only through this process can voluntary change be induced. At Ellenbrook a realistic approach has been taken. Minimal environmental improvements have been imposed and further improvements encouraged through the provision of information and inducements, such as free landscaping work. This approach will slowly move the sustainability agenda forward and will remain accessible to everyone, even those as yet unaware of the issues.

Timber decking as an alternative to water-hungry plants.

Waterwise garden display with explanatory board.

Chapter 3
Health and Well-being

3.0 Introduction

Health is a state of complete physical, mental and social well-being not merely the absence of disease.

(World Health Organisation 1946)

3.0.1 Attributes of a healthy life

– a clean and safe environment

– time for rest and recreation

– a reasonable living standard

– freedom from chronic worries

– hope for the future

– an adequate level of self-confidence and autonomy

– having a worthwhile and fulfilling job
(Mitchell 1984)

3.0.2 Causes of ill health

At least I know this, that if a person is overworked in any degree they cannot enjoy the sort of health I am speaking of; nor if they are continually chained to one dull round of mechanical work, with no hope at the other end of it; nor if they live in continual sordid anxiety for their livelihood; nor if they are ill housed; nor if they are deprived of all enjoyment of the natural beauty of the world; nor if they have no amusement to quicken the flow of their spirits from time to time; all these things, which touch more or less directly on their bodily conditions, are born of the claim I make to live in good health.
(William Morris 1884)

3.0.3 Baubiologie

Baubiologie was developed in Germany in the 1950s and aims to create buildings in harmony with the environment, which address the biological, physical and spiritual needs of their inhabitants. The building envelope, also considered the third skin (the second being clothes), should breathe, insulate and protect, while ensuring a healthy indoor climate.

In respect of creating a healthy building, the Baubiologie movement considers indoor air pollutants, humidity, light, colour, harmonic proportions, earth energies, ergonomics and electromagnetic fields. The movement combines traditional and contemporary building methods.

The concept that enjoying good health implies more than simply not being ill is well understood; as is the fact that the causes of ill-health are very wide-ranging. What is not fully appreciated by many in the building industry is that the built environment can significantly affect human well-being; and that environmentally-linked ill-health can be addressed through interventions in the built environment. In 2002, 30 per cent of deaths globally resulted from communicable disease, 60 per cent from non-communicable disease, and 10 per cent from injuries (WHO 2003a). In other words, 70 per cent of deaths are related, not to infectious and parasitic disease, including respiratory infections, but to environmentally and socially linked aspects of life. The extent of the impact of the social and physical environment is best described in the US Department of Health and Human Services' definition of environmental health, to be found in their 2001 document *Healthy People 2010*, which states:

In its broadest sense, environmental health comprises those aspects of human health, disease, and injury that are determined or influenced by factors in the environment. This includes not only the study of the direct pathological effects of various chemical, physical, and biological agents, but also the effects on health of the broad physical and social environment, which includes housing, urban development, land-use and transportation, industry, and agriculture.

(DHHS 2001)

This definition recognises that the character of an environment can determine and influence lifestyle choices, the proximity of individuals to pollution, the potential for contact with viruses and bacteria, the opportunities for social interaction, the sense of self-worth of individuals, and much more: all of which affect human well-being.

The UK government's Green Paper on health issued in 1998 identifies four main health issues of current concern: mental health, accidents, cardiovascular-related illness and cancer. These illnesses are linked to lifestyle and environmental health issues, and can often be prevented. Among the UK government's initiatives to address the causes of these illnesses was the introduction of healthy living centres that focus on preventing ill-health by encouraging healthier lifestyles through education, physical exercise, counselling, drug prevention programmes, stress management, child and parent support, dietary advice, gardening and other community activities. However, when many individuals suffer from the same problems, such as cardiovascular disease or depression, the cause for their ill-health is unlikely to be only personal, and may also be linked to the built environment they inhabit (Jackson 2003). Therefore, to support health-promoting initiatives that focus on changing life habits, there is a need to provide communal and personal environments designed to encourage the implementation of a healthier lifestyle, for example, by providing green spaces for walking, cycling and relaxation.

Improving personal health may not be in the power of all individuals. Other aspects of life, such as poverty, social exclusion, lack of employment and education, and poor housing have also been recognised as having a significant impact on human health (Molyneux 2001; Crown 1998).

While political initiatives are necessary to tackle many of the health-related aspects of life, those involved in developing the built environment are well placed to make a significant contribution towards improving public health. Many of the sustainable design approaches illustrated in previous chapters have a positive effect on health as well as benefiting the environment. For example, the potential for building projects to address social exclusion, which can be linked to ill-health, was illustrated in Chapter 2. Car use is not only associated with CO_2 emissions, but also with ground-level ozone and particulate pollution, increased congestion and traffic accidents, and the inactive lifestyles associated with cardiovascular health problems. The urban measures identified in Chapter 1 to reduce car dependency, which benefit the environment, also benefit public health. The examples of the integration of green spaces in cities, included in previous chapters, provide both amenity spaces and encourage healthier lifestyles. In fact, many aspects of sustainable communities and buildings are thought to contribute to good health and well-being (Srinivasan et al. 2003).

This chapter examines how buildings can provide healthy environments for living and working that enhance human well-being and help prevent ill-health.

Creating healthy buildings

Built environment characteristics, which range from the chemical make-up of building materials to the spatial and semantic characteristics of a building design, affect people. Some characteristics have an immediate impact on the inhabitants and very noticeable outcomes. For example, the fact that a building is uncomfortably cold, and even so cold as to cause illness, does not generally go unnoticed; likewise entering a brightly lit space has an immediate impact, generally making people feel invigorated and cheerful. On the other hand, certain building characteristics are difficult to identify and their effects on health may become evident only years after the exposure to them, as with carcinogenic materials such as asbestos. It is not only negative characteristics that can remain elusive; the positive characteristics that make a building feel pleasant, can also be difficult to identify sometimes. This is because the effect of a building on an individual is often the result of many different building characteristics acting together.

A case in point is the phenomenon of Sick Building Syndrome (see 3.0.5), where several building characteristics, such as air quality, lighting and building control, act

3.0.4 Further reading

The Healthy House
Bower, J. (2001) The Healthy House Institute, Bloomington

Materials: A Guide to the Selection of Environmentally Responsible Alternatives
Curwell, S. et al. (2002) E&FN Spon, London

Spirit and Place
Day, C. (2001) Architectural Press, London

The Sickening Mind: Brain, Behaviour, Immunity and Disease
Martin, P. (1997) Flamingo, London

Building-Related Sickness: Causes, Effects, and Ways to Avoid It
Palmer, A., Rawlings, R. eds. (2002), Building Services Research and Information Association, Bracknell

The New Natural House Book
Pearson, D. (1998) Conran Octopus Limited, London

Cutting the Cost of Cold
Rudge, J., Nicol, F., eds. (2000) E&FN Spon, London

Eco-Friendly House Plants
Wolverton, B.C. (1997) Phoenix Illustrated, London

3.0.5 Sick Building Syndrome/Building-Related Sickness

These terms refer to a set of symptoms that affect a significant number of building occupants during the time they spend in the building and diminish or go away during periods when they are not in the building. The symptoms cannot usually be traced to specific pollutants or sources within the building.

Symptoms

– allergies

– asthma

– eye, nose and throat irritation

– fatigue

– headache

– nervous-system disorders

– respiratory congestion

– sinus congestion

Employer responsibility

In the UK, under the Management of Health and Safety at Work Regulations 1999, employers are required to undertake a risk assessment of their place of work, which should include considerations regarding building-related disease. (Palmer and Rawlings 2002)

3.0.6 Materials and indoor air quality

Research on the effects of materials on health has resulted in the development of a number of material labelling schemes that classify low emission products. The main building products covered by such schemes are flooring, panelling and finishing materials.
(Yu and Crump 2002)

– Blue Angel Ecolabelling (Germany): flooring materials, wall panelling, furniture, paints and varnishes.

– GuT, Environmental quality Marks for Carpets (Germany): emissions from carpets.

– Nordic Swan Ecolabelling programme: floor finishes.

– EU Ecolabel Scheme: sets maximum emission levels for paints and coatings.

– GEV EMICODE: labelling scheme for adhesives, primers and levelling compounds (www.emicode.com).

– Finnish M1 label for finishing materials (www.rts.fi): sets maximum emission levels for flooring finishes, paints and coatings.

– Danish voluntary labelling scheme (www.dsic.org): sets maximum emission levels for flooring finishes, paints and coatings.

3.0.7 Improving urban environments

CREATING HEALTHY URBAN ENVIRONMENTS

– Ensure ample and accessible green spaces for the community and green residential roads.

– Create pedestrian and cycle routes protected from vehicular noise, pollution and the danger of accidents.

– Support independence from cars by providing an efficient and affordable public transport system.

– Create environments of human scale.

– Provide community gardens or allotments.

ADDRESSING SOCIAL CAUSES OF ILL-HEALTH

– Address lack of education, unemployment and social exclusion through inclusive building projects.

– Provide affordable, low running cost housing to help reduce the limitations of poverty.

– Provide centres for marginalised individuals.

– Create safe neighbourhoods.

together to create an unhealthy building environment. Sick Building Syndrome is mainly associated with office buildings, but can also be experienced in other building types. Air-conditioning is thought to be linked to the occurrence of Sick Building Syndrome, as are other building characteristics such as: fluorescent lighting and limited natural light; sources of indoor air pollution such as photocopiers, office machinery; finishes, fixtures and fittings that off-gas fumes that are damaging to health; excessively dry air-conditioned air; poor air quality resulting from insufficient air changes or dirty air filters; lack of views to the outside; and lack of the occupants' ability to control the temperature, humidity or lighting. While the combination of several of these factors can create an environment that negatively affects its occupants' health and well-being in an apparent way, each individual characteristic can on its own affect people's well-being in a less noticeable way. For example, individuals working in an otherwise healthy building, but without natural light, will fail to experience much natural light throughout their day for several months of the year and may feel sluggish. While this can be considered a minor ailment, over time and with particular individuals, the feeling of sluggishness may become a cause of depression, which in turn can significantly affect their well-being.

There are a number of difficulties in studying the impacts of the environment on health. These include problems associated with testing individual characteristics of an environment in isolation, which consequently requires the collection of very large amounts of data to create reliable statistics; the fact that people react differently to situations and environments depending on their character and circumstances; and the relatively recent nature of many environmental characteristics thought to impact negatively on health, such as some modern materials and contemporary lifestyles. Despite these difficulties, there is an increasing body of research into environmental health and the related field of environmental psychology that points to a number of building-related health issues.

Buildings have physical, chemical and biological characteristics that affect the physiological and psychological health and well-being of their occupants. Chemical and biological disease agents, which range from formaldehyde gas from building materials to dust mites, and are generally known as indoor air pollutants, can affect the physiological health of an individual. Their effects are well understood, even though the medical profession has not reached consensus in respect of the level of risk to health associated with certain agents (Geisler 2001; IOM 2000). These agents of disease are not easily detectable by the building occupants. As with Sick Building Syndrome, it is the symptoms of illness and not the agents of illness that are evident. Other building-related agents of disease that are not readily recognisable include electromagnetic fields and other radiation. The effects of certain forms of radiation on health are disputed, but some researchers concerned about electromagnetic fields warn that their health impact is significant (Saunders 2002). Some well-established approaches to minimising the impacts of these insensitive agents of disease are discussed in Chapter 3.2.

Other characteristics of buildings are more easily identified. Physical characteristics such as temperature, humidity and light levels affect how comfortable a building is, but can have also physiological effects, as Seasonal Affective Disorder (SAD), hypothermia or heat exhaustion. The lack of comfort may not seem a sufficient cause for ill-health; however, it can indirectly affect the physiology of an individual. As with many building-related health issues, it is not the discomfort *per se*, but the length of exposure and the lack of prospect for improvement that affect the mental well-being of an individual, which in turn can affect physiological health. A brief unwanted noise may prove unpleasant, but will not have long-lasting effects, while continuous, uncontrollable, unwanted noise, the duration of which is unknown, can prove disruptive and stressful. Chronic stress can affect the immune system, making people more susceptible to illness. Similar reactions have been studied in respect of internal building temperatures. Where building occupants have the ability to change their environment, for example, by opening windows, they are more tolerant of variable temperatures than occupants without this ability (Baker 2001). The physiological and psychological effects of comfort and the lack of it are discussed in Chapter 3.1.

The human desire for control extends to many aspects of life, and a perceived lack of control can be frustrating and stressful, and may affect an individual's sense of self-worth. Chapter 3.3 illustrates how physical and spatial characteristics of buildings can facilitate all individuals, regardless of their circumstances, to take charge of their lives and be more independent. Having a feeling of control over one's life is as psychologically important as having a feeling of privacy, safety, belonging and self-worth; and carefully designed buildings can address all these human needs.

Healthy buildings should not only be designed to prevent both physiological and psychological ill-health, but should aim to enhance the inhabitants' sense of well-being. Environments that delight, that uplift the spirit, that relax or that provide contact with nature can benefit individuals. They can help to counteract the pressure of contemporary life, characterised by excessive speed and lack of time, or simply enhance an individual's life experience and well-being. Uplifting and restorative environments, as discussed in Chapter 3.4, should be included in every building.

Healthy buildings indirectly benefit the community as a whole: healthy and happy individuals are more likely to live a fulfilling life, allowing them to enjoy, but also to participate in and contribute to their community.

DESIGNING HEALTHY BUILDINGS

– Consider health and safety on the building site.

Physical comfort levels

– Consider the indoor temperature relative to outside temperatures.

– Consider relative humidity levels and their impact on temperature.

– Provide ample natural light and good quality lighting without glare.

– Ensure sound separation between buildings and to the outside and within buildings.

– Design environmental systems that enable the users to control their environment.

Keeping the living environment pollution-free

– Avoid building boards and other materials containing formaldehyde.

– Use low VOC paints and finishes or avoid the use of finishes.

– Avoid materials, such as carpets, that encourage dust mites.

– Consider treating timber only if necessary and using the least toxic treatments possible.

– Ventilate spaces sufficiently to avoid a build-up of indoor air pollutants.

– Consider the risk associated with EMF.

Independence and identity

– Create environments that help disadvantaged individuals to be and feel independent.

– Design buildings that demonstrate consideration of all users and their particular requirements.

– Ensure building users are able to personalise and demonstrate ownership of their building.

– Create environments that enable individuals to grow old comfortably and without disruption.

Restorative environments

– Consider including peaceful and restful spaces that help rejuvenate and calm individuals.

– Provide opportunities to enjoy nature.

3.1 Comfort

3.1.1 Sources and levels of sound

Sound pressure level (dB)

0-10	Threshold of hearing
10-20	Insulated broadcasting studio
20-30	Bedroom at night
30-40	Library
40-50	Living room in suburbia
50-60	Typical business office
60-70	Normal conversation at 1 m
70-80	Average traffic on main road at kerb
80-90	Inside bus, noisy office
90-100	Inside underground train
100-110	Noisy factory, motorcycle
110-120	Pneumatic drill
120	Threshold of pain
130-140	Jet engine at 30 m, hydraulic press

3.1.2 Reducing noise levels in buildings

– Consider the building fabric construction and internal finishes. The Building Regulations for England and Wales consider the impact of airborne, impact and flanking sound and its transmission through buildings.

– Plants can help dissipate sound waves internally.

– Consider the orientation of the building and the internal spaces away from sources of noise.

– Existing windows can be sound insulated by installing secondary glazing 150-200 millimetres from the existing window and acoustic panels around the jam, head and sill of the opening.

– Externally earth mounds, vegetation and turf roofs can help create a barrier, absorb and dissipate noise.

3.1.3 Achieving thermal comfort

The human body adopts a number of mechanisms to balance the heat generated with the heat lost by the body, and maintain its vital inner organs at approximately 37°C (the body limbs tolerate a range in temperatures of +/-5-10ºC without adverse effects). These moderating mechanisms alter the amount of heat exchanged with the environment, through evaporation, convection, radiation and minimally through conduction; and the amount of heat produced by the body by altering the metabolic rate or the bodily activities.

Comfort is defined as 'a state of physical ease' (*Oxford Dictionary*). The definition may seem straightforward, but achieving a state of physical ease is a complex task. Comfort is affected by many parameters including temperature, humidity, air movement, air quality, lighting, noise, culture, habit, personal preference, the ability to control the environment, clothing and activities. Buildings can determine many of the physical parameters listed above and influence some of the psychological parameters. There is guidance on how to design buildings that are comfortable, but it is constantly changing. In terms of certain aspects such as noise, guidance and regulations are becoming increasingly stringent, while in respect to thermal comfort, the past couple of decades have brought a shift towards a more comprehensive, but also more flexible, approach to creating comfortable spaces.

A lack of comfort is generally not life-threatening. However, there is no clear distinction between uncomfortable and unhealthy environments, and experiencing particular uncomfortable environments for long periods of time can have significant impacts on an individual's health. Indoor temperature is an example: in the UK, fuel poverty, which results in inadequately heated houses, is associated with tens of thousands of additional deaths in winter compared with the yearly average, primarily due to cardiovascular and respiratory disease (Wilkinson *et al.* 2000). In 2002, 24,000 additional deaths were recorded during the winter and, of these, over 21,000 were people over the age of 65, who are likely to be less physically aware of their environment, including constant low indoor temperatures (Thakrar 2003a).

Noise is another example of a comfort issue that can become a physiological problem. In terms of comfort, noise is unwanted sound, with the potential for causing annoyance even at very low volume. The causes of annoyance relate to the volume, predictability and perceived control of the noise; whereby the higher the volume and the lower the predictability and control over the source of noise, the higher the annoyance. Noise can also have physiological impacts: mental and bodily fatigue can be experienced even at levels of 65 dBA if the noise is interfering with mental activities; rising blood pressure can be experienced at levels over 80dBA and heart stress at levels of 90 dBA, typical level of street noise; hearing loss can begin to occur at levels between 90–120dBA; and very loud sounds over 145 dBA can rupture the eardrum (see 3.1.1). High and constant levels of noise experienced in factories, from traffic or services can cause a number of other psychological and mental problems including: hypertension, sleep problems, headaches, nausea, irritability, anxiety, deteriorating memory and reduced comprehension. The increased understanding of the effects of noise on health and well-being has prompted the introduction of more stringent building regulation requirements in England and Wales for noise separation in and between dwellings. Designing for comfort is not a luxury, but a prerequisite for creating healthy environments.

Experiencing comfort, as mentioned above, is affected by a number of parameters, including personal and psychological ones. Research into thermal comfort has extensively explored this aspect. Guidance on indoor air temperature, published by the UK Chartered Institute of Building Services Engineers, recommends winter and summer temperatures for offices of 21-23°C and 22-24 °C respectively (CIBSE, 1999). However, research suggests that these restrictions of indoor temperatures are in practice neither necessary nor desirable (Nicol 1993); and that achieving thermal comfort is possible in a number of different environments and at a wider range of temperatures. First, temperature is only one of the different parameters that affect thermal comfort and which are also interrelated. Air movement, radiant heat, and relative humidity affect comfort levels without affecting temperature (see 3.1.3). An increase in air velocity of 0.3 metres per second, increases the temperature considered comfortable by 1.5°C. On the other hand, temperature and humidity can affect other aspects of comfort, for example, by altering the perception of indoor air quality: hot spaces feel stuffier, cool spaces feel fresher and humid spaces seem more odorous (Palmer and Rawlings 2002). Air movement also gives a feeling of freshness to the air.

One of the parameters, which appears to have a very significant impact on the thermal comfort perception by individuals, is people's ability to alter their circumstances (see 3.1.3). This ability affects people in two ways: it enables them physically to change the parameters for comfort, and it also provides the reassurance that any uncomfortable situation could, if wanted, be altered.

The importance of having control over one's own environment was illustrated by research, by Oseland in 1994, which tested individuals in climate chambers, at their work place and at home. The research showed that people felt comfortable at home at a temperature 3°C lower than in the test chamber, and 1-2°C lower than in their work place. Other research suggests that even if alterations to make a space more comfortable are not implemented, the fact that they could be implemented increases the tolerance to the environment (Baker 2001) (see also 3.3.1).

In addition to the ability to adapt an environment, comfort is also affected by cultural issues, individual short-term and long-term habits, and personal circumstances, which make individuals become more or less sensitive to their environment. People from certain cultures, such as Eskimos in North America and Lapps in Scandinavia, have adapted to cold environments and are comfortable at temperatures considered uncomfortable in other parts of the world. The perception of comfort is also affected by recent environmental experiences. After a hot spell of 25°C, temperatures of 20°C may feel cool, while the same temperature may feel warm after a few days at 10°C. This effect can be observed throughout the seasons: in summer people tend to feel comfortable at warmer temperatures than in winter (Nicol 1993). Furthermore, many people consider a variety in thermal experiences to be energising and stimulating, and therefore desirable.

Considering the various building-related parameters that affect comfort, including thermal, visual and acoustic comfort, and the fact that comfort is dependent on personal factors, one conclusion has to be that adaptability is a fundamental prerequisite to creating comfortable environments.

To avoid excessive heat loss, the body can:

– increase metabolism to generate heat. Metabolism is measured in Met. 1 Met produces 58 W/m² of body surface. A normal adult has a surface area of 1.7 square metres. Metabolic rate ranges from 0.8 Met during sleep to 10 Met during sports activities.

– increase generated heat through shivering or other activities

– make more blood available to the vital organs while removing it from non-essential extremities

– produce goose bumps and erect the hairs of the skin to increase the thin layer of insulating air close to the skin and help to minimise heat loss through convection

– increase insulating effect by changing posture (Insulating clothing could be worn. The unit used for measuring clothing's insulation is the Clo unit. The Clo scale is designed so that a naked person has a Clo value of 0.0 and someone wearing a business suit has a Clo value of 1.0.)

To increase heat loss, the body can:

– sweat (cooling by evaporation)

– increase breathing levels to lose heat

– dilate blood vessels near the skin surface, to remove heat from the vital organs and dissipate it through evaporative and convective cooling

– change posture to increase losses

– decrease physical activity

These bodily adjustments are affected by the surrounding environment. For example, an environment with high relative humidity does not have the capacity to absorb water from sweat, therefore sweating is ineffective and other means of cooling are required, such as air movement, which increases convective losses. The human body perceives its heat loss rather than the actual temperature. Therefore, environments where the body's adjustment mechanisms are hampered feel uncomfortable. For example, 38°C and 60 per cent humidity are perceived as more uncomfortable than 38°C and 15 per cent humidity, where sweating provides effective cooling.

The ability to change the comfort parameters increases the likelihood of feeling comfortable. Adjustments may be personal (increasing insulation by putting on more clothing), or environmental (increasing evaporation and convective losses through increased air movement, or decreasing radiant heat from the sun with shading).

Case study: Natural light

Design Centre
Linz, Austria

Client: Design Centre
Architect: Herzog & Partner
Lighting specialist: Bartenbach Lichtlabor
Interior design: Verena Herzog-Loibl
Landscape architect: Annaliese Latz
Project management: Heinz Stogmuller
Structural engineer: Ingenierbüro Sailer &
Stepan/Ingenierbüro Kirsch Muchitsch & Partner
Completed: 1994

3.1.4 Lighting levels

Recommended illuminance levels adapted from Palmer and Rawlings 2002 and Goulding *et al.* 1992 Typical room type	Standard service illuminance (lux)	Daylight factor minimum values (%)
Rarely used spaces	50	
Storage spaces	150	
Church halls		1
Domestic kitchen and living rooms, entrances	200	2
Teaching spaces, libraries, sports halls, moderate visual tasks	300	
Offices, retail shops, commercial kitchens, painting and spraying	500	
Drawing offices, ceramic decoration, meat inspection	750	
Industrial assembly tasks, cabinet making, supermarkets	1000	5
Industrial precision tasks, inspection of graphic reproduction	1500	

Humans are greatly affected by natural light and still generally live in tune with daily and seasonal light cycles, being most active with the sun, and resting and sleeping at night. Effects of natural light on people include feeling energetic and positive when it is sunny, and feeling sluggish, even depressed when it is grey and dark. Light also affects the ability to undertake particular tasks.

Natural light affects the circadian rhythm, the pattern of physical functions that influence body temperature, sleep and hormonal changes. In humans the circadian rhythm is 25 hours long and is constantly reset to match the 24-hour day by exposure to lighting levels of 2,500 lux for short periods or 1,200 lux for at least three hours. Typically, buildings provide natural light levels from less than 1 per cent to rarely over 10 per cent daylight factor. The daylight factor expresses internal light levels as a percentage of light levels measured outside under a uniformly overcast sky. Even on a bright day, the average office, with 2 per cent daylight factor, does not achieve 2,500 lux. As more time is spent indoors, particularly in winter, an increasing number of people may not be experiencing sufficiently high light levels during the day.

At dusk and during darkness hours, the body releases melatonin, which causes sleepiness. With increasing time being spent indoors, this natural process is affecting more people in an unnatural way, with feelings of fatigue and sluggishness occurring throughout the day. This syndrome, known as Seasonal Affective Disorder (SAD) manifests itself through the occurrence of sleepiness, fatigue, depression, carbohydrate craving and weight gain. In some individuals SAD has been successfully counteracted with the use of full-spectrum artificial lights.

The Design Centre viewed from the partially planted public area.

A 1,300-square metre exhibition gallery is located over a convention hall. Artwork is an integral part of the building.

3.1.5 Sustainable design features

Site and ecology
The building made use of a brownfield site.

Community and culture
The Design Centre Linz provides the city with an international venue, which benefits the city economically. The building includes artwork integrated within the structure.

Health
See main text.

Energy
Thermally spilt steel sections reduce the building heat loss. Fresh air supply is through floor inlets and low level vents at the perimeter of the building envelope and is exhausted at high level. During the heating season the stale air is extracted mechanically and the heat recycled through a heat recovery system. In hot weather the air is exhausted to the outside through a roof ventilator that induces the Venturi effect.

Just as insufficient light can have negative impacts on health, so do excessive light levels. Exposure to UV lighting is beneficial in small doses, but in larger amounts it can cause premature aging of the skin, eye damage and skin cancer. Inside buildings, excessive or highly contrasting light appearing in the field of vision can cause glare. Disability glare occurs when a bright light source, such as a light bulb in a dark room or a bright window, makes it difficult to see the detail around the light source. Discomfort glare occurs when bright lights, direct or reflected, are in the field of vision, but not the focus, such as with computer screens in front of windows. The vision is not impaired, but long-term discomfort glare can cause mental fatigue, headaches and tension.

Environments where people spend most of their time, such as work places or living rooms, should have ample natural light and a varied light environment that provides interest throughout the day. Good daylight designs, which should energise people and engender positive feelings, have been used in commercial and retail buildings to boost sales. In the Greenwich Sainsbury's store in London (see case study, p.232), natural light floods the supermarket aisles. At the Design Centre, an exhibition centre in the Austrian city of Linz, natural light has been used in a building type that often relies almost entirely on electrical light. For visitors, and in particular for exhibitors, who can spend several days in exhibition halls, access to natural light is highly beneficial.

The Design Centre is not only almost completely naturally lit, but the light is of the highest quality. Glare is excluded, even on a bright sunny day, and the impression is of being under a high, thick tree canopy. The space feels like being outdoors: bright and invigorating.

The 200m-long building opens up onto a paved area, which links it to the conference hotel.

The roof has a soft glow when the sun is shining.

The Design Centre structure consists of a flat arched structure, 12 metres high and spanning 76 metres, covering an area of 80 x 200 metres. The whole structure is largely covered with glass and the 3,456 glazed elements have been carefully engineered to achieve maximum natural light without glare, while also preventing the exhibition space from overheating. The double-glazed units include a 16mm-deep injection-moulded plastic grid coated with a thin layer of highly reflective aluminium, which is sandwiched between two panes of glass. The reflective grid allows only indirect daylight into the building, protecting it from direct sunlight. Each grid has a different inclination depending on its position on the slope of the roof, and their design had to consider the orientation and location of the building. The grid was developed for the Design Centre using computer technology that is now available world-wide and has been integrated in other buildings.

The Design Centre benefits from a highly versatile building programme, which, spread over three levels, can accommodate independent exhibitions and conferences at the same time, as well as banquets, balls, concerts and other performances. This, combined with a building design that provides an uplifting environment and dramatic space, has created a very successful venue for the city of Linz.

The 4,300-square metre exhibition hall, like most of the building, benefits from indirect daylight.

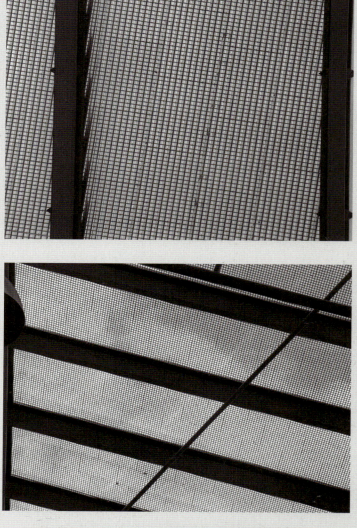

The small lighting shafts formed by the square grid always face north, and are therefore see-through when looking north and opaque when looking south.

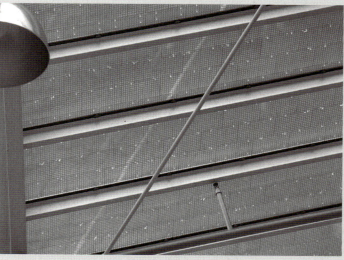

Case study: Thermal comfort

Dyfi Eco Park
Machynlleth, Wales, UK

Client: Welsh Development Agency
Architects Units 1-3: Acanthus Holden Architects
Energy consultant Units 1-3: Peter Warm
Quantity surveyor Units 1-3: Davies, Langdon and Everest
Completed: Unit One – 1996, Unit Two - 1998, Unit Three – 1999, Units Four and Five – 2002, Units Six and Seven - 2005

3.1.6 Natural ventilation and solar gain

Natural ventilation has been shown to effectively lower internal air temperature. At Unit One the natural ventilation strategy proved very effective, and was able to reduce the number of days with internal temperatures in excess of 25°C by 64 per cent, the number of days with internal temperatures in excess of 27°C by 79 per cent and completely avoid temperatures in excess of 30°C. The passive solar heating also proved effective, when, with an external temperature of between 0-3°C, the temperature in the unoccupied and unheated building rose to 20°C.

Dyfi Eco Park is a 'green' business park on the outskirts of Machynlleth, a small town in Wales. The development, located on the site of an old goods yard adjacent to Machynlleth Railway Station, began in 1995 with the first of a series of energy-efficient and ecologically sound light industrial and office units. In 2004, the seventh of these units was under construction. Each one- or two-storey unit consists of a combination of office, workshop and storage facilities.

The environmental strategy for the development considered resource use and occupant comfort and health. The buildings were designed to minimise heating, cooling and lighting energy requirements, and their performance was monitored after completion (see Chapter 5.2). Materials were also carefully selected to minimise environmental impacts and provide a healthy environment for the building occupants.

To achieve thermal comfort, an environment should be within an acceptable comfort range (humans can easily adapt to temperatures between 16°C and 25°C), and opportunities should exist to moderate the environment as required. Building design can affect the main mechanisms of the body to exchange heat with its environment through convection, radiation and evaporation; and these comfort modifying elements should be able to be adjusted and operated by the occupants. These are two key characteristics of comfortable environments (Bordass 1995).

In cold weather, the main aim of a building design in terms of thermal comfort is to reduce heat loss while maintaining good air quality and light. At Dyfi Eco Park the buildings are well insulated and sealed, minimising fabric and ventilation losses, while still providing sufficient glazed areas for good natural light. The amount of insulation was increased with each new unit (see 3.1.8), reducing the total heat loss from the building and the period required for the building to heat up each day and after a weekend without heating. After a typical weekend, Unit One required more than six hours to achieve an acceptable 18-20°C, but this period was reduced with subsequent units. While, in the case of Unit One, the problem was overcome by resetting the heating programme, in buildings with irregular and unpredictable occupation, long heating up times have a more significant impact on comfort.

Indoor air temperature affects convective losses, while the temperature of the building envelope affects the radiant heat losses from the inhabitants. Radiant heat losses, which can make up 45 per cent of the body heat exchanged with the environment, are greatly reduced if the temperature of the building envelope's internal surfaces is as high as the internal air temperature. Radiant losses are low in well-insulated buildings and high in poorly insulated buildings or near poorly insulated building elements, such as windows. Less critical in winter are heat losses through evaporation, even though in heated buildings, where relative humidity tends to be low, excessive evaporation can cause symptoms of dehydration.

Dyfi Eco Park buildings are designed to provide a comfortable environment and the means to regulate it. Radiators can be adjusted locally and windows can be opened. Personal changes, such as changing clothing or moving to a warmer or cooler part of the building, are possible in certain instances.

Units One, Two and Three.

3.1.7 Requirements for a pleasant and invigorating environment

– Indoor environments should be kept as cool as possible without compromising comfort.

– Internal air velocity should be about 10 m/min in winter and higher in summer. Velocities less than 6 m/min can make a space feel stuffy.

– Air movement should be variable and provide stimulation for the occupants.

– The relative humidity should not exceed 70 per cent and should preferably be below 50 per cent.

– The temperature of internal radiant surfaces should be above the air temperature.

– The air temperature at head height should be cooler than near the floor.
(Pearson 1998)

Sealing a building well to minimise heat loss may affect air quality, and make a space feel stuffy and even odorous (see also Chapter 3.2). All Dyfi Eco Park units are naturally ventilated. Trickle vents, integrated in the windows, supply fresh air, which is exhausted through rooflights. In cold weather the rooflights were kept mainly closed. The post-occupancy surveys, which asked the occupants their views regarding comfort in respect of building temperature, building humidity, air movement, air freshness and light levels, highlighted that the spaces were felt to lack air movement and sometimes felt slightly stuffy. Despite this issue, which could be addressed by introducing mechanical ventilation for part of the year or a permanent passive vent at roof level, 37.5 per cent of Unit One occupants considered the building very comfortable in winter and 62.5 per cent rated it comfortable. Their tolerance of minor problems was affected by their knowledge that they could control their environment: if it got too stuffy, they simply opened a window. Their attitude to the building was also affected by the satisfaction they felt at being in a sustainable building.

In summer, buildings need to be kept cool, and passive measures are the most environmentally friendly approaches to achieve this, although they do have some limitations (see Chapter 5.1). The Dyfi Eco Park units have large roof overhangs and solar shading to prevent excessive heat gains, and passive stack and cross-ventilation cools the open plan office spaces, while single-sided ventilation cools the cellular offices. In the open plan spaces the air rises as it is heated by internal gains, is exhausted through

See also: lighting 1, 2 **Chapter 5.1**

See also: performance targets and post-occupancy monitoring **Chapter 5.2**

3.1.8 Sustainable design features

Site and ecology
A brownfield site was used. It was landscaped with native plants and a willow wall protects Unit One from the noise from the adjacent road.

Community and culture
The client aimed to provide employment opportunities for the local people.

Health
Materials used are mainly natural and non-toxic, such as low VOC paints and stains and natural floor finishes. The design provides ample natural light.

Materials
Natural, low-embodied energy and locally resourced materials were used. The buildings use a breather wall system with recycled cellulose fibre insulation, plywood internally and bitumen-impregnated fibreboard externally. Other recycled materials include the Onduline roofing sheets made of bitumen-covered recycled cellulose corrugated panels. Timber and slates were locally sourced. The embodied energy of the materials used was calculated by Davies, Langdon and Everest.

Energy
The units are low-energy, passive designs. They are well insulated and built to be airtight. Large south-facing façades maximise solar heat gains in winter and large rooflights provide sufficient natural light to obviate the use of electrical lighting during sunlight hours. Natural ventilation provides cooling. All three units have small gas-fired condensing boilers and Unit Three has underfloor heating within the insulated concrete slab.

Fabric insulation

Units	Walls thickness and U-value	Roof U-value
One	0.25 W/m²K (R23)	0.2 W/m²K (R28)
Two	0.2 W/m²K (R28)	0.2 W/m²K (R28)
Three	0.2 W/m²K (R28) (500-mm flank walls- 0.1 W/m²K (R58))	better than 0.2 W/m²K

Energy consumption

Units	Gas	Electricity
One	48 kWh/sqm yr	21 kWh/sqm yr
Two	67 kWh/sqm yr	41 kWh/sqm yr
Three	22 kWh/sqm yr	82 kWh/sqm yr

Water
Low flush WCs were installed.

the rooflights and draws fresh cooler air in from outside. This simple mechanism ensures that the internal temperature generally remains within a comfortable range. The air movement also cools the occupants by increasing evaporation rates and convective losses. Control is with the occupants who can open and close the windows and rooflights. If external temperatures are very high, cooling through evaporation and convection may still be effective, but eventually the internal temperature may become uncomfortably high. On rare occasions, this occurred at Dyfi Eco Park, but the overall effect on the occupants' perception of comfort was limited, 25 per cent still considering the building in summer to be very comfortable, 37.5 per cent comfortable and 37.5 per cent slightly uncomfortable.

A revealing fact was that, of the three occupied buildings, there seemed to be a correlation between the awareness of environmental issues among the occupants and the level of their satisfaction with the building. Unit One is occupied by Dulas, a company specialising in renewable energy and dedicated to environmental issues. They are the most environmentally aware occupants of the three building, and were eager to see the building succeed in its environmental ambitions. They adjusted the building to fine–tune its performance, but were also very tolerant of its limitations and proved to be among those most satisfied with their environment. Once again, issues of control, ownership and even ethics affect people's experience of comfort.

The two-storey units have a long rooflight and glazed south-facing elevations.

Unit Two, secluded by planting.

Case study: Relative humidity

The Pishwanton gridshell (see case study, p.138) included the use of clay-based materials for the construction of some of the walls.

Internally, the gridshell has an exposed timber roof and a timber floor.

The gridshell roof structure comprises three layers of 12-millimetre thick timber planks fixed on top of a slender timber shell. The timber is left exposed internally.

Relative humidity (RH) is one of the environmental characteristics of which people are least aware. When asked whether a space has adequate relative humidity, most individuals will not know. In fact, an environment can be perceived to be dry, when in reality it is either too hot or has poor air quality. However, relative humidity is of importance as it has a significant effect on thermal comfort and can indirectly impact on the indoor air quality of a space and on its occupants' health.

As discussed in 3.1.3, humidity levels affect the human body's ability to cool itself through evaporation and consequently, hot and humid environments feel hotter than less humid environments at the same temperature. While most relevant in hot climates, this principle is used in air-conditioned environments in temperate climates, where spaces can be made to feel more comfortable by reducing the RH rather than reducing its temperature, an approach that helps to reduce energy use.

While RH remains an intangible characteristic, its impacts do not. Recommended levels of RH are between 40-50 per cent. Levels below 35 per cent, especially if experienced for long periods, can cause dryness of the eyes, nose, and throat, and the sensitising of mucous membranes, which can in turn result in elevated risk of virus infection and allergy attacks. Static energy also increases at low RH levels. Low levels can be experienced in heated interiors during winter, when cold air is warmed up when entering a building, reducing its RH significantly.

Relative humidity at levels above 70 per cent is also problematic, as it supports condensation and biological contaminants, such as fungi and mites. These are related to allergic diseases, such as rhinits and asthma, toxic reactions, and Sick Building Syndrome effects (see 3.0.5, 3.2.3 and 3.2.5.).

The RH in a building is the result of a number of conditions acting together including: the building fabric insulation, the materials used internally, sources of humidity, ventilation rates and heating. These, plus the occurrence of cold-bridging, affect the potential for mould growth.

Cooking and washing are the main domestic sources of humidity and therefore kitchens and bathrooms are most at risk of excessively high RH levels and mould growth. However, insufficiently insulated buildings with inadequate ventilation are at risk of mould growth even in spaces with only slightly elevated humidity. In particular, humidity in conjunction with cold-bridging can cause mould growth. Uninsulated north-facing walls and poorly insulated windows are typical examples of areas at risk. However, where RH levels are sufficiently high, mould can grow on any cellulose-based material regardless of temperature. Even in well-insulated modern homes, inadequately ventilated spaces with high RH levels can have mould growth.

If internal temperatures are sufficiently high, generally above 16°C, humid environments can also harbour dust mites. In highly humid environments, such as in bathrooms, carpets and other absorbent building elements may be prevented from drying out and create a perfect environment for mould growth and mites.

Ventilation is therefore essential to prevent excessive RH, as is adequate insulation. The internal building materials are also of importance. Not only does their ability to support mould growth and dust mites vary, but they can also affect the actual relative humidity in the building. Materials can be more or less hygroscopic, which refers to their ability to absorb and release moisture. Highly hygroscopic materials include clay, cork, timber, lime plaster, cellulose fibre insulation and natural fibres. These materials will readily absorb moisture when internal RH levels are high and then release it when levels drop. This can avoid excessively high humidity and helps moderate the humidity, keeping internal RH levels within the recommended 40–50 per cent. Coupled with appropriate ventilation and heating, an environment free of biological indoor air pollutants can be achieved.

Other materials, such as wood particle boards, plasterboard, cement, bricks, and stone, are also hygroscopic, but to a lesser degree. At the other end of the spectrum are materials that are not hygroscopic at all, such as glass and ceramic tiles. Hygroscopic materials should be left unfinished or should be finished with vapour-permeable finishes to maintain their hygroscopic characteristics.

Hygroscopic materials were used in a number of buildings included in this book. The Pishwanton gridshell, Piney Lakes Environmental Centre and Thurgoona Campus buildings all made use of clay-based materials for the construction of some of the internal or external walls. In some of the timber-framed houses, such as the Schreiber house, the Carlisle Lane house and the Solarsiedlung houses, elements of the timber structure and panelling were left exposed and untreated. The clay and timber not only help regulate the internal humidity, improving the comfort levels and creating a healthy environment, they also contribute to the building aesthetic.

3.1.9 Maintaining relative humidity (RH)

Avoiding excessively high RH

To avoid mould growth and dust mites the RH level is recommended to be kept at below 50 per cent. This can be done by:

– providing adequate ventilation and focus on areas with sources of humidity, e.g. bathrooms and kitchens. The moisture produced in a house of four can amount to 10.43 kilos per day (Oreszczyn and Pretlove 2000)

– insulating well and avoiding cold-bridging

– avoiding the use of materials conducive to mould growth and harbouring dust mites (e.g. carpets)

– considering using hygroscopic materials (e.g. unfired clay, timber, natural fibres, cork) finished with permeable finishes (e.g. wax) to avoid sealing the hygroscopic materials

– considering using vapour-permeable wall constructions that allow excessive vapour to escape the building

Avoiding excessively low RH

– introduce planting into an environment (a low-energy and natural approach)

– keep winter temperatures as low as comfortable (this will make a space feel fresher and will diminish the temperature difference between outside and inside, which typically cause the reduction in RH)

– consider the use of a humidifier (these can, however, harbour fungi and bacterial growths)

The Solarsiedlung houses (see case study, p.244) are timber-framed structures, with timber cladding externally. Internally, the ceiling timber structure is left exposed providing a large surface of a hygroscopic material.

3.2 Insensible Agents of Disease

3.2.1 Indoor air quality and health

Allergies, Sick Building Syndrome (SBS) (see 3.0.5) and Multiple Chemical Sensitivity (MCS) (see 3.2.2) are some of the main health problems associated with poor indoor air quality.

Allergy

Allergy is a state of immune hypersensitivity that exists in an individual who has been exposed to an allergen and has responded with an overproduction of certain immune system components.

An allergy is an immunological mechanism that causes symptoms of disease when an individual comes into contact with a particular substance. Allergy is also used more widely to describe a hypersensitivity to a substance that causes symptoms of disease without an immunological mechanism.

The process of developing an allergy begins with the foreign matter entering the body, which develops antibodies to it. While at this stage the allergic reactions do not occur, the sensitisation of the individual has taken place. Having become sensitised, a second and repeated interaction with the same material can eventually trigger an allergic reaction.

Allergic reactions commonly include irritation to eyes, nose and skin and respiratory problems, but can also include loss of energy, appetite, aches of the bones, muscles and joints. Reactions range from mild to disabling.

House mites, fungi and yeast are potent sensitisers.

A number of construction materials have the potential to cause allergic reactions, including adhesives, concrete, mortar mixes, cleaners for stone and brickwork, treatment materials, sealants and insulants (Greenberg 1990).

3.2.2 Multiple Chemical Sensitivity

Multiple Chemical Sensitivity (MCS) describes the state of hypersensitivity that occurs after a period of exposure to chemical gases.

Individuals suffering from MCS often suffer reactions and a set of symptoms that are not recognisable as a typical allergy. The symptoms can occur when in contact with synthetic materials and gases, including car fumes, fragrances, plastics and printers. Owing to their hypersensitivity, MCS sufferers may develop reactions at extremely low chemical concentration levels, which may not even be measurable.

MCS may develop as a result of a single extreme incident of exposure to pollutants; it may develop after an illness; or during a period of stress and immune deficiency.

As technology evolves, new building materials and services systems are integrated into buildings. While, at the time of installation, these may have appeared safe, experience has shown that first impressions can be misleading. Asbestos is a case in point. Exploited for its incombustibility, resistance to chemical attack and other useful properties from around 1900, with time it became evident that exposure to asbestos could cause respiratory disease, lung cancer and mesothelioma, a rare tumour associated only with exposure to very fine fibre asbestos. However, the diagnosis of such illnesses can take place 15–50 years after the exposure to asbestos, and at the time of exposure the individual affected would have been oblivious to the risk placed on their health (Addison 1990).

Asbestos is one of the well-recognised insensible disease agents associated with buildings. Others include: the legionella pneumophila bacterium, which can cause Legionnaires' Disease, a form of pneumonia; silica dust, which can cause silicosis and may lead to lung cancer; and other materials, such as mineral wool, which are recognised irritants. Recognition of these health risks has resulted in the introduction of legislation and precautionary working methods for various high risk materials and installations. In the UK, health and safety legislation requires construction workers to adopt safe working practices to minimise the risk to health of all materials. In practice, despite legislation, a risk to health, albeit reduced, may still exist. For example, the legionella pneumophila bacterium is still responsible for a significant number of deaths each year in the UK, caused primarily by poor maintenance that contravenes legislation. In 1997, of the 226 reported cases of Legionnaires' Disease in England and Wales, 28 resulted in death (Picton 1999).

New materials and technologies continue to be used unabated, and a full assessment of their risk to health tends to lag behind their use. While the individuals most at risk are those working with these materials, there is an increasing concern for building occupants who are subject to them. The increased use of new and untested materials combined with the fact that buildings are designed to be increasingly airtight and mechanically ventilated, can result in indoor air that can be as much as ten times more polluted than outside air (Wolverton 1997; Coward *et al.* 2001). Indoor air pollution, the sources of which are both internal, including building materials, equipment and consumables, and external, including traffic pollution, radon and pollen, has been recognised as affecting health, but remains uncontrolled by legislation. The reasons for the lack of legislative control include the fact that the effects of indoor air pollution, while reducing human well-being and proving, in extreme cases, debilitating, have not yet proved to be fatal (see 3.2.5).

The effects of indoor air pollution on health are exacerbated by contemporary lifestyles. Contact with indoor air pollution is increased as people, particularly in developed countries, can spend more than 90 per cent of their time in their homes, work places and cars. The increasing contact with chemicals and biological agents of disease is thought to be associated with the rise in the number of people with allergies. Individuals with immature, weakened or declining immune systems, including unborn babies, infants up to 5 years old, those suffering from illness and elderly people, are more liable to develop a sensitisation when coming into contact with biological agents, such as dust mites or mould, or chemical pollutants. This sensitisation may remain undetected for years, and later develop into an allergy (see 3.2.1) (Crowther 1994). Furthermore, stress, one of modern life's diseases, can negatively affect the immune system, and chronic stress can result in long-term inactivity of the immune system, leaving the body unprotected from disease agents (see 3.3.1).

While research in the field of health and indoor air pollution only cautiously makes links between volatile organic compounds and asthma and Sick Building Syndrome, recommendations on how to improve indoor air quality are unequivocal: the most effective method of controlling indoor pollutants is to remove their source and, in certain cases, is the only way to control pollutants (IOM 2000). In addition to removing the sources of pollutants, buildings should be designed to avoid the accumulation of agents of disease, by providing adequate ventilation and eliminating spaces and materials that attract or harbour them.

Research into the field of healthy buildings is slowly building up a body of knowledge from which to draw statistically sound conclusions about the links between the environment, materials and health. As evidence becomes available, more materials and building technologies are added to the list of potential hazards to health. Ten years ago, medium density fibreboard (MDF) was put under scrutiny as a potential cause of respiratory disease and, in the event, it was concluded that precautions taken when working the material would be sufficient to reduce the risk to health to acceptable levels. In recent years concerns regarding toxic moulds alerted the building industry to another health hazard (see 3.2.3). This trend is unlikely to change, and it would not be surprising if more materials currently in use were identified as being hazardous to health. Designing healthy buildings needs to address these risks by adopting a precautionary principle, avoiding the use of materials and systems whose health impacts are in question.

The same precautionary principle may be appropriate in respect of other building and environment-related physical characteristics thought to constitute a risk to health. The effects of ion imbalances in the air and electromagnetic fields are not fully understood, but some research suggests they may be associated with serious health issues (see 3.2.13).

In line with the WHO definition of health and the current understanding of connections between human well-being and the susceptibility to disease, taking a precautionary approach in respect of material selection and indoor air pollution is a responsible way forward (see 3.2.4).

3.2.3 Toxic mould

Toxic mould (*Stachybotrys Chartarum*) is a greenish blackish mildew which grows on materials with high cellulose content. While health problems linked to mould growth are not new, in 2002–03 toxic mould became the focus of much attention when a number of multimillion dollar compensation cases in the US were won by individuals who were suffering from its effects. Most of the cases were linked to ventilation systems that had been inadequately designed or installed.

The mould spores enter the building through open doors and windows and through ventilation and air-conditioning systems. To flourish, the mould requires sufficiently high humidity. *Stachybotrys Chartarum* produces mycotoxins, which can be inhaled, affecting sufferers by suppressing their immune system or as a result of their toxigenic characteristics. The effects of *Stachybotrys Chartarum* include cold-like symptoms, rashes and the aggravation of asthma, and, in extreme cases, it is also linked to pulmonary hemosiderosis.

The Royal Institute of Chartered Surveyors estimated that three million homes in the UK could be affected by mould, but not necessarily toxic mould.

Recommendations to minimise risk of mould include reducing relative humidity to below 50 per cent, ensuring adequate ventilation, not carpeting bathrooms, and avoiding cold-bridging and other sources of condensation. (Thakrar 2003b; Littlefield 2003).

3.2.4 The precautionary principle

The precautionary principle states that if negative effects of an action cannot to be excluded, then that action should not be taken.

3.2.5 Some of the main disease agents found in buildings

Types of disease agents	Some sources found in buildings	Health impacts
Biological		
Bacteria (legionella pneumophila bacterium)	– Water systems – cooling systems, whirlpool baths, humidifiers, water misters	Legionnaires' Disease is a type of pneumonia that principally affects people susceptible due to age or weakened immune system. 28 Legionnaires' Disease deaths in 1997 in England and Wales, and over 1,000, or 20% of all lung disease deaths, in Germany.
Fungi, moulds, spores (There are more than 100,000 mould species, of which fewer than ten are toxic.)	– Mould spores come from outside environments through open windows and doors. Any cellulose-rich material, such as wood, paper, wallboard, thermal and acoustic insulation and furnishings, will support mould growth if the humidity is high enough.	Moulds can affect people in 3 ways: by growing on or in a person; by producing toxins (mycotoxins) primarily ingested with food, but that can also be inhaled; and by producing an allergic reaction, including sensitisation and immune responses such as hayfever or asthma, after inhalation of mould particles. The latter is the most common building-related effect and the typical symptoms include sneezing, watery eyes, coughing, wheezing and the like. A single high exposure to airborne mould can develop Organic Dust Toxic Syndrome.
House-dust mites (HDM)	– Carpets, beds, upholstered furniture or other material that contains human skin scale provide a food source for HDM. – HDM thrive at RH levels above 73% and above 25°C. They survive between 16-26°C. At RH levels below 50% HDM tend to die after 6-11 days.	House dust mites can cause eye, nose and throat irritation. Dust mites account for 50-60% of asthma cases and are responsible for causing sensitisation and allergic attacks of asthma. – Asthma affects ca.3.7 million children in the USA. 1,400 people die each year from asthma in the UK and over a third of these are people under 65 (Asthma UK 2004).
People	– Bio-effluents (CO and VOCs)	See below
Chemical		
Oxides of nitrogen and sulphur (NOx and SOx).	– Combustion of cooking and heating appliances – Tobacco smoke	NO and SO2 cause irritation of the mucous membranes in the eye, nose, and throat. High concentrations of NO2 may cause pulmonary edema and lung injury.
Carbon monoxide (CO)	– Incomplete combustion of cooking and heating appliances – Tobacco smoke	Low concentrations of CO cause fatigue in healthy people and chest pain in people with heart disease. Higher concentrations can impair vision and coordination and cause headaches, dizziness, confusion and nausea. Very high concentrations can be fatal. An article in the *British Medical Journal* suggested that faulty gas appliances could be poisoning as many as 25,000 people each year in the UK.
Radon – radioactive gas	– The main source of radon is underground uranium. Certain areas of the UK, such as Cornwall and Devon. are particularly affected. – Some materials give off insignificantly low amounts	Radon can cause cancer of the lung (10% of lung cancer in UK is attributed to radon) if inhaled in sufficient qualities. In the USA it is estimated that between 7,000 and 30,000 lung cancer deaths yearly are caused by radon.
Ozone	– Copier machines and printers – Electronic air cleaners and ionisers	Ozone can cause eye, nose and throat irritation, coughing, choking, headaches and fatigue.
Formaldehyde (Half life of formaldehyde offgassing lasts up to six years)	– The glue or adhesive in pressed wood products – Preservatives in some paints, coatings and cosmetics – The coating that provides permanent press quality to fabrics and draperies – Ureaformaldehyde foam insulation	Formaldehyde has been classed as a probable human carcinogen by the US EPA. It can cause watery eyes, burning sensations in the eyes and throat, nausea and difficulty in breathing in some humans exposed at elevated levels (above 0.1 parts per million). High concentrations may trigger attacks in people with asthma. Formaldehyde can also cause sensitising to other materials.
Volatile Organic Compounds (VOCs) (VOCs take 6 months to several years to be fully liberated)	– Building materials (PVC) – Preservatives, sealants, adhesives, mastics – Finishing products (paints, solvents, carpets) – Furnishings – Combustion – Tobacco smoke – Personal care products, cleaners – Correcting fluids, reprographic facilities	The health effects of organic chemicals vary from those that are highly toxic, to those with no known health effect. VOCs can cause eye, nose and throat irritation, headaches, loss of coordination, nausea, damage to the liver and kidneys and the central nervous system. Some organic compounds are known animal carcinogens and suspected human carcinogens.
Semi Volatile Organic Compounds (SVOCs) (SVOCs may take 15-30 yrs to offgas)	– Pesticides used in gardens and indoor planting – Insecticides, fungicides	SVOCs can cause headaches, dizziness, muscular weakness and nausea. Some compounds are considered possible human carcinogens.
Chlorine	– Dissolved in potable tap water	The by-products of chlorination and chlorinated organic compounds are animal carcinogens.
Lead	– Paints (dust and flakes) – Water pipes – Petrol (lead fumes)	Lead poisoning can cause headache, nausea and anorexia, constipation, fatigue, personality change and hearing loss. In children lead toxicity can cause developmental deficits.
Heavy metals (cadmium, lead, arsenic, mercury)	– Contaminated land	Cadmium can affect the kidneys and bone structure. Mercury can damage the nervous system.
Particulate	– Soot from combustion and tobacco smoke	Particles are breathed in and can lodge in the lung causing irritation and lung damage. Charged particles, such as radioactive radon, can attach themselves to particles and be carried into the lung.
Fibres	– Asbestos – MDF, timber	When disturbed, asbestos can cause respiratory disease, lung cancer and mesothelioma. Deaths from mesothelioma are on the increase. There were 2,317 cases between 1980–85, and 6,475 cases between 1996–2000, in the UK. Dust from working with timber and timber products can cause respiratory diseases.
Physical		
+ve/-ve ion imbalance		Ion imbalance can cause depression, tension and headaches.
Electromagnetic fields (EMFs)	– Electrical equipment – Overhead electricity distribution cables	EMFs are thought to disturb sleeping patterns, trigger allergies, upset metabolism, cause stress and may be linked to increased occurrence of cancer.

(Bower 2001, EPA 1994, EPA 1995, HSE 2001, Pearson 1998, Stauffer 1996, Yu 2002)

Case study: Deleterious materials

The manufacturing process, installation, use, disposal and destruction of materials can all affect the health of individuals exposed to the materials. Polyvinylchloride (PVC) is a material notoriously associated with environmental and health impacts at virtually all stages of its life-cycle, from its production, through its use, to its disposal. PVC is used in buildings as flooring, panelling, windows, cladding, rainwater goods, below- and above-ground drainage pipes, and sheathing for wiring.

The manufacture of PVC involves using chlorine, a highly toxic gas, to chlorinate ethylene, an oil-based and therefore scarce material, to produce ethylene dichloride. This process produces dioxins, which are persistent organic pollutants (POPs) (see 6.0.5) and classified as probable carcinogens and powerful hormone disruptors. Ethylene dichloride is then converted to vinyl chloride monomer, a human carcinogen, also affecting both male and female reproductive systems. Chloride monomer is polymerised into polyvinylchloride. PVC requires the addition of plasticisers, stabilisers, pigments, optical brighteners, flame retardants, biocides, fillers, foaming agents and lubricants, which can make up over 50 per cent of the final product. Many stabilisers and pigments contain heavy metals such as cadmium, tin or lead, known to affect the nervous system. Plasticisers contain phthalates and in particular DEHP (di-ethyl-hexyl-phthalate), which has been identified as a hormone disruptor and possible human carcinogen.

The production process is not the only source of toxic emissions. Phthalates can leach out and off-gas from PVC products, such as PVC flooring and children's toys. This has been recognised and the use of PVC in toys intended to be sucked by children is currently banned by the European Union. The burning of PVC, whether accidentally in a fire or through incineration, releases dioxins, heavy metals and chlorine gas which can form hydrogen chloride and hydrochloric acid. The elevated risk of PVC in fire is the reason for London Underground, Channel Tunnel and other underground construction projects banning the use of halogenated cables of all types (Greenpeace 1997, 2001, Berge 2000)

Only the Swedish government has initiated a move towards banning the use of PVC. On a regional scale a number of local governments and cities have placed restrictions on its use and initiated a phase-out of PVC in public buildings. Linz has achieved an 85 per cent phase-out of PVC in public buildings (Greenpeace 1997).

The solarCity follows this principle and the 1317 mixed tenure dwelling units are PVC-free. The binding project contracts, signed by the housing associations developing the scheme, include the exclusion of PVC and halogenated products. Other banned materials include PUR (polyurethane foam) and PIR (polyisocyanurate foam) sprays, while the use of local, natural, renewable, recycled and recyclable materials is encouraged.

PVC is not the only material associated with considerable risks to health. For example, the manufacture of steel is also associated with significant dioxin emissions. However, risks associated with PVC are easily avoided. Replacements for PVC products are not only available, but can be used without detriment to building quality and performance.

solarCity
Pichling, Linz, Austria

Project details, Chapter 1.1, p.20

3.2.6 Fatalities in the construction industry

Workers in the building industry are exposed to a multitude of risks to health. Some health risks have delayed consequences, while others have very immediate consequences. The construction industry is one of the most dangerous of all industries. In the UK in 2002/3 71 construction workers were fatally injured. This is an improvement from the previous two years, when 80 and 103 people were fatally injured. The causes of death included: falls from heights (47 per cent), being struck by falling objects (15 per cent), electricity (10 per cent), being struck by moving vehicles (7 per cent), and collapse (7 per cent). (HSE 2003)

The community centre at the solarCity.

See also: comprehensive planning **Chapter 1.1**

See also: sharing nature **Chapter 1.3**

See also: electromagnetic fields **Chapter 3.2**

See also: sewage as a resource **Chapter 6.3**

See also: sustainable urban drainage **Chapter 6.3**

Case study: Avoiding chemical and biological disease agents

Adam Joseph Lewis Center
Oberlin College, Oberlin, Ohio, US

Client: Oberlin College
Architects: William McDonough and Partners
Structural and services engineers: Lev Zetlin Associates
Landscape architects: Andropogon Associates
Completed: 2000

The Adam Joseph Lewis Center for Environment Studies is the teaching facility for Oberlin College's environmental studies programme. The building is a demonstration of the commitment of David Orr, the course leader, and his team, who realised their ambition to teach in an environment consistent with their life views. They succeeded in convincing the college to support the development, gained independent funding for the project, developed a sustainable building brief and appointed an ecological architect with expertise in the field. The completed building, which includes 1,260 square metres of classrooms, offices and an atrium, is not only resource efficient, with the potential to export energy (see 3.2.8), but creates a harmonious relationship with the natural environment and a healthy indoor environment for the occupants. The building also acts as a learning tool for the students who can experience at first hand how an environmentally sound building operates.

Providing a healthy learning environment was one of the design aims for the centre. Living and working in healthy indoor environments is not only a basic human right and environmentally beneficial, but can also bring financial gains. A survey of research on the effects of office design on productivity concluded that healthy workplaces can increase staff productivity by 15 per cent (Arnold 2004). In educational environments research has shown that learning improves in naturally lit environments with good indoor air quality (Edwards 2003).

The classrooms are well lit and the paints and finishes are low VOC.

The main block comprises the classrooms and offices and the smaller block comprises the lecture room and the living machine.

3.2.7 Paints and VOCS

In terms of indoor air pollution, the solvent used in paints, which can be water or an organic hydrocarbon solvent, determines whether VOCs are emitted during and after its application. The manufacturing process may also be associated with other environmental impacts:

– Water-based mineral paints use potassium silicate as a binder and quartz, feldspars and inorganic mineral pigments. Mineral paints are fungus resistant and can be used in 'wet' areas such as bathrooms. Being water based, they produce virtually no harmful VOCs when drying.

– Natural paints use natural plant- or animal-based materials as pigments and organic hydrocarbon solvents. They emit VOCs when drying. They often have a high solid and low solvent content, which reduces emissions.

– Water-based acrylic paints use acrylic resin as a bonding agent and water as a solvent and emit minimal VOCs when drying. They can contain harmful additives, such as biocides and emulsifiers that can be detrimental to the environment. They can be micro-porous and vapour permeable.

– Solvent-based synthetic paints use alkyd resin and organic solvents. Their manufacturing impacts tend to be high and they emit VOCs when drying. High solids versions have reduced emissions.

The Lewis Center's indoor environment benefits from ample natural light, maximum fresh air through automatically openable windows, and minimal indoor pollutants through the careful selection of building materials, fixtures and fittings. Moreover, the contact with nature provides opportunities for relaxation for the building's occupants.

To minimise sources of indoor air pollution, materials that off-gas compounds harmful to health were avoided. All paints and adhesives contain low volatile organic compounds (VOCs) (see 3.2.7). The office furniture and the auditorium chairs, designed by Design Tex, make use of an upholstery material designed by William McDonough and Partners, which is completely non-toxic, safe and biodegradable. After having removed sources of indoor air pollution, the air quality is monitored and fresh air introduced as necessary. In the classrooms, carbon monoxide monitors and motion detectors are linked to the mechanical ventilation and regulate the supply of fresh air, while maximising energy efficiency. The lecture hall ventilation is also regulated by carbon monoxide monitors, which are set at a level 20 per cent lower than recommended by ASHRAE, ensuring a high indoor air quality

Comfort levels are further enhanced by allowing individuals to control their immediate environment by opening windows in their office spaces as desired.

To ensure the building retains its healthy environment, non-building sources of indoor air pollutants also need to be controlled. Cleaning materials (see 3.2.5) can be major sources of pollution. A maintenance protocol establishes cleaning products and practices to ensure the healthy environment is maintained in the long term.

The indoor air quality was also monitored by the National Institute of Standards and Technology (NIST), who used the Lewis Center as a test-bed for new methods of

See also: living machine **Chapter 6.3**

The entrance hall can be naturally ventilated.

measuring and modelling ventilation and indoor air quality. The study showed that the very high air exchange rates could be reduced from the current 100 per cent fresh air circulated every four hours, without affecting indoor air pollution.

Creating a healthy environment has made the Lewis Center accessible to individuals with elevated chemical sensitivities and allergies. One such student was able to visit the building, while it was being completed without suffering adverse effects. He later enrolled at the college in the knowledge that he could attend teaching activities in a healthy building.

The building has been a success in terms of creating a healthy, attractive and inspirational place to enjoy. Its role as a model has affected more than just students. In 2004 Oberlin College adopted an environmental policy that aims to reduce the college's net CO_2 emissions to zero. One of the first initiatives is to finalise agreements to purchase more than 60 per cent of the college energy consumption from 'green' energy sources. The policy also aims to encourage alternatives to the car and requires new buildings to be LEEDS certified (see 2.5.1). A second generation Lewis Center design may also be built some time in the future.

The furniture upholstery in the lecture room is non-toxic and biodegradable. The lecture room is also fully accessible, with a ramp leading to the front where seats can be unhooked from the ground to allow space for wheelchairs.

Low level vents with actuators.

Automatic high level vents.

3.2.8 Sustainable design features

Site and ecology The new college building stands on a previously used site. The external areas include an indigenous landscape, an artificial wetland, an orchard on the partial berm on the north side of the building. and a vegetable garden, which is cared for by students.

Community and culture The brief was developed in consultation with students, staff and residents and 13 design charrettes were undertaken. The main entrance area is used for community occasions, such as banquets, as well as college activities, such as public lectures. The building is used as a learning tool for students.

Health See main text.

Materials Local materials were employed where possible, such as the external façade bricks. The external paving was reclaimed from the existing 1960s building. Interface recyclable carpets were installed in first-floor areas. These are leased and not owned by the college, and will be sent back for recycling when they are worn out. Other materials with recycled content include the steel frame, aluminium roof, toilet partitions and tiling. All construction timber and most of the furniture is FSC certified.

Energy The building is designed to benefit from passive solar energy with all teaching and communal spaces facing south. Exposed internal masonry acts as thermal mass. On the north side at first floor level are offices and at ground level are the kitchen, toilets and mechanical rooms. The building envelope is well insulated with triple-glazed atrium curtain walling and double-glazed windows elsewhere. The north elevation is partially bermed to provide additional insulation.

Fabric U-values:
Walls – 0.30 W/m^2 C (R19)
Roof – 0. 19 W/m^2 C (R30)

When external temperatures are appropriate, windows automatically open to allow fresh air in. In the atrium low-level windows and north-facing clerestory windows open automatically to provide natural ventilation. A closed loop geothermal system, with 24 76-m deep wells, circulates constant heat ground water to heat pumps in each room to provide heating and cooling. Additional heat is occasionally required in the atrium and provided by means of a water-to-water heat pump feeding an underfloor heating system. Motion sensors, light sensors and individual controls reduce the amount of energy used for lighting. A grid-connected PV array with 360 units, covering the 370-square metre roof, provides 45 kW of electrical energy. The building performance was monitored after completion. Energy use in the third year of occupation was measured to be:

94 kWhr/m^2/yr (29.8 kBtu/ft^2/yr), of which 5 per cent is provided by the PV array.

Water See Chapter 6.3.

Case study: Avoiding chemical disease agents

Carlisle Lane housing
Carlisle Lane, London, UK

Client: Pringle + Richards
Architects: Pringle Richards Sharratt
Structural engineer: Alan Baxter & Associates
General contractor: DF Keane
Specialist contractor: Eurban & Finnforest Merk
Completed: 2004

3.2.9 Chemical disease agents

Type and use:	Health impacts
f = fungicide i = insecticide p= pre-treatment r = remedial	LD50 = lethal dose to kill 50% of a given population
Copper/ chrome/ arsenic CCA f/i/p (Product name Tanalith)	Skin damage, skin cancer, damage to peripheral nerves causing loss of movement or feeling. Produces toxic ash when burnt.
Creosote f/i/p/r Oil-based preservative Banned in US for non-professional use	Skin and eye irritation, acute bronchitis from spray mist, nausea, headaches; cancer of skin and lungs.
Dieldrin i/p Banned in US	Poisons through skin, nerve poison, causes cancer.
Lindane f/i/p/r Banned and severely restricted in many countries	Poisons through skin, irritant, allergen, brain and nerve system poison, causes epilepsy, suspected leukaemia, damages blood system, animal carcinogen, possible human carcinogen. LD50 = 88 mg/kg
Pentachloro-phenol (PCP) f/p/r Solvent-based. Banned in many countries. (Product name Protim)	Poisons through skin. Contains dioxins. Acute effects: rise in body temperature, collapse, death. Chronic effects: local paralysis. Possible human carcinogen. LD50 = 27mg/kg
TBTO - Tri-butyl-tin oxide f/p/r DIY products/ Banned as boat paint as it stops marine animals reproducing	Irritant, burns skin and eyes, causes painful rashes. Nerve poison
Permethrin i/p/r Accepted by English Nature for bat roosts	Associated with nerve damage and allergy
Boron f/i/p/r Accepted by English Nature for bat roosts 40 mm penetration rather than typical 3-8 mm	Nerve poisons LD50 = 4500-6000 mg/kg

Timber, despite being a natural material, can have harmful effects on health. In addition, timber is often treated to protect it from fungal and insect attack, using materials that in order to achieve their purpose have to be toxic. Health hazards associated with untreated timber include dust from working the material and volatile resin vapours from some particularly odoriferous species. These are associated with skin, lung and heart disease from the dust and irritation to the nose, eyes and throat from the vapours, in susceptible individuals. The risks to health associated with timber treatments vary according to the treatment product used, and range from very low, as with boron-based treatments, to very high, as with pentachloro-phenol (PCP) (Curwell *et al.* 2002). Many timber treatments as well as surface finishes are dissolved in hydrocarbon solvents that affect indoor air quality, mainly during applications, but potentially also during occupation (see 3.2.5).

To avoid the need for treatment, a number of approaches can be taken. The choice of timber affects what treatment is required: hardwoods, such as oak, being generally more resistant to insect attack and water. Some softwoods, such as western red cedar, European larch and douglas fir, can also be used externally untreated. Regardless of what timber species and treatment is used, timber elements should always be detailed so the timber can dry out. This is done by detailing the timber elements to allow drainage and ventilation. Preventing the moisture content from remaining above 20 per cent for long periods of time inhibits the growth of mould. Before treating timber, it is worth considering the impact that deteriorating timber would have on the building. For example, if exterior cladding deteriorates, it can easily be replaced, with minimal impact on the building as a whole. Treatment should remain a last resort after considering all other aspects of design.

If treatment is required, one of the less dangerous treatments should be selected (see 3.2.9), such as Permethrin, ACQ, which avoids the use of arsenic and chromium, or boron, currently the solution preferred by many environmentally sensitive designers. Boron is a naturally occurring material, which is part of human and animal diet in minute amounts of 1–3 milligrams per day. In much larger amounts, 1000 milligrams, it is effective against rot and insect attack. In addition to its lower health risks, boron has other advantages, such as that it penetrates deeper into the timber, 40 millimetres compared to the typical 3-8 millimetres, and it can be used to treat dry rot *in situ*.

In recent years a treatment system that does not use chemicals has also been developed. ThermoWood® are timber products treated without natural or artificial chemicals. Treatment is by means of a method developed by the Finnish State Research Centre, which involves the use of heat and steam in a three-stage process. A first treatment stage, which reaches temperatures of 130°C, brings the moisture content of the timber to almost zero. This is followed by a second stage where temperatures are kept at between 185°C and 215°C for two to three hours, and a third stage where the temperature is lowered and the timber re-humidified to reach 4-7 per cent moisture content. The treatment changes the chemical structure of the timber by removing the timber resin on which the rot-forming bacteria and fungi grow. The result is a timber resistant to decay, slightly darker in colour, more stable and with improved insulation properties.

ThermoWood can therefore provide an environmentally sound product that is safe to handle, safe to dispose of, and safe for building occupants if used internally. These were some of the reasons for its selection as external cladding material on a small housing development near Waterloo Station in London.

The development consists of four small flats, two 35-square metre and two 45-square metre flats, and will provide some affordable units for rent or sale in the city of London, where housing is often too expensive for many people on low and medium incomes. The flats, on two floors, look out on a narrow private courtyard, which also provides access to the flats.

Timber is the main construction material of the development, used for the structure and cladding. The structure comprises prefabricated cross-laminated solid timber panels and laminated timber beams made with untreated timber. The panels are sealed and create an airtight envelope and the external insulation provides good thermal qualities. The low-embodied energy structure was largely prefabricated reducing construction time on site. Internally, most of the solid timber wall panels will be clad in plasterboard to provide fire and sound protection, except the roof panels which will remain visible and were left untreated.

The use of ecologically treated timber reduces the negative health impacts that occupants and workers might otherwise experience. Timber can also contribute to the occupants' well-being in an indirect way: its warm character helps to create a comfortable external courtyard space, more likely to encourage building inhabitants to spend time outdoors in bright sunlight and fresh air.

3.2.10 Sustainable design features

Site and ecology
The site was previously used as a warehouse and two external walls were reused. It is a car-free development near public transport.

Community and culture
The scheme provides four affordable units for rent and or sale in the centre of London.

Health
See main text.

Materials
The ThermoWood timber cladding is sourced from a sustainably managed source. The Merk structure uses a small section of timber glued together with a melamine resin. The structure is insulated with recycled cellulose and jute insulation. The roof is covered in recyclable tern-coated steel.

Energy
Fabric U-values:
  Walls - 0.15 and 0.23 W/m²K (R38 and R25)
  Roof – 0.19W/m²K (R30)
  Windows – U-value 1.1 W/m²K (0.19 Btu/ft²h°F)

Water
Dual flush WCs were installed.

The large windows provide good natural light to the living space and face on the private courtyard.

The four flats are accessed from a courtyard. A spiral stair leads to the top floor flats.

The ThermoWood creates an interesting contrast to the painted timber windows.

Case study: Purifying air with plants

Glashaus
Herten, Germany

Project details, Chapter 2.4, p.84

The balconies and walkways in the Rotunde are covered in planting.

The Glashaus community centre, in Herten, comprises primarily a library, but also houses seminar and activity rooms, a restaurant and a multifunction room. The multifunction room, the Rotunde, can be rented out for private and public functions. It has become very popular with the residents of Herten as well as with people from other towns. The 42-square metre, four-storey glazed space is very impressive. At each level are balconies which act as viewing galleries during functions and, with its glazed roof and largely glazed walls, standing in the Rotunda is like being outdoors. The feeling of being outside is not only a result of the light levels: the air quality is fresh and the space is filled with plants. It is like being in a large conservatory.

The air quality is in fact a result of the plants in the space. Plants have the ability to absorb organic gases and purify the air as well as adjust the humidity levels around them.

Plants support cultures of microbes around their roots. These microbes degrade complex organic structures such as those found in leaves, but also organic gases found in the air. Gaseous organic substances are both absorbed by the leaves and through the microbes in the soil. The leaves absorb the gases through small pores, called stomata, which are situated on the top or both on the top and bottom of the leaf. They then digest the gases and convert them into primarily amino acids, organic acids and sugars. Gases are also absorbed directly through the soil. As the plants transpire water vapour through the leaves, air is drawn into the soil. The gaseous organic substances contained in the air are then converted into plant material by the microbes around the roots of the plants.

The microbes that convert these organic gases into other material react to the availability of such gases. An increase in gas levels triggers the production of new microbe colonies and consequently increases the ability to digest these gases. The plant effectively adapts to its environment and changes its absorption ability accordingly.

The National Aeronautics and Space Administration (NASA) has undertaken extensive studies of air and water treatment methods that could be used in space. Following results that showed plants effectively cleaning air, further research was sponsored by the Plants for Clean Air Council and Wolverton Environmental Services, and 50 plants were tested for their ability to remove chemical vapour from test chambers. Formaldehyde, an abundant gas in buildings, was used as a standard, but the

The library spaces also benefit from the fresh atmosphere of the Rotunde.

See also: focal spaces for communities **Chapter 2.4**

The inside of the Rotunde. Balconies overlook the main areas and plants hang down from the balconies.

3.2.11 Overall rating of house plants

Overall rating of 50 plants tested in terms of total chemical absorption, transpiration rate, ease of growth and maintenance and resistance to insect infection. Rating range 1–10.

Lady palm	8.5
Bamboo palm	8.4
Areca palm	8.0
Rubber plant	8.0
Dracaena 'Janet Craig'	7.8
English ivy	7.8
Dwarf date palm	7.8
Ficus alii	7.7
Boston fern	7.5
Peace lily	7.5
Corn plant	7.5
Golden pothos	7.5
Kimberley Queen	7.4
Florist's Mum	7.4
Gerbera daisy	7.3
Dracaena 'Warneckei'	7.3
Dragon tree	7.0
Red emerald philodendron	7.0
Syngonium	7.0
Dumb cane Exotica compacta	6.8
Parlour palm	6.6
Weeping fig	6.5
Schefflera	6.
Wax begonia	6.3
Lacy tree philodendron	6.3
Heart-leaf philodendron	6.3
Snake plant	6.3
Dumb cane Diefenbachia Camilla	6.2
Elephant ear philodendron	6.2
Norfolk Island pine	6.2
King of Hearts	6.0
Prayer plant	6.0
Dwarf banana	5.8
Christmas and Easter cactus	5.8
Oakleaf ivy	5.7
Lily turf	5.5
Dendrobium orchid	5.5
Spider plant	5.4
Chinese evergreen	5.3
Anthurium	5.3
Croton	5.3
Poinsettia	5.1
Dwarf azalea	5.1
Peacock plant	5.0
Aloe vera	5.0
Cyclamen	4.8
Urn plant	4.8
Tulip	4.7
Moth orchid	4.5
Kalanchoe	4.5

(Wolverton 1997)

absorption of acetone, methyl alcohol, ethyl acetate, benzene, ammonia, trichloroethylene and xylene was also tested (Wolverton 1997).

Of the 50 plants tested, the Boston fern and the Florist's Mum proved most effective at reducing formaldehyde levels. The areca palm, the dwarf date palm and the moth orchid proved most effective at reducing toluene and xylene levels. The lady palm absorbed by far the most ammonia.

The research also tested the ease of growth, resistance to infection and the transpiration rate. Plants are also very effective at adjusting the humidity levels in interior environments. As natural humidifiers, plants will give off more moisture as the humidity decreases, subject to being adequately watered. The areca palm, bamboo palm, Boston fern and the Kimberley Queen had the highest transpiration rates.

The plants in the Rotunda help to clean the air and humidify it, thus contributing to cooling the space. The plants also create areas of shade. One commonly experienced difference between growing plants inside and outdoors is that in the absence of outdoor climatic pressures plants growing inside tend to grow faster and taller. At Herten the gardeners had to cut the tops of some of the trees to stop them reaching the roof.

The ability of plants to improve the environment also applies to external environments. Trees in cities have the ability to trap dust and act as a sink for pollutants. The larger the leaves and bigger the canopy, the better the tree will act as a filter and air purifier. Both internally and externally, plants are vital elements for creating clean air and healthy environments.

Case study: Appropriate ventilation

Toll House Gardens
Fairfield estate, Perth, Scotland, UK

Client: Fairfield Housing Co-operative
Architect: Gaia Architects
Ventilation monitoring: Gaia Research with Strathclyde University
Structural engineer: Allen Gordon & Partners
Mechanical engineer: Gaia Architects
Contractor: Foreman Construction
Completed: 2003

Large glazed areas bring ample natural light into the houses.

View of the Toll House Garden houses from the street. The chimney-like structures on the roof are the dynamic insulation ventilation inlets.

The Toll House Gardens housing is one of the latest phases of the Fairfield estate redevelopment in Perth, Scotland. Fourteen one- and two-storey units are grouped around a private, landscaped and car-free courtyard just off the main road and access to the housing estate. The cottages and houses, with one to three bedrooms, are designed to accommodate the needs of elderly persons and people with special needs. As part of an increasingly sustainable design agenda, his particular building phase of the Fairfield redevelopment aimed to provide affordable low allergy houses appropriate for asthma sufferers.

The National Asthma Campaign warns that the number of asthmatic sufferers in the UK is growing and that currently 1 in 10 children and 1 in 12 adults suffer from asthma (Asthma UK 2004). There is also a clear recognition that the incidence of asthma is linked to unhealthy living conditions. Children growing up in humid and inappropriately ventilated houses are more at risk of developing asthma.

During asthma attacks, the difficulty in breathing is a result of a restriction of the airways to the lung which occurs spontaneously or as a result of a triggering agent. Triggering agents include house dust mites, pollen, dust from feathers and animal fur, sulphur dioxide and other gases. Moreover, predisposition to asthma may occur as a result of a respiratory virus infection or other sensitising agents encountered in childhood or, sometimes, in adulthood. Some of the triggering agents may also act as sensitising agents.

Many of these agents can be found in typical houses, but their occurrence is preventable. Appropriate building design can help to avoid both agents that predispose individuals to the illness and agents that trigger asthma attacks. There are three approaches to avoiding asthma triggers. First, materials containing and offgassing triggering agents should be avoided. Second, the living environment should not be conducive to supporting the growth of triggering agents. Third, the environment should avoid the accumulation of triggering agents.

These same approaches can be applied to create healthy indoor environments even when not needing to address any particular illness. While asthma is one of the most studied illnesses linked to indoor air quality, indoor air quality also affects people in other ways (see 3.2.5).

The design of the Toll House Garden houses addresses these three issues. Materials that are known to offgas formaldehyde and other volatile organic compounds were avoided. For example, formaldehyde-free chipboard was installed and water-based paints and finishes were specified. Further common sources of formaldehyde are typical kitchen cupboards and other furniture made with chipboard or medium density fibreboard (MDF).

Second, the house environments are designed to avoid mould growth and dust mites. Both are liable to trigger asthma attacks and thrive in humid environments. Dust mites, found in carpets and fabrics, need an environment with an internal temperature of between 20-25°C and relative humidity between 65-85 per cent to breed. Equally high levels of humidity are required for mould to develop. By ventilating appropriately and removing warm stale air from kitchens and bathrooms, the relative humidity in a home can be kept between the recommended levels of 40-50 per cent.

Ventilation also addresses the third issue: the accumulation of asthma triggers. Adequate ventilation removes traces of airborne pollutants, pollen, dust and other potential allergy triggers. The Toll House Gardens units are also designed to facilitate cleaning and avoid the collection of dust as well as removing airborne particles.

At Toll House Gardens the design team has undertaken a comparative study of different domestic ventilation systems. Four dwellings are designed with conventional ventilation systems, five units were fitted with MVHR (mechanical ventilation with heat recovery) and five use dynamic insulation. Ventilation with dynamic insulation works by pressurising the roof void. Fresh air is introduced into the roof void through an air vent (see photo) and passed through an air-permeable insulated ceiling panel into the living spaces. Moisture finds its way out of the building through permeable areas of the building fabric. By passing the fresh air through an insulated ceiling panel, the heat loss is minimised, while the fresh air supply is maximised. Gaia Architects' sister company, Gaia Research, and Strathclyde University monitored the performance of each system for its effect on the indoor air quality. The dwellings with MVHR and dynamic insulation were found to have similarly low levels of indoor air pollution, while the traditionally ventilated unit had slightly higher levels.

The triple-pronged approach to the minimisation of allergens proved successful and technical tests were supported by current residents suffering from asthma who have reported health improvements since moving into the new housing.

3.2.12 Sustainable design features

Site and ecology
The housing is part of the regeneration of a notorious estate involving the refurbishment of many existing buildings, the demolition of selected blocks and the construction of new units on the demolition sites.

The regeneration includes new landscaping of the whole estate.

Community and culture
The design involved a community consultation and resulted in a tenant-managed housing cooperative. Tenant participation is always encouraged.

Health
See main text.

Materials
Materials were chosen for their effects on the health of the occupants. Timber was treated with borax rather than CCA. Timber sections were screwed rather than nailed to enable their dismantling. The walls are insulated with recycled cellulose insulation. The use of PVC and materials offgassing formaldehyde or VOCs was avoided.

Energy
The houses make use of solar passive gains, are well insulated and use a breather wall construction. Both ventilation systems installed are energy efficient. MVHR systems typically recycle 70-85 per cent of the outgoing heat and transfer it to the incoming heat.

Water
Low water WCs and spray taps were installed.

The Toll House Garden houses are located around a planted courtyard.

On the roof are the ventilation inlets for the houses with dynamic insulation.

See also: community consultation **Chapter 2.1**

Case study: Changing technology

solarCity
Pichling, Linz, Austria

Client: Neue Heimat – Gemeinnützige Wohnungs- und Siedlungsgesellschaft
Concept architects: Foster and Partners
Architects: Erich Weismann
AND
Client: WAG
Concept architects: Herzog+Partner
Completion planned for 2005

The WAG housing was designed to minimise negative impacts on health.

See also: comprehensive planning **Chapter 1.1**

See also: sharing nature **Chapter 1.3**

See also: deleterious materials **Chapter 3.2**

See also: sewage as a resource **Chapter 6.3**

See also: sustainable urban drainage **Chapter 6.3**

Many environmental health hazards are a risk to human health, less because of their nature than because of their increased quantity or frequency. Many natural materials or phenomena are either innocuous or even beneficial to health in small quantities, but in unusually large quantities can be very detrimental, for example, UV radiation, boron, minerals, electromagnetic fields or ions. In the same way as some modern materials have proved to be a risk to health, certain technologies appear to have altered aspects of the natural environment and these alterations are thought to potentially affect human health. Such changes are understood to different degrees: the occurrence and effects of atmospheric ions are reasonably well understood, while those of electromagnetic fields remain disputed. At the extreme of current understanding are other impacts, such as that of the current technological world on the structure of water.

Air ions are one such example. They are positively and negatively charged molecules and occur naturally in a ratio of 2,000 positive ions per cubic centimetre to 1,800 negative ions in coastal areas or 1,200 positive to 1,000 negative ions in rural areas. The effects of ions are not fully understood, but it is thought that air containing a substantial amount of negative ions in a relation of 5 positive to 4 negative ions is beneficial in terms of inducing a general sense of well-being, creating a feeling of calmness and alertness and improving recovery time from illness (Saunders 2002; Pearson 1998).

An ion imbalance can result from natural conditions or as a result of artificial and built environments. Natural conditions include activity before thunderstorms and the effects of certain winds, such as the Föhn, north of the Alps, which induce feelings of tension, irritability and depression. These natural occurrences are well documented and some susceptible individuals avoid undertaking demanding tasks in these circumstances. In built-up areas, depending on the pollution levels, the concentrations of ions can be significantly reduced to 800 positive and 700 negative ions in lightly polluted urban environments, and to 500 positive and 300 negative ions in city centre areas. In buildings, negative ion levels can be even lower. Negative ion depletion occurs in a number of ways: negatively charged ions are earthed through steel frames or metal air-conditioning ducts; positively charged TV and PC screens attract negative ions neutralising their charge; static charges from synthetic fibres and materials deplete negative ions; and tobacco smoke particles attract negative ions and deposit them on various surfaces, removing them from the air (Palmer and Rawlings 2002). To increase ion levels, ionisers have proved partially effective, as has the introduction of indoor planting to counteract low relative humidity levels, which exacerbate electrostatic charges.

Ion imbalances, while affecting feelings of well-being, are not generally thought to be seriously dangerous to health. The situation is different when considering the effects of electromagnetic fields (EMF). These too exist in nature, occurring in underground watercourses, geological faults and mineral veins. The human body is well adapted to these forces, but this natural electromagnetic environment has been altered in the past century by the proliferation of man-made sources of electromagnetic fields, such as overhead power-transmission cables and electrical equipment. The effects on humans of the increased levels of radiation are not well understood, but concerns are increasingly being voiced. The distortion of natural electromagnetic fields and the exposure to EMFs from domestic appliances and overhead transmission cables is thought liable to disturb sleeping patterns, trigger allergies, upset the metabolism, increase blood pressure and cause nervousness and stress, while some low frequencies can act as triggers to allergy sufferers, causing sickness, headaches and nausea (Pearson 1998). More serious effects such as cancer are also thought to be associated with overhead power-transmission cables (Saunders 2002).

The typical approaches to minimise the effects of EMFs on building inhabitants include: installing shielded cables and conduits; installing isolating switches that isolate all or some electrical circuits; avoiding aligning electricity consumer units with sleeping areas; and avoiding keeping radios or other electrical equipment close to where people sleep.

At the solarCity some of these aspects of healthy living have been taken on board by a number of the housing associations. The WAG housing association has built flats with low indoor air pollutants and with minimal electromagnetic impact, while the Neue Heimat housing association has used 'revitalised' water in the concrete manufacture. Revitalised water is thought to restructure the molecular form of water, damaged by environmental effects. Due to its more stable structure and lower surface tension, 'revitalised water' is used in swimming pools to minimise the use of chemicals, in the production of bread to reduce the amount of water needed, in heating systems to reduce deposits, and in the manufacture of bricks and concrete to improve the malleability of the mixture. While rare, these approaches represent an extreme implementation of the precautionary principle (see 3.2.4).

The concrete on the Neue Heimat blocks was made with revitalised water.

3.2.13 Electromagnetic fields

Electromagnetic fields occur naturally and result from human activities. They have measurable strengths and frequencies. The Earth's magnetic field pulses at around 7.83 Hz, compared to electrical equipment, which has a frequency of 50 Hz in Europe and 60 Hz in the US. Medium wave radio frequencies are between 3 and 300 kHz, microwave ovens, TV broadcasting and mobile phone transmissions use high-, extra high- and super high-frequencies between 3-300 gHz.

The strength of the electromagnetic field is measured in microtesla (mT) or in milliGauss (mG), where 1 mG = 0.1mT. The strength of the field will diminish as the distance from the source increases. A 'safe' strength has not been agreed, although Sweden, following research on childhood leukaemia, has suggested a safe level for electromagnetic fields at 0.2 mT, while Powerwatch believes it should be below 0.01 mT.

While there is no consensus on the effects of EMF on health, numerous research projects from the UK, the US and other countries show a clear correlation between exposure to electromagnetic fields from overhead distribution cables and childhood leukaemia and brain cancer.

Electricity is not the only source of electromagnetic fields of concern. Mobile phones are also thought to affect human health, and are of particular concern due to their proximity to the user.

(Saunders 2002; Borer and Harris 1998; Pearson 1998)

Electromagnetic field strength measure in microtesla (mT)	Source of electromagnetic and 'safe' levels *overhead electricity distribution, measured at ground level
160 mT	Hair dryer at 30 mm
150 mT	Microwave oven at 30 mm
100 mT	Fluorescent light at 30 mm
47mT	Natural levels of geomagnetic fields
40 mT	400kV *
24 mT	Radio clock at 30 mm
11 mT	132kV *
1 mT	415V *
0.4 mT	240V *
0.4 mT	Microwave oven at 1 m
0.2 mT	Safe level suggested in Sweden
0.15 mT	Hair dryer at 1 m
0.1 mT	Fluorescent light at 1 m
0.02 mT	Radio clock at 1 m
0.01 mT	Safe level according to Powerwatch

3.3 Identity and Independence

3.3.1 Stress

There is growing evidence that psychological factors, such as stress, affect the immune function which in turn affects the physical health of an individual. Stress is the reaction of an individual to external demands, which the individual feels or fears to be incapable of coping with. Sources of stress range from bereavement or unemployment, to issues of seemingly lesser consequence such as public speaking or uncertainty regarding normal situations. Merely thinking of something unpleasant can be stressful. About half a million people in the UK have become ill due to work-related stress, while five million suffer mild symptoms. Control is of great importance. How controllable a stressor is perceived to be has a significant impact on its effect.

The physical reaction to stress is for the body to focus on immediate issues, neglecting its future wellbeing. This involves the release of over 30 hormones including adrenaline, noradrenaline, and cortisol, which, among other things, have the effect of suppressing the immune system.

Prolonged stress results in prolonged depression of the immune function, which can increase the susceptibility to illness (particularly respiratory infections), and increase psychological distress and depression. Other effects of stress include:

– impaired performance on complex tasks
– decrease in problem-solving abilities
– increase in general negativity
– impatience
– irritability
– feelings of worthlessness
– addiction
– anxiety
– depression
– coronary heart disease

A disabled accessible bathroom in the Environmental Showcase Home in Phoenix (see Chapter 6.1), designed to a high quality.

The spatial characteristics of the built environment, as well as their aesthetic and semantic characteristics, affect how people feel in and about the spaces. Buildings should address general practical needs, such as storage, as well as the special needs of specific individuals, such as those of wheelchair users, individuals with a visual impairment or mothers with buggies. Whether or not a building addresses these needs affects how demanding life becomes for the building inhabitants, but it can also be read as a reflection of the value given to their well-being.

The aesthetics of built environments are laden with meaning. The nature of a space can represent attitudes, suggest social and anti-social activities, have personal and cultural associations, and engender feelings of fear, alienation or comfort and security. Philip Johnson observed that some people found chairs beautiful to look at because they were comfortable to sit in, while others found chairs comfortable to sit in because they thought they were beautiful to look at (Lawson 1990). How liveable buildings are, as well as their expression, changes how people feel about them.

Ill-designed environments can be detrimental to health. Environments that are difficult to negotiate can cause frustration, stress (see 3.3.1) and depression and induce feelings of low self-worth. Buildings with negative associations can cause anxiety, stress and depression. Such neuropsychiatric conditions, which are interrelated, are currently the main cause of non-fatal illness globally (WHO 2003) (see 3.3.2). Chronic stress can suppress the immune system, making people more prone to disease, but even low levels of stress or frustration can reduce an individual's quality of life and well-being.

Creating buildings that address the users' needs and that demonstrate care for their well-being can contribute positively to their health.

Accessibility and independence

Addressing users' practical requirements, particularly where it can help them live independent lives, is particularly important for individuals disadvantaged through age, infirmity or disability, or who have children and additional responsibilities. Independence is greatly valued, bringing with it, among other things, financial benefits and an increased sense of self-worth. The freedom of unaided movement and unaided communication are two prerequisites for a sense of independence. Basic accessibility for all members of society through the provision of appropriate space standards, access configurations and services, is required in the UK as part of standard building regulation requirements, but further design and technical improvements can provide additional help. Cooking, personal hygiene, safety and communication can be facilitated through the use of technical solutions, for example, height-adjustable sinks, basins and worktops; walk-in showers, baths with doors and combined bidets and WCs; central systems that secure all windows and doors at the touch of a button; door entry systems connected to the television and the room lighting; and automatic lighting that switches on when one enters a room. As reduced mobility and other personal limitations become more widespread within an increasingly ageing population, making buildings easily adaptable increases the potential for adapting existing environments in future to make them more accessible. Lifetime Homes, a concept developed by the Joseph Rowntree Foundation for a flexible house able to accommodate changes in the circumstances of its inhabitants, has been estimated as having the potential for saving £5.5 billion over 60 years, in adaptation and residential housing costs. Reduced rehousing and healthcare requirements would also be expected (JRF 2004). Lifetime homes benefit individuals by enabling them to remain in their existing home and community, near their support group of friends and family. They also minimise the disruption to the individual's life, which can otherwise seriously affect their health, particularly in the case of elderly individuals.

Identity and self-worth

As important as the practical needs of individuals are their psychological needs, including those for safety, privacy and identity. These fundamental needs are key to enjoying a healthy existence with a high quality of life. An environment that feels unsafe, lacks privacy, has no contact with nature, and no aesthetic quality can prove demoralising, even stressful for its inhabitants, negatively affecting their sense of identity.

Sense of identity is related to what people believe others think of them. The environment built for particular groups of individuals can be seen as reflecting what society believes these individuals are entitled to. The quality of the built environment, therefore, reflects one judgement of its inhabitants, which is likely to influence their sense of identity. Neglected architecture not only creates unwelcoming, perhaps unsafe environments with little aesthetic appeal, but perpetuates a feeling of low self-worth and a lack of identity among its inhabitants.

Explicitly demonstrating recognition of the value of individuals in a community helps to increase their sense of self-worth and identity with the community. While this has much to do with the activities that take place the built environment can support such efforts by providing environments that demonstrate respect for their inhabitants.

Many of the buildings included in this book have addressed these issues. Respecting individuals, their needs and their identity is reflected in the way the buildings are designed and is understood by those who use them. Educational buildings such as the Adam Joseph Lewis Center, community centres like the Robin Hood Chase or the Glashaus, and housing developments like Slateford Green, were designed with care for their inhabitants. These buildings produce positive signals which suggest that society does value their inhabitants. Environmental psychology suggests the relationships between people and places are determined by the place's physical characteristics, the social activities housed by it and the cultural and personal associations with the place (Bonnes and Secchiroli 1995). As was demonstrated at Robin Hood Chase community centre, positive associations will engender positive relationships and behaviours; and buildings that show care for their inhabitants will in turn be cared for by them.

3.3.2 Neuropsychiatric conditions

Neuropsychiatric conditions are the main non-fatal disabling conditions experienced globally. The leading contributing cause for this condition in women is depression. Women also suffer from anxiety, migraine and senile dementia. A quarter of the neuropsychiatric conditions in men result from alcohol and drug abuse.

(WHO 2003)

Artwork produced by local community groups is exhibited in the Glashaus library.

At the Glashaus in Herten local residents, including foreign immigrants, have been involved in community art projects, which are now exhibited in the entrance to the library.

Case study: Lifetime homes

21st Century Homes
Aylesbury, UK

Client: Hightown Preatorian Housing Association
Architect: Briffa Phillips
Structural engineers: Structural Design Consulting engineers
Services Engineers: Jarvis Heating
Main contractor: Jarvis Contracting
Completed: 2004

The brick and timber cladding give the houses a familiar yet contemporary appearance.

Three of the eight units face a quiet road and benefit from rear gardens.

3.3.3 Design requirements to create accessible and lifetime homes

The spatial design should allow for:
- level access to the house and to a ground-floor living area; slopes should be gentle if unavoidable
- sufficient circulation space for wheelchairs
- sufficiently large doors for wheelchair users relative to the access corridor width
- wheelchair turning spaces in living areas
- ease of access to bath, WC and washbasin

The following additional spaces should be included:
- a space for a ground-floor bedroom
- a wheelchair-accessible ground-floor WC
- a 3.3-metre wide car parking space (if car parking is included)

Provision should be made for a future installation of:
- a ground-floor shower room
- bathroom and toilet grab rails
- a stair lift
- a hoist from a main bedroom to the bathroom

The use of the house should be improved by:
- providing a well-lit and covered entrance area
- lowering window sills to 800 millimetres
- making windows and doors easy to operate
- locating all switches, sockets and service controls between 450–1200 millimetres above finished floor level

(Adapted from a set of full criteria of Lifetime Homes published by the Joseph Rowntree Foundation www.jrt.org.uk)

Addressing people's needs now and in the future is an underlying concept of Lifetime Homes. A house designed to such standards provides a flexible building that is easily altered, enabling its inhabitants to remain in occupation regardless of future changes in their circumstances. Flexible homes also provide benefits for residents when first they move into a house, by enabling changes to the building configuration to suit their particular needs.

At the 21st Century Homes developments at Aylesbury and Hemel Hempstead, Hightown Preatorian Housing Association wanted to provide for its tenants' current and future needs. The brief for 21st Century Homes stipulated that the homes had to comply with the Lifetime Homes standards, as well as being environmentally friendly, affordable to run, and well designed and constructed.

Keeping within the cost limitations of housing association work, a prefabricated timber frame construction was selected for the eight three-bedroom houses. The building envelope is well insulated and, externally, a mixture of brick and timber cladding give the houses a warm and durable feel. The internal areas are spacious and include a double-height living area and stairwell.

In respect of the Lifetime Homes principles (see 3.0, 3.3.3), the design was developed to address the potential needs of notional occupants, throughout their lifetime. The houses are designed to accommodate the needs of a young couple with small children, families with teenage children, couples with no or grown-up children, elderly couples and single individuals. This is achieved by including some rooms and open spaces that can be used in different ways. All internal walls are non-loadbearing, allowing them to be removed and repositioned as required. Open-plan rooms can be sensibly sub-divided and an area is designated for a future lift installation.

On the ground floor to the front of the house, one room is designed so it can be used as a play area for toddlers, a work room, a dining room or a bedroom for a teenager or an elderly or disabled member of the household. To the rear of the house an open-plan kitchen, dining and living room can be divided into three separate rooms to allow more acoustic separation and privacy when, for example, a family has teenage children. Opposite the entrance door is an alcove that can be used to store buggies, sports and other equipment, or, alternatively, could be made into a small computer area. The ceiling of the alcove can be easily removed to allow the installation of a lift. The corresponding space on the first floor could be integrated within one of the bedrooms, should more bedroom space be required. The whole house is wheelchair accessible with sufficiently large corridors and doors. A toilet is included on the ground floor, which means that with plumbing in position a shower can be retrofitted and the ground floor can become the main living space for an elderly or disabled individual. Tenant feedback showed that the uses that the architects had envisaged did materialise. The front room, while mainly used as a bedroom, is also a play area. The space opposite the entrance is used as storage, play area, office, and hobby space, and one tenant had a lift installed, while another was planning to install a lift for an ageing relative.

Lifetime Homes have many advantages. What became evident as a result of the tenant feedback at Aylesbury was that many of the features of Lifetime Homes make them more attractive to the tenants. The size and arrangement of the circulation spaces, for example, was liked very much by the tenants and in particular by those with little children and storage needs for pushchairs. But it was not only the practical aspects that they liked; the tenants liked the feeling of the space, its airiness and brightness. The tenants also appreciated the energy-efficient features: the lower energy costs and the fact that the spaces are warm and draught-free.

Combining Lifetime Homes standards with an energy-efficient design can create resource-efficient and attractive homes that are likely to retain tenants for a long time. When asked how their new house compared to other houses, all the respondents at Aylesbury thought it was an improvement. Overall they were very satisfied with their new flexible, generous, warm and affordable homes.

3.3.4 Sustainable design features

Community and culture
The architects consulted the future tenants before designing the housing. The houses are affordable, both in terms of rent and also in terms of operating costs for energy and water.

Health
Passive ventilation combined with double height spaces in the stair area and in the living room helps improve the air quality and gives an impression of airiness and space. All spaces are well lit.
The bedrooms are built either side of the stairwell, thus increasing sound separation and privacy.

Materials
The main structure is a timber-framed and prefabricated cassette system. This should reduce material use and waste on site. Timber windows were used.

Energy
The house design was developed to minimise heat loss and a number of options were analysed before deciding on the final design. A SAP rating of 100 was targeted and an actual rating of 108 was achieved.
Fabric U-values:
    Wall – 0.2 W/m² (R28)
    Roof – 0.19 W/m² (R30)

Passive stack vents are used to extract air from the bathrooms and kitchen, and trickle vents provide fresh air to the living areas. A condensing boiler provides hot water and space heating.

Water
Dual flush WCs were installed.

All entrance areas are well lit, have level access and are protected from the rain.

Case study: Accessible homes

Slateford Green
Edinburgh, UK

Project details, Chapter 1.2, p.26

The housing surrounds a planted courtyard with a water feature. The courtyard provides a private external place to enjoy and can be viewed from most living rooms in the development.

In 1996, Canmore Housing Association ran a competition for a housing development in Gorgie Road, Edinburgh, in a disused railway yard next to the freight line. The brief reflected their high environmental ambitions and listed numerous design targets including a car-free development with a 100-year life span, low maintenance buildings, energy efficiency and the use of alternative energy sources, optimum sunlight to the homes, rainwater recycling and sustainable use of materials.

The competition was won by Hackland and Dore who developed the scheme into a courtyard development with a community centre. The teardrop-shaped courtyard is enclosed by a continuous curved block ranging from two to four storeys high. The development of 120 flats includes equal numbers of one-, two- and three-bedroom flats with average sizes of 42, 75 and 96 square metres, of which 13 were sold outright, 30 are in shared ownership and the rest are rented. By excluding car parking (see Chapter 1.2), the courtyard could be landscaped and made available to the residents to enjoy. The houses are energy efficient and make use of cheap district heating.

Four flats were designed for wheelchair use and 14 for the residential and support accommodation for the Edinburgh Deaf Society. In the UK there are 11.5 million people with some form of disability, nearly 20 per cent of the population. Included are people with sensory impairments, limited mobility, mental impairments and wheelchair users, who make up 5 per cent of disabled people in the UK. Some form of hearing impairment affects 7.5 million people. Many of these individuals can lead unassisted lives if their environments are designed to accommodate their needs.

At Slateford Green the 14 flats for the Edinburgh Deaf Society make independent life easier for their occupants in a number of ways. For people with hearing impairments, auditory functions need to be substituted with visual ones. For example, fire alarms, CO monitors, burglar alarms and doorbells can be linked to the lighting system, which flashes when activated. Loop and infrared systems, usually found in public spaces, can be used in the home to filter the sound from televisions or hi-fis. Video-phones enable visual links, while text-based systems allow written communication. At Slateford Green, the tenants can communicate visually with people outside their home by using a system that links a web camera to a computer and monitor. Similar principles apply to door-entry systems. Here the solution was to include a fish-eye lens camera within the door entry system and link it to a spare channel on the television within each flat.

In addition to these facilities, the tenants supported by the Edinburgh Deaf Society, like all tenants, appreciate the low water and heating bills. They also value the community spirit of the development, in which they can now participate more easily.

 See also: car-free development **Chapter 1.2**

The door-entry system has a fish-eye camera to facilitate communication.

The entrance to the flats is from the pedestrian perimeter road.

Case study: Accessible public spaces

Akademie Mont-Cenis
Herne, Germany

Project details, Chapter 5.3, p.243

The guidance strip at the entrance door.

All public buildings need to be fully accessible to all members of the community, and in the UK, as of 2004, existing public spaces also need to be fully accessible. How to design spaces for accessibility is well understood, but relevant facilities are sometimes not fully integrated into the building design. At the Akademie Mont-Cenis, Herne, Germany, the architecture subtly includes guidance for the visually impaired and access elements for those in wheelchairs or with mobility problems.

For those with mobility impairments and in wheelchairs, spaces and openings have to be generously and appropriately sized. Level, ramped or lift access should be provided and walkways should include stopping points and resting supports. Door handles, basins, switches and any other building elements that have to be regularly used need to be accessible from a wheelchair.

Aids for the visually impaired include communication assistance such as door-entry systems and lift controls with contrasting lettering, Braille and acoustic information, and telephones with large dial buttons which may be backlit. They also include navigation aids that can be tactile and based on the use of colour. Colour changes between walls and ceiling or skirtings can be used to help define the size of a space; colour or texture changes in the floor can help define routes; openings can be highlighted with changes in colour of doors or frames; and in toilets and bathrooms fittings should be differentiated from their background through colour. Matt surfaces are preferred as shiny surfaces can reflect too much light and confuse the viewer.

The Akademie Mont-Cenis comprises a community library, community hall, social welfare centre and a café, plus the government's research, education and accommodation facilities, all of which need to be fully accessible. The facilities are enclosed in a 12,600-square metre glass and PV roof, which creates a moderated and very pleasant internal environment, giving the development the atmosphere of a town square. Consequently, the spaces between the buildings have to be easily accessible as well.

From outside the building, people with visual impairments can find their way by following a strip of cobbles set within the concrete finish. The strip leads to the main entrance door. Once inside the building a ribbed stone strip leads the visitor to an orientation board and then guides them on their journey. There are several orientation boards in the complex, which consist of a timber model, showing where all the buildings are located, and information in Braille. Where timber decking is used as a floor finish, the guidance strip is made by turning the decking material at 90 degrees to the main floor finish – a simple and elegant solution. Equally appealing and practical are the ramps that lead to the different building blocks.

See also: Waste heat and PV **Chapter 5.3**

The orientation boards comprise a timber model of the complex and information in Braille.

A glazed canopy with PVs covers individual buildings. Guidance strips on the ground, made of different colours and textures, lead the visually impaired around the complex.

A shallow ramp leads to the entrance of the buildings of the complex.

3.4 Restorative Environments

3.4.1 Oxford Dictionary

Health *n*. 1. state of being well in body or mind

Happy *adj*. 1. feeling or showing pleasure or contentment

High up, seemingly suspended in mid-air and surrounded by planting is the seating pod in the Solar Fabrik in Freiburg, Germany, which provides a quiet place for employees to enjoy.

Physical and psychological health are interrelated, and people's health and well-being affect their sense of happiness. Equally a sense of happiness affects people's well-being (Martin 1997).

Happiness is influenced by people's expectations, experiences and sense of self-worth. Humans desire acceptance, respect and security. While in developed countries the pressures of fighting for survival no longer affect most people, other pressures have taken their place (Layard 2005). The media portrays glamorous lifestyles, successful individuals and a life to aspire to. To achieve becomes paramount and, in particular, to achieve more than friends or colleagues. However, many people's expectations, inflated by overrated opportunities and unrealistic goals, remain unattainable; and failing can be stressful and depressing, and may reduce an individual's happiness.

Self-imposed pressures to succeed in life are aggravated by the ever-increasing speed of modern society. The race to achieve more, fuelled by what Alain de Botton calls 'status anxiety' (de Botton 2005), leaves little time to appreciate what already exists and what people already have.

The world has much to enrich people's lives and all that is needed is to take time to notice and enjoy; but it is often precisely the availability of time that does not or is perceived not to exist. Time is needed to contemplate priorities and interests, to appreciate the surrounding natural environment, to enjoy solitude and company, to appreciate beauty and to relax. And with the time there has to be the physical opportunity and the personal will to contemplate these valuable aspects of life. Some designers have succeeded in providing a physical environment for these activities, by creating havens of tranquillity in their buildings. Others have had the luxury of dedicating their building to the well-being of the mind.

Comfortable seating is provided in the pod.

View of the entrance lobby and café at the Solar Fabrik in Freiburg, Germany.

However, designing spaces to enhance human well-being requires an understanding of how people respond to their environment. People associate memories, thoughts, and feelings with individual buildings, styles of building, materials, light quality, atmosphere and perceived meaning. Responses to buildings are linked to culture and personal memories, and are determined by the individual's character. Dark spaces can feel cosy to certain people and threatening to others. Introverted people may find cluttered and busy environments disturbingly over-stimulating, while extroverted people may thrive in such environments and find minimalism monotonous and depressing. It is impossible to make a universally appealing building that enhances everyone's well-being, but certain communal responses do exist, as has been discussed previously in respect of comfort, independence and identity.

An increasing number of people seek environments, both natural and built, where they can relax from stress and regain a status of mental well-being. Sustainable architecture should make such experiences not location- and time-dependent, but rather part of everyday life. Buildings should be designed to be uplifting and elicit positive feelings as well as providing places where people can retreat and enjoy quiet moments of reflection or relaxation. Beautiful buildings are enjoyable, just as unusual designs can be intriguing and provide interest. Buildings can and should elicit feelings of wonder, discovery and pleasure.

While they may be difficult to analyse, the effects of the built environment on people are significant. Certain environments can improve people's health. The ambition should be that they all do.

The concrete base supports timber seats around the perimeter of the pavilion (Architect Dan Hoffman).

The Cranbrook Academy of Art pavilion is situated near a brook surrounded by trees.

The pavilion can be enjoyed for quiet reflection.

Case study: Places of the spirit

Goethean Science Centre Craft Workshop
Pishwanton, Scotland, UK

Project details, Chapter 2.1, p.60

The craft workshop appears to have grown out of the land.

The materials and details of the building are in harmony with the character of the site.

Some argue that places have an atmosphere, an aura or a spirit – whatever name one uses it is that quality that affects the feelings and senses of those experiencing the place or even those only recalling it. The atmosphere of a building can be invigorating, calming, depressing, uplifting, inviting or hostile or may elicit many other feelings. The spirit of a place can, by inducing particular feelings, positively or negatively impact on a person's well-being.

Christopher Day has written about this somewhat elusive characteristic in his book *Spirit and Place* (Day 2001). He believes that places can be designed to be spiritually uplifting. Through his consensus design techniques, Day brings together a group of people who design buildings through obtaining the consensus of all involved. His technique, which acknowledges the contributions every member can bring, aims to understand the spirit of the place before building and even finalising the brief for the building. By doing so, the design can respond to the spirit of the place and create buildings that positively affect people.

Day used his consensus design technique for the design of the Life Science Trust project. The initial site investigation combined two complementary techniques for site analysis: one developed by Margaret Colquhoun of the Life Science Trust and the other one developed by Day. Colquhoun's technique focuses on the existing character of the site and Day's focuses on the future possibilities for the development of the site.

In Pishwanton six individuals embarked on this process of site investigation, which involved several site visits. Each member of the group would quietly walk the site, absorbing impressions and information about the surroundings and then report back and discuss with the group. The first evening visit aimed to gather general impressions, and mood-maps were produced once away from the site. The following day, the site visit began by focusing on the physical nature of the site, the topography, planting type, colour and size. After the first walk, maps were drawn from memory. The second walk on the second day focused on the history of the site, evidence of glaciation, changes from forest to farming and, more recently, dying trees and horse grazing were recorded. Learning about the past of a site can shed light on its atmosphere and mood. Considering the past of a site also brings up questions about the future. Each intervention or lack thereof will result in a different landscape in a short period of time. The group considered how the site should be affected. Studies of the physical and the historical characteristics were followed by an analysis of its mood. Each area studied elicited different feelings, some areas felt protective, others calm, gloomy or airy.

On the third day, after having slept on the newly acquired information, the group was ready to address some fundamental questions. Different areas of the site had different moods, but what was its overall character and what did it need? What would a Goethean Science Centre include and how could the Goethean Science principles of learning through respectful observance of nature be reflected? How could the spirit of the site and its future activities become mutually supportive?

See also: community self-build **Chapter 2.1**

There was a feeling that the site had been neglected and needed a new life and that the Goethean Science Centre would help to give it new life. The activities for the centre were decided and allocated on the site according to how their character matched that of the site. During the first day the group had begun to attribute body parts to different parts of the site: an area had become the heart, another the spine or the lung. Humans have historically anthropomorphised events and elements, including nature, to come closer and better understand them. During the third day, the activities were distributed on the anthropomorphised site accordingly: the study centre at the head, the herb and vegetable garden at the heart, and so on. By the end of the third day, the buildings had been pegged out on site.

The group made clay models of the proposed buildings. As the design process progressed, the clay models were changed and so were the pegs delineating the buildings on site. Sketches of the future buildings were made and discussed to establish the height, colour, mood and materials of the buildings, how they sat in the landscape and how the planting would be. The final sketches were of buildings that, as Day says, 'wanted' to be there. The workshop building was later built by volunteers and looks as if it had emerged out of the site; the building is welcoming and peaceful.

This process of analysis and design is special in the way it avoids compromise and the imposition of one individual's power, knowledge, preconceptions or interests on others. According to Day, avoiding subjectivity while contributing knowledge enables the 'right' design for the site to emerge, right in terms of purpose and nature. The details are decided and adjusted at a later time. In fact, the communal study, including considering a use for the centre, resulted in few disagreements. Each individual's knowledge, skills and experience had been fed into the process and become part of a communal basis for making decisions.

The lack of personal focus and personal agendas freed the group's minds to recognise the spirit of the place, letting it drive the design process and create buildings that respond to it. All places have an aura, which comes from the use of a place, be it a hospital or a home, and the values and emotions associated with it, and the buildings at the Life Science Trust have reinvigorated the spirit of the place by giving it a new purpose, new uses and new and positive associations. By identifying and working with the character of the site, the new buildings have also brought out the beauty and the magic of the place. There is no doubt that the centre is an example of a building that lift the spirits of the visitor and users.

The handcrafted character of structure of the workshop expresses a philosophy that appears to be shared by the craft workers who use the workshop. The space is uplifting and invigorating with a tangible air of creativity, but at the same time it is a peaceful space, calming and reflective.

The building and its surroundings are a constant source of fascination.

The barn currently under construction also appears to grow out of its surroundings.

Case study: Health and nature

Loudoun EcoVillage
Taylorstown, Virginia, US

Client: EcoVillage
Architect initial house design: Ensar group
Completed: first houses completed in 2002, building ongoing

The double height living space is bright and airy. All windows have views of the countryside.

A meadow surrounds one of the houses.

See also: enhancing native flora and fauna **Chapter 1.3**

EcoVillage of Loundon County, Virginia, US, is a 50-unit co-housing development on the edge of the village of Taylorstown in the Northern Virginia countryside. The development has two main aims: to provide an environmentally sound development that benefits the residents and the environment and to create a community where people can enjoy a safe neighbourhood and the company and support of community members, while still retaining their privacy. To achieve these aims, a holistic approach to the development was adopted. The approach included considering the land use and ecology of the site and the resource use, including energy, water and materials. It also aimed to create a supportive and cooperative community and provide a healthy life for the residents.

Providing a healthy environment was a product of a variety of measures. On average, people in developed countries spend an increasing amount of time indoors, an average of up to 90 per cent of their time. This can impact on health in a number of ways. Air pollution levels can be higher indoors than outdoors (see chapter 3.2), natural light levels in buildings are one tenth to one hundredth of those outside and spending time indoors is usually associated with a sedentary lifestyle, lack of exercise and associated health issues. The EcoVillage houses counteract these risks to health by ensuring good indoor air quality through minimising the use of toxic materials, materials containing formaldehyde and other volatile organic compounds; ensuring all internal spaces have good natural light (even the rooms in the semi-basement are bright and airy); and encouraging residents to spend time outside and enjoy nature.

Contact with nature has been found to be beneficial to health, at a conscious and unconscious level, and there are thought to be a number of reasons for this. Natural environments are considered to be calming and reduce stress owing to their less complex nature with reduced numbers of stimulants compared to urban environments. People's positive responses to nature are also thought to come from a deep-seated evolutionary preference for natural environments, in particular savannah-like landscapes, that resemble the environment where primitive humans first developed. Natural features that during the early evolutionary period would have supported the survival of humans, such as plants that bear fruits, water features, paths that provide safety, all induce feelings of security and reduce anxiety and fear. Support for this evolutionary theory comes from various studies, including where savannah-like park landscapes were found to have a preferred spatial configuration providing depth of view, openness and sufficient interest (Kaplan 1992); and studies where photographs of savannah landscapes were found to be more effective than other scenes of natural landscapes at reducing stress, even on people who preferred other landscapes or even disliked the savannah scenes (Wise and Roseberg 1988).

The restorative effects of nature have been shown in numerous studies. Feelings of fear and anger among students studying for exams who had views of plants were found to be reduced and positive feelings were increased (Ulrich 1979).

Physiological impacts, such as reduced blood pressure, skin conductance and muscle tension, were also measured. These positive impacts were found to occur after only a few minutes of viewing nature and plants (Ulrich *et al.* 1991; Harting and Evans 1993). Several other studies found that stressed individuals actively seek out nature and feel calmer and more balanced after being in planted environments (Francis and Cooper Marcus 1991; Barnes 1994; Olds 1985). Even simply viewing images of natural environments rather than the real thing, was found to be beneficial in studies of hospital patients. Studies of office workers with windows facing buildings or nature and those without windows found reduced stress, headaches and ailments and increased job satisfaction among workers with views on natural environments. The mood of office workers and their life satisfaction were also found to be positively affected by the presence of plants (Leather 1997; Kaplan 1993). Actively interacting with nature as in gardening or caring for a wood combines the psychological benefits of the closeness to nature with the advantages of physical exercise, which in itself has been shown to help counteract depression (Ulrich 1999). Nature was also found to have spiritual associations for some people. Whether viewing nature as one part of the unified earthly organism, or as a link to a spiritual being, some people appreciate the contact with nature at an intellectual level.

EcoVillage is designed to benefit from the contact with nature in many ways. The houses are designed to visually and physically reconnect with the outdoors. All windows have views of the surrounding natural environment; shaded verandas off the living rooms provide an outdoor space for eating, working or relaxing; and during the hot summer periods an outdoor sleeping veranda protected from rain makes it possible to sleep in the open. The site location and design also encourage interaction with nature. By positioning the car parking away from the houses a few minutes' walk in nature is assured each time one leaves the home and more active interaction is also possible through the reforestation work, the removal of invasive species and the general maintenance of the site as well as the individual gardens.

EcoVillage's development approach successfully creates an environment where residents can benefit physically, psychologically and spiritually from nature. It does so not in a purely anthropocentric way, but while recognising the stewardship responsibilities that humans have towards the natural environment.

3.4.2 Sustainable design features

Site and ecology
The site was selected to be close to all basic services. It is 400 metres from Taylorstown village centre and five miles from the Point of Rocks commuter train to Washington, DC. Parking is restricted to communal parking areas off the main access road, thus creating a pedestrian-oriented environment. External lighting is designed to minimise light pollution. The native biodiversity is being restored (see Chapter 1.3) and covenants ensure the whole site is gardened organically.

Community and culture
Community participation in the planning and management of the site is encouraged and residents can join a number of committees that share the maintenance work for the whole site. The EcoVillage common house includes mailboxes and a kitchen where communal meals can be prepared, a children's playroom, laundry facility and guest rooms. The development aims to facilitate collaborative relations while ensuring individual privacy. It is designed to be a safe environment.
The contractors were trained in sustainable land development and construction.
The EcoVillage, with its informative website, also actively promotes sustainability. Hundreds of people have visited the village and a number of green initiatives have developed from the activities of the community association.

Health See main text.

Materials
Durable materials were selected where possible. 150-millimetre insulated timber panels (SIP) and other natural and biodegradable materials were used for the construction. Recycled materials include recycled PVC and sawdust roof tiles. Waste minimisation in construction was reduced through minimising offcuts and careful material handling. Communal recycling and composting facilities are envisaged.

Energy
Standards for energy performance have been set by the Architectural and Environmental Design Guidelines to which all residents are bound. The homes are designed to be passive solar and well insulated and use geothermal energy to heat and cool the buildings. One house has PVs and others are wired for installation at a later date.
Fabric U-value standard house:
  Walls – 0.23 W/m²K (R24)
  Roof – 0.14 W/m²K (R40)
  Windows – 1.4 W/m²K (R4)

Water
Water is taken from local wells. Local authorities do not allow rainwater to be used for drinking purposes, despite the ample rainfall (95,000 litres/roof/yr). Low water use fixtures are installed. Sewage is treated on site with septic tanks and secondary treatment.

The open air sleeping terrace enjoys views of the woodland and the hills beyond.

Chapter 4
Materials

4.0 Introduction

4.0.1 Life Cycle Assessment (LCA)

Life Cycle Assessment (LCA) is the assessment of the impacts associated with materials from their resourcing and manufacturing to their disposal. In their book *The Green Guide to Specification*, Anderson, Shiers and Sinclair illustrate the assessment process by using a brick wall as an example and listing the processes that need to be considered to establish the environmental impact of the brick wall over its total lifespan.

The environmental impacts associated with the following issues would have to be considered:

– the extraction and transport of clay to the brickwork

– the manufacture and transport of ancillary materials

– the extraction and distribution of natural gas for the brick kiln

– the mining and transport of fuels for the generation of electricity for use in the factory

– the production and transport of raw materials for the packaging

– the manufacturing and transport of packaging materials for the brick

– the manufacturing of the brick in the brickwork

– the transport of the bricks to the building site

– the extraction of the sand and production of cement for the mortar

– the building of the brick wall

– the maintenance of the wall, such as painting or repointing

– the demolition of the wall

– the future of the materials in the waste stream

Materials, energy and water are the three main resources required to construct and run buildings. A sustainable building design approach has to consider these three resources in terms of their depletion and the environmental and social impacts associated with their use. This chapter considers design practices that help to minimise the impacts associated with materials use, and Chapters 5 and 6 analyse the use of energy and water.

Environmental impacts of material use

Materials are used throughout a building's life, initially and primarily during the construction phase and subsequently for maintenance or for alterations. Materials have a substantial impact on buildings ranging from the aesthetics and appeal of a building to its buildability and cost. During the past 30 years an increased understanding of materials and their characteristics has brought to light other less obvious impacts associated with materials, which affect people and environments well beyond the building envelope.

The potential remoteness of the impacts of material use makes the link between the cause (e.g. the use of tropical rainforest timber panelling in Europe) and the effect (e.g. the deforestation of the Amazon forest and the consequential displacement of communities and extinction of species) more difficult to comprehend and substantiate than more immediate cause and effect relationships such as that between car use and increased pollution. The impacts associated with materials can be remote with regard to both location and time. For example, timber might be used thousands of kilometres from where deforestation occurs and the detrimental effect of asbestos on health only becomes apparent decades after contamination took place. The resourcing of materials, their manufacturing processes, transport requirements, use and final disposal can involve wide-reaching environmental and social damage, including global warming, pollution, depletion of natural resources, destruction of natural habitats, extinction of plant and animal species, waste production, destruction of communities and health problems. To assess these impacts, material specifiers must consider the chain reaction and long-term effects of using any material, even those that may appear unlikely to be associated with negative environmental impacts.

Life Cycle Assessment (LCA)

The assessment of all environmental impacts of materials from their manufacture to their disposal, or as it is often described, from 'cradle to grave', is known as a Life Cycle Assessment (LCA) (see 4.0.1). Assessing the complex nature of the impacts associated with materials use has proved enormously difficult and only recently have convincing assessment methodologies and data been made available to designers. In the 1990s, the Building Research Establishment, in consultation with the building manufacturing industry, developed the Environmental Profile Methodology and Database, a method designed to evaluate the environmental impacts of construction elements. The system, now accessible through the internet (www.bre.co.uk/envprofiles), considers and quantifies the impacts of the use of materials in terms of climate change, fossil fuel depletion, ozone depletion, waste disposal, water extraction, mineral extraction and pollution to humans and ecosystems.

As already mentioned, the impacts of material use are extremely far-ranging and complex. Even the excellent Environmental Profile system does not address all material impacts, for example, it does not consider biodiversity, social issues or resource depletion apart from fossil fuel. Moreover, in common with other assessment systems, the Environmental Profile system allocates weightings to the environmental issues considered. These weightings give more importance to some environmental impacts than others, with, for example, issues affecting global warming given the highest weighting. The Environmental Profile weightings were agreed with a broad range of interested parties, from architects to environmentalists; however, weightings are, by definition, subjective. An individual may wish to prioritise issues other than those given most prominence by means of the weighting system, and, for example, in certain instances occupant health or support to local manufacturing may be felt to be more important than global warming. Designers must develop a basic understanding of the sustainability issues relating to materials and consult a selection of information sources to ensure their material choices reflect their own personal views and priorities.

There are currently a number of different types of publication on sustainable material selection to help designers specify sustainably (see Further reading). These include publications such as the *Handbook of Sustainable Building* which provide the reader with a sustainability rating system for material selection and basic principles of sustainability; publications such as the *Green Building Handbook*, which include a rating system and detailed background information illustrating the reasoning behind the publication's recommendations; and, finally, publications such as *Ecology of Building Materials*, which cover ecological issues affecting material specification. While the rating systems provide a quick reference tool for busy practitioners, more detailed information helps develop an understanding of the sustainability issues associated with material use. The remainder of this introductory section outlines the sustainability issues to be considered when selecting materials, and 4.1–4.6 outline different approaches adopted by architects to minimise the impact associated with the materials of their buildings.

Issues to consider when selecting materials

Material resourcing

Building products are derived from natural materials that are harvested or extracted and then processed. The first issue to consider is the availability of the material resource, the risk being that resources may become depleted, leaving future generations without that particular resource and, therefore, at a disadvantage.

4.0.2 Further reading

Contemporary Natural Building Methods
Adams C. and Elisabeth L. (2000) John Wiley & Sons, London

Principles of Design for Deconstruction to Facilitate Reuse and Recycling
Addis, W. and Schouten, J. (2004) CIRIA, London

The Green Guide to Housing Specification
Anderson, J. and Howard, N. (2000) BRE Watford

Handbook of Sustainable Building
Anink et al. (1996), James and James, London

Ecology of Building Materials
Berge, Bjørn (2000) Architectural Press, London

The Whole House Book
Borer, P. and Harris, C. (1998) Centre for Alternative Technology, Machynlleth

The Reclaimed and Recycled Construction Materials Handbook
Coventry, S., Woolveridge, C., Hillier, S. (1999) CIRIA, London

The Art of Natural Building
Kennedy et al., eds. (2002) New Society Publishers, Gabriola Island, Canada

The Good Wood Guide
Magin, G., (2002), London and Cambridge: Friends of the Earth, Fauna and Flora International

The Green Guide to Specification
Shiers et al. (2002) Blackwell Science, Oxford

The Green Building Handbook Vols. I & II
Woolley. T. et al. (1997/2000) E&F Spon, London

4.0.3 Cork

Cork oak grows in southern Europe. At 25 years old trees are mature enough for their bark to be peeled off without damaging the tree. The harvested bark is used primarily for wine corks and in the building industry as an insulating material or as a floor or wall finish.

The bark can be harvested every 8 to 15 years and this is organised by a process of harvest rotation. More frequent harvesting would not deplete the resource as the trees would regenerate within a decade, but is likely to endanger the cork industry by creating an income gap of several years, which the industry is unlikely to be able to bridge. The consequence of a decline of the industry could then trigger the reduction of cork oak trees or even the replacement of cork oak with another crop.

Only by managing the resource, ensuring a regular production and producing regular income for the cork farmers can this natural renewable resource have a sustained future.

Why is retaining cork oak desirable?

Trees in general are regarded as the world's lungs and are desirable for their ability to transform CO_2 to oxygen and by doing so help to counterbalance the greenhouse effect. The replacement of cork oak with another crop would affect the established and balanced ecosystems developed around cork oaks and their destruction would involve the loss of biodiversity.

The loss of the cork industry would be the loss of a traditional craft, which contributes to the local culture. The immediate effect of the industry disappearing would be unemployment, possible break-up of communities and perhaps a migration to cities.

As a building material, cork is one of very few natural insulation materials (others include sheep's wool and timber fibre). Cork is a healthy material in that it does not emit unhealthy compounds and is biodegradable, therefore does not contribute to long-term waste problems.

Materials are usually classified into renewable and non-renewable materials. Non-renewable materials include those with regeneration cycles of millennia (e.g. stone, coal, oil, metal ores), and renewable materials include those with regeneration cycles of decades or less (e.g. timber, flax, hemp, cork). Materials can be plentiful or scarce: sand is considered to be a plentiful resource, while oil reserves are limited and are estimated to last anything between 40 and 60 years (some estimates are for more than 60 years) depending on consumption rates. Renewable resources are generally considered plentiful. However, if a renewable material is over-harvested, it may become scarce and ultimately even depleted, cork and timber being relevant examples (see 4.0.3). To avoid over-harvesting, resources have to be managed. For timber, a number of organisations, such as the Forest Stewardship Council (FSC), monitor and accredit forests that implement a successful sustainable management system (see Chapter 4.3). Therefore, while renewable materials should be used in preference to non-renewable ones, this is subject to the renewable sources being sustainably managed.

Apart from the amount of resource available, the extraction or harvesting process itself can affect the surrounding environment and can be associated with pollution, the destruction of natural habitats and the reduction of biodiversity. The effects of small-scale quarrying or mining on the local ecology can be and often are reversed, as with clay or sand pits restored to wetlands. Large-scale mining, on the other hand, can cause more permanent changes: mining of bauxite strip to produce aluminium is associated with the flooding of valleys to produce hydroelectric power schemes, causing loss of rainforest habitat and, consequently, the loss of biodiversity. Pollution of water, soil and air can also be a consequence of material extraction: the extraction of oil is associated with air pollution from flaring and marine or groundwater pollution from oil leaks and spills.

Increased concern about the environmental impacts of mining and resources extraction has resulted in some improvements in these practices, increasing numbers of forests are being managed sustainably and there is a move towards small-scale mining in preference to large scale. However, there is still scope for improvement and by taking these issues into account when specifying materials, consumers can help push the market to adopt ever more sustainable practices.

Manufacturing process

Materials are rarely used in their completely natural state. Some preparation or manufacturing is generally necessary to create a usable building product. The impacts associated with manufacturing can include pollution to air, water and ground. Manufacturing also generally requires energy, which is mainly derived from fossil fuel and is associated with global warming and pollution.

At one end of the environmental impact scale there are 'natural' materials. These are materials that are found in nature (e.g timber or stone) and that require minimal processing before use. A material with such minimal manufacturing impacts is the adobe brick made with earth and water and dried in the sun, a process that makes use of a plentiful naturally occurring material, uses manual labour and the sun's heat rather than burning fossil fuels and consequently produces almost no pollution or waste.

At the other end of the scale there are materials such as metals and plastics. The metal smelting industries and the chemical industry are the two top industries in terms of total emissions of toxins to the environment, including pollution of the air, land and water. The production of PVC, one of the materials highlighted by environmental groups such as Greenpeace, as being seriously environmentally damaging, is associated with emissions of organic chlorides, dioxins, PCBs, furans, ethylene dichloride and vinyl chloride monomers, as well as mercury pollution resulting from the production of chlorine.

Similar to the improvements in mining and harvesting processes, manufacturing pollution and energy use are slowly decreasing. Energy-efficient improvements are being implemented and encouraged by government initiatives (e.g. the UK Climate Change Levy) and some manufacturers are now operating Environmental Management Systems and are seeking external party accreditation (e.g. ISO 14001). By demanding environmental information and accreditations from manufacturers, specifiers can emphasise to the manufacturing industry the importance of considering environmental issues in order to succeed in an increasingly competitive environment.

Materials, energy and transport

Unlike the example of the adobe construction given earlier, most building materials require energy for extraction and manufacture. Energy is also required to transport the material to site, maintain it and finally dispose of it. The total energy used is known as the embodied energy. Energy is still mainly produced by burning fossil fuels and is therefore associated with global warming and pollution. Specifying low-embodied energy materials is therefore generally desirable. Unfortunately, estimates for the embodied energy of materials can vary depending on the method used to calculate it and can be misleading. Embodied energy calculations do not generally differentiate between energy produced with fossil fuels and that produced by alternative means not associated with CO_2 emissions; they sometimes include the energy for the transport of materials to site, for their maintenance and disposal, and sometimes they do not. When they include these, assumptions have to be made regarding the distance of transport and the life span of an element. Embodied energy figures also fail to take into account that different materials are required in different amounts to achieve the same purpose. Despite their limitations, embodied energy figures do give an idea of what are high and low energy materials. Low-embodied energy materials should be used in preference to high-embodied energy materials, but embodied energy should not be used as the only selection criterion. It should be seen as an element of the total energy consumption of a building over its life. A building's running costs are still generally significantly higher

4.0.4 A sustainable material selection

Minimising the need for materials
– Build only when really necessary.
– Build small.
– Design for effective use of materials.
– Design for durability and for reduced maintenance.

Use existing materials
– Reuse existing buildings.
– Reuse existing building components.
– Use recycled materials.

Design to enable future buildings and material reuse and recycling
– Design for flexibility and desirability to maximise the building life.
– Design for durability and desirability to maximise building component life.
– Design for recycling or to enable the biodegrading of materials.

Select new materials with care
– Specify renewable materials with short regeneration cycles.
– Specify timber from managed and accredited sources (e.g. FSC accreditation).
– Specify plentiful resources and avoid scarce resources.
– Specify materials mined, harvested or extracted with minimal impact on local and global environment.
– Specify materials associated with low manufacturing pollution.
– Specify materials associated with low levels of CO_2 emissions over the life of the building considering their impact on saving running energy.
– Consider manufacturers' environmental policies, track record and reporting.
– Specify materials that do not pollute the indoor air.
– Select locally produced materials requiring minimal transport

Material disposal and waste minimisation
– Segregate timber, inert, metal and soil waste during construction and demolition and ensure their recycling.
– Arrange for excess material ordered and where possible waste material to be taken back by material suppliers.
– Include recycling provisions in buildings.

than its embodied energy. Consequently, the specification of certain materials with relatively high-embodied energy, such as extruded plastic insulants, can be justified due to their significant contribution to lowering building running energy costs, whereby their embodied energy is recuperated many times over the life of the building.

A substantial reduction in the building's total embodied energy can be made by reducing transport requirements. The transportation of materials from the manufacturer to the building site is generally by road and is associated with CO_2 emission and air pollution. Reducing this transport energy requires material specifiers to select manufacturers located as close as possible to the building site.

Materials in use

Maintenance of materials requires both energy and materials and is associated with similar impacts as the construction of buildings albeit on a smaller scale. Minimising requirements for maintenance by designing for durability and longevity helps to reduce the life impacts of materials. Materials can also affect the building users in terms of comfort and health (these impacts are considered in Chapter 3).

Material disposal

The building industry in the UK is currently responsible for 70 million tonnes of construction and demolition waste every year, most of which is sent to landfill. There are numerous problems associated with landfill sites, including the use of land, toxic materials leaching into groundwater, emissions of explosive gas and structural instability. Appropriate site waste segregation, designing to enable reuse and recycling, and using reclaimed and recycled materials all contribute to diverting waste from landfill and other polluting waste disposal options.

Building design can also encourage recycling of domestic or commercial waste by providing appropriate recycling facilities in the building.

4.1 Design for Longevity

The production of new materials is inevitably linked to environmental and social impacts. To minimise the need for new materials, it is important to make maximum use of materials already in existence. Furthermore, making use of existing materials, which would otherwise have entered the waste stream, reduces the impacts associated with waste disposal.

The three main opportunities for making use of existing materials are: reusing existing buildings, reusing building components, and using recycled materials. Examples of buildings that have been reused or that have incorporated reused or recycled materials are illustrated in 4.2.

What makes it possible for a building or component to be reused or recycled? First, in order to be able to reuse buildings or components, they must be in a good state of repair, but that is not enough. If we examine buildings that have been in use for hundreds of years, we find that they serve an existing need, fit into the urban or rural landscape, are often liked by the community and are also often good quality buildings. The deterioration of a building is not its only downfall. If a building becomes dilapidated, then it may have to be demolished, no matter how much the community would like to retain it, and if a building no longer has a use, retaining it would not make economic sense.

To ensure a long life for a building it is therefore essential to design in sympathy with the environment, but also to provide a building that can accommodate changes of use and has a durable building fabric that is easily maintained and upgraded.

In the UK, for example, there are many buildings that are several hundred years old. Ranging from small cottages to large public buildings, many of these have retained their original use, while others have undergone one or more changes of use. As the economy shifts, requirements for different types of building change and, to accommodate these changes, Victorian warehouses are refurbished into offices, 1960s offices into housing, and agricultural or industrial buildings into exhibition spaces. Even when the use of the building nominally remains the same, as with housing, the needs of users have changed over the years, resulting in trends, such as converting from cellular to open-plan living. Flexibility has become of prime importance and buildings that can accommodate change are likely to have a long life.

The ability to alter the internal layouts of buildings is perhaps the most important issue in terms of providing a flexible building, but structural flexibility may also be necessary. The British Council of Offices recommends designing offices to cope with a variety of loads, which may mean over-designing the structure in order to take larger loads in the future. Increased structural loads may result from a change of use or an extension on top of the existing structure, an approach that is becoming common in cities.

4.1.1 Recommendations for designing for dismantling, reuse and recycling

Guidance for designing to enable dismantling suggests that the following be considered:

Information
Provide As Built drawings and a Maintenance Log including identification of points of disassembly, component and material. Also identify materials and points of disassembly on elements.

Access
Provide easy and safe access to building elements and fixings with minimal machinery requirements.

Dismantling process
Simplify fixing systems and enable removal by means of small hand tools and handheld electrical tools, avoiding specialist plant. Use mechanical rather than chemical fixing. Provide realistic tolerances for assembly and disassembly. Design joints and components to withstand dismantling process.

Hazards
Make components suitable for safe handling and provide means of handling and locating. Avoid toxic materials.

Time
Minimise number of parts, fixings and types of fixings. Allow for parallel disassembly of different building elements.

Guidance for designing to enable the reuse of building elements and, alternatively, their recycling if reuse is not possible, recommends the following:

Reprocessing
Use materials that require minimal reworking. Avoid non-recyclable materials (e.g. composite materials), treatments and secondary finishes that complicate reprocessing. Minimise the number of component types. Ensure that inseparable sub-assemblies are from the same material, and that components of different materials are easy to separate.

Hazards
Minimise toxic content. If toxic content is unavoidable, ensure the ability to release it in a controlled manner. Make components sized and of a weight to suit the means of handling and provide means of handling and locating.

Durability
Use sturdy and avoid fragile material. Design joints and components to withstand repeated use.

Information
Provide identification of material and component types. Provide product details and installation instructions.

The ability to change internal layouts relies on internal partitions being non-load-bearing and easily dismantled. Buildings supported by a framed structure or external walls can lose all internal walls while remaining structurally intact. Building products such as relocatable office partitions offer off-the-shelf flexible wall systems, but more traditional partitions, such as blockwork or plasterboard partitions, can be and often are removed to allow internal changes. The difference between a proprietary relocatable partition and a traditional one is that the relocatable partition can be reused, in theory at least, extending the life of that building element.

Designing for flexibility ensures that the main structure of the building has the potential for a long life. Designing for reuse and recycling goes a step further and ensures that all building components can have a long and useful life.

In designing for reuse and recycling, it is important to consider the life span and frequency of replacement of building components and to detail components, liable to be replaced sooner than others, so as to enable their removal without affecting the rest of the building. Components are often removed from buildings despite still being in good working order and can be reused subject to not being damaged during their removal. The use of simple fixings and durable materials helps enhance a building component's ability to be installed and dismantled several times.

Even if a component is removed perfectly intact, it may still not be reused. This may be due to a lack of aesthetic appeal, as with standard sanitary ware; difficulties in providing warranties, as with roofing membranes; or incompatibility with contemporary building methods, as with non-metric-sized doors or bricks. The reuse of building elements is as affected by technical limitations of dismantling and reinstalling as by market demand, building standards and the cost of removal. Building components that are currently reused, such as period fireplaces or reclaimed slates, tend to be aesthetically and culturally desirable, which warrants their higher cost. The relatively slow, labour-intensive dismantling process, which contributes to the high cost of reclaimed materials, could be accelerated through detailing components to facilitate their removal. In addition, the use of good quality, aesthetically pleasing materials will enhance the products' desirability.

The UK government formulated a waste hierarchy as part of their *Waste Strategy 2000 for England and Wales* (DETR 2000c), which puts waste avoidance as the top priority to minimise waste. This is followed by reuse of waste, then recycling, downcycling (see 4.2.1), incineration to produce energy and, finally, landfilling. Reusing building components is therefore preferable to recycling them, but where reuse is impossible or economically unfeasible, recycling material provides another resource-saving option which diverts material from the waste stream. Eventually most building components will no longer be able to be reused and at that stage should be recycled.

Recycling is facilitated if the material to be recycled is as pure as possible. Metals are already extensively recycled owing to the ease of metal recycling, the minimal effect of contaminants and the resultant high value of recyclate. Recycling timber, on the other hand, is more labour intensive, requiring de-nailing and cleaning, and is consequently less lucrative. Composite materials, such as sandwich cladding panels, and materials treated with toxic substances make recycling difficult and expensive or even impossible.

Designing buildings so that components can be removed and replaced is not only beneficial in terms of sustainability: general maintenance is facilitated and made less costly, as is upgrading building elements or periodic refurbishment.

Designers, aiming to create a building that will act as a material resource for the future, should consider the potential life of their building and building components and design them for their optimal life span and recycling or reuse option. This could involve designing the main building structure for durability and eventual recycling; services for ease of dismantling and recycling; and internal partitions or external cladding that may need to be changed to accommodate a change of use or fashion for ease of dismantling, reuse and eventual recycling.

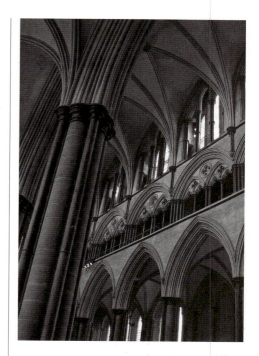

From Edinburgh housing to Salisbury Cathedral, some buildings have been in continuous use for hundreds of years.

Case study: Design for reuse and recycling

Glencoe Visitors Centre
National Trust of Scotland Visitors Centre Glencoe, Scotland, UK

Client: National Trust of Scottish
Architect: Gaia Architects
Landscape architect: Gaia Architects
Quantity surveyor: Ralph Ogg & Partners
Main contractor: R.J. McLeod
Completed: 2002

View from the covered entrance area towards the museum and viewing platform.

The timber sections of the covered entrance area are bolted or screwed to facilitate their dismantling.

Gaia Architects were commissioned in 1994 by the National Trust of Scotland to design a new visitors centre for their site at Glencoe, the site of the massacre of the MacDonald clan. Following a consultation period with the local community and the Trust itself and a lengthy search for funding, the construction of the new centre started in 2000 and was completed in 2002.

The Trust wanted the building to be 'green' and the brief was therefore developed by the architects to cover sustainability issues regarding the site, resources, energy and health. Gaia Architects considered the use of materials and focused on the principle that the most effective way to reduce the use of materials is to maximise the life of the building. This aim was pursued by following the principle of building in layers, a concept put forward by Stewart Brand in his book *How Buildings Learn*. Brand promotes a layered construction where each layer is designed to be as independent as possible, providing both flexibility and the ability to upgrade or modify the exposed layers.

The theory of building in layers was put into practice at Glencoe by designing the structural frame, the services and the finishes as distinct elements with minimal interconnections. A timber portal frame was chosen and designed to be structurally independent from internal partitions. This produced a flexible internal layout, where internal partitions could be repositioned without affecting the structural frame, thus facilitating future changes to the internal layout and use. The frame is built as a breather wall construction with a waterproof layer externally fixed to a processed timber board, with insulation between framing elements and a board internally, and constitutes both the essential structural and weather-protecting layer of the building. The external cladding and the internal finishes are two layers independent of the main structural frame, which can be maintained, upgraded and altered without affecting the frame. To enable the various layers to be accessed, all fixings are generally bolted or screwed and adhesives are avoided altogether. This enables elements to be removed without damage. The dismantled elements can then be reused elsewhere or, if reuse is impossible, recycled.

Fixings are generally left exposed to facilitate their access. Speed of disassembly not only facilitates the dismantling of a building, it makes dismantling more economically viable and facilitates maintenance by reducing maintenance time and therefore costs. Owing to cost constraints, the external timber cladding is nailed rather than screwed: this concession was made taking into account that the cladding will be removed when the timber has deteriorated and can at best be recycled, but not reused. The cladding is fixed with only two nails per board, which allows the timber to move, but also reduces the number of fixings and potential contaminants should the timber be recycled.

The layering approach was also used for building services. Between the frame and the internal finishes are voids located in the floors, walls and ceiling that house the electrical wiring and heating pipes. The voids are easily accessed through skirtings and a specially detailed flooring system, which again relies on exposed fixings. The flooring system involved rebating each floorboard and locating a fixing trim between two rebated edges, and has already proved its worth during the fit-out contract, which required the repositioning of services.

In order to maximise the potential for recycling, materials were specified without coatings or finishes where appropriate, and composite materials were avoided. Timber was used rather than chipboard and mill–finished aluminium rather than coated steel.

A few areas of the building remain traditionally inflexible and not capable of being dismantled. The rendered exterior finish and the tiling to the wet areas are traditional single use finishes. The plasterboard internal finish, while screwed with taped joints, would prove difficult to disassemble and the boards are notoriously impossible to reuse. Solutions to these culturally sensitive finishes are still in their infancy. Perhaps, in this primarily timber building, a timber boarding with exposed fixings as an internal finish could have made this building virtually 100 per cent recyclable.

4.1.2 Sustainable design features

Site and ecology
The existing building was demolished and recycled and the new building, located on the site of an old caravan park, was designed to nestle in the landscape. The original site was returned to natural use, an existing culverted stream was reopened and native planting reintroduced.

Community and culture
The design involved a community consultation. The materials used are mainly local, both in character and production, thus supporting the regional economy.

Health
The timber was not treated, avoiding preservative and relying on appropriate detailing and the correct choice of durable timber for each purpose. PVC was not used and glues associated with volatile organic compounds offgassing were kept to a minimum.

Materials
The timber specified was a locally grown Scottish timber.

Energy
The building structure has a U-value of approximately 0.14 W/m^2K and was detailed to be air-tight. The heating is supplied by a woodchip boiler, making the development, including the caravan site, carbon neutral.

Water
Water is supplied to the building from a spring-fed reservoir. The water is not chlorinated but treated with silver copper ionisation. The sewage system, which is linked to the camp site, was upgraded to return clean water to the River Coe. Low flush WCs, aerating taps and other water-saving approaches were included.

View of the village-like grain of the visitors' centre.

Timber floor showing the cover strip screwed to the subfloor with exposed fixings.

View of the external wall and roof timber boarding.

Case study: Design for flexibility

INTEGER House
Building Research Establishment, Watford, UK

Client: 30 partners across the building industry
Architect: Cole Thompson Associates, Bree Day Partnership, Paul Hodgkins Associates
Fit-out architects: Cole Thompson Associates and IKEA
Structural engineer: Antony Ward Partnership
Services engineer: Oscar Faber
Intelligent technologies: i&i Ltd.
Quantity surveyor: Andrews Partnership
Main contractor: Wilcon Homes
Completed: 1998

The house includes intelligent technologies such as automatic control for the shading devices in the conservatory and the second-floor room, which automatically adjust in response to the sun.

Located in the grounds of the Building Research Establishment, the house is partially bermed on the north side.

➤ **See also:** minimising waste on site **Chapter 4.6**

In 1996, a group of designers joined forces to consider how to address the changing requirements for housing design in the UK. They focused primarily on two contemporary issues: the impact of communication technology on everyday life and the increasing awareness and need to design sustainable buildings. The group's aims were to demonstrate how these issues could be addressed in a way that could be replicated on a large scale, beyond demonstration designs. They also wanted to counteract the industry's scepticism based on its experience of house buyers' lack of interest in radical innovation, the unavailability and high cost of innovative technologies, and the financial risk of such developments. The design of the house should, therefore, not only include technological and environmental features, but should also appeal to the typical house buyer, keeping construction costs within standard ranges.

To achieve these aims, the group set up the INTEGER Project team, the name intending to illustrate the combination of 'intelligent' and 'green' designs. Approximately 30 organisations joined the INTEGER Project as partners and over 100 building industry companies donated time, materials, and expertise. The project development involved an exchange of information and experience among the whole team, setting targets and developing solutions as a group. The resulting building includes a wide variety of environmental design technologies (see 4.1.3) and contemporary lifestyle design features.

The design considers how to improve the occupants' comfort, security, safety and control of their home. 'Green' technologies were used as well as so-called 'intelligent' features, such as automatic operation of the ventilation, heating and shading; programmable controls for water level and temperature in the bath; light systems with different mood settings, central room switches and light level sensors; whole house audio systems; internet access and security observation via the television.

The design also addresses the increasing need for flexible space. As the needs of the users change as a result of new members of a family being born or needing to work from home or becoming less mobile, the INTEGER house can change as well.

The house was designed to allow changes in the use of the rooms and the configuration of the rooms. The external walls incorporate a small void created with 38mm battens behind the plasterboard inner lining, used to run cabling for information technology and electricity. The services running in the void are joined at the base and pass within ducts behind the skirting, one duct for the electrical wiring, the other for information technology. These can be accessed easily by removing the surface fixed skirting boards. This system facilitates reconfiguring the space, adding sockets and upgrading services as new technologies are developed.

Another innovative measure to increase the flexibility of the home is the introduction of a partition wall between two of the bedrooms which can be repositioned as required. This internal partition is made of 900mm–wide drywall panels with two adjustable feet and is suspended centrally on a ceiling-mounted track. To install the wall, the panels are rolled along the track and fixed into position by adjusting the feet. The skirting element is then mechanically fixed with screws or with hidden magnetic catches, completing the wall. Two rooms can be made into one room or the sizes can be adjusted, making one room larger and one smaller, in accordance with the current user's needs.

Flexible systems not only facilitate change, but also reduce waste and the need for new materials when alterations are undertaken. Because building changes are less onerous, occupants are also more likely to make the required changes rather than live in an unsuitable building or move house. Introducing such flexibility, common in commercial buildings, into housing design is a simple way to reduce the environmental impacts associated with materials, while contributing to the occupants' quality of life.

The house is designed to be passive solar and also includes active solar technologies.

The panels making up the partition wall between the two bedrooms can be moved along the tracks set flush in the ceiling.

The wall's skirting is screwed in position.

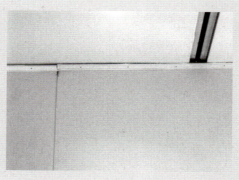

The top section of the wall includes a trim and the track used to move the partitions is recessed in the ceiling

4.1.3 Sustainable design features

Site and ecology
The building has a green roof planted with alpine species.

Community and culture
The house was used as a demonstration for a selection of environmentally friendly building methods and technological innovations. The construction process was filmed and shown on television inspiring viewers and informing them about environmental building-related issues.

The intelligent technology includes improved security systems and smart keys that allow limited access to the house for delivery purposes.

See also main text.

Health
The furniture in the house was selected from IKEA on the basis of their environmental approach. The largely MDF furniture was thought to have the potential to affect the indoor air quality, which was then monitored and proved acceptable.

Materials
The building was largely prefabricated, including panels and bathroom pods, which helped minimise waste and construction time on site. See also Chapter 4.6.

The structure is a timber frame filled with recycled cellulose insulation. The external cedar cladding does not need treatment.

Energy
The building structure is well insulated. A solar thermal panel provides hot water to the house and a small PV panel provides power for the mechanically assisted passive stack ventilation. A closed loop ground source heat pump system, comprising two vertical boreholes and a water-to-water heat pump, supplies warm or chilled water to an in-floor convector system

The house should use 50 per cent less energy than the average new house.

Water
Water use is minimised through the use of water saving automatic taps and water-efficient kitchen appliances. Greywater is recycled to flush the 3/6 litre dual-flush WCs. Water use should be 30 per cent lower than in comparable new houses.

Rainwater is collected to irrigate the conservatory plants and part of the garden. The rainwater tank is kept clear of algae by using an ultraviolet light, which operates intermittently using off-peak electricity.

Case study: Ageing gracefully

Environmental Discovery Center of Sonoma County
Spring Lake Regional Park, Santa Rosa, California, US

Client: Sonoma County Water Agency
Architect: Obie G. Bowman
Main contractor: CWB Christensen-Williams-Bohn
Completed: 1992

The Environmental Discovery Center in Spring Lake Park offers children and adults alike the opportunity to learn about the natural environment by examining the centre's displays, including animal displays, playing traditional and computer educational games, and listening to the centre staff talk about nature. All this takes place in the middle of 130 hectare of wooded hillside. Including a lake has been devised as a flood control facility for the local area. The centre, which is just inside the entrance to the Spring Lake Regional Park, was originally designed as a visitors centre for the park to provide information about the local environment and while the centre's remit has broadened, its ethos of engendering a sensitivity towards the natural environment remains. In addition to the permanent displays, it also organises special exhibits relating to environmental issues, such as recycling, water use, health and the summer heat, and is a favourite venue for school groups as well as being open to the general public.

View of the park beyond the centre.

The concrete and stone have mellowed and seem to have developed from the site.

The centre appears to fit comfortably on the hillside of the Spring Lake Park among the oaks and buckeyes.

Timber louvres are designed so as to allow maximum natural light through the glazed structure, but prevent direct solar penetration, heat gain and glare.

The six air vents and the flue from the wood-burning stove are located on the roof.

While the displays in the building promote a harmonious relationship with nature through education, the building itself exemplifies how to build in response to the characteristics of a site while impacting minimally on the environment. The heavy concrete base reflects the stone boulders dotted on the sloping site of the park and the progressively finer grid of timber louvres, shading the glazed façade, represents the change in scale of the surrounding oaks and buckeyes.

While grounded visually, metaphorically the building treads lightly on the earth. It is very energy efficient and has minimal water requirements (see 4.1.4). In addition, the materials for the building were carefully selected. The redwood shading and the concrete are durable materials, which have required little maintenance, while ageing very well. The natural growths on the concrete make it look even more like the rocks in the area and the timber shading has acquired a beautiful silver colour, virtually identical to the bark of the oak trees. The materials were allowed to age naturally and as a result the building has gained even more character than it already had. These material qualities and the way the design of the building successfully links it to the site will ensure its long life, but it is also its innovative aesthetics, unique character and the quality of the spaces that give this building an architectural quality worth preserving.

4.1.4 Sustainable design features

Site and ecology
The site was selected to minimise impact on the forest and the trees cut during construction were used to create a canopy for a storytelling cavern in the park.

Community and culture
The centre provides an educational facility for the local community and in particular for local schools.

Health
The internal space benefits from high levels of natural light, while completely avoiding any glare.

Materials See main text.

Energy
The building is naturally ventilated and makes primarily use of solar gains for heating. In the summer, cool air is drawn through low-level earth tubes, which help cool the air. As the fresh air warms up inside the building, it rises and is extracted with the assistance of a fan through a vent in the ceiling. The hot air is also extracted via the solar collector. The glazed solar collector heats the air which rises within the sloping collector and is exhausted through the six vents on the roof. As hot air is exhausted from the attic plenum, cool air is drawn into the bottom of the solar collector, which is halfway up the building interior, thus creating a continuous throughflow of air to cool the building.
In winter, the air heated up in the solar collector is supplied to the visitors centre through exposed ducts and is used as the main means of heating the building. A wood-burning stove, using wood waste from the site, provides back-up heating.

Water
Water requirements are minimal for this type of building.

Internally the centre is brightly lit entirely by natural light. This light and airy yet shaded space is reminiscent of the shade of a large tree protected from the scorching sun. The duct visible in the corner of the space brings the solar-heated air from the solar collector into the space.

4.2 Waste as a Resource

4.2.1 Reuse, recycling and downcycling

Reuse Putting to new use a previously used building component taken from a building or other source. The building component can be made of a single material (e.g. brick, slate tile, timber joist, precast concrete floor) or more than one material (e.g. door with ironmongery, composite wall panels, precast concrete foundations). It can require no processing (e.g. a roof tile) or significant processing (e.g. paint stripping and finishing doors).

Recycling Reprocessing a material or component to form the same or an equivalent material or component (e.g. metal roofing recycled to make new metal roofing or wall cladding).

Downcycling Reprocessing a material into a lower grade use material (e.g. concrete or brick into hardcore, timber into chipboard).

The Oxo tower in London was transformed from a warehouse to flats, shops and a high quality restaurant with views on the Thames.

The building industry is one of the biggest consumers of materials. In the UK the industry is responsible for the extraction of 260 million tonnes of minerals, equivalent to 90 per cent of minerals extracted annually for non-energy purposes (Addis and Talbot 2001). Measures to reduce this substantial use of virgin materials and the associated environmental impacts need to be extensively implemented. One way forward is to design buildings to be capable of being dismantled and enable the reuse or recycling of their component materials at the end of the building's life, thereby making secondary materials available and reducing the need for virgin materials. This not only reduces the impacts of resourcing and manufacture, but also the impacts associated with landfill sites and incineration. However, for this approach to be effective, there has to be a balance between the reused and recycled materials available to the construction industry and the demand for them. Unless there is sufficient market demand for recycled and reclaimed materials, they will simply end up, at best, unused in expensive storage and, at worst, landfilled.

To create a viable closed material resource loop, where materials are reclaimed from buildings and then reused in new buildings, designers must both design buildings that can be dismantled, and specify reclaimed building products or products with recycled content. Increasing the demand for recycled and reused materials will strengthen the market for such materials, increasing their manufacture or reclamation, making them more affordable and ultimately diverting more waste from landfill. Making use of building elements made of materials diverted from municipal waste also reduces other sources of waste.

The type of 'waste' available to the building industry can be divided into four main groups, namely: whole buildings; reclaimed building elements; recycled building materials; and building products made with recycled material from non-building sources.

Existing buildings may not have been designed with their future recycling and reuse in mind, but many currently act as sources of reusable or recyclable building materials. When considering the development of a site with an existing building in place, reusing the whole building is the most environmentally desirable option, as it most effectively minimises waste and the need for new materials. In Europe, there is a long tradition of reusing buildings, which has also helped maintain the character of many cities. However, reusing a whole building may be problematic. The energy performance of many existing buildings is poor compared to current standards for energy-efficient buildings. One of the priorities of a sustainable refurbishment is to upgrade building performance, but in certain cases this may not be feasible. In terms of economics and marketability, the existing building may not be aesthetically desirable. If such drawbacks preclude the reuse of the building as a whole, then the retention of the building structure should be considered. If the structure is not reusable, the building should be dismantled for recycling or reuse rather than demolished and landfilled. Fixtures and fittings can be offered to charitable organisations; reclaimed finishes such as timber floors have good resale value; all metals are easily recycled; structural timber can be visually graded for structural strength; and concrete structures can be recycled or downcycled. Careful dismantling can take more time, but is less noisy, dirty and disruptive than standard demolition, and therefore more appropriate in densely populated areas. Waste disposal taxes, such as the Landfill Tax in the UK, act as financial incentives to segregate waste, which is facilitated by careful dismantling of buildings.

Reclaimed materials are available from a number of sources. Architectural salvage yards deal with reclaimed items ranging from paving stones, bricks and timber sections to sanitary ware, furniture and decorative elements of historic interest, such as fireplaces or iron pieces. Some are sought after for their character and many, such as timber doors, are often made of higher quality materials than newer versions. Reclaimed materials can also be sourced directly from demolition sites and a number of internet sites help this process of materials exchange by advertising available and wanted recycled materials (e.g. www.bre.co.uk/waste, www.salvo.co.uk). The potential for using reclaimed materials is not being exploited. In the UK, for example, an estimated 500,000 tonnes of reclaimable timber is landfilled each year, of which 50,000 is tropical hardwood (Magin 2002), and 2500 million bricks are used, of which only 150 million are reclaimed (BRE 2003).

Reusing building products is the most environmentally preferable option. However, certain materials are either financially, aesthetically, or technically impossible to reuse, but can be recycled. Metal sections should be reused whenever possible, but high scrap value makes it simple and cost-effective to reintroduce waste metals into the standard manufacturing process. Faded plastic windows or sanitary ware could be reused, but have minimal resale value. *In situ* concrete cannot physically be reused, but can be recycled to substitute natural aggregate in new concrete. Recycling materials is always preferable to downcycling them. Concrete can also be downcycled to a lower-grade use such as hardcore, although recycling it saves more energy and materials.

Typical barriers to the use of reclaimed and recycled materials include cost, which is still often higher than new material; availability, which can in certain cases be erratic; and the compliance with performance standards. Remanufactured metals have the same performance characteristics of virgin metals and therefore comply with the same standards. Recycled concrete aggregate has different characteristics from natural aggregate and even though research shows that replacing up to 20 per cent of the natural aggregate with recycled does not negatively affect the concrete, widespread use of recycled aggregate has not taken place. Reusing timber cladding may not prove problematic in terms of complying with standards and warranties, but reusing a roofing membrane almost certainly will. Nonetheless, increased use of reclaimed and recycled materials, combined with financial and legislative inducements, is slowly eroding these typical barriers and making the use of such products increasingly competitive.

4.2.2 Dismantling buildings for maximum reuse and recycling

- Fixtures, furniture and fittings can be sold or donated to organisations in need of secondhand items.

- Services should be tested for their suitability for reuse, including an assessment in respect of their energy efficiency. If not reusable, they should be recycled.

- Finishing boards, roof tiling, timber, bricks, stonework, architectural features, doors and windows and ironmongery all have good reuse potential.

- Finishing materials that are not reusable for aesthetic reasons should be recycled.

- Pre-cast concrete, steel and timber structural elements can be reused.

- Metals are recycled very cost-effectively.

- Non-reusable materials should be recycled.

The Building Research Establishment Building 16 is a model of maximum reuse of demolition material. The building, located at the Building Research Establishment in Watford, near London, was designed by Feilden, Clegg, Bradley Architects. The existing building on the site was dismantled and 96 per cent of the materials by volume were reused or recycled: fixtures, fittings, and furniture were given to charities; roof sheeting, slate cladding and cast iron drainpipes were reclaimed; metals and timber were recycled; and masonry was downcycled. The new building (above) used reclaimed timber floors, bricks and aggregate in the structural concrete.

Case study: Reuse of whole building

Sanders Eco-Renovation
Phoenix, US

Client: Diane, Barry and Mattie Sanders
Architect: Sol Source
Completed: 2004

A newly formed external space provides a partially shaded seating area.

One of the extension elements made of SIP, rendered and painted in purple. Other extension elements are painted in muted green and yellow.

The Sanders' house is situated in an older central suburban area of Phoenix. The 1950s house had become too small for the family and, rather than demolishing it, architect Tom Hahn carefully and skilfully extracted the most out of the existing structure to produced a seemingly new building. By inserting a number of rectangular, flat-roofed extension elements, the house not only gained the additional space necessary, but lost the typical, but dated, ranch-style aesthetics and assumed a contemporary feel.

As with all of Hahn's work, the refurbishment also addressed the environmental performance of the building. The extension elements were made with a structural insulated panel (SIP) system, consisting of two processed timber boards with insulation between, which helped improve the insulation of the building as a whole. The panels were rendered and each one painted in different muted colours in character with the dry desert landscape. Frameless windows, including a corner window, frame views to the outside.

The existing structure of the building was also adapted and renovated. The old windows were replaced with energy-efficient windows made with fibre and resin, which not only provide more insulation, but are also more durable in a climate where timber tends to deteriorate quickly. With the introduction of the extension elements in selected places, natural light was brought into all areas of the building, improving energy efficiency by reducing the need for electrical light and creating a healthier interior environment. The relation between indoor and outdoor spaces was also improved. An external seating area was formed between the existing building and a new garage. The garage, positioned between the house and the street, makes good use of a previously unusable driveway and protects the house visually and acoustically. The area, protected from visual intrusions, provides a private external seating area for the family to enjoy.

View of entrance. The addition of extension elements alters the aesthetics of the building, giving it a contemporary feel.

The refurbishment was designed to make the most of the finances as well as the existing building. Waste materials were used inventively to create useful building elements of interest. Drilling rods, which have to be discarded at regular intervals to comply with safety regulations, were used to fence off the property and also to direct the rainwater from a steel downpipe to the earth. Reclaimed timber was used to make a pivoting door integrating small square glass sections which bring shafts of light into the entrance area.

Through simple and sensitive means, the existing building was given a new character and a new life that promises to be a long one. This is not only because the house now satisfies the family's practical requirements, but also because the quality of space and the delightful design touches create a building that the owners will be proud of and will love for a long time.

4.2.3 Sustainable design features

Site and ecology
The refurbishment minimises the impact on land by reusing the existing building footprint.

Community and culture
The design incorporates a number of artistic architectural interventions, including a sculptural rainwater outlet celebrating the nature of rain, while the bathroom includes a window feature made by sandblasting four layers of glass to create a three- dimensional effect, bringing light into the shower area while acting as a privacy screen.
The unusual approach to refurbishing a building raises awareness of the advantages of refurbishments and environmental design among the community.

Health
Natural light is brought into all areas of the building. Healthy materials were used in preference to those offgassing VOCs.

Materials
Reclaimed and recycled materials were used where possible. Bathroom tiling is made with recycled glass, drilling rods were used as fencing material, reclaimed wood was used to make the entrance door, waste metal was mixed as aggregate in the concrete kitchen tops. The kitchen cabinets are made from wheat-straw particleboard and have bamboo doors and drawer fronts. The new interior structure was made with reclaimed timber from the existing building or with metal studs with recycled steel content. The interior flooring finishes include cork, recycled rubber, and reclaimed broken concrete pavers from the driveway.

Energy
The energy performance of the building envelope was improved. The cooling system, which is considered essential in the Phoenix climate, was upgraded, improving its efficiency.

Water
Low flush 5-litre WCs were installed. Low water native vegetation minimises water needs in the garden. Rainwater is collected to water the garden.

A new corner window provides a view of the tree in the garden.

The main entrance door incorporates small glass elements and reclaimed timber.

Sandblasting of the window provides a screen to the shower area while admitting good daylight.

Rainwater is directed along the reclaimed rods to the ground.

Case study: Reclaimed materials

Using reclaimed materials has many environmental benefits. The resourcing of virgin materials and the associated energy use, pollution and impacts on the natural ecosystems are avoided; the manufacturing processes with their associated energy use and pollution are replaced by generally low impact cleaning, resizing and treatment processes; and transport requirements can be substantially reduced.

In an ideal situation, reclaimed materials would be sourced from the development site itself or a nearby location and require no treatment before reuse. Materials that require minimal processing include roof tiles and loose-laid paving. They are self-finished and have minimal fixings, which result in a fast and cost-effective dismantling process. Such materials also benefit from being small standard components, which can be integrated within any configuration and do not impose restrictions on the building design. At the BCZEB headquarters building, the roofing tiles were reclaimed from the existing building, stored on site and installed on the new roof. New nails were required to install the tiles, but otherwise the environmental impact of reusing the tiles can be considered close to zero.

The Building Research Establishment Building 16 used 80,000 reclaimed bricks for the external walls and some internal walls.

BCZEB, the new RES (Renewable Energy Services) headquarters building, made use of reclaimed roofing tiles. (see Chapter 5.3, p.248).

The reclaimed tiles are an environmentally sound material selection and have character.

Reclaimed materials are more likely to be used if this does not affect the building layout, size of openings or other design-related features. Bricks, like roof tiles, provide this design flexibility and, if bedded in lime mortar, are relatively easily to reclaim. Despite being relatively time-consuming to reclaim and prepare for reuse, and therefore often more expensive than new bricks, reclaimed bricks are commonly used because of their aesthetic appeal and the design flexibility they offer.

Using larger reclaimed components, such as doors or structural beams, may involve adjusting the design in terms of the size of building openings or structural spans to suit the reclaimed element sizes. Alternatively, the reclaimed building elements can be resized to fit the design requirements; however, this can involve additional costly work. In practice, larger reclaimed elements tend to be used on smaller projects where a direct interaction between designers and contractors is possible, where programmes are more flexible or where the design can be based on the reclaimed materials.

As important as the integration into the design of reclaimed materials, is the integration into the construction programme. The availability of reclaimed materials

The Building Research Establishment Building 16, designed by Feilden Clegg Bradley, is a ground-breaking building in terms of environmental performance in general. In addition to using recycled and reclaimed materials, it is designed to be energy efficient through the use of natural ventilation in the offices and ground water cooling in the lecture room. It also has a PV array.

needs to be confirmed in respect of the amount of recycled materials available and the timing of delivery. On large projects it may be difficult to find enough reclaimed doors of the same design, or sufficient reclaimed bricks of the same type. Delivery times may also be longer than for new materials. Investigating the availability, delivery time and cost well ahead of time is therefore important.

Many of these limitations can be overcome by careful planning. On the BedZED housing project, Bioregional, an environmental consultancy, helped the architects to source reclaimed materials. With this additional assistance on the project it was possible to source 54,000 metres of reclaimed timber studwork, 98 tonnes of reclaimed structural steel, 700 square metres of reclaimed floorboards and reclaimed ply shuttering. Following on from their BedZED experience, Bioregional (www.bioregional–reclaimed.com) now offers a sourcing and supply service to designers and builders who want to include reclaimed materials in their projects.

The Macoskey Center (see Chapter 4.6) comprises a couple of small buildings refurbished with much care. The barn roof is covered with reclaimed tiles and the barn structure is a reclaimed timber frame.

The Macoskey Center chicken house makes use of a reclaimed cart, timber sections, timber boards, and offset printing sheets.

The Hidden Villa chicken house is designed to make use of reclaimed doors, windows and timber studs, rafters and joists.

The roof tiles of the chicken house are made of reclaimed metal offset printing sheets.

The BedZed's environmental strategy includes the use of recycled materials.

Case study: Recycled materials

A window sill made with recycled post-consumer glass set in a resin mix at the Shorebird center in Berkeley, California, US (see case study, p.242).

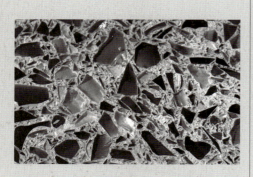

Close up of recycled glass window sill.

As discussed in the introduction to this section, building materials with recycled content make use of waste material that would otherwise be disposed of in landfill sites or through incineration. Waste material from domestic and commercial activities is increasingly used to make consumer products as well as building products. As the demand for recycled building products rises, so will the price paid for the waste material used in their production, which will in turn help finance more effective collection systems, increasing the amount of waste recycled and diverted from landfill.

In the past, manufacturers were sometimes reluctant to admit to including recycled materials in their products. Now, recycled content is a selling point. When considering specifying recycled products it is, however, worth examining the products carefully. Materials advertised as recycled materials can have anything from 100 per cent recycled content to as little as 20 per cent and less. The type of recycled content included is often not specified. Recycled products can contain post-consumer waste or manufacturing waste. Post-consumer waste includes used plastic bottles, glass containers, newspaper, metal cans, clothes, vehicle tyres, packaging and more. Manufacturing waste includes waste from the manufacturing process of anything from yoghurt containers to rubber flooring or slate roofing tiles, as well as by-products of steel, power and other industrial production processes.

Manufacturing waste is perhaps the simplest waste to deal with as it tends to be very pure. However, following waste minimisation priorities that put avoidance of waste before its reuse or recycling, improvements in production efficiencies should be implemented in preference to simply recycling the waste. Rather than producing new materials made of manufacturing waste, some companies recycle their manufacturing waste by mixing it with the virgin material as part of their normal manufacturing practice, an approach that may not be advertised and may only be evident in the company's environmental policy. Manufacturing by-products, such as pulverised fuel ash from power stations or blast furnace slag from steelworks, are difficult to reduce through increased efficiencies and are often used as low grade material substitutes in landscaping, road building or masonry products production.

Post-consumer waste can come from a variety of sources including municipal sources and packaging from industry. Treatment may be more complex than with manufacturing waste because of contaminants, but the environmental benefits are high as the alternatives are limited to incineration and landfilling.

While recycling is generally considered to be environmentally positive, there are counter-arguments to using recycled materials. The main argument suggests that the ability to recycle certain environmentally questionable materials is being used by their manufacturers to argue for their environmental acceptance. Other arguments suggest that the ability to dispose of manufacturing waste may counteract efforts to make manufacturing systems more efficient; recycling packaging counteracts incentives to reduce the amount of packaging used; and recycling materials may, in certain cases, simply postpone their disposal in landfill or incineration by a few years.

Recycled materials can help raise awareness of environmental issues. Panels made out of recycled yoghurt pots, CDs, clothes hangers, plastic cups, crisp packets, timber fibre, expanded polystyrene packaging, flexible sheeting made from recycled rubber boots and paving with colourful crushed glass may be aesthetically pleasing, flamboyant or brash, but they tend to attract attention and underline just how many applications there are for recycled materials.

Not all recycled materials are obvious. Some are hidden in the building fabric: recycled polyethylene damp proof courses, pulverised flue ash used as cement substitute in concrete blocks, insulation bats made of recycled denim and cotton fibres, recycled cellulose (newspaper) fibre insulation and carpet underlay made from recycled rubber from tyres. Other recycled materials are visible, but indistinguishable from non-recycled ones, for example, rubber flooring made with manufacturing and post-consumer waste, pinboards made of recycled cellulose, timber-like sections (for anything from retail trims to outdoor furniture) made of recycled plastic and slate tiles containing waste slate dust.

Some of the recycled products, such as recycled cellulose fibre insulation, have been fully tested and are now commonly used. Others are more experimental and the high costs of testing may not be warranted for small production runs. Only through increased use can many of these products be further developed and their use ultimately become common practice. With increased awareness of recycled materials, including through recycling-focused websites, such as www.ecoconstruction.org, building with recycled materials could soon become commonplace.

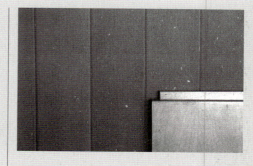

Trex used as decorative panel on the kitchen counter of the Environmental Showcase Home in Phoenix, Arizona, US (see case study, p.262).

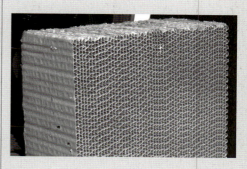

Cardboard honeycomb insulation made from recycled paper fibre at the Schreiber House (see case study, p.230).

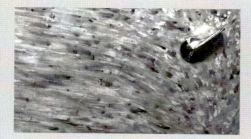

WC access panel made of recycled plastic bottles

Metal strands in concrete kitchen top (see case study, p.160).

Wall cladding made of recycled plastic bottle in the Sainsbury's store in Greenwich (see case study, p.232).

Recycled metal in concrete kitchen top at the Sanders house (see case study, p.160).

Trex post-consumer thermoplastic mixed 50/50% with recycled timber fibre used as an external decking material at the EcoVillage in Loudon County (see case study, p.140).

4.3 Avoiding Resources Depletion

4.3.1 Outstanding resources of materials

Material	Outstanding resources
Arsenic	21 years
Aluminium/ Bauxite	200 years 600 years of bauxite reserves at current rates of consumption / 80 years of economically exploitable ores (1)
Boric salts	295 years
Cadmium	27 years
Chrome	105 years
Copper	36 years
Gold	22 years
Iron ore	200 years of supply at current rates of consumption/100 years of supply at exponential growth rates of consumption(1)
Lead	20 years
Nickel	55 years
Sulphur	24 years
Tin	28 years
Titanium	70 years
Zinc	21 years
Oil	41 years (2)
Gas	60 years (2)
Carbon	Coal (hard) – 326 years/Coal(soft) – 434 years (2)

Plentiful materials

Sand	Clay	Gypsum	Perlite
Gravel	Earth	Lime	Quartz
Stone			Silica

(Crawson 1992, (1) ECRA 1995, (2) Meadows 1992)

Sustainability is very much about considering the future and thinking long term. In selecting virgin building materials, non-renewable resources should be used with care. Not only do they require millennia to form, but the conditions under which some of the non-renewable materials were formed no longer exist. Outstanding resources of selected non-renewable resources are listed in 4.3.1, which suggests that current economically viable and known stocks of certain materials will be depleted in as little as a single generation. Some non-renewable materials are considered plentiful. The environmental considerations when using plentiful materials should focus on the resourcing impacts, which in many cases are temporary and can be reinstated. The alternative to using plentiful non-renewable materials is to use renewable ones.

Renewable resources are those that regenerate, mainly through photosynthetic activity, within a human lifetime or less. They are also biodegradable if appropriately treated and not combined with non-biodegradable materials. Renewable materials, including plants and grasses, which grow anew every year or season, trees that require several decades to mature, and animal hair, can be used for a multitude of functions. In contemporary construction, timber, straw and bamboo are used for structural purposes; mixtures of hemp and straw are used to infill external wall frames; straw, cork, flax and sheep's wool make good insulation materials; timber and soya can be made into finishing or structural boards; timber is commonly used to make fittings and can even be used to make bathtubs and sinks; jute is used for carpet backing and wall coverings; sea grass, sisal, coir, cotton and wool are made into carpeting; flexible floor finishes are made of pure cork and cork mixed with wood flour, powdered limestone, linseed oil and natural resin to make linoleum; bamboo and timber make rigid floor finishes; and roofs can be covered with timber and thatch. With minor additions of non-renewable materials such as glass, it is possible to construct a building entirely with renewable materials.

What is significant about renewable materials is that they are grown with minimal environmental impacts and harvested using non-destructive processes at time intervals that allow the material to regenerate.

As the cultivation of renewable materials intensifies, agricultural processes can become less environmentally friendly. Pesticides are used on a number of crops including timber. Cotton growing often involves high use of pesticides and fertilisers; today, however, a growing number of organic cotton plantations avoid such practices. Sisal is a strong soft plant fibre extracted from the agave sisalana bush and used for carpeting. Its intensive cultivation, resulting in nutrient depletion and soil degradation, has been a cause for concern.

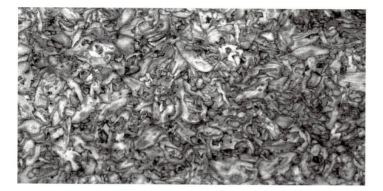

Board made of recycled newspaper and sunflower hulls bound in soybean resin.

4.3.2 Forest ecosystems and deforestation

– Forests are vital to the balance of CO_2 and oxygen in the Earth's atmosphere. They also serve as watersheds, soil erosion controllers and temperature modulators. Forests are home to many species of plants and animals.

– Habitats closer to the equator have increasing numbers of species of flora and fauna. Wilson had identified 43 species of ants on a single tree in Peru, approximately the same number as in the whole of the British Isles. The tropical rainforests cover 6 per cent of the land surface, but contain half the known species of organisms.

– Today forest cover globally is half of what it was at the beginning of the agricultural revolution 8000 years ago. Sixty per cent of temperate hardwood and mixed forest, 30 per cent of conifer forest, 45 per cent of tropical rainforest and 70 per cent of dry tropical rainforest have been lost.

– Clearing forests is one of the forms of habitat destructions that has the most devastating consequences in terms of loss of plant and animal species. Harvesting timber through clear-cutting removes all vegetation including the nutrients in the above ground biomass, leaving the ground prone to soil erosion and nutrient depletion. On average, the loss of nine-tenths of habitat causes a decline in flora and fauna of 50 per cent. As habitats are fragmented, an increasing number of reduced size habitats, housing 50 per cent of their original number of species, are in danger of being wiped out all together.
(Mackenzie 1998; Seager 1990; Wilson 2002)

The frequency and methods of harvesting are also of importance. Appropriate harvesting intervals depend on the material. (see 4.0.3). For instance, in its natural environment, bamboo grows an incredible 25 and 30 centimetres in one day once the plant is well established. When the bamboo has reached its full size, it transforms the sugars and water into cellulose and silica in three years, after which it can be harvested. Cultivated plants such as jute, soya, sea grass, sisal, hemp, flax and cotton can be harvested one or more times each year. Timber thinnings can be harvested every 5-20 years, while mature deciduous trees can be harvested after 30-60 years, and some hardwoods need to be over 100 years to mature. The harvesting process can also have environmental impacts. Sea grass grows among mangroves and coral reefs and the harvesting procedures, as well as the harvesting frequency, can unbalance this ecosystem.

Of particular concern, in respect of renewable materials, are the harvesting procedures and frequencies of timber. The versatility of timber makes it an extremely sought-after product. In 1994, 4.4 billion cubic metres of wood were consumed globally, 43 per cent of which was burned as fuel and 57 per cent of which was used for building, paper and other products. This huge demand fuels extensive deforestation, which has significant environmental impacts (see 4.3.2).

Deforestation is generally characterised by the long-term or permanent removal of forest cover and conversion to non-forested land uses. Older forestry practices applied on a large scale can contribute to this process. For instance, slash and burn was historically restricted to small areas, leaving long intervals for re-growth. Today, large-scale slash and burn is a major cause of deforestation and is still being undertaken in the developed countries, such as in the US, where 25,000 hectare of primary old-growth forest is clear-cut annually (Mackenzie 1998).

To preserve forest ecosystems as well as timber resources for the future, it is vital that sustainably managed forestry be implemented globally. This forestry uses alternative methods that aim to protect the forest ecosystem by removing limited amounts of timber, as little as 2 per cent per year, and allowing the forest to regenerate naturally. Select felling, where selected trees are felled, leaving the forest habitat intact, is applied.

4.3.3 Comparison of timber certification schemes

(V = variable)

(Friends of the Earth 2002)

	Fully participatory & transparent?	Performance-based standards?	Credible inspection and monitoring?	Individual forest units assessed?	Credible label and chain of custody?
Forest Stewardship Council	yes	yes	yes	yes	yes
Pan-European Forest Certification	no	V	V	V	V
Canadian Standards Association	V	no	yes	yes	no
Sustainable Forest Initiative	no	no	no	yes	no

Trees are not felled where erosion might take place without the trees in place, and where felling would pollute waterways. Roads are kept to a minimum and portable handheld tools are used in preference to large machinery to avoid the destruction of the forest floor and minimise soil compaction. Leaves and small timber sections are left to return nutrients to the forest and also provide a living environment for animals.

Timber from sustainably managed forests is identified through a number of certification schemes. The Forest Stewardship Council (FSC) is perhaps the most stringent certification system, which considers environmental and social issues relevant to local communities, workers and indigenous people. The Programme for Endorsement of Forest Certification (PEFC), previously known as the Pan–European Forest Certification, is a rapidly expanding scheme that groups together 13 national certification schemes. The national schemes differ in their detailed requirements, which overall are considered less onerous than those of the FSC scheme. While currently only a small percentage of the timber available is certified, demand for certified timber should encourage more producers to undertake the certification process.

Whether using renewable or non-renewable resources, there are always potential pitfalls that can only be addressed by verifying the material sources, probing suppliers, and requiring written documentation. This will not only ensure the delivery of the most sustainable materials possible to site, but will also help educate the supply chain.

Case study: Timber

The Weald and Downland Open Air Museum, opened in 1970, houses a collection of historic buildings from the local area, many of which are centuries – old traditional oak – framed structures. The buildings in the museum have all been saved from destruction, renovated and re-erected in the museum's grounds. In 1995, the need for a new workshop to house the renovation work was identified. It took another six years to appoint a design team, including a specialist carpentry firm, secure some funding from the Heritage Lottery Fund, develop the innovative design that stands there today, and finally begin construction in 2000. The new building, completed in 2002, includes a workshop and an archive for storing historic agricultural and other artefacts. Located on the sloping site next to the museum's car parks, the lightweight timber gridshell structure, shaped like a triple bulb hourglass and housing the workshop, is supported on a heavy and high thermal mass concrete structure housing the archive. The archive is built partially underground and thermally linked to the surrounding earth.

The workshop is 50 metres long, 16 metres wide and 7.35–9.5 metres high, and is large enough to erect timber building sections as part of the building renovation process. The large sliding doors at both ends of the workshop allow access to the workshop for materials and visitors. Two enclosed rooms at one end of the workshop provide heated teaching spaces.

One of the design aims was to use environmentally friendly materials and in particular investigate the use of local timber in an innovative and efficient way. Many of the UK's forests are still relatively young, having been substantially felled during and following the Second World War. Forest thinnings, young, small-diameter trees, currently make up approximately half of the annual timber crop in the UK, but are generally considered inappropriate for use in construction. Despite this, Cullinan Architects and Buro Happold had used this renewable and sustainable resource on a previous project: the Westminster Lodge in Hooke Park. For the gridshell the design team took a different approach to using timber efficiently and drew on Buro Happold's chairman, Michael Dickson's experience of gridshell structures, which dates back to the timber gridshell designed by Frei Otto for the 1975 Mannheim Garden Festival, Germany.

Double curved shells are the most material-efficient shell structures. In addition, timber gridshells enable irregular forms with large spans to be created that can accommodate openings where needed and can be prefabricated. However, previous experience had highlighted some problems with timber gridshells, which may account for the Weald and Downland shell being only the fifth such structure in the world. The design team not only decided to adopt the gridshell solution, but also to further develop and monitor its design and construction and make such a material-efficient and environmentally friendly structure type more accessible to the building industry.

The shell construction comprises four layers of 35 x 50mm timber laths forming two connected mats. The use of four thin layers, rather than two thicker ones, was due to the need to create a specific curvature that proved too small for the thicker and stiffer timber sections. The in-plane shear strength is provided by laths of oak running parallel to the

Weald and Downland Gridshell
Chicester, UK

Client: Weald and Downland Open Air Museum.
Director: Christopher Zeuner followed by Richard Harris
Architect: Edward Cullinan Architects
Structural & services engineer: Buro Happold
Quantity surveyor: Boxall Sayer
Carpenter: The Green Oak Company
Contractor: EA Chiverton
Completed: 2002

View of the west entrance of the gridshell.

View of the north elevation. The timber gridshell is supported on the concrete archive and store. The cedar cladding and the polycarbonate glazing allow for movement of the structure. Rainwater is collected from the valleys and discharged on the ground.

4.3.4 Sustainable design features

Site and ecology
The building respects the Area of Outstanding Natural Beauty within which it is located.

Community and culture
A traditional joinery company was employed, helping to keep the traditional craft alive.

Health
The oak is not treated. Natural light provides a healthy work environment.

Materials
All materials were to be biodegradable, reusable or recyclable. The oak structure is not fire treated. The walls comprise a thin foil-backed layered insulation with the same insulating properties of 200-millimetre mineral wool, a breather membrane and untreated western red cedar vertically lapped cladding sourced 25 miles from the site. The roof cover included an area of Roofkrete (sand and cement mixture over steel mesh). Waste timber from the construction was made into door stops and sold in the museum shop.
The ash floor is laid over a 6-millimetre cork insulating layer over 80-millimetre larch structural deck.

Energy
The uninsulated ground floor links the building thermal mass to the ground taking advantage of the thermal lag of the ground. Underground pipes draw air into the building preheated by the earth. Minimal heating is required in the store area to counteract changes in temperature and humidity caused by visitors.
The workshop is naturally ventilated.

Water
There are minimal water requirements.

ground and diagonally to the grid; they also provide a fixing element for the cladding. The mats and shear laths are connected with a purpose-designed galvanised steel node clamp developed collaboratively by the design team. The green oak structure was sourced from the closest location providing the appropriately grown oak, which was just over 200 kilometres away in France. In order to make maximum use of timber, short timber sections, approximately 600 millimetres long, were finger jointed using a fully automatic system and a Swiss-made glue to make 6-metre lengths. These were transported to site in a single lorry, where they were scarf jointed to form sections up to 37 metres long for the mats and 50 metres long for the shear laths.

The clamp   Finger-jointed section.   The internal wall.

The spacing of the grid laths varies between 0.5 and 1 metre, whereby the narrower spacing is located where the majority of the stresses were identified by means of an advanced computer modelling software, essential for maximising design efficiencies. The installation involved laying the gridmats out flat on a scaffolding structure at high level, and over a period of six weeks dropping the scaffolding to form the shell. The bracing laths, which also act as fixing battens for the cladding, were subsequently fixed to the clap nodes along the length of the building.

The innovative project, which pushes the boundaries of current technology, while also making use of traditional technologies, exemplifies how to use a sustainable natural resource efficiently. The success of the project was only possible as a result of the enlightened commissioning and continuous support of the client, as well as the close collaboration of a dedicated design and construction team.

Internal view of the workshop.

View of the east entrance and the south elevation with its cedar cladding, polycarbonate clerestory and central roof ribbon made of Roofkrete.

Case study: Straw bales

**Hidden Villa,
Wolken Education Center**
Los Altos Hills, California, US

Client: Hidden Villa
Architect: San Luis Sustainability Group (Ken Haggard and Polly Cooper)
Straw bale expert: Scott Clark
Energy consultant: Jennifer Rennick
Main contractor: John Swearingen of Skillful Means Inc.
Completed: 2000

The straw bale walls have been covered with a layer of mesh and render and lime washed.

Near the entrance there is a viewing window showing visitors the straw bale material.

Straw is the stalk of cereals and grasses including rice, barley, oats and wheat. Straw is a by-product of farming that can be used for animal bedding and for conditioning soil, but currently the amount produced exceeds the amount needed for these purposes. In the 1800s, the settlers in Nebraska started building with this waste product creating houses of load-bearing straw bales. Today, besides its agricultural uses, straw is baled and used as wall construction material; mixed in with clay-based building materials; compressed and faced with kraft paper to make non-load-bearing internal partitions; used for thatched roofs; and bonded with non-formaldehyde resin to make building boards of comparable strength to plywood.

In the Central Valley in California, rice straw is considered a waste product and is often burnt on the fields, creating serious pollution problems. This was one of the numerous environmental reasons for choosing straw as a building material for the Wolken Education Center at Hidden Villa.

Hidden Villa is an environmental and multicultural education centre set in a nature reserve and organic farm of approximately 650 hectare. Founded in 1924 by Frank and Josephine Duveneck to promote multicultural understanding, Hidden Villa was donated to the community in 1984 to continue its activities. Today, Hidden Villa offers multicultural summer camps, environmental education, volunteering opportunities, access to the nature reserve and more. The buildings on the site are demonstrations of sustainable building practice, providing education and inspiration for visitors of all ages as well as minimising their environmental impact.

Materials for all the buildings had to be selected following a set of environmental criteria, considering the whole life of a material. Materials with low-embodied energy, natural, recycled, reclaimed and local materials were preferred. Straw fitted the criteria well, being a natural and waste material resourced locally.

The Wolken Education Center uses straw bales within a timber frame. The frame supports the roof and the straw is non-load-bearing. A load-bearing straw bale construction would also be possible. Straw bales vary in size between two-string bales of 360 x 460 x 920 millimetres, and the larger three-string bales, which are 600 millimetres thick. The Wolken Center uses two-string bales laid flat. Bales can also be laid on edge. The bales have to be tightly compacted and tend to settle after construction. However, with non-load-bearing bale construction, most of the settlement occurs within the construction period and before the finishes are applied and is therefore generally not a problem. They are set on a concrete foundation elevated off the ground, stacked like bricks and pinned vertically through the bales from the foundation to the wall plate. Materials appropriate for pinning the bales range from metal bars to hazel, willow or bamboo rods. Here metal was used.

Window and door openings were made with wood and the windows are fibreglass and have low-e double glazed units.

The Center walls are finished externally with a cement render on a metal lath. Internally a cement plaster with a thin finishing coat avoids the need for a paint finish. Once plastered on both sides, straw bale walls provide good resistance to fire. Alternative finishes would have been clay and lime plasters and renders. These are more vapour permeable, allow the structure to breath and can be applied directly to the bales without a lath, owing to their more flexible nature.

Straw has a good insulating capacity and a 600-millimetre thick rendered straw bale wall is said to provide a U-value of 0.12–0.09 Wm²°C (0.018 Btu/ft²h°F). This has contributed to an overall energy-efficiency strategy that has proved very successful. The Wolken Education Center is expected to save 73.5 per cent of the energy used in a traditionally built option and to have a total annual energy consumption of 41 kWh/m² (13 kBtu/sqft): a high performance with a low tech material.

The overhanging roof provides protection for the bale structure and solar shading for the building. It also creates a seating area in the shade.

View of the Wolken Center from the south. In front is the vegetable growing area. The solar hot water panels, the PV and the clerestory windows are on the south-facing roof.

The soft curves of the straw walls give the interior a cosy feeling. The propane heater provides heat for extremely cold weather. The clerestory brings light into the rooms.

Below the windows and the horizontal strip are the water tanks providing thermal mass.

4.3.5 Sustainable design features

Site and ecology
The building is designed to be as small as possible to reduce overall impacts.

Community and culture
The Hidden Villa's main objectives include promoting multicultural understanding.

Health
The internal plaster finish was left unpainted to avoid volatile organic compounds associated with standard paints. Ample natural light creates a healthy indoor environment.

Materials
Metal was used on the roof for its durability (four times that of shingle roof) and recyclability. The countertops in the conference rooms were made of recycled newspaper and sunflower hulls bound in soybean resin. Recycled cellulose insulation was used in the roof. Recycled glass tiles were used in the bathroom.
All timber was either reclaimed or FSC certified. The kitchen cabinets and other fixtures and fittings used trees that had fallen in a hurricane or other bad weather conditions. The roof structure is a truss that utilises smaller pieces of certified wood.

Energy
The highly insulated building is orientated to take advantage of solar heat gains. The sun penetrates the building and heats up the thermally massive floor and the 230-mm thick water tanks integrated within the thickness of the wall under the windows. The plaster finish was also designed to provide thermal mass. These absorb the sun's heat throughout the day and release it once the sun has set.
Hot water is provided by a solar hot water panel. A propane heater provides back-up heating for hot water and space heating.
Good natural light reduces the need for electrical lighting. All lights are compact fluorescent and a super-efficient fridge designed to operate with PVs was installed. A grid-connected 4.6 KW peak output PV array provides electricity to the centre, selling surplus to the grid and buying back electricity when required. The PV panels are washed weekly to reduce the dust build-up, which occurs particularly in summer.

Water
The building is designed to collect rainwater from the building roofs and use it for flushing WCs. However, county permission has not been forthcoming until now. An underground holding tank will be installed once permission is granted. The plumbing allows for future collection of greywater for irrigation purposes.

4.4 Minimising Manufacturing Impacts

When selecting new building materials, as opposed to recycled or reclaimed ones, consideration should be given to their source, whether it is renewable, non-renewable or plentiful, and to the manufacturing processes involved in their production.

All building products are derived from natural materials – even those considered synthetic, like plastics, are made from a natural material, which, in the case of plastics, is oil. However, the manufacturing processes range from simple to extremely complex. Timber needs minimal processing, while steel derived from iron ore, which is cleaned, sintered, smelted out, and reduced at 1700-1800°C, is associated with far more intense processes. Manufacturing processes require energy and can also be associated with pollution to air, water and ground. In the UK, the manufacture and transport of construction materials are responsible for 10 per cent of CO_2, 0.7 per cent of volatile organic compounds including methane, 2.5 per cent of nitrous oxides and nearly 8 per cent of sulphur dioxide emissions to air (Howard 2000). The more complex the manufacturing process, the more likely it is to be associated with environmental impacts.

As discussed in the previous section, many renewable materials require minimal processing, but there are also non-renewable materials that can be used in their natural state. Construction systems, including rammed earth, earth bricks, adobe, earthbags and cob, make use primarily of earth with minimal additives and can be constructed by hand. Materials such as clay plasters also make use of essentially unprocessed natural materials. Stone and slate are also generally used in their natural state; however, their resourcing and manufacturing impacts can be considerable. Mining can substantially change the natural landscape and while mining areas can be restored, in particular smaller ones, the process can permanently affect the local flora and fauna and even alter the ground water conditions. The mining and finishing of stones are increasingly mechanised, therefore are energy intensive, and the weight of the material means that its

The Autonomous Environmental Information Centre at the Centre for Alternative Technology.

transport is also energy intensive.

Earth materials, on the other hand, are plentiful and their resourcing impacts limited. The earth has to be dug up from just below the top soil, a process that can have similar impacts to slate and stone mining. Earth construction can, however, make use of earth resourced from the building site itself, if of appropriate quality, which substantially reduces the resourcing and transportation impacts.

By minimising or simplifying the manufacturing processes, the embodied energy of the materials and the pollution during manufacturing is reduced. For example, earth bricks can be sun dried or kiln dried, the difference being the amount of energy used, which increases by 0.2 MJ/kg for every 100°C increase in firing temperature (Berge 2000), and the pollution from the firing process, which produces sulphur and nitrogen oxides, as well as fluoride and chloride gases, depending on the type of clay. The environmental impacts of the mechanised manufacture of fired bricks are therefore far higher than those of handmade air-dried bricks.

While unfired earth construction is not appropriate for all situations, its use is increasing in developed countries and adding to the vast number of existing earth dwellings that house a third of the world's population. The methods of earth construction vary depending on the materials and technologies locally available, but there are two basic variations: monolithic and brick construction, including adobe and compressed bricks (see 4.4.2).

Monolithic constructions include rammed earth construction (see Thurgoona Campus case study, p.177) and constructions that mix clay with fibres such as cob (see Eden case study, p.180), hemp or light earth construction. These can be used as structural materials and also as infill materials, typically within a timber frame. The traditional infill materials for timber frames is wattle and daub, where timber laths are formed into a grid within the timber frame and plastered with earth plasters. Hemp, light earth and rammed earth construction are less labour-intensive and present promising alternatives for more widespread use.

The above construction systems are not often perceived as compatible with the contemporary construction requirements for maximum speed and for technologies that are familiar to the general workforce. It is, therefore, necessary to ensure that the standard materials and technologies are associated with the minimal manufacturing impacts possible. Increasing environmental awareness has resulted in some building material manufacturers considering how to improve their manufacturing processes. A number of brick manufacturers in the UK, for instance, have begun to address issues of energy efficiency and pollution emissions. Manufacturers can be encouraged to improve their environmental performance, by requesting them to formulate and implement an environmental programme, and seek certification through an environmental management system such as the ISO 14001:1996 Environmental Management System.

Certain materials with particularly high manufacturing impacts, such as steel, PVC, aluminium, cement or concrete, can be substituted with materials with reduced impacts,

4.4.1 Some environmental impacts of resourcing and manufacturing aluminium and PVC

Environmental impact of resourcing aluminium
Bauxite strip mining to produce aluminium causes loss of rainforest and the flora and fauna in it. Most bauxite is mined using hydropower, which is associated with the flooding of areas of rainforest. Red mud has to be disposed of in the process and is sometimes disposed of in lagoons where it leaches alkali and amphoteric metals into the water.

Environmental impact of manufacturing aluminium
Aluminium production is associated with emissions to air of nitrous oxides contributing to global warming, acid rain and photochemical smog; sulphur dioxide associated with acid rain; discharges of heavy metals into sewers; discharges of sludge containing fluoride and carbon to land; emissions of fluoride and carbon monoxide to air; emissions of fluoride, hydrocarbons and solids to water.

Embodied energy required in manufacture of aluminium
Aluminium manufactured from ore requires 180-250 GJ/tonne 77 per cent of energy due to electrolytic reduction and 17 per cent due to alumina refining. Aluminium manufactured from recycled material requires 10-18 GJ/tonne.
(ECRA 1995)

Environmental impact of resourcing PVC
Crude oil is processed into naphtha which is processed to produce ethylene. The impact of oil resourcing includes pollution from flaring, marine and land pollution from oil spills and leaks (particularly from tanker accidents) affecting the flora and fauna. Oil transport is associated with major environmental accidents
Natural gas can also be processed to produce ethylene.

Environmental impact of production of PVC
The manufacture of PVC begins with chlorine, which is a poisonous gas, used to chlorinate ethylene to produce ethylene dichloride. This process produces dioxins, which are classified by the US Environment Protection Agency as probable carcinogens and powerful hormone disruptors, associated with a reduction in sperm count in animals. Ethylene dichloride is converted to vinyl chloride monomer, a known carcinogen, and then into polyvinylchloride. PVC often requires the addition of plasticisers, fillers and heavy metals such as cadmium and lead, known to affect the nervous system. The most common plasticisers used are phthalates, which have been identified as possible human carcinogens and as hormone disruptors that mimic the female hormone oestrogen (see also Chapter 3.2 for impacts in use).
(Greenpeace 1997, EPA 1994, ECRA 1995)

4.4.2 Earth brick construction

Adobe buildings are made from bricks of wet mud with enough clay content to bind the clay. Straw or sand may be added to adobe bricks to reduce the shrinkage caused by the clay. The bricks, approximately 350 x 2 50 x 100 millimetres, are made by hand by placing the mixed mud in a form, and air-drying them for several weeks. They are used to construct walls by binding the bricks with a clay mortar. Machines can also be used and the bricks can be fired, all of which adds to the embodied energy of the material. Well-maintained adobe structures can have a long life.

Compressed earth bricks make use of pressure rather than water to shape the bricks. These bricks, which may or may not make use of a stabiliser such as cement or lime, are made by manually or mechanically pressing subsoil into moulds made of timber or other material. Stabilised bricks are left to cure in a damp environment and unstabilised bricks are dried slowly to avoid cracking. Natural or cement mortars and plasters can then be used to build and finish the construction.

Earthbags, which make use of loose earth, were developed into a viable building system by architect Nader Khalili, who was initially interested in options for construction on other planets using local materials, minimising the transportation of materials from the earth. The system developed makes use of polypropylene or jute or hemp bags, filled with the soil from the development site, and used like bricks to form strong and even earthquake-proof dome-shaped structures.

The rammed earth wall supports the roof.

such as recycled steel and aluminium, and, in the case of cement-based products, lime-based products. Cement and concrete are ubiquitous in the construction industry, but are associated with high CO_2 emissions. The manufacture of cement involves firing the raw materials (limestone or chalk, silica and clay containing alumina) in kilns at peak temperatures of 1400°C, where the calcium carbonate from the limestone or chalk is transformed into the oxides of calcium, silicon, aluminium and iron, while giving off large quantities of CO_2. Because of this process, the cement industry is responsible for 8–10 per cent of CO_2 emissions globally. Like cement, lime manufacture is also associated with CO_2 emissions, albeit reduced compared to cement. However, unlike cement, its curing process reabsorbs a significant amount of CO_2.

Commonly used substitutes for cement include lime mortars and renders. Less common is the use of lime to make concrete, yet it has been used successfully in a number of projects, including the Autonomous Environmental Information Centre, at the Centre for Alternative Technology (CAT) in Wales. The CAT is one of the first environmental centres in the UK and has more than 25 years of experience in experimenting with new materials and technologies. The Information Centre made use of Limecrete rather than concrete, has a rammed earth internal wall and avoided the use of PVC.

There aren't always simple solutions to selecting materials with low manufacturing impacts. Reliance on formal certification, such as the ISO 14001, may prove misleading, as such certification is expensive and beyond the means of many small, but potentially environmentally sound, manufacturers. Apart from building with natural, minimal impact materials, architects will have to verify their sources. While asking for environmental credentials is time-consuming, it sends a powerful message to the industry that environmentally sound materials are wanted.

Case study: Rammed earth

In 1993, Charles Sturt University bought a site from the Albury–Wodonga Development Corporation for the development of a new university campus. The new site is near Thurgoona, 10 kilometres north of Albury, a town on the Victoria–New South Wales border. In 1996, the first new building, a student pavilion, was completed and set the sustainable design agenda for the whole campus design. The new campus, which by 2007 should house the staff and students from the Albury city campus in addition to the 500 students and 100 staff currently on site, was designed to be as autonomous as possible and minimise its impact on the environment.

By 2000, various other buildings were completed, including a new teaching complex with a 200-seat lecture theatre, an administrative building and a teaching block for the School of Environmental and Information Sciences for 100 staff, accommodation facilities for 32 students, and a laundry block. A further two student cottages, including two rooms for students with disabilities, and a recreation building were completed in 2003 and a new teaching block for the School of Business is due for completion in 2005.

The sustainability strategy for the whole campus addressed the use of materials, water and energy while producing a healthy and attractive environment for students and staff. In addition to creating an energy- and water-efficient development, the grounds are landscaped in an environmentally sensitive way. They include areas designated for revegetation with the site's original vegetation and an arboretum containing plants from different geographic regions in the world that were originally part of Gondwanaland and Eurasia.

The approach to material selection aimed at minimising resource use and embodied energy, and maximising the use of materials that do not negatively affect human health. The healthy materials used included wool insulation in the roof, wool and linoleum flooring, and specially prepared non-toxic paints and natural oil timber treatments. The use of PVC was minimised. Renewable, recycled and low-embodied energy materials were selected, such as recycled timber supplemented by plantation timber for the joinery, including all windows. Reclaimed library shelving, steel and glass were sourced from a state library in Sydney.

In line with the desire to use materials with minimal impacts on resources, energy and health, the main construction material for the development is rammed earth. Rammed earth is a natural, non-toxic and healthy material that can provide thermal mass to a building. If sourced locally, it can also have a very low-embodied energy.

At Thurgoona, the solid unreinforced rammed earth external and internal walls are 300–600 millimetres thick. They support the *in situ* first-floor concrete slabs and roof structure and are intrinsic to the energy strategy since they provide thermal mass to the building. The external walls are uninsulated, as is usual for the local climate. The application of external insulation may have improved the thermal performance of the external walls, but would have been detrimental to the aesthetic integrity of the scheme.

Thurgoona Campus
Charles Sturt University, Albury, New South Wales, Australia

Client: Charles Sturt University
Architect: Marci Webster-Mannison
Engineers: Advanced Environmental Concepts, Branco Boilers and Engineering
Completed: 1999 – 2007

Rammed earth piers to student building.

See also: natural ventilation **Chapter 5.1**

See also: solar thermal 1,2 **Chapter 5.3**

See also: composting toilets **Chapter 6.1**

See also: sustainable drainage **Chapter 6.3**

Small glazed opening in rammed earth wall.

Earth is a naturally occurring and abundant material. It does not give off harmful gasses and does not leach toxins into the earth or water course. Rammed earth walls therefore do not contribute to the depletion of scarce resources and pose no health risks to the users and the environment. The rammed earth walls also have the advantage of being fire and termite resistant and reasonably durable in the southern Australian climate. They require only minimal maintenance.

Suitable earth, described as 'road dirt', for the walls at Thurgoona campus was sourced from a nearby quarry as the soil on site was not suitable. Rammed earth structures can involve mixing a stabiliser, typically cement, with the earth to improve material cohesion. At Thurgoona the earth was mixed with 5 per cent cement and water to achieve the appropriate consistency. The walls were produced by compacting earth in between prefabricated plywood formwork that was reused throughout the project and replaced as necessary. Some of the walls are now several years old and have aged well, without substantial degradation and retaining their aesthetic appeal.

The rammed earth walls panel junction detail.

Teaching block with rammed earth end walls, roof vent and window shading.

Rammed earth walls being erected for the new teaching block.

4.4.3 Sustainable design features

Site and ecology
The site had been cleared for farming, causing erosion and the degradation of soil. The new development is restoring native planting.

Community and culture
The campus is used for educational purposes and is developed for ecotourism.

Health
Natural light is provided throughout. Healthy materials are used where possible. See main text.

Materials
Renewable, reclaimed, recycled and low-embodied energy materials are used. See main text.

Energy
The buildings are orientated east–west, maximising northern heat gains in winter. Roof overhangs and corrugated metal window shields shade windows from the summer sun. Insulation is installed within the ceiling construction to reduce heat loss in winter and heat gains in summer. Walls are uninsulated.

Thermal mass helps stabilise the daily temperature fluctuations. Roof-mounted solar hot water panels circulate water through concrete slabs to provide space heating in winter as well as cooling, by dissipating the heat to the clear skies at night, in summer.

Cooling is also provided through natural ventilation assisted by ceiling fans and spray misting of the lecture theatre ventilation (see Chapter 5.1). Night ventilation to cool the thermal mass is provided through automatic vents below windows and through shafts at high level.

Water
Rainwater is collected for use in the laundry and for watering the landscaping. A strategy of treating greywater and rainwater in the wetlands on site and the use of composting toilets obviates the need for a sewer connection.

Case study: Cob

Eden Centre, bus shelter
Cornwall, UK

Client: Eden Centre
Designers: Jackie Abey and Jill Smallcombe
Main contractor: Back to Earth
Completed: 2002

The cob walls are protected by an overhanging corrugated steel roof.

The cob sits on top of a stone base to prevent it becoming saturated with moisture.

The Eden Centre is a very popular garden visitor attraction located in a disused china-clay mine in Cornwall, comprising three large-scale greenhouses with tropical and desert plants. The complex is surrounded by local flora and served by a visitor centre and other supporting structures. One of these structures is a delightful cob building designed by the artists Jackie Abey and Jill Smallcombe. The building provides a shuttle bus waiting area and toilet facilities. The structure is essentially open to the elements, with larch thinnings to support the corrugated steel roof; underfloor heating provides protection against frost and minimal comfort levels. The use of cob, a natural low environmental impact building material, is in line with the ethos of the Eden Centre, which concerns itself with the protection of plants and the environment.

Cob buildings date back to the fifteenth century and are particularly common in south-west England and in Wales. Cob is made with a mixture containing 3–20 per cent clay subsoil, straw, water and sometimes sand or crushed flint. The materials are mixed into a homogenous mass, originally by treading onto the mixture, but can also now be done by using a tractor. The walls, generally 600 millimetres thick, are formed in lifts of 450 millimetres. The lift is left to dry for a couple of weeks before the next lift is formed, creating walls of up to 7 metres in height. Windows and doors are formed with timber as the structure is erected. The cob walls can be plastered and rendered with lime products or left uncovered depending on the use of the structure. Over 40,000 cob buildings, mainly historic ones, are thought to be in existence in Devon alone. In the 1800s, as fired bricks became more affordable, cob was abandoned, but with the Kevin McCabe cob house built in 1994, cob began enjoying a revival.

The environmental advantages of cob include the use of a natural plentiful material, clay, and the use of a renewable material, straw. If the materials can be sourced locally, the transport impacts are also reduced, and if it is built manually, the overall embodied energy is minimal. In addition to the environmental credentials, the cob construction has a very tactile appeal. The rounded edges of the walls are reminiscent of plastered straw bale, but here the texture of the material is more evident. At the Eden Centre's cob building the structure's rich textures and the play of light provide interest and would make waiting inside it a pleasant experience.

The cob structure creates captivating plays of light and texture.

Reclaimed buckets are used to make openings.

4.4.4 Sustainable design features

Site and ecology
The Eden Centre made use of an abandoned china-clay mine and has restored the site through extensive replanting.

Community and culture
The building makes use of a traditional material and building technology. By displaying the material's potential the building contributes to keeping the tradition alive and promoting its use. By specifying cob crafts people are also given the opportunity to ply their trade.

Health
The building has good natural light and has the potential to enhance the visitor's wellbeing by providing interest and comfort.

Materials
See main text.

Energy
Minimal energy is needed for this type of structure. Lighting is energy efficient and the underfloor heating efficiently provides the minimal heat required for the structure.

Rainwater is collected in a standard rainwater gutter.

The larch thinnings support the roof, their natural texture matching that of the cob.

4.5 Materials and Energy

4.5.1 Embodied energy comparison

US study of energy needed to manufacture and build a 2200 m² warehouse

(Timber Trade Federation 1995)

Construction type	Energy in GJ	Scale
Timber throughout	1480	1.0
Concrete block, timber roof	2550	1.7
Prefabricated steel throughout	3150	2.1
Concrete tilt up walls, timber roof	4030	2.7
Prefabricated steel, aluminium cladding	4830	3.3

4.5.2 Energy needs and savings associated with materials

Energy requirements of materials and building products	Building operational energy savings through materials use
– Resourcing activities (e.g. mining, harvesting)	– Reduced heating and cooling requirements (e.g. insulation and thermal mass)
– Manufacturing processes (including operating machinery, running a business)	– Increased efficiencies of machinery (e.g. MVHR, boilers)
– Transport of base resource to manufacturing plant and from the plant to the site	
– Installation on site (e.g. machinery)	
– Maintenance requirements (e.g. transport of spare parts, machinery)	
– Demolition requirements (machinery, transport and disposal)	

The manufacture of building products requires energy, materials and, often, water. The embodied energy of a material is the energy required to harvest or mine materials, transport them, process and manufacture them and finally install them in a building. Minimising this energy, which is generally still produced by burning fossil fuels, contributes to reducing CO_2 emissions responsible for global warming (see Chapter 6).

The method for calculating the embodied energy of materials has not been standardised and consequently different values for the same material can be found. The differences are the result of a number of discrepancies in the calculation methods. Embodied energy values can refer to the primary energy used, i.e. the calorific value of the fuel supplied to the energy-generating plant; or the delivered energy, the energy used at the point of manufacture. Considering that the production of electricity has an efficiency of approximately 30 per cent, in other words the primary energy is three times the delivered energy, this difference in calculation can result in significant discrepancies. The measure used can also vary; embodied energy values can be kWh per tonne or per volume or per building element. Furthermore, different materials will be required in different amounts for the same purpose; for example, the weight of a wall constructed in timber will be much lower than if constructed in concrete, so comparing the embodied energy of a kilogram of concrete with one of timber will not be an accurate representation of the embodied energy of the two wall options.

Everything else being equal, materials with the lowest embodied energy should be selected. However, to overcome the discrepancies mentioned above, it is necessary to assess the construction of the building as a whole, using the same type of energy values (delivered or primary energy). This was done in the study illustrated in 4.5.1 that calculated the energy needed to build a 2,200m warehouse using a selection of different building systems.

The embodied energy of materials should not be considered in isolation, but rather in the context of the total energy needs of a building including its operation. The embodied energy of a building has been estimated to make up between 6 per cent and 25 per cent of the total energy consumption for a building over 50 years. This percentage depends on the life span of the building and the operating energy requirements. As buildings become more energy efficient to run, the embodied energy becomes a more significant percentage of the total. Conversely, the longer the life span of a building, the less significant the embodied energy becomes, making up a reduced percentage of the overall energy requirements. If the embodied energy makes up 6 per cent and the running energy 94 per cent of the total energy use in the first 50 years, over 100 years the embodied energy will have dropped to 3 per cent.

It is also important to remember that certain relatively high embodied energy materials contribute to lowering the running energy of buildings. For example, concrete is a material associated with high levels of CO_2 emissions resulting from the relatively energy-intensive manufacturing process and the chemical reaction necessary to manufacture cement, which emits CO_2 as a by-product. Concrete is, however, also a material that can provide the high thermal mass used as part of a low energy strategy to absorb internal and external heat gains and reduce cooling loads. The embodied energy of concrete is often less significant than the operating energy saved through its use over the lifetime of a building.

Similarly, when considering the insulation of buildings in cold and temperate climates, more insulation increases the building's embodied energy and lowers the operating energy. For example, the yearly heat loss of a dwelling with a highly insulated external envelope comprising 300 millimetres of cellulose insulation was calculated to be 1090 kWh/yr, which was two-thirds of that of the same dwelling with only 100 millimetres of insulation. The additional insulation was calculated to have an embodied energy of 1416 kWh, which was three times the energy saved through its use, resulting in a three-year payback period. Using insulation with a higher embodied energy would have longer payback periods, but would still be significantly advantageous considering a 50- or 100-year life span. Other calculations suggest that for domestic construction in Britain, the optimum insulation thickness is approximately 600 millimetres (Borer and Harris 1998). Higher insulation levels would result in embodied energy values that may not be recuperated through reductions of operating energy.

A similar consideration is required when considering transport energy. In most cases selecting materials manufactured close to the construction site reduces the need transport these materials. When building in Wales, using Welsh slates clearly involves less transport than using slates imported from Spain. Using local materials often does not affect the design of the building; for example, clay bricks from the south of the UK are not dissimilar to those from more northern regions. Using local materials also has some community benefits, in that it can help support the local economy and skills. On the other hand, when it comes to certain technologically demanding building elements it may not be possible to source an appropriate quality material or technology locally. If such building products affect the energy efficiency of the building, more energy may be saved over the lifetime of a building by installing a high quality, energy-efficient building element sourced from further away, which therefore requires more transport energy, than a locally sourced energy-inefficient building element. As environmental impacts associated with materials are better understood, the outdated reliance on embodied energy as the only measure to assess the environmental credentials of materials is replaced with a more holistic assessment method. Nonetheless, embodied energy remains one of the criteria for sustainable material selection, encouraging the use of materials manufactured locally, with low resourcing, manufacturing and transport energy requirements.

4.5.3 Embodied energy of selected materials

Material	KWh/tonne (1)	KWh/m³ (1)	MJ/kg (2)
Fletton bricks	175	300	2
Non-fletton bricks	860	1462	3
Engineering bricks	1120	2016	3.5
Clay tiles	800	1520	8
Concrete tiles	30	630	2
Local stone tiles	200	450	0.3
Local slates	200	540	0.1
Single-ply membrane	45,000	47,000	70
Concrete 1:3:6	275	600	1
Concrete 1:2:4	360	800	
Lightweight blocks	500	600	4
Autoclaved blocks	1300	800	4
Natural aggregate	30	45	
Crushed granite aggregate	100	150	
Lightweight aggregate	500	300	
Cement	2,200	2,860	
Sand/cement render	277	400	
Plaster/plasterboard	890	900	5
Steel	13,200	103,000	25
Copper	15,000	133,000	70
Aluminium	27,000	75,600	184
Imported softwood	1450	7540	3
Timber local air-dried	200	110	
Timber local green oak	200	220	
Glass	9200	23,000	8
Plastic	45,000	47,000	
Polyethylene (PE)			67
Polyvinylchloride (PVC)			84
Plastic insulation		1125	
Expanded polystyrene			75
Ureaformaldehyde			40
Polyurethane			110
Cork			4
Mineral wool		230	16
Cellulose insulation		133	21
Straw bale (3)			0.13-0.25
Woodwool		900	20

((1) Talbott 1995, (2) Berge 2000, (3) ACTAC 1998)

Case study: Minimising transport

BedZED
Beddington, UK

Client: Peabody Trust
Environmental Consultants: Bioregional
Architect: Bill Dunster Architects
Services engineers: Ove Arups & Partners
Structural engineers: Ellis and Moore
Quantity surveyor: Gardiner and Thoebald
Completed: 2002

4.5.4 Energy use of different means of transport

Type of transport	MJ/ton/km
Diesel road transport	1.6
Diesel sea transport	0.6
Diesel rail transport	0.6
Electric rail transport	0.2

The development makes use of energy from a CHP system and building-integrated PVs.

The Beddington Zero (fossil) Energy Development (BedZED) is a mixed tenure housing development located in Beddington, in the London borough of Sutton, which aims to address sustainability issues in a holistic manner. The design of the scheme considered issues ranging from land and transport use, to materials and operational resource consumption. The scheme benefited from the enthusiasm of a progressive client and a dedicated design team, but was also supported by the local authority. The Sutton Borough argued against selling the development land to the highest bidder on the basis that other benefits resulting from the sustainability features of the BedZED proposal would outweigh the loss in the sales revenue. This enlightened approach from the Borough involved employing an environmental economist to assess these benefits, which were identified as resulting primarily from reductions in CO_2 emissions in the first 20–25 years of operation, and were given a monetary value based on the cost of achieving the European Union targets for reductions in CO_2 emissions. As part of its planning permission requirements, the Borough also imposed legal obligations on the development to implement a Green Transport Plan; and a Section 106 agreement required the developer to build a football pitch adjacent to the site for the enjoyment of the whole community.

The development built on a 1.7-hectare site and comprising 82 dwellings (271 habitable rooms) and 2500 square metres of commercial and community spaces achieves high development density of 48 dph or 159 hrh. Impact on the local flora and fauna was minimised and efforts were made to provide planted communal areas for the residents to enjoy; and the proximity to public transport combined with the provision of work units on site encourages reduced car dependence. The development addresses resource issues, but above all it aims to become virtually CO_2 neutral. It has been estimated that when all the energy-efficiency features are fully implemented and when about half of the residents have reduced their car use to 8,500 kilometres per year and switched to electric cars charged from the building-integrated PVs, total CO_2 emissions of the development could be a mere 4 per cent of equivalent suburban developments.

View of south-facing residential units from the main road.

The building aesthetics advertise its environmental aims.

View of the communal open space.

The aim of reducing CO_2 emissions affected all aspects of the design including the selection of materials which, where possible, were selected to be natural, recycled or reclaimed and have low resourcing impact and low embodied energy. As a result most of the timber was sourced from certified suppliers and a variety of reclaimed and recycled materials was used, including reclaimed timber studwork, reclaimed structural steel, reclaimed floorboards, reclaimed ply shuttering, recycled crushed glass sand and 2,100 tonnes of recycled crushed concrete.

In order to reduce the embodied energy of the materials, one of the targets set was to procure all materials within a 60-kilometre radius. Limiting the distance from which the materials are sourced reduces the energy use and pollution and also supports the local industry; 52 per cent of the materials were sourced from this target distance, including most of the heavy materials, such as bricks, blocks aggregate, 50 per cent of the concrete and the imported topsoil. The weatherboarding was locally sourced and 90 per cent of the internal studwork was reclaimed. Exceptions were made, when using local materials would excessively compromise cost or the construction programme. Windows were an example: the high performance windows are Danish as UK-manufactured windows would have proved too expensive.

As a result the average sourcing distance was 107 kilometres compared with the national average of over 160 kilometres. Construction-related haulage in the UK accounts for 30 per cent of all road freight and produces 28 million tonnes of CO_2 (Freight Transport Association). By selecting local materials BedZED's CO_2 emissions are 120 tonnes less than equivalent developments. This also represents a reduction in embodied energy of 2 per cent.

4.5.5 Sustainable design features

Site and ecology
The development is on a brownfield site and integrates working spaces, so residents can work close to home. Space not needed for work was converted into dwellings. Existing ecology has been protected and enhanced. The planners imposed a Green Transport Plan and as the development is on a main street with several bus links and only 700 metres away from a train station, it is almost within the recommended distances for encouraging the use of public transport (see 1.2.3). The London City Car Club has three cars at BedZED and two in Wallington, and allows residents the use of a car without the need for car ownership. Electrical car recharging points are available.

Community and culture
Residents are issued with a handbook that explains the operation of the buildings and natural features of the site. Local labour was used where possible. The mixture of dwelling sizes should encourage a mix of resident types. A childcare facility has moved into the development.

Health
Carpets were avoided.

Materials See main text.

Energy
The building structure is airtight and well insulated. Living spaces face south, making use of solar gains, while work spaces face north to avoid overheating. The houses have small conservatories the full height of the building and are ventilated by means of a wind-driven ventilation with heat exchanger that recovers 70 per cent of the heat.

Fabric U-values:
  Walls – 0.11 W/m² K (R51)
  Floors and roof – 0.10 W/m²K (R58)
  Windows, doors and rooflights – 1.20 W/m²K
  (0.21 Btu/ft²h°F)

A combined heat and power (CHP) district heating system, burning local tree surgery and timber waste. provides domestic hot water and some of the electricity. The system, which includes building-integrated PVs, is grid connected and can export and import electricity as required. Average space heating requirements are 16.2 kWh/m²/yr, almost achieving Passivhaus standards, representing a reduction of 73 per cent compared to UK new-build homes. A 44 per cent reduction in domestic hot water consumption and a 25 per cent reduction in electricity were also achieved.

Water
Water-saving appliances have been installed, including dual flush 3/5-litre WCs. Rainwater is collected to flush WCs. The water meter is installed where it can easily be seen and monitored by users. Average water use per dwelling per day is 76 litres, a 50 per cent reduction compared to UK average consumption. Sewage is treated in a Living Machine and SUD is applied throughout the site.

Case study: Materials to help save running costs

PowerGen HQ
Coventry, UK

Client: PowerGen plc.
Architect: Bennetts Associates
Services engineers: Ernest Griffiths and Son Consulting engineers
Structural engineers: Curtins Consulting Engineers
Quantity surveyor: Midlands
Main contractor: Laings
Completed: 1995

The exposed ceiling coffers house the lighting rafts and smoke detectors.

The offices are arranged around the atrium.

The PowerGen headquarters office, in Westwood Business Park near Coventry, was one of the first buildings in the UK to employ the building's concrete structure to provide thermal mass as part of an energy strategy. Despite concrete being a high embodied energy material and cement, in particular, being associated with high levels of CO_2 emissions, the concrete thermal mass was selected as part of a sustainable low energy strategy for the building.

The PowerGen headquarters building, now owned by Eon, houses over 600 people in 14,000 square metres of office space and has proved to be a very popular building with its occupants. The aim of the building design was to provide an energy-efficient and comfortable environment, promoting the well-being of the occupants while minimising the building's environmental impact.

Located on the edge of a nature park in quiet surroundings, the building benefits from an ideal setting for natural ventilation. Three office floors are arranged on 10.8-metre floor plates around a central 113-metre long atrium. This set-up made cross-ventilation across each floor plate possible. However, for the natural ventilation to work effectively, internal heat gains had to be minimised. Cores with stairs, toilets, refreshment points, and copier rooms were located at both ends of the building and at its centre, segregating activities with high heat gains from the main office spaces. Other typical sources of internal heat gains, such as lighting, were also designed to be as efficient as possible and reduce heat build-up. External heat gains were minimised through the use of shading on the south elevation and the roof.

To further reduce the effects of heat gains, the concrete structure is left exposed to absorb heat throughout the day. The *in situ* concrete coffers are the main exposed concrete element, as the concrete floor is covered with a raised floor to house services. The windows are divided into three panels, of which the two bottom ones are manually operated, allowing the building occupants to adjust the ventilation and avoid desktop draughts. The top one is operated by the building management system to provide night-time ventilation and cool the concrete soffits, dissipating the heat absorbed during the day and enhancing the cooling capacity for the next day. In the event, the concrete was found to retain its capacity to absorb heat over a period of several days, without night cooling. During the heating season, the concrete can also contribute to reducing heating needs by absorbing excessive internal heat gains and reradiating heat when the air temperature drops below the concrete temperature.

The natural ventilation and high thermal mass strategy have proved very successful, and even during excessively hot spells the average internal temperature is several degrees lower than the outside temperature, with indoor temperatures being as much as 5°C lower than peak outside temperatures. Other buildings that have also used concrete as part of their cooling strategy have reported similar results: exposed concrete thermal mass can reduce internal temperatures by between 3-4°C, effectively providing a cooling capacity of 25 W/m2, and peak temperatures are delayed by up to six hours (BCA 2001).

Other materials can also be used to provide thermal mass. Dense materials such as stone, brick or rammed earth may seem more environmentally friendly options; however, at PowerGen concrete provided other benefits. The concrete coffers could be shaped to maximise the surface area and the temperature exchange with the air, and in economic terms a concrete structure proved very cost-effective. But the biggest advantage is that the thermal mass could be provided by the building structure, a substantial element of the building with spans of 10.8 and 7.2 metres over four levels. Material specification has to take into account the context within which the buildings are commissioned. Modern office buildings are often framed, multistorey structures, commonly built in concrete. While domestic size offices may be able to take advantage of other low-embodied energy construction systems, large buildings will continue to depend on concrete or steel structures. In these cases the sustainable approach is to use each building element in the most efficient way possible, making one element work in more than one way. Taking into account the need to provide a structure and thermal mass, concrete, despite its embodied energy, is a solution that works effectively. The system used successfully at PowerGen was subsequently used in many other buildings, and is now a common low energy approach to providing cooling in buildings.

4.5.6 Sustainable design features

Site and ecology
The natural surrounding environment has been retained and enhanced.

Health
The spaces benefit from ample natural light and the atrium creates a naturally-lit relaxation area. The close proximity to nature also provides views towards nature and the ability to relax within natural environments.
The office spaces benefit from both direct and indirect light from the integrated lighting raft, which also includes smoke detectors and sound absorbers, whose elliptical form helps avoid acoustic focusing and creates a comfortable environment in respect of sound.

Materials
See main text.

Energy
The building is oriented with the long elevations facing north and south. The south-facing façade has extensive solar shading. At the west end of the building are the computer facilities which are the only air-conditioned spaces in the building.
To heat the building, heat sources from the building, such as excess heat from the computer facilities, or from the air, are used in the underfloor heating in the atrium.

Water
A rainwater-retaining pond and water-porous areas are installed externally.

View of the south-facing elevation.

The escape stairs are clad in metal mesh and break up the over 100-metre long façade.

The south façade is protected from the sun by aluminium louvres. Pre-fabricated panels of stack bonded bricks form the wall cladding.

4.6 Waste Minimisation

4.6.1 Waste management

Landfill sites

Landfill sites are associated with environmental problems including: expenditure of land, toxic materials leaching into ground water, emissions of explosive gas and structural instability of the sites.

Landfill sites are a source of land and air pollution. Capping and lining landfill sites do not necessarily ensure the containment of the toxic materials or the site stability. Toxins such as cyanide, dioxins, mercury, hydrochloric acid, sulphuric acid and lead may potentially leach into the ground and ground water. Air pollutants from landfill sites include volatile organic compounds, methane, toluene, benzene, chloroform and vinyl chloride. Methane gas, produced from anaerobic decay of organic waste, including construction timber, can combine with CO_2 to produce an explosive landfill gas. It is also a potent greenhouse gas. Where organic waste is mixed with rubble, hollows may be left in the structure of the landfill site as organic waste disintegrates, increasing the risk of collapse.

Incineration

Incineration generates a number of toxic air pollutants including dioxins, furans, heavy metals, acid gases and particulates, and also generates contaminated ash, which is generally landfilled. The residue consists of up to 70 per cent of non-combustible material such as glass or metals and is often toxic.

Small 250-millimetre diameter containers and plastic bags made of corn are supplied by the local authority of Busto Arsizio, in Italy, to collect biodegradable waste. Communal bins for each block of flats, containing biodegradable waste, glass and paper, are emptied on different days of the week.

The increasing amount of waste is not only a construction industry problem, but one affecting all aspects of life. The average municipal waste produced per capita in countries of the Organisation of Economic Cooperation and Development (OECD) and the European Union is approximately 550 kilos per annum, but the US produces 51 per cent more per capita than any other OECD country (Worldwatch 2004; DEFRA 2004b). However, household waste represents only a relatively small percentage of the total waste produced. In the UK, household waste accounts for 26 per cent (49 million tonnes) of all controlled waste, which includes commercial, industrial and construction and demolition waste, or 13 per cent of all waste, which also includes agricultural, mining and quarrying waste (ODPM 2004c). UK construction and demolition (C&D) waste is estimated to be between 90-120 milion tonnes of waste per annum (BRE 2003).

Problems associated with waste include the energy and transport impacts of transferring materials and the environmental impacts associated with the disposal methods (see 4.6.1). Waste minimisation can help to reduce these disposal impacts and, by recycling waste, less new material is required, so waste minimisation can also help to reduce the impacts associated with material production. Appropriate building designs and building construction processes can contribute to reducing both municipal and C&D waste.

Recycling targets for the UK, set out by the *European Landfill Waste Directive 1999/31/EC*, include reducing, by 2010, municipal waste by 25 per cent compared to 1995 levels. By 2013, this figure should rise to 50 per cent, and by 2020, to 65 per cent. The *UK Waste Strategy 2000* aimed to bring these targets forward and achieve recycling rates of 25 per cent of municipal waste by 2005 (DETR 2000c). However, 2002/3 recycling rates were only 14 per cent and the 2005 targets are unlikely to be achieved. Moreover, the total amount of municipal waste, which is now 20 per cent greater than ten years ago, continues to rise. Making the recycling of household waste simple and effortless is crucial to overcoming the apathy towards recycling.

Two-thirds of the recycling collection in the UK occurs at bottle and can banks. For these to be used, adequate storage inside the house is required, and can be provided by multiple waste containers integrated in standard kitchen cabinets. Kerbside collections, where all recyclable waste is stored mixed in one box, are increasing and do not require the waste to be separated, but need storage space for the box. Where kerbside collection is not available and the development is large enough, installing on-site recycling banks and arranging for regular collection should be considered. Composting is not unusual for dwellings with gardens, but where individual composting is impractical, communal systems should be encouraged. In certain parts of Italy, the council provides all households with a small container for biodegradable material, plastic bags made of biodegradable corn material, and large communal bins, which are emptied three times per week.

While municipal waste makes up a quarter of the controlled waste in the UK, C&D waste makes up about half. Of this, 15-20 million tonnes are thought to be construction waste, most of which currently goes to landfill (BRE 2003), while the rest is demolition waste. Approximately half of the inert waste is used as fill materials in landscaping and road building, but as little as 3 million tonnes of the total C&D waste is reclaimed for reuse in the building industry (McGrath *et al.* 2000).

With the UK Landfill Tax of £15 per tonne on mixed waste in 2004, and likely to rise to a maximum of £35 per tonne, minimising waste during building construction and demolition is increasingly recognised as a financially rewarding approach and particularly valuable for an industry that suffers from low profit margins. Taking into account that the total cost of waste includes, not only the disposal cost, but also the purchase cost of the material wasted, its delivery, and the cost of handling it, reducing construction material wastage from 10 per cent to 5 per cent could save the house building industry £1,400 per house unit (BRE 2003).

All stages of a building's life, starting with the building design and finishing with its demolition, offer opportunities to minimise waste. Simple building designs that avoid over-complex and excessive decoration, efficient structures, and appropriately sized buildings are less wasteful. At detail design stage, considering standard sizes of materials and the potential to use offcuts, will later reduce site wastage. Once on site, the combination of good site practice and a thought-through design should reduce the amount of offcuts, abortive work, and materials that are delivered to site, not used and then landfilled. Over-ordering materials should be avoided; good and safe material storage will keep damaged and lost materials to a minimum; while minimising changes to designs and careful workmanship will reduce abortive work. Selecting materials from manufacturers that operate an environmental management system can also help address the waste associated with the manufacture of materials, estimated to amount to 12 million tonnes annually (Howard 2000).

Both construction and demolition sites can reduce waste by segregating it, which facilitates recycling and attracts reduced disposal charges. Typically, skips are used for metal, timber, and inert materials; glass and plastics may also be recycled. Manufacturers are becoming more attuned to waste minimisation issues and operate take-back schemes for offcuts and packaging. Packaging, in particular, makes up 25 per cent of the typical construction waste on site (BRE 2003). Materials, such as plasterboard, that are likely to be classified as hazardous waste in the near future in the UK should be dealt with separately, and the waste material preferably returned to the manufacturers. To avoid the problems associated with biodegradable waste in landfill sites (see 4.6.1), opportunities for composting C&D waste on site, potentially including treated biodegradable materials, should be considered.

Implementing waste minimisation can be encouraged and facilitated through the provision of information. Monitoring site waste provides records of the amount of waste produced and recycled, and the cost of disposal. This can be used to identify areas for improvement and ultimately reduce waste and disposal costs. A number of waste monitoring systems have been developed for this purpose and have been used successfully (see INTEGER house case study, p.192).

4.6.2 Minimising construction and demolition waste

Design stage

- consider size and architectural design of building
- maximise efficiency of structure and other building elements
- rationalise design to make use of full-size standard building elements where possible
- include recycling facilities for municipal waste in all building types
- consider accommodating opportunities for recycling commercial waste

Site operations

- establish a waste minimisation plan and waste minimisation targets
- if demolishing a building, undertake a demolition audit
- train sub-contractors and other building team members and raise awareness about the waste minimisation targets
- segregate waste
- provide good and safe storage
- avoid over-ordering
- arrange with manufacturers for take-back schemes of offcuts and packaging
- consider on-site composting
- consider monitoring waste

Off-the-shelf kitchen waste bin with multiple compartments.

Case study: Minimise waste by design

Resourceful Building
Emeryville, California, US

Client: Emeryville Redevelopment Agency
Architect: Siegel & Strain Architects
Structural engineer: Komendant Engineering
Services engineers: Davis Energy Group
Environmental life cycle assessment: Boustead Consulting Engineers Ltd
Quantity surveyor: Baker Pre-construction
Completed: 1998

The window is shaded from the high summer sun. The cement-fibre cladding reduced the use of solid timber.

One unit is on the street edge and the other two are set back and accessed through a courtyard.

The Emeryville Resourceful Building (ERB) is a housing development comprising three units in the City of Emeryville, located between Berkeley and Oakland, California. It is the result of a thorough analysis of how to create environmentally sound affordable housing. The development is part of Emeryville's first-time home buyers' programme, an enlightened initiative whereby affordable housing is developed by the Redevelopment Agency on underdeveloped or abandoned sites around the town. The opportunity to apply environmental design approaches to the project came about when the Alameda County Recycling Board and the Alameda County Waste Management Authority offered grants to fund green demonstration projects. The architects took this opportunity and were granted the funding. They then set ambitious targets for the development in terms of reducing the running energy of the buildings, providing a low maintenance building, designing for material efficiency and waste minimisation, providing a healthy indoor environment, and developing a model for environmentally sound affordable housing.

The additional grant money covered the research and the additional cost of the construction. However, a key concept was that the design developed should not substantially add to the typical cost of construction. In addition, it should not reduce the building quality and should use construction technologies familiar to traditional builders.

The initial project stage involved an in-depth research of current and alternative design options to enable the architects to make informed decisions about the most cost-effective, energy efficient and environmentally sound designs.

The research involved a number of activities. The design team developed between three and four specification options, including standard and environmentally preferable construction specifications for floors, walls and roof, which were compared in terms of construction cost. A selection of the construction materials were also analysed in terms of their life cycle impacts. Their manufacturing energy and material inputs, the associated waste and emission, and the long-term costs associated with maintenance were assessed and compared. A payback analysis of different energy–efficiency measures was made, whereby the final selection of measures resulted in an operational costs saving for the residents of $182 per annum. Finally, a material-efficient timber-framing design was engineered.

The construction specification options were developed with the aims of: minimising material use, using durable materials, minimising the operational energy of the building and using materials from sustainably managed sources. In response to these aims, the design team undertook a study of the timber frame for the main structure, which aimed to minimise the amount of timber used. Most affordable housing in the area is timber framed. While timber is renewable and biodegradable, there are concerns regarding its over-harvesting and the environmental impacts of non-sustainable harvesting methods. Reducing the amount used is, therefore, environmentally desirable. Furthermore, using less material would also reduce costs and offset the additional cost of other sustainable building measures.

The design team devised an optimised framing system for the buildings, drawing on the 'Optimum Value Engineering' framing methods of the National Association for Home Builders. The improved frame design included studs at 600-millimetre centres instead of the traditional 400 millimetres. It enabled the use of offcuts and precut studs and joists, used engineered timber for large sections, used built-up headers rather than oversized headers and roof trusses rather than rafters. An important measure that was not possible on this project was to build on a 600-millimetre grid to ensure the openings would coincide with the framing. Changing the spacing of the wall studs saved 19 per cent of the material and cost. Using trusses rather than rafters saved 10 per cent of the materials and 6 per cent of the cost. Using engineered floor joists rather than solid timber saved 25 per cent of the materials and 6 per cent of the cost.

By avoiding material wastage through design, the house overall has 50 per cent lower embodied energy, is associated with reduced manufacturing waste and in future will produce less deconstruction or demolition waste. Although this was not measured, it will also have produced less construction waste. Not wasting materials saved enough money to install additional insulation and some energy-efficient appliances. The changes in specification were estimated to increase the overall cost by 3 per cent, but once the project was tendered the lowest bid was within budget.

This project carefully analysed ways to build to save material and reduce waste and through its dissemination programme contributed significantly to promoting a more sustainable way of building. Timber frames in the UK use the more material-efficient frame spacing of 600 millimetres as standard. It is interesting how experience on one side of the Atlantic does not seem to reach the other. There is clearly scope for improving the long-distance exchange of information and it is precisely these types of well-researched projects that would benefit building designers and architects globally.

View of the house unit on the street side.

4.6.3 Sustainable design features

Site and ecology
The development is located within a residential neighbourhood, on a relatively small brownfield site and achieves a development density of nearly 60 dwellings per hectare, which is comparable to recommended sustainable development densities in Europe.

Community and culture
The houses provide energy-efficient housing at affordable prices, and running costs are also reduced, making running as well as purchasing the homes affordable.

Health
Low VOC paints were used throughout and adhesives and sealants with low VOC carpets.

Materials
All the timber used was FSC-certified timber from local suppliers. Durable materials such as tiled kitchen tops, rather than plastic laminate were selected. Recycled materials, such as recycled glass tiles and recycled cellulose insulation in the walls, were also used where possible.
Laying durable linoleum flooring avoided the use of PVC. Timber was treated with ACQ to avoid the use of arsenic and chromium.
To reduce the use of timber, cement-fibre cladding was used, which also provided the advantages of low maintenance and durability.
See also main text.

Energy
High efficiency air-heating furnaces were installed with sealed and insulated ductwork. Water heater insulation blankets were also used.
Peak indoor summer temperatures are reduced by 2.5°C (4.5°F) through increased building fabric insulation, window shading, solar insect screens on the south and west windows and energy-efficient lighting and appliances.
Fabric U-values:
   Walls – 0.28 W/m² C (R20)
   Glazing – 2.0 W/m² C (0.35 Btu/ft²hF)
CO_2 emissions were estimated to have been reduced by 23 per cent compared to the standard design.

Water
Water-saving taps, showerheads, dishwashers, washing machines and WCs were installed, as well as a drip irrigation system.

Case study: Minimising waste on site

INTEGER house
Building Research Establishment,
Watford, UK

Project details, Chapter 4.1, p.154

The conservatory is made with a standard prefabricated curtain walling system.

Internal view of conservatory.

The INTEGER house was built to demonstrate how housing could be made to be environmentally friendly and offer a contemporary lifestyle, taking advantage of modern technology.

The project was also experimental and forward-looking in respect of the choice of building processes adopted. Many of the building systems used are prefabricated. This responds to the lack of building skills experienced in the building industry and the desire for a faster building process, higher quality building and reduced waste. Prefabrication transfers much of the manufacturing to the factory and therefore reduces the on-site building processes, which can be unpredictable, are liable to delays due to weather, and are therefore less controllable. Factory manufacturing offers a better working environment for the workers and more control over the building quality. The comfortable and controlled building environment results in a better quality building product. Factory manufacturing can also reduce the amount of waste resulting from the manufacturing processes and in the factory any waste that does arise can more easily be recycled. Overall prefabrication can contribute to sustainable construction by reducing waste, improving working conditions and reducing the impact of building processes on their immediate surroundings.

Transferring much of the building processes off-site reduces the construction time on site. This was an advantage that was particularly important for the INTEGER project as the construction was to be filmed and screened on television and, therefore, had to take place within a 12-week period. Consequently, the basement is made of pre-cast concrete elements, the timber frame superstructure is made of prefabricated panels, the bathrooms are prefabricated pods, delivered with all finishes and fittings installed, and the conservatory is made with prefabricated curtain walling elements. Prefabrication also helped reduce two of the main causes of waste production on site, namely over-ordering materials and the production of offcuts. In the factory materials not used on one project can be used on the next, and any offcuts can be stored and either used on different work or recycled.

Other waste-reducing approaches, in addition to prefabrication, were also adopted on the INTEGER project. Keeping the site organised and tidy makes it easier to allocate safe storage space for materials, inappropriate storage of materials being another source of waste on site. Careful on-site workmanship avoids waste through mishandling of materials or incorrect construction, just as careful detailing by the designers reduces waste by avoiding changes once construction has begun. Finally, packaging waste makes up a large percentage of the waste typically produced on site. At the INTEGER site a radical approach was taken to address all these issues. No skips were made available and all the waste had to be removed from site each day. The sub-contractors were made aware of the environmental aims of the project and each one was made responsible for their own waste.

See also: design for flexibility **Chapter 4.1**

Construction waste, as opposed to demolition waste, is relatively low in amount and on small developments, like the INTEGER house, an effective approach to reducing waste is to avoid producing it in the first instance. Prefabrication, careful ordering and safe storage help achieve this aim. However, in larger construction projects and demolition projects, waste needs to be segregated.

Waste is generally collected into different skips for timber, metal, plastics and inert materials. The skips should be colour-coded or marked in another clear manner to avoid contaminating waste. Skips for returnable materials can be an option if manufacturers are prepared to take back offcuts of materials such as plasterboard, which can be reintroduced in their manufacturing processes. Packaging is often reusable and should be sent back to the manufacturers. All this requires considering waste at the start of a project. The site has to be organised to allow space for multiple skips, take-back schemes have to be agreed with manufacturers in advance and site staff need to be educated.

Education and awareness raising of the aims of any initiative are key to its implementation. At the INTEGER project, the Building Research Establishment (BRE) monitored the building efficiency with a system they developed called CALIBRE. By logging on-site activities throughout the building process, unproductive time was identified and ways of improving considered and later implemented on subsequent INTEGER projects. Similar learning processes have been developed by the BRE for waste minimisation. Knowing what waste is produced and where the waste comes from is the first step to reducing it. The BRE SMARTwaste system helps achieve this. The system records the number and the content of skips leaving site as well as monitoring site activities in relation to the production of waste. Sites using this system can compare their performance to national averages and other sites and take action accordingly. Increased awareness, combined with rising waste disposal costs should, with time, encourage less wasteful site practices in mainstream construction.

The lessons learnt throughout the INTEGER project are now benefiting others. The INTEGER house was the test bed for a specific approach to designing and constructing sustainable and contemporary houses. The system has now successfully been used, with the necessary modifications to achieve true market potential, in the social housing sector and, to a lesser extent, in the private housing sector. The architects have applied the same principles to refurbishment projects and extensions, and to an educational development. They have also exported the know-how by integrating it in new-build housing projects in China and Hong Kong.

4.6.4 Types and quantities of construction waste

Classification according to SMARTwaste and percentage of UK construction waste

Packaging	**25.9%**
Cardboard, paper, timber, plastics, metal	
Timber	**13.8%**
Timber general, plywood, MDF, chipboard, waferboard, hardboard, formwork, panelling	
Plaster and cement	**11.5%**
Plasterboard, mortar, cement, screed, external cladding	
Concrete	**10.2%**
Reinforced and un-reinforced concrete, rubble (concrete with bricks), blocks	
Miscellaneous	**9.6%**
Office waste, canteen waste, sweepings	
Ceramic	**8.6%**
Bricks, tiles, drainage pipes, sanitary ware	
Insulation	**7.5%**
Mineral wool, glass fibre, polystyrene, styrofoam, purlboard, wool insulation, insulation materials including asbestos	
Inert	**7.1%**
Topsoil, sub-base soil, sand, clay, gravel, natural stone, aggregate, glass	
Metal	**4%**
Aluminium, copper, galvanised metal, tin, cables, zinc, brass, lead, iron	
Plastic	**3.2%**
uPVC windows and doors, plastics membranes and sheeting, cordek sheets, polythene sheets	

Internally the fact that much of the structure is prefabricated cannot be seen.

Case study: Waste minimisation in use

Gallions Ecopark
Thamesmead, London, UK

Client: Gallions Housing Association
Architect: Splinter Architechon
Sustainability consultants: DHV
Main contractor: Wilmott Dixon
Completed: 2003

Eight flats for market rent were included in a block.

The flats for sale are situated on the north-west corner of the site together with the visitors' centre.

Gallions Ecopark is a housing development in the regeneration area Thamesmead, south-east of London. The development constitutes an affordable element of a larger development by Gallions Housing Association (HA), the Reach Urban Village, which will include 1500 new homes plus shops and a school. The mixed tenure development of 39 homes for social rent and eight flats for market rent is designed to provide sustainable solutions, which can be replicated on a wide scale.

To achieve a replicable design, the sustainable design aspects of the development needed to be affordable. The low-cost environmental options that were therefore selected and implemented, increased the overall development cost by only 5 per cent. Furthermore, by using a partnering contract during the procurement phase, Gallions Ecopark was developed on a cost parity with traditional schemes. The basic structure is well insulated and the homes are heated with efficient condensing boilers and solar thermal panels. Ventilation is either passive or by means of mechanical ventilation with heat recovery. Water-efficient appliances were installed throughout and one house features a greywater recycling system.

Gallions Housing Association has committed itself to a dissemination programme which includes promoting energy efficiency to local schools, builders, developers and residents, with the ultimate aim of increasing the uptake of energy-efficiency measures in the Thamesmead area. Drawing from their Dutch experience, where buildings that achieve a specific level of environmental sustainability are supported with additional funding from government, they also intend identifying regulatory and financial vehicles to facilitate the integration of energy-efficiency measures in housing and support the market of these products. Gallions HA are not only sharing their general knowledge with others, they are also sharing their experience from this project, both good and bad, established through post-occupancy evaluations. They are open about the successful items as well as how they intend addressing less successful design aspects in future developments.

This proactive approach has been adopted at various levels. Thamesmead is a brand new development area and a supporting network of essential facilities such as transport, recycling and leisure facilities is still largely at the planning stage. In view of this situation, Gallions HA decided not to wait for a structure to be provided by the council, and they provided a recycling facility within their development.

The housing is arranged around a courtyard, originally intended as a communal garden, but used for car parking instead. In this area four underground recycling containers have been installed to collect glass, plastic, paper and cans. These have a capacity of the estimated recycling waste of 600 homes. Gallions HA approached the recycling company, arranged for regular collections and provided householders with a stack of recycling boxes and a space in the kitchen to store the recyclable materials. The effort of disposing of the material in the central banks is minimal. As with several other design items, Gallions HA is going to improve on its design in future, including multiple waste containers in the fitted kitchens, facilitating further the storage of recyclable materials.

The east–west housing has relatively small windows.

The south-facing houses have a fully glazed elevation to take advantage of the solar gains.

The recycling collection banks are located in the courtyard between the houses and are easily accessible and relatively unobtrusive. Future planting will further improve the aesthetics of the development.

The plastic collection bank.

The box on the kitchen counter is the typical box provided to the householders to collect glass and aluminium. Future developments will include fully fitted multi-compartment waste bins in the kitchen cabinets.

4.6.5 Sustainable design features

Site and ecology
The development is situated on previously used and contaminated land. A reduced parking allocation of one car per dwelling was applied.

Community and culture
The development includes a visitors centre which demonstrates some of the principles and technologies used, and gives some environmental background information explaining the reasons for the approach adopted. The centre is the starting point for many visitors from the social and private housing sector as well as from schools. One of the houses has been kept as a demonstration house.

Health
The condensing boilers are Class 5 low NOx emissions boilers.

Materials
The houses are timber-framed structures.

Energy
Fabric U-values:
 Walls - 0.25 W/m² C (R23)
 Glazing – 1.10 W/m² C (0.19 Btu/ft²h°F)

Solar thermal panels preheat hot water for domestic use. A condensing boiler is used to further heat the domestic hot water and water for space heating. South-facing houses make maximum use of passive solar gains through large glazed conservatory spaces and are passively ventilated. East-west-facing houses have underfloor heating with MVHR.

Electricity consumption is thought to have been reduced by 45 per cent compared to similar projects, and gas consumption by 60 per cent.

Water
Water-saving devices have been installed including dual flush WC (2.5/4 litres) and spray showers (8.5 litres/min). Small baths and flow restrictors in taps were also installed but will be replaced with standard baths and spray taps in future developments. Each house has a water butt for rainwater harvesting. One house has a greywater recycling.

Case study: Composting

Macoskey Center
Slippery Rock, Pennsylvania, US

Client: Slippery Rock University
Architect: Sustainaissance International
Engineers: Spring House Energy
Completed: work ongoing

View of the renovated farmhouse with the organic farm in the foreground.

A movable chicken house and electrical fence powered by a movable PV.

A PV-powered cart is used for community and information event.

See also: greywater treatment **Chapter 6.3**

The Robert A. Macoskey Center is an educational facility and a 'living laboratory' for testing ideas and technologies for sustainable systems. Located a couple of miles outside Slippery Rock town, Pennsylvania, it is part of the Slippery Rock University, but has also become a focal point for the local community. The Master of Science in Sustainable Systems (MS3) degree as well as other university-based environmental courses make use of the centre's facilities, as do children from the local schools. The centre also provides a venue for community events and meetings of environmentally oriented organisations.

The Macoskey Center, located on 33 hectare belonging to the Slippery Rock University campus, was the brainchild of the late Robert Macoskey, Professor of Philosophy, and was developed by the Alternative Living Technology and Energy Research (ALTER) project, a community organisation. It includes a small-scale organic farm and a collection of buildings, including classrooms, workshop, laboratory and student residences. The main building is a renovated farmhouse that now accommodates offices and teaching facilities.

The centre develops environmental educational programmes for children of various ages. Students from the university are encouraged to link their course work to the centre by investigating issues related to the centre, such as legislation pertaining to the use of compost from composting toilets or the quality of treated greywater. Students are also involved in the building projects that gradually take place on site with minimal financial support. Initiatives, such as creating a path to connect the centre with the main university campus, are real projects the students can learn from.

The centre operates a mini organic farm of approximately 0.4 hectare. It is taken care of by students and relates to other activities of the centre, such as the promotion of a market for local produce, 'good food lunches' for school children, and other events that encourage organic and local food production. The community composting is part of the organic farming ethos.

The community composting started on a large scale when, in 1995, Slippery Rock University received a Pennsylvania Department of Environment Protection Grant for the restoration of the hillside in conjunction with setting up a community composting that would support the restoration. The hillside had been stripped of its top soil as part of the construction requirements for a new football stadium across the road. Without top soil the acidic clay subsoil was exposed to erosion. The grant enabled the university to purchase a leaf vacuum, which is used to collect leaves from the town in autumn, and set up a windrow (elongated piles 1.5 metres in width) composting system. The restoration replaced the top soil and stopped the erosion and compost was used as a soil conditioner and fertiliser. The hill is now covered with native grasses that support native butterfly and bird species.

The compost system works by placing the collected leaves in three windrows on a 1 hectare site at the centre. These are mixed with approximately 450 litres of food waste from the two university cafeterias. Three times per week buckets of food waste are delivered to the centre as are coffee grounds from the union coffee shop. Students manually mix the food waste in the leaf rows and monitor the decomposition process.

The rows are approximately one square metre in section to ensure there is sufficient material decomposing to raise the temperature to between 32-60°C and accelerate the rate of decomposition.

A compost turner is used to turn the compost rows, adding water or dry adsorbent material as required to adjust the moisture content and achieve as close as possible to the ideal moisture content of 40-60 per cent for rapid decomposition.

After one year of decomposing the compost is used in the organic farm and for other university uses. It is, as is everything at the centre, also a teaching vehicle and students can compare its operation with other compost systems at the centre, which include: a simple plastic domestic-sized compost bin; a four-compartment multi-compost system made with recycled timber pallets; and a vermicomposting bin, which relies on redworms to transform the waste into compost. These systems are also available for the community to investigate and learn from.

As with many environmental initiatives, the advantages are manifold. Students learn about the technologies, the university has free compost, the city has a leaf collection service and, not least, waste from several sources is diverted from landfill.

4.6.6 Sustainable design features

Site and ecology
The existing buildings were kept and renovated. The organic farm includes a nature trail on the renovated hill. The trail leads through areas planted with native species and includes information tables for the visitors.

Community and culture
The design involved a community consultation. The materials used are mainly local both in character and production, thus supporting the regional economy.

Health
Mainly natural and low toxicity materials were used.

Materials
The timber used is mostly reclaimed or FSC certified. Recycled glass tiles were used in the entrance to the centre. Reclaimed roof tiles were used on the refurbished barn, which also makes use of salvaged timber frame construction, straw bales and clay straw infill. The new springhouse makes use of recycled concrete blocks.

Energy
The centre has a small PV array. A masonry stove is used to heat the refurbished farmhouse with locally sourced timber.

Water
Water use is minimised by the use of a composting toilet.

The compost turner aerates the compost, ensuring sufficient oxygen for aerobic decomposition.

The roller on the compost turner mixes the leaf rows by turning them over.

The centre is on Harmony Road, a fact reflected in the pattern of the reclaimed roof tiles of the workshop.

The compost rows are spaced out sufficiently to allow access to the turning machine

Chapter 5
Energy

5.0 Introduction

5.0.1 Greenhouse gases

The emissions of the first six greenhouse gases listed here are controlled by the Kyoto Protocol, while CFCs have been phased out under the 1987 Montreal Protocol on Substances that Deplete the Ozone Layer.

Carbon dioxide (CO_2)

Half the global warming is caused by CO_2 of which 6,000 million tonnes are emitted to the atmosphere each year as a result of burning fossil fuel to produce energy in power stations, factories, cars and homes.

Methane (CH_4)

Methane is the second most significant greenhouse gas, it is 20 times more powerful than CO_2, but emitted in lesser qualities. It is the resultant gas from carbon-based metabolic systems and is produced by rotting vegetable matter also found in landfill sites, ruminants' digestive systems, or in waterlogged areas such as swamps or rice paddies.

Nitrous oxide (N_2O)

A powerful greenhouse gas accounting for 10 per cent of greenhouse effect. It has a life of 200 years. It is produced through burning fossil fuels and the breakdown of chemical fertilisers. Nitrous oxide also contributes to acid rain.

Hydrofluorocarbons (HFCs)

HFCs are potent greenhouse gases. They have replaced CFCs in the manufacture of insulants and refrigerants as they have a reduced ozone depleting affect compared to CFCs.

Perfluorocarbons (PFCs)

Perfluoromethane and perfluoroethane are the most important PFCs in global warming terms. They have a life of 50,000 and 10,000 years respectively.

Sulphur hexafluoride (SF6)

This is used as an insulator and is a powerful greenhouse gas with a life of 3,200 years.

Chlorofluorocarbons (CFCs)

CFC is also a long-lasting greenhouse gas, 10,000 times more powerful than CO_2.

Perhaps the most pressing environmental issue today is global warming. The international scientific community overwhelmingly supports the view that global warming is the result of human activities, and that its effects will be both of great financial and human cost. It has also become clear that global warming is taking place at a faster rate than previously believed. It is therefore necessary to address energy use, worldwide, as a priority.

Greenhouse gases

The main cause of global warming is the increase in greenhouse gases in the atmosphere. These gases admit solar radiation into the lower atmosphere and absorb and re-radiate a portion of the infrared radiation emitted from the Earth. As the concentration of greenhouse gases increases, more heat is trapped in the lower atmosphere causing global temperatures to rise.

Greenhouse gases include carbon dioxide (CO_2), methane (CH_4), nitrous oxide (N_2O), hydrofluorocarbons (HFCs), perfluorocarbons (PFCs), sulphur hexafluoride (SF6), chlorofluorocarbons (CFCs) and water vapour (see 5.0.1). Antarctic ice cores have revealed that CO_2 concentrations have been increasing since the 1800s and CH_4 since 1700s; and fluorine-based compounds have been increasing in the atmosphere since the 1960s. CO_2 is the main greenhouse gas resulting primarily from the burning of fossil fuels, such as coal, gas and oil, for energy. In 2002, 6.44 billion tons of carbon, in the form of CO_2, were released into the atmosphere (Worldwatch 2003). Buildings are associated with the burning of fossil fuels to power their construction and operation. In the UK, operating buildings is responsible for 50 per cent of all CO2 emissions, construction processes for 10 per cent (Rao *et al.* 2000). In the US, buildings are associated with 36 per cent of the total energy use and 65 per cent of the total electricity consumption. World-wide, buildings contribute 30 per cent of global CO_2 emissions (IPCC 2001).

Global temperature changes and the effects of global warming

Temperature on the Earth has varied in regular patterns, as is evident from the 100,000-year cycle of ice ages, as well as abruptly and unexpectedly as a result of solar activity and volcanic eruptions. On the basis of existing patterns, the expectation is that the global climate should be cooling; however, just the opposite is happening. In the past 100 years, the world's average global surface temperature has increased by 0.4–0.8°C. 1998 was the warmest year since records began in 1860, in the warmest decade of the century. 2003 was the second warmest. Evidence of heating up is to be found world-wide from Mount Kilimanjaro, where 82 per cent of the ice caps have melted since 1912, to Siberia, which has experienced a rise in temperature of 5°C (see 5.0.2). Current predictions suggest global temperatures will rise a further 1.4 to 5.8°C by the end of the twenty-first .century, depending on population growth, energy consumption and energy conservation (DEFRA 2004a).

Levels of CO_2 are measured in parts per million by volume (ppmv) and prior to the industrial development there were between 200-275 ppmv of CO_2 in the atmosphere. In 1959, when a study of atmospheric CO_2 concentrations began at the Mauna Loa Observatory in Hawaii, levels were just under 316 ppmv, today they have reached 375 ppmv, for the first time in 420,000 years, and they continue to rise at 2 ppmv per year. The European Union member states have decided to aim to prevent concentrations from exceeding 550 ppmv, which would limit the rise in temperature to no more than 2°C above pre-industrial levels (Crown 2003). This recognises the fact that global warming is happening now and cannot be stopped, but that it should be feasible to slow it down. However, between 2001 and 2003, researchers at the Mauna Loa Observatory observed rises in levels of CO_2 that were higher than what was to be expected from anthropogenic CO_2 emissions alone. While this could simply be an abnormal peak, it could also suggest the start of the 'runaway greenhouse effect', a scenario which would challenge any effort to slow global warming down (HAC 2004).

The 'runaway greenhouse effect' is an extreme scenario, where rises in temperature, caused by global warming, affect natural sources and sinks of CO_2. These, in turn, further increase CO_2 levels and trigger a self-perpetuating process. Oceans, for example, can absorb CO_2, and, together with terrestrial plants, absorb half of the global CO_2 emissions. But as ocean temperatures rise, this ability decreases, which increases atmospheric CO_2, and raises temperatures still further. Other mechanisms that increase greenhouse gases as a result of rising temperatures include evaporation from the oceans, which add water vapour to the atmosphere; and the thawing of the permafrost layer, which releases methane.

The 'runaway greenhouse effect' may seem an extreme outcome, but even if atmospheric CO_2 were stabilised immediately, rising global temperatures would persist for several decades (Smith 2003). The impact of climate change can be seen already, and has had significant human and financial costs, in recent years. In the UK, in past five years storm and flood losses have totalled £6 billion, twice as much as the previous five years (FOE 2004), and the floods in the autumn of 2000 cost £1 billion (Crown 2003). In 2003, 14,800 people died in France from the effects of a heatwave, where temperatures repeatedly rose over 40°C (Worldwatch 2004) and fatalities have also occurred as a result of flooding, storms and other extreme weather events. Similar events involving more widespread and frequent heat waves, violent storms, forest fires, droughts, and flooding are to be expected, as global warming increases at an unprecedented speed (see 5.0.2).

In the UK, rising sea levels, shifting rain patterns, and associated storm conditions are expected to have the biggest impact. In some areas of the UK sea levels may rise up to 900 millimetres by 2080, and by the end of the century, extreme high water levels could be 10 to 20 times more frequent on some parts of the east coast. Rainfall is expected to

5.0.2 Past and future effects of climate change

Effects of climate change in the twentieth century
- Ice caps are retreating from many mountain peaks like Kilimanjaro.
- Global mean sea level rose by an average of 1-2 millimetres a year during the twentieth century.
- Summer and autumn Arctic sea ice has thinned by 40 per cent in recent decades.
- Global snow cover has decreased by 10 per cent since the 1960s.
- El Niño events have become more frequent and intense during the past 20-30 years.
- Usage of the Thames Barrier has increased from once every two years in the 1980s to an average six times a year over the past five years.
- Weather-related economic losses to communities and businesses have increased ten-fold over the past 40 years.

Expected impacts of climate change
- Sea levels are expected to rise between 100–900 millimetres, mainly because of the increase in volume as the water temperature rises. Many coastal areas, such as the island nations of Kiribati and the Maldives as well as New Orleans and New York, will be at risk from the rising sea. In Bangladesh a 450-millimetre rise would result in a loss of 10 per cent of the land and the displacement of five million people.
- In the extreme case that the polar land-based ice should melt, sea levels would rise by 5 metres, well above the levels of many large cities.
- Habitats would shift. While animals may be able to migrate, the rate of climate change is so fast that, unlike after the last ice age when trees were able to follow the retreating ice sheets, extensive forest demise is to be expected.
- Northern climates will be lost entirely and with them species such as reindeer and polar bears.
- Certain insects such as termites and the malaria mosquito will expand their habitats affecting an increasing number of people.
- Agricultural land will be affected by changing temperature and rising sea levels, causing increased risk of famine and conflict. A 1-metre rise in Bangladesh will flood half the country's rice fields.
- Glacial fresh water reserves will be reduced, as droughts and irregular rainfall affect water availability and increase water stress.
- An estimated 150 million climate change refugees would be expected.
(Crown 2003; Smith 2003)

5.0.3 Plant as CO₂ sequestration

For every dry ton of new plant biomass produced through photosynthesis, approximately 1,273 kg (1.4 tons) of oxygen are added to the atmosphere and approximately 1,636kg (1.8tons) of carbon dioxide are removed. Russian space agencies show that astronauts consume approximately 0.9kg (2lb) of oxygen and exhale approximately 1.1kg (2.4lb) of carbon dioxide every 24 hours.
(Wolverton 1997)

5.0.4 Global CO₂ emissions

	% of global CO2 emissions as a country	Tons of carbon emissions per person
USA	24	5.2
Germany		2.75
UK	2 (Crown 2003)	2.5
Japan		2.5
China	12	0.5
India		0.3

(Worldwatch 2003)

increase up to 35 per cent in winter and decrease in summer by up to 35 per cent. The reduced summer rainfall, combined with increases in summer temperatures of up to 3°C, will increase the incidence of water shortages and, consequently, the need for agricultural irrigation (Hollman *et al.* 2002). The UK Climate Impacts Programme also predicts that in housing, indoor temperatures in excess of 28°C will occur on 14 days per year by 2020 and on 68 days per year by 2080, a significant increase from only six days in 1989.

While most climate predictions for Europe forecast an increase in temperature, this may not be the case. The Gulf Stream, known as the conveyor belt, transfers warm water near the surface of the ocean towards the European coast, keeping Europe several degrees warmer than it would otherwise be, and returns it at low level once it has cooled. As the polar caps melt, there is the risk that excessive amounts of fresh water might mix with the salt water, making it too buoyant to sink to the ocean floor and continue its cycle. Should this conveyor belt cease to operate, Europe would experience a dramatic cooling of the climate.

Addressing climate change

Climate change cannot be prevented, but by stabilising concentrations of greenhouse gases, the most extreme effects can be avoided. Individual countries alone will not make enough difference, but a global coordinate effort should. In 1998 the UN Environmental Programme and the World Meteorological Organisation formed a panel of experts, the Intergovernmental Panel on Climate Change (IPCC), to research the causes and effects of climate change and possible strategies to counteract its impacts. The IPCC issued three reports, in 1990, 1995 and 2001, that informed the decisions taken at an international level.

In 1992, as part of the Earth Summit at Rio de Janeiro, the UN Framework Convention on Climate Change (FCCC) was drawn up. It set out an overall framework for strategies to address climate change and requires specific agreements to be formalised through protocols and amendments. The FCCC, signed by 186 countries, including the EU member states and the US, required industrialised countries to stabilise their greenhouse gas emissions to 1990 levels by 2000. The EU achieved this target.

The Kyoto Protocol is a protocol to the FCCC and was signed at the Kyoto Conference in 1997. Its signatories agree to reduce their collective emissions of greenhouse gases by 5.2 per cent below 1990 levels by 2008-12. The 15 EU member states, which include the UK and Germany, have agreed a target to reduce emissions by 8 per cent below 1990 levels, and the UK set a national target of 12.5 per cent reduction. For the Kyoto Protocol to come into force, it had to be ratified by a minimum of 55 nations and the nations responsible for at least 55 per cent of the 1990 greenhouse gases emissions. With Russia signing the Kyoto Protocol in 2004, it was ratified; however, the US, which has 5 per cent of global population and is responsible for 24 per cent of CO_2 emissions (Worldwatch 2003), has not ratified the Kyoto Protocol, opting instead for voluntary domestic targets, which critics believe will increase emissions by 30 per cent rather than decrease them. Australia has also opted out of the treaty.

One of the Kyoto Protocol's implementation mechanisms is emissions trading. Developed countries that have ratified the Kyoto Protocol will be given a greenhouse gas allowance, the Assigned Amount Unit (AAU), which will become a tradeable commodity. In preparation for 2008, the EU Emissions Trading Scheme came into force in January 2005. The scheme covers emissions from the main industrial emitters, accounting for 46 per cent of EU emissions. The industries covered include: power stations, paper and pulp, steel and iron, glass and ceramics, cement, and industrial facilities with a capacity greater than 20 MW. A cap is set on the emissions from each country, and emitters are allocated tradeable allowances. If an emitter over-achieves, it can sell its credits, and if it fails to achieve its targets, it can purchase credits. Trading can occur between industries and between countries. Emitters can also use credits from emission-saving projects undertaken outside the EU (TCT 2004).

Independent from the Kyoto Protocol, the UK has also set further domestic targets, including a 20 per cent reduction of greenhouse gases by 2010, and other more specific targets, such as reducing CO_2 emissions from homes by 4-6 million tonnes a year by 2020. These targets would reduce the total CO_2 emissions by 135 million tonnes from 1990 levels of 600-700 million tonnes of CO_2. To achieve these aims the UK government has introduced a number of fiscal, regulatory and voluntary initiatives.

The UK government has also adopted the recommendations of the Royal Commission on Environmental Pollution (RCEP) for a reduction in CO_2 emissions of 60 per cent from current levels by about 2050 (Crown 2003). It is this level of reduction, which is recommended by the scientific community, that should be the aim for all developed countries.

5.0.5 Further reading

Energy Efficiency Best Practice Programme

A collection of building-related publications. BRE, Garston, Watford

Energy and Environment in Architecture

Baker, N., Steemers, K. (2000), E&FN Spon, London

Energy Efficient Office Refurbishment

Burton, S. ed. (2001) James and James, London

Energy Conscious Design: A Primer for Architects

Goulding et al. (1992) Batsford, London

Sustainable Housing: Options for Independent Energy, Water Supply and Sewerage, Application Guide AG 26/97

Smerdon et al. (1997) BSRIA, Bracknell

Sustainability at the Cutting Edge

Smith, P. (2003) Architectural Press, Oxford

Introduction to Architectural Science: The Basis of Sustainable Design

Szokolay, S. (2004) Architectural Press, Oxford

Environmental Design

Thomas, R. ed. (1999) E&FN Spon, London

5.0.6 Designing to minimise CO₂ emissions and pollution

Reduce energy requirements
- Design with the natural environment:
  - Orient building to maximise or protect from solar gains depending on requirements (e.g. maximise south-facing glazing and minimise north-facing glazing in the northern hemisphere).
  - Orient building to make use of planting and landscape to protect it from or take advantage of prevailing winds.
  - Consider using planting to provide shading and to moderate internal environments.
  - Orient the spaces in a building that can benefit from solar heat gains on the south side and spaces that can remain cool on the north side (in the northern hemisphere).

- Design the building envelope to moderate internal temperatures:
  - Minimise heat loss through appropriate insulation and building airtight.
  - Minimise unwanted heat gains with solar shading, insulation and reflective finishes.
  - Consider using thermal mass to moderate daily temperature variations and as a seasonal heat store to make use of summer heat in the winter.
  - Provide lobbies and conservatories as buffer zones.
  - Provide natural ventilation and cooling.

- Design the building envelope to minimise electrical lighting needs:
  - Provide ample natural light

- Encourage a resource-saving lifestyle:
  - Use showers rather than baths.

Use energy efficiently
- Use energy-efficient equipment:
  - Provide heating and cooling through energy-efficient mechanical appliances.
  - Use energy-efficient lights and appliances
  - Provide communal heating and electricity where possible (e.g. district heating, CHP).
  - Set energy design targets and monitor building performance.
  - Educate users and implement energy-saving policies.

Use 'green' energy sources
  - use 'free' energy sources (e.g. wind, sun, ground heat).
  - use renewable energy sources (e.g. timber from managed forests, rape oil).

Energy and sustainable building

The aim of sustainable building in respect of energy is to enable the occupants of a building to maintain and, if possible, improve their quality of life, while producing the least possible amount of CO_2 emissions. The most direct solution is to change the source of energy from fossil fuel-based systems to renewable sources with low CO_2 emissions. However, considering the economic and technical barriers, this approach on its own is unlikely to be a realistic solution.

To minimise the environmental impact of energy use, a three-stage approach should be adopted. First, how energy is used in buildings should be analysed and building fabric design alternatives selected to provide the same performance with reduced energy requirements. Second, if a zero energy design solution is not possible, active systems should be selected that uses energy in an efficient way. The Third Assessment Report of the IPCC estimates that a 30 per cent reduction in projected increases of CO_2 could be achieved by 2020, and 60 per cent of these reductions could be achieved through more efficient appliances and increased insulation (IPCC 2001). Third, the resulting reduced energy requirements should be provided by alternative, low CO_2–emitting energy sources. By first minimising the energy requirements, the use of renewable energy to provide the very much reduced amount of energy becomes feasible. This chapter illustrates these three approaches.

5.1 Minimising Energy Needs

The energy associated with buildings includes the operational energy and the construction energy. The construction energy, known as the embodied energy, is discussed in Chapter 4. The operational energy is the energy used to heat, cool, ventilate and light the building, provide hot water, and run appliances and equipment.

The operational energy varies depending on building location, climate and season, and building use. The climate and season have the biggest impact on the building's requirements for heating and cooling, but all factors have to be considered. Designing buildings to minimise energy needs means adopting measures that primarily affect the building envelope and the spatial design. These are passive measures that include: orientating the building in relation to the sun, the wind and the site characteristics; insulating the building and providing heat storage according to climatic needs; integrating systems to passively cool and ventilate the building; and providing appropriate natural light to minimise the need for electrical lighting.

Passive measures also include considering the real needs of the building's inhabitants. In particular, the space requirements and comfort standards have a significant impact on the building energy use and can be tailored to individual needs. Increasing per capita space requirements and decreasing household sizes are two of the drivers for the increase in total energy used in the building sector (IPCC 2001). Buildings are often bigger than they need to be, using more energy than is necessary. The comfort standards used to design buildings also affect their energy use. Degree-days are used to establish the heating requirements in a particular location based on historic climatic parameters. In the south of England, the design degree-days, a measure used to describe the amount of heating required for a building, is about 2,000 to achieve a base indoor temperature of 18.0°C; if the base is reduced to 15.5°C, it is about 1,500. Reducing internal temperature by 2.5 per cent reduces heating needs by 25 per cent. Similar energy reductions can be achieved by adjusting the cooling temperature of air-conditioned buildings (Nicol 1993).

Even thought climatic parameters affect the design and the energy use of buildings, the principles of energy efficiency can be applied in the same way in different climates, while adjusting the detail implementation to suit the climate. The case studies that follow illustrate how passive heating, cooling and lighting strategies can minimise energy requirements.

In Northern Europe, the US and Southern Australia, buildings need to be heated for certain periods during the winter. Globally, heating is the dominant energy use in both residential and commercial buildings (IPCC 2001). Space heating in the UK accounts for 26 per cent of total UK energy use and 60 per cent of energy used in housing (Crown 2003). Buildings gain heat from internal incidental sources, such as people and equipment; external sources, such as the sun; and auxiliary sources, such as heating and ventilation systems. To minimise the need for auxiliary heating, requiring energy, buildings have to be designed to harness solar radiation, and to retain the heat within the building.

5.1.1 Passivhaus standards

Passivhaus aims

Passivhaus is a house that provides a comfortable environment without auxiliary heating. Key performance features include:

– maximum heating requirements – 15 kWh/m$_2$a

– energy requirements should be covered by alternative energy forms.

Designing to Passivhaus standards

– The building envelope should be compact and well insulated with U-value of less than 0.15 W/m$_2$K (R38) and minimal cold bridging.

– U-values of windows including glass and frame should not exceed 0.8 W/m$_2$K (0.14 Btu/ft$_2$h°F).

– The building envelope should be well sealed, providing a maximum 0.6 air changes per hour.

– Living spaces and maximum glazing should face south, and overshadowing should be minimised.

– Fresh air entering the building should be passively pre-heated (e.g. through earth ducts).

– Mechanical ventilation with heat recovery with over 80 per cent efficiency should be used.

– Water should be heated through alternative heat sources such as solar panels and heat pumps.

– Energy-efficient appliances should be used.

5.1.2 Typical energy use in housing

	% of total energy use	
	AU (Rearson 2001)	UK (Yannas 1994)
space heating and cooling	39	60
water heating	27	23
electrical light and appliances	21	10
refrigeration	9	
cooking	4	7
Total CO_2 emissions per average family	8000 kg/yr	4000 kg/yr

Orienting glazed openings in the south side of a building (in the northern hemisphere) allows the maximum possible solar radiation to enter the building, and creating a well-insulated and airtight building envelope will retain heat within the building. These three principles are fundamental in creating buildings that do not require auxiliary heating at all and can rely on solar and internal gains to provide an adequately heated interior. Numerous buildings have successfully implemented these principles, which have been formalised by the Passivhaus standards.

The Passivhaus standard, widely adopted in Germany, Austria and Switzerland, sets targets for heating energy and overall energy use of buildings (see 5.1.1). Originally developed for housing, the standard has also been used for other building types. Zero heating buildings exist in many countries, but in Germany alone the number of buildings constructed to Passivhaus standards is expected to rise to 15,000 by 2006 and to 137,000 by 2010 (IBO 2004). These buildings are, as the name suggests, passive solar, but typically make use of some 'active' technology such as: mechanical ventilation with heat recovery, PV panels, solar thermal. The construction systems range from timber frame to concrete with external insulation, and the completed buildings show that the standard does not restrict design freedom. Taking into account the need for developed countries to reduce their CO_2 emissions by 60–80 per cent, Passivhaus standards should be applied more extensively.

Reducing the need to cool buildings is as important as reducing the heating needs, particularly as mechanical ventilation, fans and air-conditioning rely mainly on electricity; and electricity, because of its low generation efficiencies, produces about three times the amount of CO_2 emissions per kWh of energy than burning gas for heating.

Passive approaches to cooling include protecting the building from solar gains, reducing infiltration, and providing natural ventilation and cooling. Excluding solar radiation, which can cause a building to become uncomfortably hot, is an appropriate approach even in cool climates. Here, the combination of solar gains and internal heat gains, from people and equipment, can often raise the internal temperature well above the external. Shading to glazed areas can reduce external sources of heat. In hot climates the building fabric should be prevented from heating up and transferring heat to the inside, which can be done by using light and reflective external finishes and insulating the building fabric. Orienting the building away from the sun and shading the whole building with double layered roofs or planting can also be effective. Building an airtight envelope will prevent hot air entering the building.

Once the building is protected from solar heat gains, the type of passive approach will depend on the climate. Where internal heat gains are the main problem, and the external temperature is low enough, natural ventilation can effectively reduce internal temperatures and increase evaporative and convective cooling (see Chapter 3.1; see also 5.1.3). Wind directions and potential obstructions should be considered, and whether passive stack, cross-ventilation or single-sided ventilation is possible and appropriate. Natural ventilation is also the most energy-efficient way of supplying essential fresh air to a building. Grouping activities and equipment associated with high heat production away from building occupants can help reduce the cooling needed (see Powergen case study, p.186).

When natural ventilation is not sufficient to create a comfortable environment, then other cooling options may be possible. If the diurnal range is large enough, the cool night temperature can be exploited. Thermal mass is dense materials that heats up and cool down slowly. Cooling thermal mass overnight provides a 'heat sink' for throughout the following day. Thermal mass can also be used to harness heat and provide heating when the air temperature drops, daily or seasonally. In hot dry climates evaporative cooling can also be effective. Evaporative cooling extracts the latent heat of evaporation from the air, thus cooling the surroundings. As mentioned earlier, climate is the main determinant; in hot humid climates, for instance, neither thermal mass nor evaporative cooling are effective, and natural ventilation has to be exploited to its maximum potential.

Getting the building configuration and structure right makes the largest contribution to creating low energy buildings. It is therefore important for architects to consider the passive aspects of the design right from the start of a building design project.

5.1.3 Energy consumption and carbon emissions per m² of treated floor space per annum

*energy provided by zero-CO_2 sources
**space heating only

	Gas kWh/m²yr	Electricity kWh/m²yr	CO_2/m²yr
typical air-conditioned office	178–210	226–358	135–205
best practice air-conditioned office	97–114	128–234	77–129
typical naturally ventilated office	151	54–85	54–68
best practice naturally ventilated office	79	33–54	30–40
target values for office	47	36	25
Dyfi Eco Park Unit 1	48	21	19
Dyfi Eco Park Unit 3	22	82	42
RES	32**	43	0*
Lewis Center		94	18*
typical UK house (extrapolated values)	160–220	26–78	67
Hockerton		21–32	~0*
Passivhaus standards	15**		~0*

Typical and best practice values taken from BRECSU (2000) *Energy use in Offices: Energy consumption guide 19*, Watford: BRE.

The kindergarten in the solarCity in Linz is designed to Passivhaus standards and only uses 8 kWh/m²yr for space heating (Architect Olivia Schimek).

The Heliotrop, in Freiburg, is a low energy dwelling and work place designed to track the sun to optimise its solar orientation. Its 54 m² PV installation with a peak output of 6.6 kW exports 5 to 6 times the energy the building uses (Architect Rolf Disch).

Case study: Minimising heat loss

Chorlton Park
Manchester, UK

Client: Irwell Valley Housing Association
Architect: Stephenson Bell
Structural engineer: Whitby Bird & Partners
Services engineer: Steven A Hunt & Associates
Quantity surveyor: Simon Fenton Partnership
Main contractor: Queghans, McGoff & Byrne
Completed: 2002

The timber balconies give character to the elevation and provide an outdoor area for the residents.

The east elevation overlooks a public park.

Chorlton Park is a housing development located in a 1930s suburb four miles from Manchester city centre. The development was initiated by the Irwell Valley Housing Association, who wanted a landmark housing scheme. The aim was to provide spacious, flexible, light and warm housing that would be affordable to operate and have links to the natural environment. The Housing Association held an invited architectural competition and Stephenson Bell's design, comprising a three-storey L-shaped block and creating a secluded courtyard away from the road, was selected. One of the competition assessors, Tom Bloxham of private developers Urban Spash, decided to propose a joint venture and extend the development by adding seven two-bedroom flats for sale to the 20 one- and two-bedroom shared ownership flats provided by the housing association. The enlarged project was welcomed by both the housing association and the planners, and the financial gain made it feasible to locate the car park underground, freeing up the courtyard for landscaping.

One of the challenges was to keep construction costs within the limited budget, while providing high quality dwellings with minimal operating energy. The main approach taken was to minimise energy needs. In the UK, 60 per cent of the energy used in a typical dwelling is for space heating. Reducing heat loss from the building fabric is the first step towards providing a low energy building and this was done here by providing a highly insulated and airtight building envelope. The structure is a timber frame with 230mm glass wool insulation externally finished with acrylic render. The flat roof comprises an ethylene propylene diene monomer (EPDM) membrane mechanically fixed on 110mm extruded insulation, backed by 100mm glass wool insulation with a vapour control layer. The overall U-value is 0.11 W/m² K (R51). Composite windows were used, which are timber inside and aluminium outside, with low-e glass and argon-filled cavities. These are energy efficient and provide a durable finish. The combination of the well-insulated wall structure with the high performance doors and windows forms a very efficient building shell. Furthermore, by their very nature flats have a reduced external surface area, particularly those located centrally in the block. This also makes a significant contribution to reducing heat loss.

The second step was to maximise solar heat gains. At Chorlton Park all living spaces have large glazed areas, which admit both light and heat from the sun. The living rooms of 11 of the flats are oriented south, which maximises the solar gains, and 16 of the flats are oriented east. As is often the case when building in cities, the optimum orientation is not always possible; however, the east orientation will provide an initial boost of heat in the morning that, taking into account the low building fabric heat loss, should make a significant contribution to the heating of the flats. Solar gain is affected not only by orientation, but also by physical obstructions. In cold climates where solar gain is desirable in the winter, the position of the winter sun in relation to surrounding buildings and natural landscaping has to be considered. At a latitude of 52°N, the winter sun at its highest is at an angle of only 15°, which means an obstruction higher than three metres 11 metres away will overshadow some of the building. The ground-floor south-facing

flats will therefore be overshadowed by the buildings on the opposite side of the road for part of the year. The east-facing flats, which look onto a wide road, are free from overshadowing, but here the solar access is reduced, particularly in winter. In summer, excessive solar gain is prevented by the deep balconies, which shade the flats from the high midday summer sun (at about 60° in England), while sliding screens on the balconies provide shade from the summer when is at a lower angle.

With a heat load reduced to only 1.25 kW per flat, a central heating system was unnecessary and small electrical panel heaters were installed in the living room and bedroom providing 1 kW and 0.25 kW respectively. These will only rarely be used, as the high level of insulation will retain internal heat gains and the flats also have MVHR (mechanical ventilation with heat recovery). This provides ventilation to the flats, recovering the heat from the extracted stale air and using it to preheat the incoming fresh air. The units are fitted in an insulated cupboard adjacent to the bathroom, and a variable-speed fan reduces operating noise.

The omission of a central heating system saved £1,600 per flat, which was invested in the increased insulation and in the mechanical ventilation system. The development proved to be affordable despite the different design approach: the overall cost was £650 per square metre gross and the selling price was about £1940 per square metre.

The scheme not only shows that minimising energy needs is feasible and cost-effective, but also that it can result in quality architecture that also contributes to the regeneration of a neighbourhood.

5.1.4 Sustainable design features

Site and ecology
The development is on a site previously used by a petrol filling station. The site was contaminated and needed remedial work before work could commence. The development density is 180 dwellings per hectare. Due to the increased density it was financially feasible to include underground car parking, which allowed the internal courtyard to be landscaped.

Community and culture
The houses are affordable in terms of purchase and running costs. The courtyard scheme has also successfully created a communal spirit. The development introduces needed small dwellings to an area of primarily individual houses, enhancing the mix of residents and helping to regenerate the area.

Health
The dwellings benefit from good natural light and access to external spaces. A 300-m² timber-framed balcony structure provides external areas for the residents. Half of the flats overlook a public park. The flats have the use of the walkway on the courtyard side of the building and the planted courtyard. Bedrooms are on the courtyard side to provide a quiet environment.

Materials
The structure is made of timber, which is a renewable material with a low-embodied energy.

The oak for the balcony structure was sourced from hurricane-damaged forests in northern France.

Energy
The building is well insulated and benefits from passive solar gains. Total heat loads were calculated to be 1.25 kW per flat, and heating costs were calculated to be less than £100 per year. Water is heated by an electrical insulated water heater with a 125-litre capacity.
Fabric U-values: 0.11 W/m² K (R51)
See also main text

Sliding solar shading panel

Case study: Maximising heat gains

Solarhaus Freiburg
Freiburg, Germany

Client: Fraunhofer Institut Solare Energiesysteme
Architect: Hölken & Berghoff
Energy consultants: Fraunhofer Institut Solare Energiesysteme
Completed: 1992

The windows have motorised, manually operated external shading.

The double windows on the south elevation.

The north elevation.

The Solarhaus in Freiburg is an experimental house dating back to 1992, which was built to demonstrate the potential of using solar energy alone to power a house in the central European climate. The solar power had to be derived from installations on the building itself. It was commissioned by the Fraunhofer Institute for Solar Energy Systems and, from 1992 to 1995, the 145–m^2 four-bedroom house was occupied by a family of three. During that period the building performance was monitored. Since then the building, which was ahead of its time, continues to be used to test a range of innovative technologies and products.

In order to create a building that could be powered entirely by the solar energy that it could harness, the building energy requirements had to be minimised. This was done by methodically applying all the main passive solar principles, involving both minimising heat loss and maximising solar heat gains.

The building was designed to have a compact form with a low surface area to volume ratio of 0.76, which minimises the external building fabric area liable to lose heat. The building fabric is highly insulated and airtight. The north-facing wall is constructed with 300mm calcium silicate blocks with a timber frame and 240-mm recycled cellulose insulation on the outside of the block, finished with timber cladding. The south-facing walls are constructed with 300mm calcium silicate blocks with 120 millimetres of transparent insulation covered by an external glass panel. The north-facing windows are triple glazed and the openings on the south side are glazed with two windows, each with low-energy double-glazed units filled with krypton gas, effectively creating a four-layered glazed enclosure.

To maximise solar heat gains and minimise losses, the building is oriented south: the building plan is a circle segment whereby the smaller straight segment faces north and the larger curved segment faces south. Living spaces, which require higher indoor temperatures, are positioned on the south side of the building, while the stairs, services, and cupboard-lined walls face north. In terms of fabric heat loss, windows are the weakest element, and typically only provide a quarter to a tenth of the insulation of a solid wall. Also, transparent building elements are those that admit most solar radiation into the building. They are, therefore, concentrated on the south side of the building (24m^2), to capture the sun, and on the north side there are only two windows in the stairwell (4m^2). The enclosed stairwell, which does not need to be as warm as the rest of the house, also reduces heat loss by acting as a buffer on the cold side of the building. It also includes the entrance door and provides a lobby to the outside, reducing the heat lost when the entrance door is opened.

The south façade is designed to make the most of the solar gains. The 24 square metres of windows allow solar radiation into the house. In addition to the glazing, the solid elements are insulated with transparent insulation made of a polycarbonate honeycomb material, which allows solar radiation to pass through it and heat up the block wall. The wall is plastered both sides and painted black on the outside to absorb as much radiation as possible. It acts as a solar collector, or Trombe wall, slowly heating up during the day and storing heat until the surrounding air temperature drops below the wall's temperature. It has an eight-hour time lag, which means that when the sun sets and direct solar radiation through the windows ceases, the wall's mass will reradiate heat into the house. To prevent the wall radiating heat to the outside air, the insulating effect of the transparent insulation, which has a relatively low resistivity of 0.09 W/mK, is enhanced by lowering woven blinds with an aluminium finish. This increases the overall wall U-value from 0.51 W/m²K to 0.40 W/m²K. The blinds are also used to shade the building and prevent overheating in summer.

Sixty-five per cent of the south wall is insulated with transparent insulation, which contributes 6,000 kWh of heat per annum. On all except approximately 15 days a year, the heat provided is sufficient to keep the building comfortable. The house is ventilated by MVHR, operating at 80 per cent efficiency. The incoming air passes through an earth duct, buried 4 metres under ground. The stable ground temperature preheats the air in winter and cools it in summer. If needed, the MVHR system can heat the air.

As a result of this strategy, the energy use for space heating, including the use of the MVHR, in the three years of monitoring ranged between less than 1 and 4 kWh/m²yr. The domestic hot water is provided entirely by solar thermal panels and all the appliances are energy efficient. Consequently, the total energy use for the house was less than 12 kWh/m²yr, or 10 per cent of the average use in Germany. This energy was provided by means of a PV installation and the house was never connected to the grid.

Overall, the strategy to minimise heat loss and maximise heat gains was very successful and, even though some of the more sophisticated technologies, such as the fuel cell seasonal storage, struggled with teething problems, the Solarhaus contributed to setting the standards for other zero-energy buildings.

5.1.5 Sustainable design features

Community and culture
The pioneering design paved the way for a number of technologies such as building applied fuel cells.

Health
All internal spaces have good natural light and provide a warm and comfortable environment.

Materials
The building makes use of recycled cellulose fibre insulation.

Energy
The building is well insulated and built to be airtight to provide 0.3 air changes per hour at 50 Pa.

Fabric U-values:
   Roof – 0.19 W/m² K (R30)
   North wall – 0.16 W/m² K (R36)
   South wall – 0.51 to 0.40 W/m² K (R11-14)
   Basement wall – 0.19 W/m² K (R30)
   Basement slab – 0.18 W/m² K (R32)
   South windows – 0.60 W/m² K (0.11Btu/ft²h°F)
   North windows – 1.20 W/m² K (0.21Btu/ft²h°F)

Solar thermal panels provide hot water. All domestic appliances are energy efficient.

A mono-crystalline silicon cell PV installation of 36 square metres and 4.2 kW peak output provides the house with electricity. Batteries are used to store up to 20 kWh of electricity. A seasonal store of hydrogen to produce electricity was originally installed and operated for a number of years. The seasonal store system worked by splitting water into hydrogen and oxygen using electricity produced by the PV array. The gases were stored and when a deficiency in the PV electricity production occurred, the gases would feed into a fuel cell to generate electricity and heat. The heat from the electricity generation was used to provide hot water. Hydrogen was also used to cook and as a back-up fuel for space heating.

In summer the blinds shade the transparent insulated façade and roller blinds can be used to shade the windows.

The shading is partially drawn over the transparent insulation.

Case study: Building orientation

Pinakarri Cohousing
Hamilton Hill, Perth, Western Australia

Project details, Chapter 2.2, p.72

All houses have the main living accommodation and large windows on the north side to maximise solar heat gains.

Louvred openings on the west façade allow the cool sea breeze into the building and the hot air out of the building.

Pinakarri housing community, designed primarily to offer an alternative way of life to the typical impersonal suburb, aimed to create a sustainable development that was as energy efficient as possible.

Perth, at approximately 32° latitude, has a maritime climate characterised by hot summers and mild winters. Summer temperatures can reach 40 °C; in winter temperatures can drop to below 5 °C. Most houses do not have central heating and rely on individual room heaters to cope with colder spells. In summer, cooling is required and is typically provided through natural ventilation assisted by fans and air-conditioning.

The houses in Pinakarri are designed to provide a comfortable environment throughout the year without auxiliary heating or cooling. In such a mild climate high levels of insulation are not warranted: the roofs are insulated, but the walls are solid block walls. Nonetheless, a comfortable environment is created as a result of considering the buildings' orientation to maximise passive heating and cooling.

To take advantage of solar heat gains, the units are oriented east–west which results in the long façades facing south and north. Large windows are situated on the north façade (the main solar aspect in the southern hemisphere), while smaller glazed openings are situated on the south side. Most living spaces face north and benefit from direct solar heat gains, while secondary spaces that do not require as much heat, such as utility rooms and stairs, are located on the south side of the buildings. The solar radiation, which is admitted into the houses, heats up the space, including the thermally massive tiled concrete floors, which provide heat storage. The building fabric is sufficiently insulated to retain the heat generated through internal and solar heat gains and maintain comfortable internal temperatures.

Orientation has to be considered not only in respect of the sun, but also in respect of the wind. Particularly in climates where summers are hot, taking advantage of even light breezes can help to cool a building. The Pinakarri houses rely on opening windows and doors to provide cross-ventilation. In addition, the freestanding houses incorporate a louvred ventilator at high level on the west- and east-facing façades. These ventilators channel the cool breeze from the sea through the building and allow the hot air to escape.

The temperatures monitored in one house during the past years show that even when temperatures drop to below 5°C in July and August, internal temperatures always remain above 16°C and are generally above 17°C, occasionally even reaching 24°C. Winter averages are 3-4°C above external averages. In summer when external temperatures are above 35°C, the houses can be as much as 9°C cooler. Average internal temperatures were between 22-26°C and only 15 per cent of the time did internal temperatures rise above 27°C. While further improvements, such as additional shading and insulation, are possible, the current design, which relies largely on appropriate orientation, has proved very satisfactory.

See also: cohousing Chapter 2.2

See also: acquiring life skills Chapter 2.3

Case study: Landscaping to moderate the environment

The sun, the wind and the surrounding land forms and landscaping interact with each other and determine the microclimate of each site. Land forms influence the direction and strength of the wind, and physical obstructions affect the access to direct solar radiation. When designing for energy efficiency and comfort, existing built and natural forms must be considered and new elements can be introduced to help regulate the environment. In particular, planting can help moderate the microclimate, while also enhancing habitats for flora and fauna, preventing soil erosion, purifying the air in urban sites, providing noise protection and privacy, defining space and improving its aesthetic quality. Planting may be employed to reduce heating and cooling needs. Trees and shrubs can protect buildings from the wind and reduce convective heat losses. Shrubs located close to a building can also create a buffer of air which insulates the building envelope.

Plants can reduce heat gains by protecting buildings from direct sunlight and reflected light from streets and other buildings and by lowering the ambient temperature. Trees, planted screens and climbers on walls provide effective shading to walls and windows. Trees, depending on the species, let through 10-25 per cent of the light when in leaf and 60-70 per cent when bare (Thomas 1999). This difference can be exploited in climates where solar gain is welcome in winter and unwelcome in summer. The selection of the tree species should take into account when the trees lose their leaves, for instance, in the south of the England maples can retain their leaves until December, well into the typical heating period when solar gain would be welcome. Trellises and screens planted with deciduous climbers form a seasonal shading device similar to deciduous trees. Other seasonal changes of climbers can also be exploited. The leaves of an ivy plant growing on a wall tend to stand away from wall during summer providing shade and allowing a breeze to cool the wall. In winter they lie flat against the wall and create an insulating layer, which helps to reduce heat loss (Johnston and Newton 1997).

Plants also help cooling by lowering the ambient temperature. Vegetation uses some of the solar energy reaching the ground for photosynthesis and reduces the amount of heat reflected into the environment. The process of evaporation from plants also cools the surrounding air by extracting energy from it. The combined cooling and shading effect of trees is thought to save up to 50 per cent of building air-conditioning costs where used (Foster 1994).

The Schreiber house is growing a planted trellis as a shading device. Until the plants are sufficiently grown a reed mat is used instead.

A thin metal frame with metal wires creates a support structure for the clematis and other climbers.

At the new BCZEB headquarters building near London (see p.248), a row of deciduous trees shades the office windows in summer and allows solar gains in winter.

Case study: Shading

College Library
Sunshine Coast University, Sippy Down, Queensland, Australia

Client: Sunshine Coast University
Architect: Lawrence Neild & Ptns with John Mainwaring & Associates
Structural engineer: Taylor Thomas Whitting, McWilliams Consulting Engineers
Services engineer: Lincolne Scott Australia
Landscape architect: John Mongard
Quantity surveyor: Graham Lukins & Partners
Contractor: Evans Harch
Completed: 1996

The fully shaded north elevation.

The south elevation that does not require shading.

The reading room.

To minimise energy needs, different strategies can be applied simultaneously. For instance, to minimise heating needs, using high levels of insulation, building airtight and maximising solar heat gains all work together. Similarly, to minimise cooling needs, shading should be used in conjunction with other approaches. Where the climate permits, shading, together with natural ventilation, evaporative cooling or high thermal mass can create a comfortable environment. Where mechanical cooling is needed, shading can still help to reduce the cooling loads.

There are different types of shading devices: fixed or movable, and internal, external or integral to the building fabric. Commonly used types include overhangs, louvres, blinds, shutters, curtain, awnings, and screens, which, as discussed in the previous case study, can be planted. The choice of shading type depends on when shading is required and for what purpose. The two main reasons for needing shading are to reduce heat gains and glare.

To reduce heat gains, the building and, in particular, the glazed openings have to be protected from direct solar gains. In hot climates, where solar gains are always unwelcome, fixed external overhangs or louvres may be appropriate. In many locations, however, shading is required only during certain periods of the year. At high latitudes, for example, in England at 52° latitude, shading should block out the summer sun to minimise overheating, but let in the winter sun to maximise heat gains. To achieve adequate shading in such situations, the seasonal sunpath changes have to be considered. First, the sun angle varies throughout the year: the sun at 12 noon in summer is at 60° and in winter it is at 15°. Second, the sunpath is much shorter in winter than in summer, which means that different elevations of a building are affected by the sun at different times of the year. In winter the sun rises in the south-east and sets in the south-west (in the northern hemisphere), while in summer it rises in the north-east and sets in the north-west. In summer the east and west façades are exposed to the low morning and evening sun and receive much more direct solar radiation than the south façade. The north façade receives only minimal direct solar radiation. In winter the south elevation receives most of the solar radiation, and the east and west elevations receive only a little. Closer to the equator the difference between summer and winter diminishes, the sun angle at 12 noon nears 90° and the east and west elevations are increasingly affected by solar radiation.

Movable shading can respond to changing parameters. Louvres can be made to tilt according to the incident of the sun, and blinds, shutters, curtains and awnings can be opened and closed as required. If fixed shading is to be used, it has to be designed to respond to the seasonal changes and the elevation orientation.

An example of fixed shading that responds to solar incident can be found at the Sunshine Coast University, Brisbane, Australia. The Sunshine Coast University College Library is the symbolic centre of the new campus and the most prominent building when approaching the university. It not only houses the library and study spaces, but also an exhibition facility and a café. Its main entrance is from a covered and shaded wing open to the elements and oriented north–south, which also provides an external study space. To the north of the library is a paved plaza, to the south and east are lawn areas, and to the west is a paved pedestrian street leading to other university buildings.

The library is partially overshadowed on the west side by other buildings, but all other elevations are exposed. As mentioned earlier, a north-facing façade in the northern hemisphere and a south-facing façade in the southern hemisphere receive minimal if any direct solar radiation. For this reason the south-facing library elevation has no shading.

Instead, the east and north façades both require shading, and in both cases external shading is used. External shading prevents the solar radiation from entering the building and heating up the building fabric. This is in contrast to internal shading devices. These are appropriate to avoid glare, but allow heat into the building, reradiating only a smaller percentage to the outside, making them ineffective at reducing solar heat gains. An intermediate solution consists of using double-glazed units with a blind sandwiched between the two panes of glass, or integrating blinds within a double façade (see RWE case study, p.224). This has a similar effect to external blinds, and the blinds are less vulnerable to weather damage.

At the library, the east elevation shading has to provide protection from high and low sun. Here horizontal timber slats provide shading, and are spaced differently depending on whether more or less shade is required. The south façade has both horizontal and vertical shading, made of corrugated perforated metal panels. The horizontal shading protects the glazing from the high summer sun. The vertical shading is angled slightly towards the west so as to protect the building from the low evening sun, while allowing views out of the building.

The louvres and slats protect the library from the sun, but also bring to life its interior. A limited amount of direct sunlight penetrates the building, forming shafts of bright light in certain areas. This warm light creates an atmosphere which contrasts with the cool study areas on the north and east sides of the building. The shading reduces the cooling load of the building, and also enhances the quality of the light and the space.

The north-east façade.

The covered outside area is used as an open-air study room.

The shading on the north side, made of perforated metal, is both horizontal and vertical.

The internal work and relaxation areas.

Case study: Thermal mass and heat storage

Materials with a high heat capacity, such as concrete (with a capacity of 0.204–0.784 kWh/cubic metre), stone, bricks and water (capacity of 1.157 kWh/cubic metre) are considered to have high thermal mass. This means that they absorb more energy than a low thermal mass material before their surface temperature is affected. When exposed to a heat source, the surface temperature of material with low thermal mass will relatively quickly achieve the ambient temperature, while a material with high thermal mass will take longer. Having reached ambient temperature, when the source of heat is no longer active, the low thermal mass material will reradiate the relatively small amount of stored heat quickly. Instead the high thermal mass material will take longer to slowly reradiate a larger amount of heat. How long the thermal mass requires to absorb and reradiate the heat depends on the type of material, its quantity and its exposure to the surrounding environment. Within a daily cycle, heat will typically penetrate no more than 100 millimetres of concrete.

The ability of materials with high thermal mass to absorb and store a significant amount of heat before reradiating it is used to help cool and heat spaces.

Cooling strategies exploiting thermal mass generally operate on a diurnal cycle and are most appropriate for buildings with high occupancy, such as offices and theatres. To make use of thermal mass in this way, high diurnal temperature variations are necessary. The climate in the UK is appropriate for using thermal mass, and at the BRE Building 16 (see p.159), the Powergen headquarters (see p.186), and De Montfort University (see p.220), thermal mass was part of an overall energy-efficiency strategy. In these cases the thermal mass, provided by the concrete and brick structures, was designed to absorb internal heat gains; external heat gains having already been reduced by shading to the offices and, at De Montfort University, by limiting windows. Throughout the day the thermal mass absorbs heat from its surroundings, effectively cooling the space by a couple of degrees. At the end of the working day, after the occupants have left the building, the thermal mass can be cooled by ventilating the building with cool night air. The following day the cycle can begin again. Cool night air is therefore fundamental to the thermal mass cooling strategy. If the external night temperature is similar to the daytime temperature, such as in some tropical climates, using thermal mass for cooling is ineffective.

Night-time ventilation can be provided through automatically opening windows and vents, often at high level, or by passing air through ducts within concrete slabs, as in the proprietary system Thermodeck. Cooling can also be provided by water: in the BRE Building 16, groundwater at a constant temperature of 11°C is used to cool a high thermal mass concrete screed and slab floor.

In certain situations, rather than discharging the heat, it can be beneficially used. For instance, dwellings in the UK require more heating than cooling and are occupied at night when the external temperature drops. In such cases the thermal mass can absorb solar radiation during the day and emit heat in the evening (see the Autonomous House case study, p.270).

Whether used to help cool or heat a building, thermal mass diminishes temperature variations that could cause discomfort and increase the use of energy for cooling or heating. However, the use of thermal mass does have its pitfalls and is not always appropriate. The high heat capacity of the thermal mass, which is so beneficial when heat needs to be absorbed to keep a space cool, means that heating a space with high thermal mass requires longer than heating up a space with low thermal mass. This can be problematic in buildings occupied intermittently or where occupancy is low. On overcast days with negligible radiation from the sun, an unoccupied building will cool down throughout the day and auxiliary heating will be required when its occupants arrive. A well-insulated lightweight building will heat up quickly with little energy. Heating a high thermal mass building requires more time and energy as the thermal mass has to be heated up before the air temperature is affected. Extended periods with no solar gains or, conversely, with elevated temperatures day and night, can negate the advantages of thermal mass.

The exposed concrete soffits provide thermal mass at the Building Research Establishment Building 16, located at the Building Research Establishment in Watford, near London, designed by Feilden, Clegg, Bradley Architects.

One way to partially address this drawback is to increase the thermal mass and, rather than generate a diurnal cycle, generate a seasonal cycle. This can be done by significantly increasing the mass of the building structure or by coupling the building structure to the ground, effectively storing heat in the ground to be used in the building. Rather than insulating the building structure, the earth surrounding the structure is insulated. This principle was used at the Mile End Park (see p40), where the ground around the art and exhibition buildings was insulated and waterproofed for 6 metres, following the principle that heat transfers at approximately at 1 metre per month in dry earth. The ability of a seasonal heat storage system to continue radiating or absorbing heat, remains unaffected by short periods without sunshine or with elevated temperatures. At Mile End Park the earth's thermal capacity was also be used to pre-heat and pre-cool the air supply to the buildings. Tubes were located underground and, as the air travels through the pipes, the heat is transferred from the earth to the air and vice versa.

Seasonal storage can also be remote from the building. This approach was taken at the BCZEB headquarters building (see p.248). Here hot water is stored throughout the summer and used in winter for space heating. Hot water from fifteen 4.2 x 1.7-metre solar panels (170 m^2) and seven thermal PV panels (54 m^2) is pumped to a seasonal heat store. The store comprises a 1,100m^2 pit, lined with geotextile membrane and filled with 1,400 cubic metres of water kept at 20-50°C. The pit is surrounded by 2-metre thick chalk and clay mixture and is insulated to 1 metre below ground. The top of the water is insulated with a layer of 500-millimetre thick polystyrene. Despite the insulation the store is expected to lose 50 per cent of the heat. The solar panels are expected to generate 39 MWh of heat, of which 15 MWh is used directly in the building and 24 MWh is collected in the store, to be used to pre-heat the supply air to the 2,700 m^2 of office, exhibition and conference facilities.

Different materials to store heat are also being experimented with. Phase change materials are of particular interest. Rather than storing the sensible heat (heat associated

The solar panels at BCZEB

with a change in temperature), phase change materials can store the latent heat of fusion (the heat associated with a change in state, i.e. gas, liquid or solid). The latent heat of fusion is far greater than the sensible heat, being between 38-105 kWh/m^3 (Goulding *et al.* 1992). Paraffin has been used as a phase change heat store in a timber-framed house designed by Dietrich Schwarz in Switzerland. An experimental façade element was developed, consisting of a paraffin-filled plastic container within a double-glazed unit, providing ten times the heat storage capacity of concrete. A prismatic outer layer allows winter sun to the heat store, while shielding it from the summer sun. The installation contributes to achieving a comfortable environment within a house complying with the Passivhaus standards.

The Mile End Park art and exhibition buildings are partially located under ground and are linked thermally to the earth.

The BCZEB seasonal store has a polystyrene cover, which is weighted down with stones and some plants.

Earth ducts, used to supply fresh air into buildings, take advantage of the earth's constant temperature to heat the incoming air in winter and cool it in summer. The intake ducts here are at the Akademie Mont-Cenis (see p.243).

Case study: Natural ventilation in high occupancy spaces

Queens Building
De Montfort University, Leicester, UK

Client: De Montfort University
Architect: Short and Ford Associates
Service engineers: Max Fordham Associates
Structural engineers: Antony Hunt Associates and YRM
Quantity surveyor: Dearle and Henderson
Main contractor: Laing Midlands
Completed: 1993

The curved external wall of the lecture theatre is visible from the street. Air inlets are located between the windows, which light the workshops below. The theatre seating has its back to the street.

The main entrance to the university building

The Queens Building remains, even after more than a decade, a model for naturally ventilated buildings. Completed in 1993, the Queens Building was experimental in many ways and proved that natural ventilation is not limited to small or sparsely occupied buildings, but can successfully be used to create comfortable environments in demanding situations. The 10,000 m² building houses classrooms, drawing studios, mechanical and electrical engineering laboratories, offices and two lecture rooms. The mechanical laboratories, where testing takes place, are the only mechanically ventilated spaces and cooling is not required anywhere.

The tall chimneys provide ventilation to the teaching rooms.

The building is characterised by its ventilation chimneys and brick walls, a result of its environmental design. The building envelope incorporates 100mm insulation and internally the exposed bricks and concrete floors provide thermal mass. All spaces have good natural light provided by windows or rooflights. Shallow plans allow cross-ventilation and high ceilings generate temperature stratifications, keeping low level areas, where people work, cooler than high level areas. Where cross-ventilation is not possible passive stack ventilation is provided. The most complex areas to ventilate naturally are the two 150-person lecture theatres.

The natural ventilation strategy for the theatres assumed them to be fully occupied for eight hours per day, five days per week. The total internal heat load of occupants, lighting and equipment was expected to be nearly 100 W/m². To naturally ventilate the lecture theatres, passive stack ventilation had to be employed. The passive stack effect describes when hot air, which is lighter than cool air, rises naturally. During the design development numerous tests were undertaken and the design team cautiously concluded that temperatures in the theatres would exceed 27°C for only nine hours per year, out of term time. In practice, the lecture theatres have proved to be very comfortable. The peak daily average temperature during the monitoring period of the summer of 1994 was 22°C. Occupants, then and more recently, are very happy with the environment.

The lecture halls have raked wooden seating and carpeted floor and the walls are partially exposed brick and partially covered with acoustic timber panelling. In one of the lecture theatres fresh air enters an acoustically insulated plenum under the raked seating. Air inlets are located in the external wall at one storey above street level. Heating elements under the seats warm up the incoming air if required, and it is then supplied into the hall through grilles under the seats. Once in the theatre space, the air is further heated up by internal heat gains from people and equipment. As it warms up, it rises and is drawn up through two 13.3m-high acoustically lined chimneys. These stacks have a combined area of 4 square metres and they extend 3 metres beyond the roof line. Their vertical opening areas are approximately 8 square metres. The air inlets and the stacks have dampers that are linked to the Building Energy Management System (BEMS) and are automatically adjusted to modify the air supply and avoid excessive levels of CO_2 and high temperatures. Equally, if the temperature of the exhaust air is below 12°C, the dampers in the stack close. The natural ventilation continues operating at night, cooling the thermal mass for the following day. Night cooling is also controlled by the BEMS, which ensures the temperature does not drop below 17°C to avoid discomfort.

The second lecture hall is at 180 degrees to the first and air is introduced from the front of the lecture hall behind the speaker. A large heater in the room provides heating if required. In this lecture hall the air supply path is much more direct and sound can also travel into the hall more easily. Nonetheless, both configurations have proved to work satisfactorily.

A number of concerns at the design stage proved unfounded. For instance, it was thought that first thing on a cold morning a mass of cool air in the stack would seal the stack, and where the chimneys extend beyond the insulated building envelope, there was concern that the air might cool down and reverse the stack effect. None of these problems materialised, but during the design process a number of measures were taken to reduce the risk of the system malfunctioning. Where possible, the stacks were fully glazed so that the sun can heat the air further, and in the lecture halls a punkah fan was installed in one of the two stacks in each hall to provide assistance if needed. The fans are set up to operate if the temperature in the lecture hall exceeds 25°C and is at least 2°C above the external temperature. This has, in fact, proved unnecessary and the fans are never used.

Even using the improved computer technology and technical installations available today, it would be difficult to significantly improve the ventilation design for the lecture theatres. The theatres provide a good teaching environment appreciated by many lecturers.

5.1.6 Sustainable design features

Community and culture
The building has proved very beneficial to the university and the city, attracting interest and visitors. It enhances the university's reputation as a forward-looking institution.

Health
The occupants feel the building has a good indoor quality. The materials used are all inert and toxic materials were avoided. Ample natural light and natural ventilation create invigorating spaces.

Energy
Heating is provided by a combined heat and power unit (38 kW) plus a condensing boiler and two high efficiency boilers. Energy consumption is 143 kWh/m²yr of gas and 52 kWh/m²yr of electricity. CO_2 emissions are 65 kg/m²yr.

The chimneys for the lecture theatres are on the right of the tall stack and have glazed vertical openings.

The bottoms of the stacks are visible at high level to the right and left of the display screen.

The air grilles are located below the timber panels behind the chairs.

Exposed brick and concrete provide thermal mass.

Internal view of one of the lecture theatres.

Above the doors are the air inlets for the second theatre, which has the seating facing the street.

Case study: Natural ventilation with water cooling

Thurgoona Campus
Charles Sturt University, Albury, Victoria, Australia

Project details, Chapter 4.4, p.177

Thurgoona Campus, the new Charles Sturt University campus situated in the Murray River valley, lies on 36° latitude. The average temperature in winter is 7°C and in summer it is 22°C. The area has marked diurnal variations and in summer the average high temperature is 30°C and the average low night temperature is 14°C. Daytime temperatures in excess of 30°C are common.

In such an environment, naturally cooling sparsely occupied spaces, let alone a densely occupied lecture theatre, can be a challenge. However, despite the climate, air-conditioning is installed only in the herbarium storage and some herbarium work spaces that require very controlled environments. The student accommodation, student building, the teaching blocks and the lecture theatre rely on thermal mass, natural ventilation and night-time cooling to ensure comfortable temperatures throughout the summer.

The central vents, clearly visible over the roofs of the naturally ventilated teaching block, are used to draw air from the air inlets under the windows.

The naturally ventilated teaching block with a central vent. Note the glass louvres over the doors, which allow cross-ventilation from the office windows to the central vent.

The air inlets under the windows supply fresh air to the building. The roof and sunscreens shade the windows and minimise solar heat gains.

Natural ventilation is made possible by minimising solar heat gains and using the building's thermal mass as a heat sink. Solar radiation is prevented from entering the building by shading the windows and insulating the roof. The thermal mass, provided by concrete floors and rammed earth walls, helps to stabilise the internal temperature by absorbing heat during the day and releasing it at night. At night, cool air is drawn into the spaces through automatic vents at low level under the windows and exhausted through high level louvred shafts to help cool the thermal mass. In addition, solar roof panels used to heat the space in winter cool the concrete slabs at night by circulating water through the warm slabs and dissipating the heat to the cold clear skies.

Internal view of the lecture theatre.

To naturally ventilate the 200-seat lecture theatre a system had to be devised that could deal with the high internal gains typical of lecture theatres, where many people congregate at once, plus the potential for high solar gains. Excluding solar heat gains was of primary importance and the same basic environmental strategy used for the rest of the building was applied, but in a more rigorous way. The lecture theatre is a partially underground and has minimal glazed openings. Direct solar access is virtually impossible. The earth covering the lecture theatre roof and more than 50 per cent of the walls provides good insulation, keeping the structure cool. Inside the lecture theatre, the walls and floor are made of concrete and rammed earth and are thermally massive to absorb internal heat gains. Natural passive stack ventilation provides fresh air and cooling. Night-time ventilation is also employed to cool the thermal mass with the cooler night air.

When the external air temperature is very high, the combination of thermal mass and natural ventilation may not be sufficient to create a comfortable internal environment. The temperature of the air entering the lecture theatre has to be lowered to provide cooling, and this is achieved by evaporative cooling using a water spray around the air intake to the lecture theatre.

The intake vents for the air supply, situated below the racked seating at the rear of the theatre, are set below an external water fountain. Jets of water create a screen to the air intake vents. As the water evaporates and changes from a liquid to a gas, it absorbs energy from the surrounding air, thus reducing its temperature. The cooler air enters the theatre, is heated up by the occupants, rises as it warms up and is evacuated from the theatre through the high level vent. As the hot air exits the buildings, it draws more cool air into the building through the low level vents below the water fountain. This simple mechanism requires minimal maintenance, consisting mainly of cleaning the fountain regularly and maintaining the pumps. Animals are prevented from entering the building by the difference in levels between the fountain, the vents and the ground. Despite the simplicity of the system, it has proved successful in keeping the lecture theatre comfortable and demonstrating that natural ventilation can be made to work even in hot climates.

5.1.7 Evaporative cooling

Evaporative cooling refers to the cooling of the air that occurs when a liquid in contact with the air changes to a gas.

Latent heat is the heat that is absorbed or released when a substance changes from a gas to a liquid or a liquid to a solid and vice versa. When a liquid evaporates, it absorbs heat from the surroundings. This heat, known as the latent heat of evaporation, is the energy required to expand the liquid into a gaseous state. As heat is absorbed from the surroundings, the temperature of the surrounding air drops.

This mechanism has been used historically in hot and arid climates where water fountains or basins were used as part of a cooling strategy in buildings and courtyards.

The ledge above the vents to the lecture theatre contains spray nozzles that form a screen of water, cooling the air taken into the theatre.

On the right the earth-bermed lecture theatre with the central vent. The theatre is accessed through the circular link which connects the theatre to other teaching facilities.

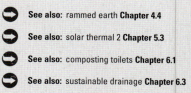

See also: rammed earth **Chapter 4.4**

See also: solar thermal 2 **Chapter 5.3**

See also: composting toilets **Chapter 6.1**

See also: sustainable drainage **Chapter 6.3**

Case study: High tech low energy

RWE AG Essen HQ
Essen, Germany

Client: RWE AG
Architect: Ingenhoven Overdiek und Partner
Structural engineer: Hochtief AG.
Services engineer: HL-Technik
Façade specialist: Gartner
Landscape architect: Klaus Klein
Main contractor: Hochtief
Completed: 1996

View from the Aalto theatre in the park on the opposite side of the main road. Behind the tower is the garden, which forms the centre of the city block, consisting primarily of six-storey office buildings. The garden is one storey level lower than the street.

The metal ventilating elements between the external and the internal glass layer let air in and out through perforations in alternative bays. Floor level detail shows heating grill and ceiling detail shows edge of suspended ceiling.

The RWE AG office building in Essen was conceived as an antithesis of the traditional high rise of the time. The concept that high-rise buildings had to have full air-conditioning and artificial lights switched on permanently and that users had to be divorced from the outside world was overturned by this elegant and restrained tower in the centre of the old industrial heart of Germany.

The tower was developed as part of an urban design competition, which addressed a larger area and originally involved two high-rise buildings. Only one tower was built, but the urban concept for a city block built around a landscaped garden was retained. The RWE tower forms one corner of the city block and its entrance is from a paved court that opens up to the street and creates a notional link to the Aalto theatre on the opposite side of the road. The garden on the inside of the city block is one storey lower than the road and here the tower gains a plinth, which houses the restaurant. The restaurant opens up on a terrace on the edge of an artificial lake in the centre of the garden. Above the ground floor entrance are 31 storeys of offices, with the top five floors dedicated to the management of the company. Two stair cores are at the perimeter of the cylinder, with services at its centre and a block with four lifts running alongside it.

Offices are located along the perimeter of the 32m diameter, 120m high cylinder (the top of the antenna is at 162 metres). The external wall of each office consists of floor-to-ceiling glass and provides views of the sky and city that stretch for miles. Artificial light is seldom necessary and the windows can be rolled open to let fresh air in. The building is, in fact, naturally ventilated for nine months of the year.

To achieve maximum natural light and natural ventilation a new façade type had to be developed: a double glass façade for a high rise building. The construction comprises two clear glass layers 500mm apart. The outside layer is made of structural glazing with eight fixings per 2 x 3.6m panel, and the inner layer is a full height glazing system with a sliding window and a U-value of 1.2 W/m²K. In the cavity are blinds that can be operated by the occupants. The cavity is naturally ventilated and an air intake and exhaust element is incorporated between each floor. Externally only a 150mm ventilation slot is visible. Internally the convex-shaped ventilation element lines up with the floor and ceiling finishes. Each slot either allows air into the floor above it or exhausts air from the floor below it. Having alternate intakes and exhausts minimises the risk of exhaust air re-entering the building. The ventilation of an office therefore occurs diagonally across two glazed units. Extensive testing of all design elements was undertaken as part of the design development. The system of a ventilated double façade, which makes energy-efficient natural ventilation to high-rise buildings possible, was pioneered at the RWE and is now in widespread use.

At the RWE, heating is provided by perimeter convector heaters supplied by the city district heating system. For the periods when natural ventilation does not provide sufficient cooling, cooling is provided through chilled ceilings with a maximum output of 125 W/m² combined with mechanical ventilation. The cooling plant is located on the eighteenth floor. The building occupants are advised of the optimum operation mode by means of a control panel in each office. A monitoring system avoids wasteful use of energy by, for instance, switching off the cooling system when a window is opened. Cooling loads are reduced through the use of the thermal mass of the structure and, at the lower levels of the building, also by adiabatic cooling from the lake.

It is self-evident that this building has been designed for the benefit of its users. The offices provide a high quality work environment with a link to the outside and to nature; and the communal spaces are equally uplifting. The building has also become an important part of the community, and seven years after its completion local people still visit the building on the open days organised by RWE to enjoy the views from the roof. The tower has become the trademark for Essen and a symbol of the city's development.

High-rise buildings are often considered unsustainable due to their significant consumption of materials and energy. However, their sustainability also has to be assessed by considering the need of humans for comfort, aesthetics, excitement and a sense of belonging and pride, which this building has achieved. Furthermore, the RWE tower set the mould for energy-efficient high rise buildings and continued technological improvements would suggest that similar buildings, built today and in future, could achieve even greater reductions in energy and resource use.

5.1.8 Sustainable design features

Site and ecology
The development is on a previously used, city centre site near the main station. The development includes an extensive new garden and lake at the centre of the new city block.

Community and culture
The building provides a symbol of modernity for the city of Essen.

Health
The building maximises natural light and ventilation, and allows the occupants control over their environment.

Materials
All the materials have been treated as little as possible to maintain their character and to allow a natural and aesthetic ageing process.

Energy
The building was designed to reduce energy requirements by 25 per cent compared to conventional buildings.

The entrance canopy is covered with 192 metal louvres with PV cells. The total installation has a peak rating of 19KWp.

The horizontal ventilation slots are located level with the floor slabs.

A 1.35m wide internal glazed element can be slid open to provide natural ventilation.

The slim ventilation slots are almost completely unobtrusive.

Case study: Lighting 1

Dyfi Eco Park
Machynlleth, Wales, UK

Project details, Chapter 3.1, p.106

5.1.9 Probability of building occupants switching on electrical lights

(Adapted from Loe and Mansfield 1998)

Daylight levels as % of daylight factor	9.00-15.00 (%)	7.00-9.00 and 15.00-19.00 (%)
10	5	40
5	10	50
2	30	65
1	40	77
0.5	60	85

The rooflight is the main source of light in the first-floor offices. At the far end is the south-facing glazed elevation which also contributes natural light.

Unit Two. Horizontal glazed openings, as in rooflights, allow more light to penetrate a building than similar areas of vertical glass.

➤ **See also:** thermal comfort **Chapter 3.1**

➤ **See also:** performance targets and post-occupancy monitoring **Chapter 5.2**

The electricity used for lighting is a function of the total wattage associated with the electrical lighting installation and the hours of use. The higher the availability of natural light, the less electrical lighting is used. In the UK, lighting typically accounts for 40-42 per cent of the electricity used in commercial offices without mechanical ventilation or air-conditioning, and 12.5-16.5 per cent of the total energy use. The higher CO_2 emissions associated with electricity, compared to gas, mean that lighting accounts for 20-25 per cent of the CO_2 emissions associated with such buildings.

Maximising natural light was therefore one of the aims of the Dyfi Eco Park design team when they formulated the strategy for the development. The first three of the six office and light industrial units were occupied between 1996 and 2002 and were monitored after completion, including an assessment of the daylight design.

Units One and Two are two-storey, 12m-wide buildings with a rooflight running the length of the building at approximately 5 metres above the first floor finished floor level. They have open plan offices on the top floor and workshops, services, and meeting rooms on the ground floor. In Unit One daylight factor levels in the open-plan office ranged between 4 and 16 per cent. Electrical lights were hardly used and only 11.4 kWh/m^2 of electricity was used for lighting. This constitutes a 20 per cent reduction compared to good practice office design and an 80 per cent reduction compared to typical air-conditioned prestige offices as set out in the Energy Consumption Guide 19 (BRESCU 2000). However, at times the light levels proved excessively high, causing glare, and sunshading had to be retrofitted to the rooflights. In Unit Two, to avoid the glare problem the specification of the glass was changed. Daylight factor levels dropped to 3-12 per cent, glare was no longer such a problem, and the energy use associated with lighting remained low.

The configuration of Unit Three is different in that it is a single-storey, 18m-wide building. Originally meant to be used as a single space, it was fitted out with perimeter cellular offices. The rooflight, similar in size to Units One and Two, is at 7,300 millimetres above finished floor level in the central open plan office space. Due to the distance to the source of natural light, and the larger floor area, daylight factor levels range from 1-7 per cent in the central space, with an average of 3 per cent. In Unit Three electrical lighting is reported to be on all the time during working hours.

Minimum recommended daylight levels for offices are set at 2 per cent, but to avoid the use of electrical light, levels need to be higher (see 5.1.9). The psychological effect of dark corners and perimeter areas, as in Unit Three, is as important as the actual light levels. Units One and Two are excellent examples of how natural light can contribute to lowering overall energy use. The CO_2 emissions associated with Unit One (22.6 $kgCO_2/m^2/yr$), and Unit Two (38.8 $kgCO_2/m^2/yr$) compare well with the lowest target values of 31.7 $kgCO_2/m^2/yr$ (BRESCU 2000). Unit Three, despite extremely low heating requirements, consumes a little more (55.2 $kgCO_2/m^2/yr$), the difference being due to higher use of electrical appliances and lighting.

Case study: Lighting 2

Providing good daylighting to minimise the use of electrical lighting can conflict with efforts to exclude the sun to prevent overheating. This is particularly problematic in hot countries where air-conditioning is prevalent and is associated with higher CO_2 emissions than is heating. The Phoenix Central Library addresses this issue and is designed to bring light into the building, while avoiding direct solar radiations and the associated problems of glare and overheating.

Phoenix Central library
Phoenix, Arizona, USA

Client: Phoenix City
Architect: William Bruder and DWL Architects & Planners
Structural engineer: Michael Ishler
Energy consultants: Ove Arup and Partners
Main contractor: Sundt Corp
Completed: 1995

The south elevation.

The five-storey library houses various book collections, reading rooms, administration and seminar facilities plus a reading room on the top floor. The floor plate is 90 x 60 metres. The 90m east and west façades are clad with a perforated copper cladding and are light impermeable, while the south and north façades are fully glazed. Protecting the east and west façades is increasingly important the closer to the equator a building is. Phoenix is at 33° latitude. At the peak of summer the sun at 12.00 is at 80° altitude, and for the rest of the day it shines primarily on the east and west façades. The south elevation is the third most vulnerable elevation. It is shaded with computer-operated louvres that adjust according to the position of the sun. Fixed vertical Teflon sails on the north façade reduce the reflected light and glare. The top floor reading room also benefits from 2m-diameter rooflights and a lighting strip at the east and west perimeter.

While some of the lower floors need electrical lighting throughout the year, the main top-floor reading room has good natural light, with task lighting used only at the reading tables and book shelves. The shading configuration protects from glare and the additional rooflights effectively light the area. The central atrium has additional rooflights with mirrored louvres within to help bring daylight down to the ground floor.

The shading strategy creates a well-lit space and reduces the cooling load for the air-conditioning. The quality of light, in conjunction with the light tension roof structure, also creates a dramatic space that is relaxing and stimulating at the same time.

The rooflights are positioned above the concrete columns that support the 'tensegrity' roof.

The north elevation

A lighting strip separates the wall and roof.

5.2 Using Energy Efficiently

5.2.1 Energy and environmental labelling

Europe

– The EU Eco-label is administered by the European Eco-labelling Board, and applies to and receives support from members of the European Economic Area. The EU Eco-label considers the environmental impacts associated with a selection of products from paper to electrical equipment. A rating of A–G is used for electrical equipment and domestic appliances, where A indicates the highest efficiency and G the lowest.

– The European Energy Performance of Buildings Directive is due to be implemented by January 2006. The directive requires minimum energy performance standards to be set for new buildings and large refurbishments, and energy certificates to be provided when buildings change ownership or tenancy. Regular boiler and air-conditioning plant inspections are also required.

US

– The Energy Star programme is operated by the United States Department of Energy (DOE) and the Environmental Protection Agency (EPA). It provides energy ratings for office equipment and domestic appliances (PCs, TVs, etc.). An Energy Star rating can also be achieved for residential and commercial buildings that save 10 per cent or more energy compared to standard buildings.

Australia

– The Energy Rating Label is mandatory for domestic appliances and states the energy consumption of the appliances. It rates appliances from one to six stars. The greater the number of stars, the higher the efficiency. A similar system to that operating in the US applies to office equipment.

5.2.2 CO₂ and carbon emissions and energy sources

Energy sources	kgC/kWh delivered energy	kgCO$_2$/kWh delivered energy	factor
Gas	0.052	0.19	1
Oil	0.069	0.25	1.3
Coal	0.081	0.30	1.6
Electricity	0.127	0.46	2.4

Zero-energy buildings are not realistic, but low energy buildings are. Even if a building is designed to provide a comfortable environment all year around through passive means, it will still require energy for lighting at night, to operate equipment and appliances, and to provide hot water. In most cases, some energy will also be required to moderate and ventilate the internal environment.

Energy-efficient building design may require the use of new design and technologies, and may sometimes mean that traditional ways of thinking are obsolete. For instance, super-insulating a building makes central heating redundant and new technology has to be employed (see Schreiber case study, p.230). Through an analysis of a building's energy needs, appropriate systems can be selected that work together in a coordinated way. Lighting, appliances, ventilation, heating and cooling should be considered together.

Particularly in respect of electrical equipment, an increasing amount of guidance is now available (see 5.2.1) and major energy savings can be achieved through, for example, the use of energy-efficient lighting systems (see 5.2.3).

Space and water heating also consumes a significant amount of energy (see 5.1.2) and efficient systems are now commonly available. Old gas-fired boilers are 50–70 per cent efficient, converting 50–70 per cent of the primary energy in usable heat. Modern efficient boilers and condensing boilers operate at efficiencies of 75–85 per cent. Condensing boilers make use of the heat from the exhaust flue gases to pre-heat the cold water entering the boiler in order to maximise operating efficiencies. The cost of efficient equipment is steadily decreasing and payback periods for condensing boilers are less than five years. Legislation is also encouraging the use of efficient equipment and in the UK inefficient boilers rated C or less are being phased out.

Another efficient heating system is a combined heat and power unit, CHP, which generates both heat and electricity. Stirling micro CHPs are smaller domestic versions of commercial models (see Sainsbury's case study, p.232). Micro CHPs are the size of a standard kitchen cabinet, are 90 per cent efficient, and currently have a ten-year payback.

Devising a system to be energy efficient not only depends on using energy-efficient equipment but also appropriate controls. This applies to lighting (see 5.2.3) and to heating. Thermostatic radiator valves, central thermostats, timers and programmers allow for optimal heating starts and temperature. The heat emitters also affect the system's efficiency. Panel radiators operate at approximately 75°C and primarily heat by convection. Underfloor heating provides mainly radiant heat that heats people and objects rather than the air. The air temperatures can therefore be kept lower without compromising comfort, and the system uses less energy. Underfloor heating also operates at a lower water temperature (45°C), which can be efficiently supplied by solar thermal panels and condensing boiler systems.

To improve efficiencies further, individual users can be grouped and supplied by a communal facility. Community heating systems can operate boilers or CHP systems and use virtually any fuel: coal, gas, oil, refuse, biofuel and waste heat from industrial processes. The CO₂ emissions of a community heating system depend on the fuel used (see 5.2.2), but central systems are more efficient than individual boilers, owing to improved equipment design, sizing and maintenance. Community heating system sizes vary from small ones serving a block of flats to large ones serving a whole city district. Community heating has successfully been used in many European countries, and a third to half of the homes in Denmark, Finland and Sweden use it. The developments included in this book that use community heating include: Slateford Green housing, SolarCity in Linz, Solarsiedlung in Freiburg, BedZED and the housing at Akademie Mont-Cenis.

Even in cool and temperate climates, air-conditioning and cooling system installations are increasing. UK statistics show that the air-conditioning system of an air-conditioned building contributes 25-40 per cent of the building's CO_2 emissions. A typical air-conditioned office produces up to 75 per cent more CO_2 emissions than a typical naturally ventilated office, and an efficiently designed air-conditioned office can save 35-45 per cent of the operational CO_2 emissions compared to a typical air-conditioned design (BRESCU 2000). In northern Europe and the US, buildings can be designed not to need air-conditioning at all; a number of examples were illustrated in the previous section. Even in some of the harshest environments, buildings can be designed to be naturally ventilated for at least part of the year. Mixed mode buildings, such as the Merrill Center (see case study, p.234), are either naturally ventilated or mechanically cooled depending on the external temperatures.

If air-conditioning is to be included, an energy-efficient system should be installed. Air-conditioning involves filtering, heating or cooling, and humidifying or dehumidifying air. It also entails distributing air throughout a building. The energy used is typically in a ratio of 1:1.5:3 for humidification:cooling:distribution. Some of these processes can be dispensed with entirely, others provided by energy-efficient means. Providing comfort cooling only and no humidification is an option that can save nearly 20 per cent of the operating energy. 'Free' cooling sources can be exploited, such as ground source heat used for heating and cooling (see BCZEB case study, p.248, and Merrill Center case study, p.234), and night air cooling in conjunction with thermal mass (see Powergen case study, p.186). Of the three main traditional cooling systems used in air-conditioning, which include vapour compression, absorption cooling and desiccant cooling, the latter operates primarily with heat produced from gas boilers and is therefore associated with reduced CO_2 emissions compared to the other modes, which operate on electricity. There is also potential for linking air-conditioning with solar power, PVs or solar thermal, as the requirement for cooling coincides with the availability of solar energy. Distributing air within a building is also energy-intensive. Reduced friction, shorter runs and fewer bends enable the use of smaller pumps and fans, which in turn reduces energy consumption. Distributing air at low velocity, as with displacement ventilation (see BCZEB case study, p.248), also reduces the operating energy consumption.

In addition to the system design, the way the system is operated by the occupants can significantly impact on its performance. Educating users, monitoring performance and regular maintenance are necessary to ensure optimum operating efficiency.

5.2.3 Light

Achieving an energy-efficient lighting system requires considering the lighting installation, using energy efficient lamps (light bulbs), and educating the users. The three approaches are interrelated.

Energy-efficient installations

– Locate lighting only where required and optimise the distance between light source and area to be lit.

– Zone lighting. Install controls for small groups of lights rather than for large areas to maximise individual control and ensure banks of lights can be switched off when not required. Zoning should take into account the proximity to natural light, banks of lights near windows being switched on separately from those further away.

– Select the light fitting with care. Reflectors and louvres have an impact on the efficiency of the lighting.

– Automatic controls can help improve efficiencies. Presence detectors switch on lights only when people are in a space. Daylight detectors switch on lights only when natural light levels are lower than a set level. Timed controls switch off lights after a set time of being switched on. Programmed controls switch lights on and off at set times in the day. Controls can be combined, for example, presence and daylight detectors are often used together.

Energy-efficient lamps

– Fluorescent tubes, in particular the newer T8 and T5 with efficacies of 60-105 lumen/watt, consume 13-18 per cent of the energy used by a tungsten bulb. Electronic ballast control gear increases efficiencies compared to older control gear. Fluorescent lighting has a long life: T8 have a life of 13,000-20,000 hours compared to 1,000 tungsten hours. The extended life not only reduces running costs, but also maintenance costs.

– Compact fluorescents have efficacies of 50-90 lumen/watt and are appropriate for domestic use.

– High pressure sodium lamps and metal halides are very efficient: metal halides have efficacies of approximately 80-90 lumen/watt. They provide high levels of light and are appropriate for large spaces and outdoors. Less powerful ceramic metal halides (35-70 W) can be used in smaller spaces as spotlights and downlights and can replace tungsten halogen spots, which have lower efficacies of 12-22 lumen/watt.

Educating users

– Inform users of the energy implications of leaving lights switched on unnecessarily and of the lighting system installed.

– Make individuals responsible for switching off lights.

Case study: Appropriate solutions

Schreiber house
Aarau, Aargau, Switzerland

Client: Familie Schreiber
Architect: Theresia Schreiber
Energy consultant: Energiesysteme Aschauer
Completed: 1999

The south-facing block on the left is clad in glass, while the north-facing block is clad in larch horizontal boarding. All east-facing windows benefit from impressive views of the valley below.

The cardboard honeycomb insulation

The Schreiber house is a zero-heating house located in the northern part of Switzerland. The house is built using some well-established and some more experimental environmental strategies.

The house is on the east-facing slope of a hill overlooking a valley and the mountains beyond. It is situated among traditional housing and is partially hidden by trees and planting. It is divided into two offset rectangular blocks, one facing south and the other north, each treated differently according to its orientation. The north block, which houses the entrance, stairs, bathrooms and ancillary rooms, is built with traditional timber frame technology and clad in larch horizontal boarding. The south-facing block houses the spaces that can benefit most from solar heat gains, including the living room on the ground floor and the bedrooms on the first floor. This block is also a timber frame structure, but is clad with toughened glass over cardboard honeycomb insulation. The 120mm honeycomb insulation is fixed within a timber frame on the outside of the structural timber frame, which is filled with 120mm cellulose fibre insulation. The honeycomb insulation works by trapping a layer of warm air within the honeycomb structure, which is heated up by the solar radiation passing through the glass cladding. This layer of air is warmer than the inside of the building and prevents heat loss through the structure, effectively increasing the fabric U-value to $0.0 \, \text{W/m}^2\text{K}$. When the sun is not shining, the honeycomb still contributes to insulating the house by forming a buffer zone of still air that reduces heat loss. The cellulose insulation provides a good basic level of insulation, whatever the weather or time of the day.

With such high levels of insulation a central heating system became unnecessary. A system was required that could provide minimal heating and in this case a whole house MVHR system was installed. The advantage of such a system is that it also supplies fresh air in a controlled manner that minimises ventilation losses. In ultra-low energy buildings, ventilation losses constitute a significant percentage of the overall heat loss. MVHR supplies fresh air to living spaces and extracts air from wet areas such as bathrooms and kitchens. The extracted stale warm air is passed through a heat exchanger that transfers the heat to the incoming fresh air. MVHR can be up to 85 per cent efficient. The air supply is passively pre-heated by passing it through earth ducts located a few metres under ground where the earth retains a constant temperature. Alternatives to a whole house system are individual through-the-wall fans or passive vents (see 5.2.5).

At the Schreiber house the MVHR is located in the basement of the house in a utility room. The internal heat gains from building occupants, cooking and appliances, plus solar gains are sufficient to heat the house and the MVHR ensures that the heat from the extracted stale air is recycled into the house. This has proved to provide a comfortable environment throughout recent winters, but for unexpected eventualities a wood-burning stove in the living room can provide back-up heating. In summer the honeycomb insulation structure does not allow the sun to penetrate deep into the honeycomb layer and therefore avoids excessive heat gains. A cavity in front of the insulation ensures that hot air can escape. All south-facing windows have external blinds and further solar shading for two of the four French windows in the living room is provided by a planted metal trellis.

The material selection and the spatial design provide aesthetic enjoyment and interest, a healthy environment, privacy and close contact with nature. This ultra–low energy house succeeds in providing a high quality of life with minimal impact on the environment.

All living spaces face south, benefiting from direct solar gains and overlooking the private garden.

The wood-burning stove in the living room acts as a focal point.

The external glass cladding is fixed over the cardboard honeycomb insulation.

The MVHR is in a basement utility room. The rectangular box contains the heat recovery element.

5.2.4 Sustainable design features

Site and ecology
The building development has retained much of the surrounding planting and has further enhanced it, providing areas for wildlife. Planting is used as a solar shading device.

Health
The internal materials are mostly natural with minimal finishes. All spaces have ample natural light. The Baubiologie principles were applied.

Materials
Timber, which is a renewable resource, was used. Recycled materials used include the cardboard insulation.

Energy See main text.

Water
Water-efficient appliances are used throughout.

5.2.5 Passive stack ventilation (PSV) versus MVHR

Buildings need a regular supply of fresh air and the removal of stale air to maintain appropriate air quality. UK Building Regulations set out requirements for fresh air supplies. Typically houses have one or two air changes per hour (ach), while energy-efficient airtight buildings should aim for 0.5-0.6 ach. Ventilation can be provided mechanically or with passive ventilation.

The advantages of MVHR are that it provides controlled ventilation and can recycle the heat from the building. Being able to control the ventilation is particularly important for well-insulated and airtight houses, where the energy performance depends on minimising ventilation losses. MVHR does, however, use some electricity to run. MVHR is generally used throughout the whole building, but can also be installed within individual rooms (see Autonomous House case study, p.270).

Passive stack ventilation (PSV) is a natural ventilation system, based on the natural tendency for hot air to rise. Domestic passive stack ventilators comprise extract ducts in wet areas (kitchens and bathrooms), with outlets at roof level. The hot air rises though the duct and is exhausted above the roof. External negative pressure helps draw air through the system. Trickle vents in windows supply fresh air.

The disadvantages of PSV are that it is not controlled and has no heat recovery facility, which makes it inappropriate for zero-heating houses. The advantages of PSV are that it requires no operating energy, has no moving parts and cannot be switched off. In certain low energy houses where tenants renting the property are not fully aware of the building systems, PSV provides a low maintenance easy-to-use solution (see Slateford Green case study, p.132).

Case study: Coordinated approach

Greenwich Sainsbury's
Greenwich, London, UK

Client: Sainsbury's
Architect: Chetwood Associates
Mechanical and electrical engineer: Oscar Faber
Structural engineer: WSP Consultants
Main contractor: RGCM Ltd
Completed: 1999

The south-facing entrance

Natural light floods the sales area.

The Greenwich Sainsbury's store is part of the regeneration of the Greenwich peninsula in London, which includes housing, shops, educational and leisure facilities. The 35,000m² building is the main food store serving not only the 1,300 new Greenwich Millennium homes, but also the existing community.

It was designed using principles not usually applied to supermarkets; in particular it makes use of natural light rather than the ubiquitous fluorescent lighting in the sales areas. It was also designed taking into consideration all the different sources and needs for heating, cooling and lighting and addressing these in a coordinated system. By doing so, energy requirements were reduced by 50 per cent.

The building consists of a virtually circular plan with a south-facing entrance and delivery area on the north side. The structure is mainly concrete to provide thermal mass and the east and west elevations are earth bermed.

Any large store needs a fresh air supply, heating, cooling and lighting. The lighting is the most independent environmental aspect, all the others being highly interrelated. Here a radical departure from the norm means the building makes use of natural light from a series of north-facing high-angled rooflights to provide general background lighting. North lighting provides diffuse light that does not degrade the merchandise. Additional general lighting is installed at the checkout area, and high efficiency lights are installed at the bottom of the rooflight bulkhead to provide general lighting when external light levels are low. The merchandise is lit from shelf-mounted lights, increasing the effective intensity of the light fittings. The energy-efficient lights used include T5 fluorescent tubes, compact fluorescent light bulbs and CDM metal halides.

Electrical lighting is located on the display shelving.

Additional lights are located in the checkout area.

To provide a comfortable environment in stores with refrigeration and high occupancy can require simultaneous heating and cooling, while also providing fresh air. The building is naturally ventilated. Fresh air is drawn from outside through 1,500mm-diameter air ducts under the earth berms on the east and west sides of the building. It is distributed through 600mm-diameter ducts under the floor and introduced into the sales area through grilles at the base of display cabinets. The air is supplied at only a couple of degrees below the comfort temperature and, as it heats up, the air rises and is expelled through vents integrated within the rooflights.

Heating and cooling systems are interconnected and provided by means of the ventilation system and an underfloor heating-cooling system. The main heat source is CHP; heat is also recycled from the refrigeration units. The CHP, with a generating efficiency of 90 per cent, provides 85 per cent of the required electricity, and the waste heat, together with the recycled heat from the refrigeration, is used to heat groundwater, extracted from below ground at 12°C, for space heating and defrosting. Hot water heats the incoming air, by passing through hot water coils in the undercroft area, and is also used in the underfloor system to heat the sales area. Unwanted cool air from the chiller cabinets is extracted with a fan at the base of the cabinets and used to dehumidify the supply air to the space. Cooling requirements are covered by the same underfloor system by circulating groundwater at 12°C. Groundwater is also used to help cool the refrigeration cabinets, thus reducing the electricity needed for refrigeration. Different areas of the sales space may require heating and cooling at the same time. The underfloor system is zoned to allow certain areas to be heated while others are cooled.

The coordinated services strategy is helped by the design of the building fabric. The high building mass is used to moderate temperature swings by storing solar heat and internal heat gains from occupants and lights, and the earth berm on two sides of the building increases the insulation of the structure and protects it against wind chill.

The naturally lit space with electrical light accentuating the merchandise creates a pleasant atmosphere.

The earth berm and landscaping provide a habitat for wildlife.

The scheme also addresses other sustainability issues. Some experimental recycled materials, such as wall panels made with recycled plastic bottles, were used, demonstrating their viability. The store also has a café located near the entrance on the glazed south elevation of the building. This has become a popular meeting place for the local community. A landscaped area on the east side of the building, which includes a reed pond that treats the run-off from the service access, is not used much by people and has become a small haven for wildlife. The development does have a car park with 1,150 spaces, but also provides free electrical supply points for customers with electrical cars.

The comprehensive strategy to minimise operating energy use resulted in estimated savings in the order of £60,000. As energy prices rise, the incentives to adopt similar sustainable solutions should increase; and as the confidence in such designs grows, similar solutions should become more common.

5.2.6 Sustainable design features

Site and ecology
The whole area is part of a millennium regeneration project and makes use of previously used land. The area has been landscaped to create a variety of habitats including a small woodland, a wetland meadow and a reed bed.

Community and culture
The store provides a vital facility for the existing community and the new community of over 1,300 homes.

Health
The natural lighting is particularly beneficial for the employees who spend their whole working day in the supermarket. Improved levels of comfort are also provided through the environmental strategy.

Materials
Recycled finishes, including recycled tyres entrance matting and toilet panels made of recycled plastic bottles, were used. Refrigeration uses propane to avoid the use of ozone-depleting substances.

Energy
The design was assessed using the BREEAM systems and achieved a 31 (top score) Excellent rating.
Natural light is provided through a series of north rooflights to provide minimum 5 per cent daylight factor, with louvres to avoid excessive light levels and avoid light spill at night. The rooflights also have thermal blinds to reduce heatloss at night. External signage illumination is powered by wind turbine and PV panels.
See also main text.

Water
Borehole water is used to flush the WCs. A green roof and landscaped areas, including a reed bed that cleans run-off water from the service yard, significantly reduce rainwater run-off from the building.

A small wind turbine and PV panel, which power the sign lighting, are symbolic of the sustainable building approach.

Case study: Fine-tuning buildings

Phillip Merrill Environmental Center
Annapolis, Maryland, US

Project details, Chapter 6.2, p.268

The sign tells occupants when conditions are appropriate for opening windows to cool the office.

The workspace lights are controlled by movement and light sensors to avoid being left switched on unnecessarily. The overhead lights are controlled by light sensors measuring the level of natural light and dimming the lights when needed.

The Phillip Merrill Environmental Center, commissioned by the Chesapeake Bay Foundation, is designed to have minimal impact on the environment. The building design reduces the building's impact on the land and the use of resources, including water and energy, during construction and operation.

At the Merrill Center, minimising energy needs is achieved through passive and active strategies. As important as installing appropriate building systems, is making sure they are used correctly. Building users are of fundamental importance to a building's energy performance, affecting how lighting and appliances are used. The building users have to be educated in how the building works. However, where possible, systems should operate automatically to avoid accidental misuse. Building systems should also be designed to allow some flexibility of operation, as required when people work out of hours, without compromising the energy efficiency. At the Merrill Center the ease of use and flexibility of operation were achieved through a number of measures taken at the design stage. In addition, after a few years of monitoring the building's use and operation, particular operational aspects became evident and prompted some adjustments and improvements to the building systems.

The passive measures used to reduce the need for energy include a largely glazed south elevation which makes maximum use of solar heat gains in winter, while a trellis structure with timber louvres and a row of PV panels shade the elevation in the summer and help prevent overheating. The building fabric is built to be airtight and is well insulated. The walls and roof are constructed with Structural Insulated Panels (SIPs) consisting of two outer layers of oriented strand board and an inner layer of CFC- and HCFC-free foam insulation.

The active measures include a building energy management system (BEMS) that responds to external weather conditions and switches between operating modes, including a natural ventilation mode, a heating mode and a cooling mode. In summer when the external air temperature is sufficiently cool, the windows can be opened to allow cool air into the building. The air is slowly heated by internal heat gains, rises within the office space and is exhausted at high level through the automated clerestory windows. When the external temperatures are too high to provide cooling, mechanical cooling takes over and the windows have to be kept closed. Constant temperature groundwater, extracted from 48 100m deep wells, in conjunction with a heat pump and a desiccant heat recovery wheel, cools the air supply. To inform the occupants of the current operating mode, an illuminated sign indicates when the windows can be opened. This system is both educational and helps avoid the frustration of not feeling in control of one's own environment. The BEMS automatically closes and opens high level windows to suit operating mode.

The ventilation for the main offices can function separately from the conference facility. In the conference rooms, the ventilation is optimised by using a CO_2 monitor that triggers an increase in ventilation rates only when CO_2 levels become too high, allowing the default ventilation settings to be kept low. Opening the doors also switches off the ventilation.

The glazed façade brings ample light into the large open plan office and electrical light is often not required. To avoid electrical lights being switched on unnecessarily, they are controlled by movement and light sensors, and switch on only when people are present and natural light levels are insufficient.

After having occupied and assessed the building for a while, some improvements were made. To minimise unnecessary use, the switches to the general lighting were altered to enable the independent operation of the up- and the downlighters. Settings for working out of hours were introduced, allowing for out-of-hours heating and lighting without compromising energy efficiency. Each work station was set up with a central switch linked to the lighting and computer. This has an integrated sensor, and must be switched on first thing in the morning. If a work station remains unoccupied for a period of time, the sensor switches off the desk lights and computer screen. Similar sensor-linked switches are used on the dispensing machines in the kitchen, the coffee machines and the communal photocopiers and printer. Savings of £250 per year were achieved by installing the sensor on the drinks dispenser, while the work station sensor saves 25 per cent of the energy used per work station.

The various improvements, which complemented the original design, are the result of the building owner's dedication to environmental issues, and were made possible by the resourcefulness and experience of the building manager. Buildings should be cared for and not abandoned to their users. At the Merrill Center the post-occupancy care and attention helped to fully realise the potential of the energy-efficiency strategy.

The block on the right houses the main office space and the smaller block houses the conference rooms. Each section of the building can be ventilated separately.

The long block houses the main office space, and the smaller block houses the conference rooms.

Sensors are used on all communal machines, including the drinks dispensers.

Sensor and switch for the photocopier.

The main entrance to the centre.

See also: efficient and reduced vehicle use **Chapter 1.2**

See also: rainwater for washbasins **Chapter 6.2**

Case study: Performance targets and post-occupancy monitoring

Dyfi Eco Park
Machynlleth, Wales, UK

Project details, Chapter 3.1, p.106

From the left: Units Two, Three, Four and Five. Units Four and Five have large south-facing, roof-mounted PV arrays.

Unit One with a small PV array covering a bicycle stand.

In 1996, Unit One of the Dyfi Eco Park was completed. It was the first of a series of light industrial and office buildings in a new green business park on the outskirts of Machynlleth, Wales. The client was the Welsh Development Agency (then known as the Development Board for Rural Wales) and the aim was to develop an environmentally friendly business park and attract 'green' businesses to the region.

One of the development aims, stipulated by the client, was to minimise the buildings' impact on the environment. The design team, driven by Julian Bishop, the project architect, and Peter Warm, the energy consultant, both very dedicated to designing environmental buildings, persuaded the client to undertake a comprehensive environmental analysis of the project prior to the design and post-construction stages.

The analysis involved three stages. At the design stage, an assessment of the design was made and targets for energy and resource use were set; during the construction stage, the building process was closely followed and building elements, critical to achieving the targets set, were tested on site; after completion, the building's performance was comprehensively monitored.

The design targets for reducing Unit One's environmental impacts were set by undertaking a pre-construction evaluation of the building's environmental design by means of a full BREEAM 5/93 assessment. A strategy was developed in line with these targets involving minimising requirements for auxiliary heating and lighting and using materials with a low environmental impact. The buildings was, therefore, designed to include high levels of insulation coupled with a sealed building envelope and passive solar heating to minimise heating requirements. The design also maximised the use of natural daylight to reduce electricity use for lighting, and made use of natural ventilation to cool the building in summer and avoid the need for mechanical cooling. The materials specified were generally natural, non-toxic, locally procured and had low-embodied energy so as to provide a healthy building environment for the occupants with minimal environmental impact. Unit One achieved a BREEAM score of 'excellent', which was later confirmed by the building monitoring studies.

A full embodied energy calculation of the materials specified was undertaken, and consequently renewable, recycled and locally sourced products were specified. These included timber, recycled cellulose insulation, bitumen corrugated roofing sheets with high recycled cellulose content, and locally sourced timber and slate.

During the construction stage the focus was on ensuring sufficiently good workmanship to achieve the required airtightness and insulation values. A de-pressurisation test, undertaken by Retrotec, identified areas of the building that were inadequately sealed and allowed excessive air to escape, increasing heat loss. A thermographic survey, undertaken by McKinnon & Clarke, identified areas of high heat loss. High heat loss can be a result of sagging insulation, areas where insulation was omitted, or generally insufficient insulation. On the basis of the test results, remedial work was still possible during the construction period.

See also: thermal comfort **Chapter 3.1**

See also: lighting 1 **Chapter 5.1**

After the building was completed, a comprehensive monitoring process over a period of two years was undertaken. This included monitoring the internal temperatures, relative humidity, lighting levels and energy consumption, and surveying the occupants' views on comfort. The monitoring results confirmed that the building had achieved the targets set at the start of the project. The assessment also highlighted some potential improvements to the design and was used to inform the design of the subsequent units. In Unit One, problems of excessive glare in the first-floor offices and slow heating up times were addressed in the design of Unit Two, by altering the glass specification for the rooflight and increasing the fabric insulation. Unit Two, with its improved design, was monitored over a two-year period and further changes were suggested for the design of Unit Three. The monitoring of Unit Three was completed in 2002.

The post-occupancy monitoring was particularly informative as it combined physical measurements with personal views of the building occupants. Building occupants are not only fundamental to the successful performance of the building, but are also an invaluable source of information. However, they are more likely to be open about the problems they experience, if they are talking to someone not directly involved with the building design. For this reason and to ensure impartiality, post-occupancy assessments should be carried out by independent specialists.

The occupants' surveys undertaken at Dyfi Eco Park included a structured questionnaire and open-ended interviews. In addition to assessing the buildings in terms of comfort, the occupants shed light on how building elements, including those associated with energy efficiency, were used and performed in practice. For example, to cool Unit One in summer, the windows are opened, letting in fresh air, which is exhausted through the rooflights at high level. However, the windows in the offices are at desk height, and when opened can cause draughts, displacing paperwork and causing discomfort. Consequently, in certain instances the windows were not opened and the space overheated. Another example is the feedback regarding the rooflights. In Unit One, rooflights provided a 5-16 per cent daylight factor in the offices, which may appear desirable and an effective means of reducing electrical lighting needs. However, in practice, such high light levels caused glare and discomfort to the occupants. Knowledge of practical operational issues can effectively be gained only from the building users.

The monitoring of Dyfi Eco Park highlighted how not only the overall building design, but also detail design issues, such as how the window opens, can significantly impact on the building performance. It also showed how building monitoring can help improve even already very successful building solutions.

Building designs, which are modelled on existing buildings that have not been monitored, run a risk of replicating unsuccessful strategies. Building monitoring can identify successful and unsuccessful design approaches and details. This can contribute essential information to the body of knowledge held by the design profession as a whole, and help to improve building designs in general.

5.2.7 Environmental building assessments

ECOHomes and BREEAM (Building Research Establishment Environmental Assessment Method)

The ECOHomes environmental assessment method was developed to be used for residential properties, while different versions of the BREEAM are suited to specific building types including offices, superstores, industrial buildings, health buildings, sports facilities and courts.

The assessment, undertaken by a trained assessor, gives a rating of pass, good, very good or excellent. All systems can also be used by designers as an educational tool, to set environmental targets and to monitor their design work.

ECOhomes is designed to be used for newbuild and refurbishment project, during the design phase, while BREEAM can also be used for existing buildings to improve their operation.

The issues covered by the assessment are:

- management
- health and well-being
- pollution
- energy
- transport
- water
- materials
- land use
- ecology

A number of UK organisations, including the Housing Corporation, Government Client Contractors Panel (GCCP) and English Partnerships require specific BREEAM and ECOhomes ratings for their developments.

BREEAM also provides a way of publicising successful environmental performance and can be used to improve public relations and marketability.

5.2.8 Advantages of post-occupancy evaluations

- Design targets can be verified.

- Building occupants are made aware of the environmental aims of the strategy of their building and its operation.

- Potential for improvements to the building may be identified and undertaken.

- Changes and adjustments to the building maintenance and operation can be monitored for improvements.

- Successful designs can be used as models for subsequent designs.

5.3 'Green' Energy Sources

5.3.1 Woking Borough Council

Woking Borough Council has developed a number of independent and interconnecting energy grids that supply their customers with electricity produced by renewable and energy-efficient installations. The installations include CHP systems in numerous sheltered housing developments, an integrated CHP and PV roof system, and the first fuel cell and CHP system in the UK, which provides heating, cooling and electricity to a swimming pool and leisure complex. The council has also subsidised condensing boiler installations. These initiatives have resulted in a reduction in CO_2 emissions of 6 per cent compared to 1990 and cost savings of £4.5 million (Jones 2002).

4 Times Square, New York, uses a 200 kW fuel cell to cover approximately 5 per cent of its daytime electrical needs (Fox and Fowle Architects).

A biomass boiler at the Centre for Alternative Technology in Machynlleth burns woodchips to heat the centre's buildings.

Zero-energy buildings are not realistic, but zero-CO_2 buildings are. The definition of zero-CO_2 building does require some qualification. Building materials and elements, including energy-generating installations such as solar panels and wind turbines, have an embodied energy (see Chapter 4). This embodied energy is generally associated with CO_2 emissions. The concept of a zero-CO_2 building can therefore currently only be applied to the building's operation. Moreover, a further distinction is required between zero-CO_2 energy supply technologies and renewable energy: not all renewable energy is necessarily zero-CO_2. The power from the sun, wind, rivers and tides is considered renewable, as is that derived from renewable biofuels, geothermal and ground heat. Yet for instance, once installed, a PV installation requires negligible energy to operate, while a geothermal system requires energy to operate pumps and also, sometimes, heat pumps. Geothermal energy generation plants are on average associated with emissions of 65 g/kWh CO_2, compared to 450 g/kWh for gas and 1042 g/kWh for coal (Smith 2003). At the point of use, the CO_2 emissions from an electrically operated geothermal heating system are 0.11–0.15 kg/kWh. This is only marginally less than a gas heating appliance associated with CO_2 emissions of 0.19 kg/kWh (see 5.2.2). The energy required to operate a geothermal system could, of course, be provided by PVs or other zero-CO_2 means, qualifying the whole system as zero-CO_2. Similarly, biofuel is also associated with operating energy for the harvesting and processing of the fuel crop, which may not come from zero-CO_2 sources. Taking into account this distinction, this chapter looks at renewable energy systems that aim to provide a zero-CO_2 energy source.

In developed countries, the renewable systems most commonly linked to buildings are solar thermal, PVs and geothermal. Wind power is limited by site and planning restrictions, hydro power is possible only where suitable watercourses exist, and large-scale biofuels use is constrained by the relative scarcity of renewable fuel, whereby domestic biofuel systems, such as wood-burning stoves, are widespread. These technologies are well established and are continuously being improved, while new technologies are also being developed.

A new technology of particular interest is the fuel cell. Fuel cells combine hydrogen and oxygen through an electrochemical reaction to produce water, heat and electricity. To operate these electrochemical internal combustion engines a hydrogen-rich fuel, such as natural gas, methane or pure hydrogen, is used. The fuel is fed into the cell where it reacts with a catalytic material and splits the hydrogen molecules into protons and electrons. Protons pass through an electrolyte membrane, and electrons create useful energy. A number of different fuel cell types are being developed and refined. They operate variations of this process, at temperatures ranging from 80°C to 1000°C, and use different fuels. Fuel cells that use pure hydrogen produce no local emissions of CO_2 and pollution. If the hydrogen fuel is made by electrolysis powered by PVs, fuel cells can provide a zero-CO_2 emissions energy source. The first fuel cell-operated building in the world was the Solarhaus in Freiburg (see Chapter 5.1). The Solarhaus system, which has been decommissioned and replaced with another experimental installation, generated hydrogen from PVs. The hydrogen was stored from the summer to the winter and used to power a 1 kW fuel cell during periods of low PV output. Fuel cells have been used in a number of buildings since then, they are used to power cars (see 1.2.2), and have been used as part of comprehensive energy supply systems, such as that in the borough of Woking, in the UK (see 5.3.1).

As with most renewable energy technologies, and in particular those still in development, installation costs can be a significant obstacle to their widespread use. PVs are a case in point; their cost has dropped dramatically, but is still in the order of £5,000 per kW, which, at current electricity prices, results in a payback period of up to 100 years. This is in contrast with the more cost-effective systems, such as solar thermal systems which, at £1,500 per dwelling, have a payback period of 10–15 year (Hyde 2004).

As energy prices rise, renewable energy technologies will become more cost-effective and there will also be scope for reviving less used systems. Micro-hydro does not have the environmental disadvantages of large-scale systems and is one of the renewable energy sources with the lowest environmental impacts. Micro-hydro installations are typically 100 W–500 kW and often make use of existing water wheels that used to drive mills. Small-scale hydro, which generate less than 20 MW of energy, as micro hydro, can operate by using the flow of the stream or river, without the need to dam or store water.

In addition to renewable sources of zero-CO_2 power, energy can also be extracted from various waste streams. These include sewage, agricultural waste and municipal waste. Anaerobic digestion of biodegradable material produces mainly methane gas, some CO_2 and minimal impurities. This can be used to power conventional combined heat and power generators or could be used as a hydrogen-rich fuel for fuel cells, when technologies become sufficiently developed. As general waste and sewage sludge disposal becomes more costly and controlled, new ways of using waste material to produce energy will become cost-effective. While such forms of energy generation may appear unrelated to building design, small-scale generation using, for example, agricultural waste to supply small communities, may become increasingly possible as small-scale generation technology improves.

Selecting 'green' energy systems requires comparing the energy needs with the available options for renewable energy. Certain types of renewable energy technologies complement others: one working when the other does not. Wind may be coupled with PVs; wind being more active in winter and PVs more active in summer. Simplicity has its own virtue: installations with several renewable systems ultimately providing the same type of energy (i.e. heat or electricity) are costly and risk being wasteful; not least because of the associated manufacturing impacts and the fact that technologies are improving fast enough to make systems obsolete before they have reached their natural end of life.

Where an independent renewable energy installation cannot be afforded, electricity can be purchased from suppliers that generate power through renewable technologies. Raising demand for 'green' energy will boost the renewable energy industry. It will also contribute to achieving the targets set in the UK by the Renewable Obligation, requiring all suppliers of energy to obtain 15 per cent of the energy they sell from renewable sources by 2015.

Freiburg encourages renewable energy installations. The city benefits from five 1.8 MW wind turbines in the nearby valley, numerous PV installations on public and private buildings with a total peak rating of 3.4 MW, and other small-scale installations such as micro-hydro.

In the centre of Freiburg, two micro-hydro installations, one installed in 1927, the other in 1948, both refurbished in 1992, provide a total of 25,000 kWh/yr and save 15 tonnes of CO_2 emissions.

A sign identifies the micro-hydro installation which would otherwise remain undetectable in the pedestrian streets of Freiburg.

Case study: Solar thermal 1

Millennium Green
Collingham, Nottinghamshire, UK

Project details, Chapter 6.2, p.266

On the roof above the three rooflights is an evacuated tube solar panel.

A flat plate collector.

The traditional-looking houses are high performance.

Solar thermal panels are a simple solar technology, which is well established and in common use. Solar thermal systems are primarily used to heat water for space heating and domestic hot water. They typically consist of a solar collector, mounted on a south-, southeast- or southwest-facing roof (in the northern hemisphere), and a heat store. The most common systems are water-based, but there are also air-based systems, such as the Sunwarm system. The solar panels of air-based systems heat air, which is supplied via an air-handling unit throughout the house to provide space heating, and when space heating is not needed, the hot air is used to heat water. The system can also be used in summer to cool the building.

Water-based systems are available in various types and configurations. There are two main types of collector: flat plate collectors, which can be integrated within the roof finish, and evacuated tube collectors, which are mounted on top of the roof finish. Both types can also be installed on an independent support structure. The systems can circulate the water mechanically using a pump, or can operate passively, as with thermosyphon collectors that comprise a tank above the panel, and where the hot water rises naturally into the tank without needing a pump. Small circulating pumps can be powered by a PV panel. The hot water produced can be supplied to a combination boiler, or stored in a hot water cylinder, where it may be further heated by other means, such as by a gas boiler or an electric immersion heater. In northern Europe, with an average radiation of 900–1350 kWh/m² per annum, the typical system, with efficiencies of 75 per cent, are generally designed to supply approximately 60 per cent of the hot water needs over the whole year. In countries with more solar radiation, such as Australia, up to 90 per cent of the hot water needs can be provided by a solar panel.

At the Millennium Green, both flat plate collectors and evacuated tubes were used. The development, which is one of the first commercial sustainable housing developments in the UK, considered solar thermal to be a cost-effective measure to complement others, including building a well-insulated and airtight envelope, providing auxiliary heating by means of a condensing boiler, and recycling rainwater. The solar thermal systems are designed to cover 60 per cent of the heating needs of each house, and each comprises a solar panel and a twin coil 250-litre storage cylinder. The bottom coil of the cylinder is heated by the solar panels and the top coil by the condensing boiler. The hot water is extracted from the top of the cylinder, where the water is hottest, and distributed around the dwelling. The panels are aesthetically unobtrusive, fitting in well with the traditional house designs.

 See also: rainwater for general needs **Chapter 6.2**

Case study: Solar thermal 2

Solar panels are used mainly to provide domestic hot water and are less commonly used for space heating. The main reason for this relates to the cost of solar panels and the fact that their performance, which is affected by seasonal variations, peaks when space heating needs are lowest. In the UK, at current fossil fuel prices, solar thermal installations sized to provide domestic hot water only have a payback period of 10-15 years (Hyde 2004). Installations sized to cover space heating as well, which are significantly larger and not used during the summer period, have even longer payback periods. While in climates with more solar radiation the payback period is considerably reduced, cost-effectiveness can be increased if the panels are used all year round.

At Thurgoona Campus, in Albury, a solar thermal array is used to provide space heating and space cooling and is therefore used all year round. The campus consists of a number of teaching and accommodation buildings built with uninsulated rammed earth walls and concrete floors. In the teaching blocks, underfloor heating pipes are embedded within the concrete floors and circulate water heated by means of extensive solar thermal arrays on the roof of each building. The heated water is also stored in large tanks at roof level. Separate smaller thermosyphon collectors with integrated water storage tanks are used to heat water for basins and sinks.

The concrete floors have a high thermal mass, as do the rammed earth walls. During the heating season the solar hot water is used to heat the thermal mass and provide radiant heat to the teaching spaces. The underfloor pipes are also used to cool the buildings in summer. Here the diurnal temperature difference is exploited and the solar panels are used to reradiate the heat from the building to the clear night skies. The water is circulated around the system at night, transferring the heat from the building to the outside. The thermal mass of the concrete slab and rammed earth walls is cooled and the following day it can reabsorb some of the day's heat. The combination of solar cooling and the thermal mass obviates the need for mechanical cooling, even in a climate where the summer high temperature is as high as 30°C .

Thurgoona Campus
Charles Sturt University, Albury, New South Wales, Australia

Project details, Chapter 4.4, p.177

The typical student accommodation building has two types of roof-mounted solar panels. One thermosyphon flat plate collector in the centre of the array provides domestic hot water, which is stored in a tank above the panel. On both sides of it are flat plate collectors providing hot water for space heating.

Teaching block (left) and adjacent lecture theatre (right). The teaching block has an extensive array of solar panels for space heating and cooling and one solar panel to provide water for washing. A natural ventilation chimney is centrally positioned.

See also: rammed earth **Chapter 4.4**

See also: natural ventilation **Chapter 5.1**

See also: composting toilets **Chapter 6.1**

See also: sustainable drainage **Chapter 6.3**

Case study: Photovoltaics 1

The BCZEB 54m² thermal PV array produces both hot water and electricity. The efficiency of conventional PV panels drops as their temperature rises. The thermal PV panels used at the BCZEB have a copper heat exchanger filled with water and glued to the back of the panel and painted black. The heat absorbed by the panel can raise the water temperature to about 25°C, and removing the heat from the PV panel ensures the PV-generating efficiencies remain constant.

The Shorebird Nature Center in Berkeley is a passive solar building made of straw bales. It makes use of recycled materials and timber from managed forests. It also has a solar thermal and PV installation.

The amorphous PV cells are made of plastic rolls attached to the metal roof substrate between the metal upstands.

Photovoltaics (PV) cells convert solar radiation into electricity. This occurs when solar radiation falls on a semiconducting material, such as silicon. The energy from the sun activates the electrons in the semiconductor and generates a direct current. PV panels can consist of individual (mono-crystalline) slices of a slowly grown silicon crystal, molten silicon cast in blocks (poly-crystalline), sandwiched between layers of glass or plastic, or amorphous silicon deposited on a metal, glass or plastic substrate. PV technology is improving rapidly and new manufacturing methods and materials, such as cadmium telluride and copper indium diselenide, are being tested with the aim of reducing manufacturing costs and improving efficiencies.

Of the three types of PV cells, the mono-crystalline cells are the most expensive, but have highest generating efficiencies, typically between 13-17 per cent. Experimental versions have achieved up to 34 per cent efficiency (Smith 2003). Poly-crystalline cells are approximately 12-15 per cent efficient, and amorphous cells 4-5 per cent. Individual PV panels are linked together to form an array. Panels are given a peak rating in kilowatt peak (kWp), which is measured in standards test conditions, and have a yearly output measured in kWh. The output depends on the panel's orientation, its location and the local climate. In the UK, the most energy can be harnessed by positioning the panels on a 30-40° inclination facing south, +/- 30°. The output of mono- and poly-crystalline modules can be affected by shading from buildings and planting, and all module types suffer efficiency losses when their temperature rises: 0.4-0.5 per cent efficiency is lost per 1°C above 25°C (see BCZEB panels, adjacent). The UK receives a maximum solar radiation of approximately 1 kW/m² and an average radiation of 900-1350 kWh/m² per annum. Depending on the type of PV and its installation, an array will provide between 50-150 kWh/m²/yr.

PVs can be grid connected or independent. In the latter case a storage facility is required, and is typically provided by batteries, but hydrogen has also been used (see Solarsiedlung, p.244). Independent systems may be designed to operate DC appliances directly. Grid-connected systems need a DC/AC inverter and a protector. Unless distant from a grid connection, PV systems that are grid-connected are preferable to independent ones, owing to the lower space requirements, reduced cost and higher reliability.

PVs can be installed as part of the building fabric, which partially offsets installation costs, or on a separate structure. Glazed elements can be used as wall cladding, as roof finish or as shading devices. The whole building envelope can consist of double-glazed units, some with integrated PVs (see p.243). There are also PV roof tiles which can be used instead of traditional tiles. Some PV shingles are indistinguishable from standard tiles. Increasingly, amorphous silicon is used in conjunction with flat and metal roofs. Single-ply roof membranes with integrated PVs are now available, as are flexible rolls of PVs, which can be attached to a metal roof system.

Despite the cost of PVs having dropped significantly in the past decades, high costs still remain the biggest barrier to a widespread use of PVs. However, as technologies improve and their use increases, prices will drop further, making this low maintenance, zero-CO_2 energy source more affordable.

Case study: Waste heat and PV

The Akademie Mont-Cenis is one of the buildings developed as part of the IBA (Internationale Bau Ausstellung) Emscher Park initiative for the regeneration of the Ruhr area. The Akademie houses the government's research and education facilities. Training and conferences for local government officials take place here and sleeping accommodation is also provided on site. The Akedamie also houses a community library, community hall, social welfare centre and a café, and through this expanded remit has become a focal point for the local community.

The focus of the IBA Emscher Park was energy conservation and land regeneration and the Akademie addresses both issues. The building consists of a 168 x 72m timber-framed greenhouse, located over a disused mine. It encloses nearly a dozen individual buildings and creates a microclimate, which is 5°C higher in winter than the outside air and helps reduce the energy needs of the buildings inside.

The Akademie has a building-integrated PV installation, including 9,300m² of panels on the roof and 800m² on the south elevation. The total installation has a peak rating of 1 MW and produces 600,000 kWh per year, more than twice the development's requirements, with savings in the order of 450 tonnes of CO_2 emissions per year. The excess electricity generated by the PV installation is exported to the grid.

The PVs are designed to provide shading to the buildings below. Different types of mono-crystalline and poly-crystalline panels, with efficiencies of 12.8 and 16 per cent respectively, were used to create an impression of clouds in the sky, hovering mainly over the buildings, while the central areas were kept clear to increase the natural light.

The development also makes use of the gas harnessed from the disused mines. This is a highly useful waste resource. One million cubic metres of gas are used to power a combined heat and power system, which generates 9,000,000 kWh of electricity and 11,000,000 kWh of heat per year. The heat is distributed by a district heating system to the houses in the area, which are increasing in numbers as the area is regenerated. At the centre of this continuous regeneration is the Akademie, acting as a cultural and activity centre, while also providing the community with power.

Nord-RheinWestfalen
Akademie Mont-Cenis Herne, Germany

Client: Nord-Rhein Westfalen district authority
Architect: Jourda and Perraudin
Completed: 1999

5.3.2 Sustainable design features

Site and ecology
The development regenerated a disused mine area and the landscape was reinstated.

Community and culture
The new library and other facilities provide the community with a new venue and a focal point.

Health
The Akademie provides an accessible centre for everyone in the community to benefit from.

Materials
Timber was chosen as a renewable resource.

Energy See main text.

Water
Water-saving appliances were installed.

The PVs are integrated within the glass envelope.

The inside of the Akademie is like a village centre. The café facing onto the water feature, the temperate climate and brightly-lit space create a relaxed atmosphere.

The roof above the library and the wall beyond are a combination of PV panels and clear glass double-glazed units.

The housing adjacent to the Akademie is heated by the waste heat from the mines.

See also: accessible public spaces Chapter 3.3

Case study: Photovoltaics 2

Solarsiedlung
Solarsiedlung Freiburg, Germany

Client: Solarsiedlung GmbH
Architect: Rolf Disch
Completed: 2005

The south façades are fully glazed to maximise solar gains.

The roads are used only for delivery and cars are parked at the perimeter of the site in an underground car park. The site is extensively planted with trees and shrubs.

Some of the houses have monopitch roofs with PVs that face south, and a north-facing terrace.

The Solarsiedlung (solar-community) in Freiburg, Germany, is a housing development that pushes the boundaries of sustainable living. The fundamental feature of the development is the Plusenergiehaus® concept, which embodies a forward-looking approach to sustainable building. The concept is for housing that is not only zero-CO_2, but also generates zero-CO_2 energy and exports it to the grid. The exported energy, generated from an extensive PV array, is not just a small surplus; the concept is for a roof-mounted zero-CO_2 energy-generating plant. The sizing of the PV array is therefore not based on the electricity needs, but rather on the maximum area available for the installation.

What also differentiates this development from other zero-heating and zero-CO_2 developments is its ambition and funding. The development comprises 50 houses and a mixed use block of approximately 5,000m², which includes a further 1,500m² of residential use, all of which produces zero-CO_2 operational emissions. The funding is also innovative. The Solarsiedlung is a speculative development by the Solarsiedlung GmbH, a private company. While some of the units have been bought outright, owing to the need for rental properties in the area, most units are for rent. Short-term funding was not an appropriate vehicle to fund the construction of properties for rent, and an alternative was developed. A long-term investment fund was set up giving companies and individuals the opportunity to invest in a sustainable business. The first of three Freiburger Solarfonds was set up in 2001; two more followed sequentially. All Solarfonds offer high returns based on the immediate and continuous rental income from the houses. The funds have proved to be very effective and successful for developers and investors alike.

The development benefits from the extensive experience of solar design of architect Rolf Disch and the infrastructure of a progressive city. The houses are the classic example of creating an energy-efficient envelope by reducing energy needs, and then providing the remaining energy requirements by renewable means. They are highly insulated and built to be airtight. Wall construction comprises a composite timber framed with 300mm of mineral wool insulation, providing a U-value of 0.12 W/m²K (R48) and the timber frame roofs incorporate 350mm of insulation. The houses make maximum use of solar gains: the south façade is virtually completely glazed with high performance windows with a U-value of 0.7 W/m²K (0.12 Btu/ft²h°F). Protection from the summer sun is provided by large south-facing balconies, which shade the floor below, and the top floor is shaded by the roof-mounted PV array. Heating requirements are expected to range between 10-20kWh/m²/yr depending on the size of the house, its location in the terrace and the occupants' habits. This is equivalent to a consumption of 1-2 litres of oil/m²/yr and qualifies it as superior to the '3-litre house', the German low-energy house, and on par with the Passivhaus standards. The hot water is provided by a district heating system that serves the whole area of Vauban and burns wood waste.

All the roofs are covered with PV panels. The roof is asymmetrical: the south-facing roof is larger than the north-facing roof. Each house has a PV installation with a 3-10 kW peak output, which is expected to generate 2,800-9,600 kWh of electricity per year. The modules are 13 per cent efficienct and have a 20-year guarantee. They are installed directly over a waterproof membrane on a timber deck covering the insulated timber frame.

The Solarsiedlung is not, however, simply a highly energy-efficient development. It also considers wider sustainability issues. Low utility bills are one advantage the houses will offer their residents, but the quality of life created by the development as a whole is also a great benefit. The houses allow for individual needs and tastes: there is a wide variety of possible house layouts on three or four floors, with floor areas ranging from 75m² to 270m². The houses can be bought before completion and finished to suit the buyers' needs and aesthetic taste. The timber frame structure allows a flexible internal layout enabling open plan and cellular configurations. The quality of space is high and space standards are well above what is typical in the UK: two-bedroom houses are 89m² and three- to four- bedroom houses are up to 160m². The houses are also designed to be healthy with ample natural light and no toxic materials; PVC is not used anywhere.

The development has created a good community feeling. Each house has its own garden, but many have been joined up to form a large communal facility. The Solarsiedlung community is soon to increase in size, as the Sonnenschiff (Solar-ship) is completed in 2005. The Sonnenschiff is a 125m-long, four- to six-storey block along the main road, which defines the edge of the Solarsiedlung. It will include 1200 square metres of retail and 3600 square metres of office space, plus 1500m² of flats. An underground car park and storage area are already in use. It is envisaged that the Sonnenschiff too will be covered with 1,500 square metres of PV panels, and is expected to export electricity to the grid. A number of ecologically oriented companies have already expressed an interest and some have committed themselves to moving into the development. With the Solarschiff completed and occupied by sustainable organisations, the Solarsiedlung will become a commercial as well as residential centre for sustainable living.

5.3.3 Sustainable design features

Site and ecology
The site was used by the French military and when it became available the city of Freiburg encouraged the sustainable development of the area. At the Solarsiedlung, cars are excluded from the inner areas of the site and parking is available in an underground car park, which is part of a mixed use block at the perimeter of the site.
Each dwelling has an easily accessible garden and bicycle store.

Community and culture
The houses are affordable to operate. The total utility costs are expected to be just over a third of typical costs. Reductions include 75 per cent for heating and hot water and nearly 50 per cent for electricity and water. The mixed use block will house ecological businesses as well as flats.

Health
The use of PVC was avoided in all cases. The timber is not treated and alternative protection through appropriate detailing is provided.

Materials
The timber-framed construction uses timber from managed forests. It is primarily prefabricated and therefore minimises waste and enhances the work environment for the construction team. The insulation is mineral wool.
Electrical and communications services are installed within a timber skirting, allowing for future upgrading and reconfiguration.

Energy
Fabric U-value:
Walls – 0.12 W/m²K (R48)
Roof – 0.11 W/m²K (R51)
Windows – 0.7 W/m²K (0.12 Btu/ft²h°F)
See also main text.

Water
Site drainage is minimised by applying SUD principles: much of the site is planted.
Water-efficient fixtures and fittings are installed.

Each house has an external store for garden equipment, cycles and general needs.

The houses are clad in different-coloured timber, creating a bright and friendly atmosphere.

The site has been extensively planted with trees and shrubs.

The top floor is shaded by the overhanging PV roof.

Balconies at each level provide shade to the floor below.

Case study: Wind energy 1

Beaufort Court Zero Emissions Building
RES, Kings Langley, Hertfordshire, UK

Project details, Chapter 5.3, p.248

The BCZEB turbine.

The turbine provides visual interest and does not detract from the Arts and Crafts building.

The 36m high turbine.

Wind is one of the renewable energy forms associated with the lowest embodied energy, which is typically saved within three to five months of operation. The UK has excellent potential for generating energy from wind, being the windiest country in Europe. As an island it also has many possibilities of developing off-shore wind farms. To achieve the UK government target of 8 per cent of the country's electricity needs being supplied by wind energy by 2010, an estimate of 2,000 onshore and 1,500 offshore wind turbines will be necessary, providing 8,000 MW (BWEA 2004). This is a significant increase from the current installed capacity of 897 MW and still significantly less than the installed capacity in Germany of 16,628 MW in 2004 (WPM 2005). While the cost of energy from small-scale wind turbines is still greater than that from fossil fuels, large-scale wind generation is increasingly cost competitive.

Typical wind turbines currently installed in the UK are rated at 1.8MW, larger ones are also used. Most turbines are in wind farms with approximately 20 turbines, but individual smaller turbines can be appropriate for community and individual use. Small-scale turbines rated up to 20 kW can be building-integrated. A number of helical vertical axis turbines have been installed in buildings, including the School of Built Environment at Nottingham University and the Doncaster Earth Centre, and have proved to be quiet, producing minimal vibrations. Medium turbines rated up to 600KW can power several hundred dwellings. These are currently more suitable to rural areas or small towns than cities, because of the associated noise, albeit limited, and the visual impact.

The wind turbine at the BCZEB HQ is a medium size, 225-kW wind turbine, expected to generate 250 MWh annually. The energy supplied covers the annual energy needs of the building, estimated at 115 MWh, and the excess, exported to the grid, is enough to supply the energy needs of about 40 homes. The excess is currently sold to the local energy supplier, Green Energy UK.

The turbine is 36m high and has a 29m rotary blade. It is visible from the M25 London orbital a couple of hundred metres away, and advertises the building and BCZEB activities. The BCZEB wind turbine model starts generating energy when the wind is blowing at 3.5 m/s and shuts down, for safety reasons at 25m/s.

The BCZEB turbine, like many other installations, proves many of the concerns regarding wind turbines to be unfounded. Noise and visual intrusion, two of the main concerns of people likely to live close to wind turbines, are shown not to be a problem. The noise of the BCZEB turbine is completely drowned out by that of the M25 orbital road, but even at Hockerton (see p.247) the noise of the turbine is inaudible in its rural surrounding. The turbine's visual impact is, of course, a matter of personal taste, some people like them, some don't, but the BCZEB turbine shows that in certain environments heavily affected by human interventions, such as the M25, a turbine can bring interest and even enhance the environment.

See also: geothermal energy **Chapter 5.3**

Case study: Wind energy 2

Hockerton Housing Project's comprehensive approach to sustainable living addresses many issues including energy. In this respect the development aims to be CO_2 neutral, ideally producing all the energy required on site by renewable means.

The first step towards being able to cover all energy needs with renewables was to minimise energy requirements. The design of the housing minimises heating needs by creating a super-insulated, earth-sheltered and airtight construction which takes advantage of passive solar energy through a south-facing conservatory. Ventilation is by means of mechanical ventilation with heat recovery and all appliances are energy efficient. With these measures the homes used 20,500 kWh in one year of monitoring, equivalent to an average of 4,000 kWh per house.

To supply the development with renewable energy the group had intended installing a wind turbine, expected to produce 12,000 kWhs, and a PV array. A planning application was made for the wind turbine separate from the building itself, but was rejected on grounds of noise pollution and visual intrusion. Before the end of the construction of the houses in 1998 a second application had been rejected for the same reasons. By the third application, submitted in September 1998, the issue of noise had been successfully addressed by highlighting the noise from the nearby road, which was greater than that of the turbine. However, the issue of visual intrusion was still reason enough for rejection, despite the turbine location being moved much further away from the village and the fact that there were numerous visually intrusive electricity pylons nearby. It was only at the fourth attempt that the planning approval was granted. Even on this occasion despite the support of the Director of Development and Planning, the Chairman of Planning and the Leader of the Council, three out of eight people voted against.

The 26m high, 6 kW 'Proven' turbine was installed in 2002 and to complement it a 7.6 kW PV array was installed later as part of a Department of Trade and Industry trial. The installations are all grid connected.

Having installed the first turbine, another planning application was lodged for a second wind turbine to cover the additional energy requirements of the growing Hockerton Housing Project business and for charging a community electric car. No objections were lodged against this application, demonstrating that the many fears which had delayed the approval the previous time had been allayed. The 'Proven' turbine is visually unobtrusive, being a similar height to the surrounding trees and set within a landscape of rolling hills, which often completely hide the development. In most cases noise from the turbines is inaudible above the background noise, particularly with a busy road nearby.

With the second turbine, an 'Iskra', installed in 2005, it is expected that over 20,000 kWhr per year of energy will be produced on site. The grid connection allows the surplus to be exported and, when the wind and sun are not generating sufficient power, electricity is imported. With this last addition, the development should now be largely CO_2 neutral.

Hockerton Housing Project
Southwell, UK

Project details, Chapter 1.4, p.46

5.3.4 Wind turbines

– Embodied energy of turbines can be recuperated within 3 months of operation.

– The financial payback is about two-thirds of the lifetime of the turbine, comparing favourably with other renewable forms of renewable power.

The terraces face the south and the lake. The wind turbine can be seen beyond.

See also: producing food on site **Chapter 1.4**

See also: secondary treatment with reedbeds **Chapter 6.3**

Case study: Geothermal energy

Beaufort Court Zero Emissions Building
RES, Kings Langley, Hertfordshire, UK

Client: Renewable Energy Systems
Architect: Studio E Architects
Services engineer: Max Fordham LLP
Structural engineer: Dewhurst Macfarlane & Partners
Main contractor: Wilmott Dixon
Completed: 2003

5.3.5 Geothermal energy and ground source heat

The temperature of the Earth varies from the crust to its core by 2.5-3°C for every 100m closer to the core, which has at temperature of approximately 7000°C. Current technology allows this geothermal source of energy to be utilised by pumping groundwater from hot underground reservoirs several kilometres into the earth or injecting water into areas of rock at high temperature. Electricity from geothermal energy is produced by using the hot water or stream to drive a turbine.

The ground also acts as a store of energy from the sun. The first metre of the Earth's crust varies in temperature as the air temperature changes. This first layer of earth also insulates the ground below it, which retains a constant temperature throughout the year. This source of energy can also be used to heat and cool buildings.

Ground heat systems
Ground heat can be harnessed by passing air or water through a transfer system in contact with the ground or water at a constant temperature. In summer, the ground can be used as a source of cooling, in winter, as a source of heating.

The simplest system is where 10-40m of duct work, buried 1-4m under ground, is used to pre-heat or pre-cool the supply air to a building. This system is often used in conjunction with MVHR.

More complex systems make use of a fluid to transfer heat from the building to the ground and vice versa, with the help of a heat pump.

The new Renewable Energy Systems head office, known as the Beaufort Court Zero Emissions Building (BCZEB) is located in Kings Langley, north of London, and designed to be a zero emissions commercial building. The building's wind turbine, which is visible from the M25 London orbital, is only one of a wide range of renewable technologies that are used to power the building; the others included are: PV panels, hybrid PV-thermal solar panels, seasonal ground heat store, biomass heating and ground-water cooling. While this might have been expected from a client that develops wind farms worldwide, the building also addresses other aspects of sustainability, such as land use, material selection and community issues.

The development involved the conversion and extension of a former Ovaltine egg farm into 2,665 square metres of office accommodation and a visitors' centre, including exhibition and conference facilities. The building currently accommodates 75 members of staff plus regular visitors. BCZEB's commitment to using the building as a demonstration and education medium for the public was supported by a £700,000 funding grant from the EC Framework 5 Programme, which was used for the educational facilities and the renewable technologies.

The aim was for the development to be energy self-sufficient, and an energy efficient building design was therefore essential. However, due to the proximity to one of the most trafficked roads in the UK, a naturally ventilated office was thought likely to create an unhealthily noisy environment. Consequently, the building is partially sealed and mechanically ventilated. In order to reduce the cooling and heating requirements, the building envelope had to be well insulated and airtight and unwanted solar gains had to be minimised. This was achieved, despite the reuse of an existing building, demonstrating that energy efficiency is not limited to new build.

The building is ventilated by natural and displacement ventilation and uses renewable energy to provide heating and cooling. Displacement ventilation supplies cool, rather than cold air at low velocity into a space, introducing it at low level through supply grilles set within the floor. The higher temperature and lower velocity of the incoming air improve thermal comfort. Occupants and equipment heat the air, which rises naturally and is extracted at high level; at BCZEB it naturally passes through a grille in the door and is expelled at high level through rooflights. The fresh air is not mixed with the existing air in a space, and the rising displaced air takes contaminants with it, thus improving the indoor air quality. A temperature gradient of 5-6°C is formed within the space. Apart from an improved indoor environment, displacement ventilation also has the benefits of reduced operating energy and reduced capital investment. It can also be linked to a number of energy-efficient heating and cooling technologies.

In winter, the air supply is preheated by hot water from the solar thermal arrays. If solar energy is not available, heat is recovered from the seasonal heat store, which stores hot water from the solar thermal arrays produced throughout the summer. Additional heating is provided by a biomass boiler burning an energy crop grown on site.

In summer, cooling is provided by groundwater. The groundwater at BCZEB comes from a chalk aquifer with a constant temperature of 12°C and the groundwater system used is an open loop system (see 5.3.5). The groundwater is extracted from a 200mm diameter borehole 75m deep. It is pumped up at 5 litres per second and filtered to remove any impurities. It is first used to cool and dehumidify the supply air to the building. Then, having warmed up to 15°C, the groundwater is used to cool the spaces by circulating it within chilled beams. Being an open loop system, the water is then discharged rather than returned to the borehole, and in this case it is used outside to water the biofuel crop. This means that the water is indirectly returned underground.

Ground source energy can also be used to heat buildings, whereby low grade heat is upgraded by using heat pumps. However, heat pumps operated with electricity from fossil fuels are generally not CO_2 neutral (see 5.3.5). Instead, BCZEB makes use of groundwater at its natural temperature, without requiring heat pumps. In addition, all the mechanical plant is powered by PVs and wind power, which are zero–CO_2 emission energy sources. In this way, even the BCZEB cooling system can be considered zero–CO_2.

The main ground source heat systems are: closed loop ground heat systems, open loop groundwater systems, and surface water systems.

Closed loop systems can be vertical and horizontal.

– Vertical systems require bore holes between 40-150 metres deep, containing one or more pipes.

– Horizontal systems involve laying pipes in parallel trenches 1-2 metres deep. A slinky coil configuration can minimise the trench sizes.

– Open loop systems use ground-water directly, by passing it through a heat pump or other system and disposing of it in another well or river or to the ground.

– Surface water systems make use of heat from lakes or rivers and can be open or closed systems.

In heating mode the liquid in the pipes is heated by the earth, which remains at a constant 8-12°C. The heat is upgraded by a heat pump (see below) and used to heat internal spaces. In winter, the opposite takes place: heat from the building is extracted and transferred back to earth. In cooling mode the use of a heat pump can be dispensed with, and the groundwater used directly as the cooling medium (as in BCZEB).

Heat Pumps

Heat pumps are used to upgrade low grade heat. Sources of heat can be the air, surface water, the ground and groundwater. Heat pumps operate by using refrigerant fluid, heated through compression, to transfer heat from the heat source to the building and vice versa. Since refrigerants that are associated with ozone depletion are either banned or being phased out, ammonia is being increasingly used. Heat pumps are operated with electricity and have an efficiency coefficient of 3-4: 1 kWh of electricity will release 3-4 kWh of useful heat. This means that unless the heat pump is operated with energy produced from renewable sources, the CO_2 emissions from a heat pump are comparable to those from a gas boiler.

The main entrance to the offices and exhibition areas is through a single-storey glass block, linked to the existing Arts and Crafts building.

As part of BCZEB's educational remit, the plant rooms display information panels explaining the operation of the building systems.

Biofuel is used to heat the building

The extension to the inside of the courtyard has been covered with a green roof.

See also: wind energy 1 **Chapter 5.3**

Case study: Biofuel

Solar-Fabrik
Freiburg, Germany

Client: Solar-Fabrik
Architect: Rolf & Hotz
Structural engineer: Ingenieurbüro Werner Reppel
Energy consultant: Büro für Sonnenenergie
Completed: 1999

The Solar-Fabrik viewed from the road.

PV panels on steel supports shade the glazed façade.

Light shines through the glazed façade into the entrance and café area.

The Solar-Fabrik in Freiburg manufactures PV modules and their building reflects the company's activities. Not only does the building make use of PV panels, but its environmental strategy aims to achieve CO_2 neutrality.

CO_2 neutrality generally refers to the use of biofuels. These are fuels that are either a biodegradable waste product or are renewable plants that absorb CO_2 during their growing phase, so that when they are burnt the quantity of CO_2 emitted is the same as that absorbed. Biofuels include wood, wood waste and coppiced wood, grasses, oils, ethanol from fermentation of crops, and gases from sewage plants, biodegradable municipal and agricultural waste. Wood is the most common biofuel and on a small scale, it can provide heat and is often used as a back-up heat source in very low-energy houses (see Schreiber house case study, p.230). Wood is also exploited on a larger scale as part of communal district heating systems, like the one in Vauban in Freiburg. Grasses such as Miscanthus, a type of elephant grass which grows quickly and produces large quantities of biomass per hectare, could prove a valuable biofuel once more experience is gained in its cultivation and use. Oils derived from planted crops have a higher calorific value than grasses, but are approximately twice as expensive as ground oil and therefore uptake has been slow.

At the Solar-Fabrik a combination of PVs and rape seed oil provide auxiliary power to the building, and passive internal and solar heat gains also make a significant contribution to its heating. The Solar-Fabrik consists of two interconnected blocks: a south-facing block and a manufacturing block on the north side of the site. The south-facing block faces the road and houses the offices, entrance and exhibition space, café, plus two dwellings at roof level. The building is designed to have low-energy consumption by insulating the fabric well, providing thermal mass and maximising solar gains. The external walls have a U-value of 0.22 W/m²K (R25) and the glazed curtain walling has a U-value of 1.1 W/m²K (0.19 Btu/ft²h°F). Thermal mass is provided by concrete floor slabs and a solid stone wall at ground floor. The south-facing façade is glazed along its full length and solar gains through the glazing are estimated to contribute 15 per cent (43 MWh/yr) to the heating requirements of the building. The manufacturing block is heated by means of mechanical ventilation with heat recovery and has a heating requirement of 17.1 KWh/m²yr, while the offices' heating requirement is 13.4 KWh/m²yr.

The summer operation is largely free-running. Comfort is achieved through a number of measures that ensure that the internal temperatures do not exceed the external temperature by more than 2°C. The south-facing elevation is shaded with 210 square metres of PVs, automatic windows at high level open to allow the hot air to escape, the thermal mass helps to absorb daytime heat gains and earth ducts supply cooled air to the entrance and exhibition space. The earth ducts can further cool the space by introducing cold air at night to the thermal mass. The offices can be cross-ventilated and the manufacturing block is naturally ventilated.

To cover the winter heating needs a boiler run on rape seed oil provides 50 MWh/yr, while a CHP system also burning rape seed oil provides 150 MWh/yr heat.

The CHP unit also generates 90 MWh/yr of electricity and further electricity is provided by 450m² of PVs, which generate 40 MWh/yr. With further heating needs covered by passive means, the building is CO_2 neutral.

The 30,000 litres of oil required to run the building are derived from rape seed cultivated following ecological agricultural principles on a 30-hectare site. This ensures that the building is not only CO_2 neutral, but achieves this in an ecological way.

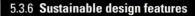

5.3.6 Sustainable design features

Site and ecology
The local landscaping, which includes a planted pond, enhances the local flora and fauna.

Community and culture
The entrance hall, exhibition area and the café have become a focal point for the local area.

Health
The space benefits from ample natural light. Natural materials were used where appropriate.

Materials
Low-embodied energy materials were selected where possible.

Energy
Fabric U-values:
  Solid walls – 0.22 W/m²K (R25)
  Glazing – 1.1 W/m²K (0.19 Btu/ft²h°F)

Heating requirement covered by

Rape seed oil boiler – 50 MWh/yr
Rape seed oil CHP – 150 MWh/yr
Passive solar gains – 43 MWh/yr
Internal gains – 35 MWh/yr

Electricity requirement covered by

PVs – 40 MWh/yr
Rape seed oil CHP – 90 MWh/yr

Water
Water-efficient appliances are installed throughout. Rainwater is used to flush WCs.

The entrance, exhibition area and café are within the south-facing glazed building element.

Some of the PV panels are integrated within the glazed elevation and some are mounted on steel supports and shade the glazing. Opening vents in the façade provide ventilation.

The air intakes, which draw air into the underground ducts are located outside the manufacturing building.

Two building-integrated PV panels between two opening vents.

Chapter 6
Water

6.0 Introduction

	Total use m³ per capita per annum (Worldwatch 2004)	Total use m³ per capita per annum (Guardian 2003)
Congo		20
Ethiopia	42	47
UK		160
Austria		281
South Africa	354	391
China	491	439
Germany	574	583
France	675	704
Australia	1250	839
Canada		1623
USA	1932	1844
Uzbekistan		2626

Note: The low levels of water consumption in the UK and the Congo Democratic Republic relate to the limited area of irrigated agricultural land (1080km² UK and 110km² Congo) compared to China (525, 800km²) or the US (214,000km²).

	Estimated demand km³ per annum	% share
Agriculture	2880	65
Industry	975	22
Municipalities	300	7
Evaporative losses in reservoirs	275	6
Total	4430	100

(MacKenzie 1998)

Water is essential for life on earth. Water is needed for plant growth and for the survival of animals, including human beings. Of the total amount of water on earth, 97.25 per cent is contained in salty seas, 2.05 per cent is contained in glacial icecaps, and most of the remaining 0.7 per cent is contained in aquifers. The amount of renewable fresh water, available through rainfall on watershed areas for consumption by humans, is very small, approximately 0.008 per cent of the total. Of this 110,300 cubic kilometres of water, two-thirds evaporates, leaving 40,700 cubic kilometres per year of rainwater run-off, feeding rivers and replenishing aquifers and available for domestic, industrial and agricultural use. It is on this resource particularly that increasing pressure is being placed (Postel 1997; Mackenzie 1998).

Endangered water resources are not the only water-related environmental issue that needs to be considered. The treatment and discharge of wastewater are associated with a number of environmental problems, which directly relate to clean water resource issues. This chapter considers the use of water and the treatment of waste water in relation to buildings, how building design can minimise the use of water, and how to reduce the amount of black-, grey- and rainwater discharged to a mains sewer system.

Water availability

Of the 40,700 cubic kilometres of fresh rainwater, 12,500 cubic kilometres falls in populated areas at regular intervals (except during floods) and can be extracted for use. This is the main renewable source of freshwater available for use. In addition, groundwater can be extracted from aquifers. Current global annual freshwater use is in the order of 4,430 cubic kilometres, of which agriculture is the biggest user.

To satisfy basic water needs, estimates of up to 700 cubic metres of fresh water per capita per year have been suggested (Postel 1997). Since, in order to maintain a stable ecosystem only 30–50 per cent of available surface freshwater should be extracted, it is generally assumed that availabilities of less than 1700 cubic metres of fresh water per capita constitute water stress. Another measure of water stress is when 40 per cent or more of a river's content is extracted for use (Perkins 2002). Current estimates of people living in water-stressed countries range from 430 million to 733 million and this figure is expected to rise to between 2.4 and 3.4 billion people by 2025 (UNFPA 2004; Postel 1997). There are also 1.1 billion people without adequate access to clean water, defined as 20 litres per person available less than 1 kilometre away from their dwelling; 2.4 billion without adequate sanitation (Worldwatch 2003); and 2 million people, of whom 90 per cent are children, dying from diarrhoeal diseases transmitted through inadequately clean water (WHO 2003b).

Among the reasons for water stress, which notably include inadequate infrastructure, is that the distribution of accessible fresh water is uneven across the world and does not coincide with population densities. Countries with low rainfall may be able to meet only a small portion of their water needs through rainwater run-off, and have to rely predominantly on non-renewable groundwater sources with limited reserves. For instance, Israel and Libya are already extracting more water annually than is replenishing their groundwater systems. This is not only unsustainable, but is associated with other environmental problems. Extracting excessive amounts of groundwater can reduce the water table levels, which in extreme cases can cause subsidence, while in coastal regions over-extracting from aquifers can result in their contamination with saltwater, which can subsequently cause land salination and affect agriculture (Goudie 2000).

Countries that have adequate rainfall, but are densely populated, can also suffer water stress. For example, the North China plain, with a population of 450 million, has a renewable fresh water supply of 500 cubic metres per capita. Britain, owing to its high population density, is one of the most water-stressed European countries, in particular in the Thames Estuary, which is the most populated part of Britain. This area receives only 500 millimetres of rainfall a year, compared to 2,400 in Wales and the Lake District. Here again, groundwater is the main alternative source of fresh water being exploited as surface fresh water fails to meet demand. Many of the world's crop-producing regions, including in the US, are now over-exploiting groundwater sources. In the North China Plain, the level of ground water is dropping at 1–1.5 metres per year (Worldwatch 2004). In the UK, aquifers in the Anglia, Severn and Trent, Thames Valley and Southern regions are being progressively depleted.

Another alternative source of freshwater is desalinated seawater. With costs of desalination dropping to $0.54–3.50 per cubic metre of water, compared to $0.11 for conventional treatment in the US, desalination is becoming a potential source of fresh water for the future; however, desalination is very energy intensive and over-reliance on it would aggravate the greenhouse effect (Joynt and Poe 2003).

As global population increases, so do the requirements for water for municipal, industrial and agricultural use. At the same time, climate change is likely to aggravate water stress, as changing weather patterns are expected to make rainwater less accessible. For instance, in the UK, global warming is predicted to cause wetter winters and drier summers. The extreme rainfall in winter, will not, however, be able to be absorbed by the already saturated land and replenish aquifers. In summer, because the existing infrastructure will be unable to collect and store sufficient water to bridge dry periods, there will be an increased likelihood of drought. Overall the already existing and problematic pressure on freshwater sources will increase.

Water pollution

In future, water scarcity and stress are expected to be the cause of political friction and even armed conflicts. But just as essential as the quantity of freshwater is its quality. Water pollution is threatening the quality of fresh drinking water and, at the same time having detrimental impacts on the natural environment.

Sources of water pollution include urbanisation, contaminated land, industrial

6.0.3 Water needs for electricity and food production

Water consumption and electricity

In the US the production of 1 kWh of electricity made from fossil fuels requires approximately 8.3 litres of water. This is needed to cool the power plant and necessary for mining the fuels.

The average household in the US uses 10,000 kWh per year which requires 83 cubic metres of water (Worldwatch 2004). In the UK 25 per cent of fresh water extracted is used by the electricity supply industry (EA 1998).

Water consumed to supply protein and calories for selected foods in California, US
(Worldwatch 2004)

Food	Water (litres) consumed to supply 10 grams of protein	Water (litres) consumed to supply 500 calories
Potatoes	67	89
Groundnut	90	210
Onions	118	221
Maize (corn)	130	130
Pulses (beans)	132	421
Wheat	135	219
Rice	204	251
Eggs	244	963
Milk	250	758
Poultry	303	1515
Pork	476	1225
Beef	1000	4902

6.0.4 Eutrophication and soil particle pollution of water courses

Eutrophication

This is a process resulting from an increased nutrient content, for example nitrates and phosphates, of the water from agricultural run-off and domestic and industrial effluent. The increased nutrient levels result in increased algae growth, followed by reduced dissolved oxygen content of the water, which is caused by the algae preventing oxygen exchange with the atmosphere and then by decay, as the algae die. Reduced light penetration and low oxygen levels will reduce flora and fauna biodiversity and, if oxygen levels drop sufficiently, fish life can be endangered.

Soil particle pollution of water courses

Soil particles washed into rivers can fill in and cover gravel beds where fish would spawn.
Soil particles, particularly from agriculture, can also absorb chemicals, in particular pesticides and phosphates, and pollute the water.
(Goudie 2000)

6.0.5 Persistent Organic Pollutants (POPs)

The Stockholm Convention, signed in 2001, bans certain pesticides, chlorinated industrial chemicals, and aims to control materials that give rise to dioxins and furans. The production, import, export, disposal, and use of POPs is to be controlled by legislation issued by the signatory governments. The convention was ratified in 2004, with more than 50 countries signing up to it.

The current list of POPs includes eight pesticides (aldrin, DDT, dieldrin, endrin, heptachlor, chlordane, mirex and toxaphene), two industrial compounds (hexachlorobenzene and polychlorinated biphenyls (PCBs)), and furans and dioxins, which are unintentional by-products mainly of the incineration of municipal waste and the iron and non-ferrous metal industries, but also derive from combustion of leaded petrol and combustion for domestic heating.

POPs have contaminated virtually all global ecosystems. They are assimilated in the food chain and their concentrations increase as they are transferred up the food chain. The health effects of these compounds can be serious. They have been linked to cancer, allergies and hypersensitivity, damage to the endocrine and nervous system, damage to the liver, reproductive disorders, and disruption of the immune system.
(UNEP 1999)

processes, mining, fire, agricultural fertilisers, pesticides and soil particles, sewage, and domestic chemicals. There are three classes of pollutants to consider: nitrates and phosphates, metals, and synthetic organic pollutants.

Agriculture is perhaps the major pollutant of watercourses, with fertilisers containing nitrates and phosphates causing eutrophication (see 6.0.4). Eutrophication normally takes place in inland watercourses, but even closed seas, such as the North Sea and the Baltic Sea, have shown increased concentrations of phosphates from sewage and agricultural discharge. Eutrophication of seas can cause excessive algae growth in estuaries, which can prove toxic to marine life. Eutrophication of coral reef areas causes overproduction of algae that competes with the coral, causing the decline and ultimate death of the coral (Goudie 2000).

Sewage also contributes to eutrophication through nitrates and phosphates from metabolic processes and from detergents. Sewage also contains pesticides and metal pollutants, such as nickel, copper, lead and zinc, which derive from water pipework, cosmetics, cleaning fluids and medicines. Pollution incidents from domestic premises, such as oil contamination of stormwater sewers or misconnections of sewage outlets into stormwater sewers from DIY work, accounted for 1,000 pollution incidents in 1995 in the UK (EA 1998).

Industrial processes, as well as landfill sites, are responsible for metal pollution, particularly lead, mercury, arsenic and cadmium, which are harmful to human health, and copper, silver, selenium, zinc and chromium, which are harmful to aquatic life. Industrial and agricultural processes also contribute synthetic organic pollutants, which are thought to be harmful to health even in small concentrations and are persistent, remaining in the environment for many years. These include synthetic organic pesticides, such as DDT; industrial products, such as PCBs; organic solvents used in industrial and domestic processes; and phthalates. Of these organic pollutants, eight pesticides and two industrial compounds are on the list of Persistent Organic Pollutants (POPs), compiled as a result of the Stockholm Convention, which aims to protect public health and the environment in respect of these pollutants (see 6.0.5).

Stormwater run-off in urban areas can contain a cocktail of pollutants from rubbish, vehicle liquids, industrial processes, garden chemicals and animal excrement, of which 1,000 tonnes is deposited on the streets of the UK each day (Goudie 2000).

Polluting substances find their way into watercourses either directly or indirectly. Rainwater falling on agricultural land can wash pesticide-polluted soil and the pesticides on the surface of the soil directly into rivers. Small amounts of pesticides may not compromise the quality of drinking water, but European Union drinking-water limits of pesticides have been exceeded on numerous occasions, for example as a result of spraying chemicals on saturated soil unable to absorb them (NRA 1995). Groundwater can be contaminated as pollutants from agricultural, industrial or landfill activities seep through the ground into groundwater. If water table levels rise, groundwater can become polluted by coming into contact with contaminated land, such as that polluted by industrial processes. Groundwater in the industrial areas of Birmingham is no longer used as drinking water for these reasons (Stauffer 1996).

Indirect pollution can occur when polluted water is collected within sewer or storm-water systems and then disposed of, untreated, in watercourses. The planned disposal of untreated sewage and sewage sludge (see Chapter 6.3) into rivers or at sea is a practice that still occurs in many countries, but since the 1998 implementation of the EEC Urban Waste Water Treatment Directive (1991), is no longer permitted in the UK. At present in the UK, the unplanned disposal of untreated stormwater or sewage into watercourses occurs occasionally when abnormally high volumes of waste water are collected, as in during a once in fifty years rainfall event. In such cases the sewage treatment works may discharge sewage in excess of their plant's capacity into the nearby watercourses. In 1996, over 2,000 overflow incidents occurred in the UK and, with increasing population and increasing storm events resulting from climate change, such occurrences could become even more common (NRA 1995). Even where storm and sewer disposal is separate, excessive amounts of stormwater can cause soil erosion and discharge sediment into watercourses, as occurs in areas of Australia.

The construction industry is also responsible for water pollution as a result of direct and indirect pollution incidents. Incidents that can chemically and physically pollute water range from washing out lorries into stormwater sewers to transferring clay-contaminated water into small watercourses.

Water pollution not only damages the natural environment, but ultimately compromises the quality of some of the available freshwater, reducing the total amount that can be used for drinking and other purposes, and therefore increases the water stress experienced.

Designing for reduced water consumption and waste

There are three main approaches, relevant to building design and water-related environmental problems, that contribute to reducing water use and pollution. First, the need for freshwater should be reduced and efficient means of using this water should be introduced in buildings (see Chapter 6.1). Second, sources of water other than mains water, such as rainwater and greywater, should be used where appropriate (see Chapter 6.2). Third, the disposal of black-, grey- and rainwater has to be considered. Pressure on the sewer and stormwater system can be reduced through rainwater retention and recycling systems, on-site wastewater treatment and SUD systems (see Chapter 6.3).

Buildings that can combine all three approaches are well on their way to becoming water autonomous. Water autonomy implies a provision of freshwater independent from mains supply and on-site sewage and stormwater treatment and disposal, obviating the need for a sewer connection. A number of buildings, including some of the following case studies, have successfully implemented such a strategy.

6.0.6 Sustainable water use and wastewater disposal

Minimising the need for water
– Use composting toilets.
– Select plants with low watering requirements.
– Encourage the use of showers instead of baths.

Use water efficiently
– Install water-saving spray or automatic taps on basins and showers.
– Install low or dual flush WCs.
– Retrofit existing appliances, e.g. upgrade existing WCs with an efficient flush mechanism or a 'hippo' (heavy duty plastic container that displaces water) in the cistern, upgrade taps.
– Install irrigation systems, grouping plants by their water requirements (see Chapter 2.5).
– Install water meters.
– Educate users and adopt a water-conscious approach (e.g. shower rather than bathe).

Recycle used water
– Install greywater collection systems from basins, showers and baths to flush WCs or water gardens.

Recycle rainwater
– Install a butt to collect rainwater for gardening.
– Install a rainwater recycling system.

Reduce the use of mains drains
– Install on-site waste water treatment systems.
– Install a Sustainable Urban Drainage System (SUD) (e.g. water-absorbent landscaping).

6.0.7 Further Reading

Urban Drainage
Butler, D., Davies, J.W. (2000) E&FN Spon, London
Sustainable Urban Drainage Systems: Design Manual for England and Wales CIRIA (2000) Construction Industry Research Information Association, London
Sewage Solutions: Answering the Call of Nature
Grant et al. (1996) Centre for Alternative Technology, Machynlleth
Rainwater and Greywater Use in Buildings: Best Practice Guidance
Leggett et al. (2001) Construction Industry Research Information Association, London
Sustainable Housing: Options for Independent Energy, Water Supply and Sewerage, Application Guide Smerdon et al. (1997) BSRIA, Bracknell
Safe to Drink? The Quality of Your Water
Stauffer, J. (1996) Centre for Alternative Technology, Machynlleth

6.1 Minimising Need and Maximising Efficiency

6.1.1 Use of treated water in the UK

Agriculture	4%
Commerce and services	12%
Industry	20%
Households	64%

(Stauffer 1996)

6.1.2 Domestic water use

The typical African family uses approximately 23 litres a day compared to more than 450 litres per person in the US. (Vidal 2003)

Estimates of typical domestic water use

	litres per capita per day
Uganda	60
Denmark	130
UK	145
Singapore	170
Australia	250
USA indoor	262
USA all	300-800+

(Worldwatch 2004)

6.1.3 Water losses through leaks

Loss type	Loss per minute	Annual loss	Annual cost in £
2 drops/sec	18 ml	9.5 m³	£6-13
Drops breaking into a stream	59 ml	31 m³	£19-42
2mm stream	277 ml	146 m³	£90-195
3mm stream	638 ml	336 m³	£210-450
5mm stream	1 litre	528 m³	£325-705

(WRAS 1999a, 1999b)

The first step in addressing water-related environmental issues is to reduce the amount of water used, which will subsequently reduce the amount of wastewater produced. Each country uses water in different ways and in some countries agriculture accounts for much of the total use, so interventions in respect of irrigation methods are a priority. In the UK, the main water users are households and virtually all the water is used indoors, with a small percentage used to water the garden, clean cars, and other external activities (see 6.1.1 and 6.1.4). In hotter affluent countries, including Australia and the US, the percentage of domestic water used outdoors is far higher. In Australia, up to 60 per cent of water is used outdoors and in the US, this figure is between 50-70 per cent. Irrigation of landscaping and lawns throughout the US uses 30 billion litres of water each day and the standard lawn uses 38,000 litres of water in a summer (Worldwatch 2004).

As with all environmental improvements, educating the users is essential. Particularly in respect of water use, water-efficient appliances need to be operated and maintained correctly to achieve high water savings. For example, a shower can use half as much water as a bath, but it is up to the user to choose which one to use; a dual flush WC can reduce overall domestic water use by 10-15 per cent, but if the users always use a full flush the saving will not materialise. Education combined with financial pressure has proved successful in minimising water use, as can be seen in metering trials in the Isle of Wight, which resulted in a 10 per cent decrease in water consumption (Butler and Davies 2000). Only 10-15 per cent of homes in the UK have water meters, suggesting a good potential for further reductions in water use. Working against water-saving initiatives is the fact that fashion trends have introduced Jacuzzi baths, hot tubs and power showers, which can use more water than a conventional bath in just five minutes, a fact that highlights again the importance of educating users.

Designing buildings to conserve water

To save water in buildings, first install water-efficient equipment (see 6.1.5 and case study Thurgoona Campus p.260), of which there is an increasing collection to choose from. Second, the users need to be educated about the importance of saving water and the facilities they have in their building. The building owner's manuals or other awareness-raising methods could be used for this purpose. Addressing external water use is particularly important in hot countries (see Environmental Showcase Home case study, p.262). Third, maintenance is vital in reducing accidental water losses, such as those resulting from system leaks (see 6.1.3). Water companies should also play their part in addressing leaks in the distribution system. Losses through leakage range between 3 per cent in Copenhagen and 50 per cent in rural France, while certain developing countries experience leakage losses of up to 75 per cent. In the UK 23 per cent of water is lost through leakages (DEFRA 2004a). If a combination of water efficiency measures, awareness raising, and leakage control were implemented, a reduction of 42 per cent of the water extracted is thought to be achievable.

6.1.4 **Water use**	% of total water use in UK per day (Butler 2000)		Typical volume of water per single use in UK (Butler 2000)	% of total domestic water use per capita per day in Germany (BGW 2000)	Efficient use possible	Greywater use possible	Rainwater use possible
	domestic (total use = 145l/capita)	commercial (%)					
flushing WCs	31% (45 l)	35	8.8 l	27% (35 l)	yes	yes	yes
washing/bathing	26% (38 l)	26	Bath 74 l Shower 36 l	35% (45 l)	yes	no	yes
flushing urinals		15	Basin 3.7 l		yes	yes	yes
drinking/cooking	15% (22 l)	9		4% (5 l)	no	no	yes
laundry	12% (17 l)	8		12% (16 l)	yes	no	yes
washing dishes	10% (15 l)	2		6% (8 l)	yes	no	yes
external use	5% (7 l)	4	116 l	15% (19 l)	yes	yes	yes
other	1% (1 l)	1					yes

Dual flush WC flush mechanism.

6.1.5 Water efficient equipment

Toilets

– Dual flush WCs are designed to flush a full flush and a half flush, whereby a full flush can be from 3–6 litres and a half flush can be from 1.5–4 litres, depending on the cistern manufacturer. Using dual flush WCs relies on the users being familiar with the system to avoid the full flush being used in all cases.

– Low flush WCs have smaller cisterns than standard ones and use 4.5 litres rather than the current 6 litres or the old 7.5 litres standard in the UK up to 2001.

– Vacuum toilets operate with air rather than water and can achieve big water savings. They need electricity to run, therefore, the energy use has to be weighed against the water savings.

– Waterless toilets, such as composting toilets, with or without electrical drying, use no or minimal water, and can save up to 40 per cent of domestic water use.

– Urine separating toilets can have as low water use as low and dual flush WCs (see case study, Chapter 6.3, p.283).

Urinals

– Urinals should be fitted with a person detector that activates the water flush, or with an integrated sensor to activate the flush. Compared to urinal systems that flush six times per hour, savings of over 30,000 litres per year per urinal can be achieved during unoccupied weekends.

– I-litre urinals save more than 65 per cent of water compared to normal urinals.

– Waterless urinals do not need to be flushed with water. A barrier and seal, which can be made of a number of materials let urine through, but stop smells coming out. There is less salt build-up and less need for maintenance. Water saving can be as high as 236,000 litres per urinal per year.

Taps

– Aerated taps, available for basins and showers, mix water with air, providing a normal water volume without using as much water as non-aerated taps. Aerated shower heads can use 9 litres instead of the usual 20 litres per minute. Aerated basin taps use 3.6 litres instead of 20 litres per minute. Spray inserts operate in a similar way.

– Flow regulators limit the amount of water coming out of a tap. The water flow can be set as required.

– Automatic basin taps with infrared sensors are only turned on when the integrated sensor identifies a hand under the tap. They automatically turn off after a set time.

– Self-closing taps are pushed to activate and turn off automatically after a set time.

Laundry and dishwashing

– Water-efficient equipment can be identified by means of an Eco-label (in Europe), whereby an A rating is awarded to the most efficient and G to the least, or an Australian Water Conservation Rating whereby AAAAA is awarded to the most efficient and A to a reasonably efficient model. Efficient washing machines use approximately 50 litres per wash, compared to more than 100 litres used by older inefficient models.

Landscaping

– Drought-tolerant species, e.g. cactus, succulents and eucalyptus reduce watering needs. If a lawn is needed, select a grass species that requires less watering.

– Automatic irrigation with moisture sensors optimises the use of water by irrigating only when required.

– Grouping plants according to their watering needs improves watering efficiencies (hydro-zoning).

– Mulching reduces water evaporation. Improving soil condition with organic material improves water retention.

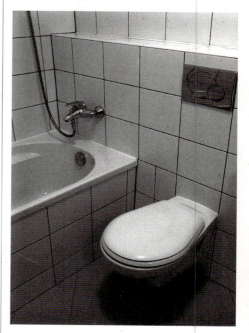

Dual flush WC in Barling Court housing (see Chapter 2.2).

Aerated shower head

Case study: Composting toilets

Thurgoona Campus
Charles Sturt University, Albury,
New South Wales, Australia

Project details, Chapter 4.4, p.177

A composting toilet in the student building. Note the plastic container with wood shavings beside the pedestal. The toilet cubicle is enclosed by the rammed earth external walls and an internal metal partition.

See also: rammed earth **Chapter 4.4**

See also: natural ventilation **Chapter 5.1**

See also: solar thermal 2 **Chapter 5.3**

See also: sustainable drainage **Chapter 6.3**

The Thurgoona Campus of Charles Sturt University is situated in the Murray River valley on the border of Victoria and New South Wales, Australia. The sustainability strategy adopted in respect of the development of the campus was very comprehensive and considered everything from materials to energy use, but put particular emphasis on the use of water.

The Murray River valley receives 740 millimetres of precipitation per annum (see Appendix 3 for comparison), 75 per cent of which falls during the winter. Summer precipitation is limited and liable to high rates of evaporation, owing to the high ambient temperatures. It was therefore necessary to adopt a comprehensive approach to collecting and saving water on the campus.

Typical university campuses, similar to the Thurgoona Campus, require water for drinking, washing (kitchens, basins and showers) and flushing WCs. Assuming the use of low flush WCs (e.g. 2–6-litre cisterns) a population of 600, such as that at Thurgoona Campus, may use 9 cubic metres of water per day just for WC flushing. In addition to building uses, water may be required to maintain the landscaping.

At the Thurgoona Campus, flushing WCs and watering the landscaping would have constituted the primary uses of water, and both these requirements were addressed in a coordinated water management strategy that considered water use and wastewater treatment together. Water use was minimised by designing WCs and the landscaping watering system to operate independently from the mains water supply. The need for water in WCs was completely abolished by using composting toilets throughout the new campus. Water for irrigation was also kept independent from the mains supply by relying on a complex stormwater collection and storage system. The use of composting toilets not only minimised the use of water, but also meant that there was no need to treat blackwater from WCs. With only greywater and rainwater to treat, it became very simple to treat all waste water on the campus site itself (see 6.3).

Composting toilets are minimum resource toilets using no water and minimal or no energy to treat human waste, transforming it into a usable compost. The treatment of faeces occurs within the collection tank and involves aerobic decomposition by bacteria and fungi, as well as invertebrates, such as red worms, simulating what would happen in nature (red worms are only there if put in by the users). Aerobic decomposition can be considered the opposite of the process that takes place through photosynthesis, whereby inorganic compounds are transformed into complex biological molecules by using energy from the sun. Aerobic decomposition, known as mineralization, decomposes the complex biological molecules into the original inorganic compounds, including nitrates, phosphates, sulphates, CO_2 and oxygen, and in the process releases energy as heat. This process transforms unpleasant and potentially hazardous material into a safe and soil-like material, reducing its volume by 80–90 per cent.

Composting toilets consist of a traditional–looking toilet with an outlet that drops straight down into a collection tank. While it is possible to purpose-build collection tanks out of brick or dig them out of the ground as in old-fashioned privies, the tanks used in Thurgoona Campus are commercially available plastic tanks. The composting toilets are installed over a small basement area where the collection tanks are situated and made easily accessible for the removal of compost. The compost that has been in the system for about a year is removed from the bottom of the tank approximately every six months.

In composting toilets the heat released through the aerobic decomposition is advantageous for several reasons. The heat kills pathogens and accelerates the decomposition process, thus reducing smells. The heat also heats the surrounding air causing it to rise. In composting toilets, as in Thurgoona Campus, the heated air is channelled to the outside through a vent pipe (see photograph) and by doing so draws air from the toilet cubicle into the collection tank and out the building. This ensures that any smells that develop in the tank are always directed to the outside air rather than back into the cubicle. The Thurgoona installations supplement natural ventilation with continuously operating electric extractor fans.

Each campus toilet has a container with sawdust in addition to the typical toilet paper dispenser and other special waste collection containers. A note explains to the uninitiated the need to drop some sawdust into the toilet after use. This is necessary to ensure the compost heap is well aerated to maintain the aerobic decomposition.

In terms of their use the toilets have proved unproblematic and very successful, especially taking into account the large population using them. This shows that the initial cultural barriers, including composting toilets' association with 'primitive' and unsophisticated ways of life, the uneasiness of sitting close to decomposing excrement, and the lack of the 'flushing ritual', can all be easily overcome.

Disappointingly, the local authority didn't authorise the use of the compost as a plant fertiliser and therefore it is simply dug into the ground on campus. This reflects the lack of familiarity with such systems still experienced by many people.

Student accommodation. Composting toilets and vent pipes are located on left side of building.

Access to the basement space with composting toilets collection tank.

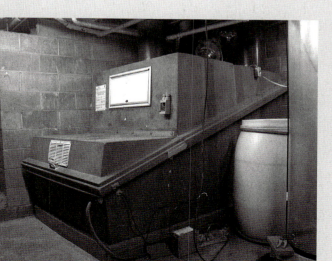

Typical compost tank size is approximately 1700 (H) x 1850 (W) x 1700 (L) millimetres. (photographed at the Macoskey Center). The front can be opened at high level to ensure the compost heap is well distributed and at low level to remove completely composted waste.

Composting toilets vent pipes on teaching block venting above roof level.

Case study: Low water landscaping

Environmental Showcase Home
Phoenix, Arizona, US

Client: Arizona Public Service
Architect: Jones Studio, Inc
Main contractor: Homes and Son
Completed: 1994

On the south elevation facing the private garden is a large glazed sliding door which links the living room with the patio.

The garden has only a minimal lawn area to the rear of the house.

Phoenix is one of the cities with the highest domestic water use, not only in the US, but also the whole world. It relies on water from the Colorado River and with over to 800 litres of water per capita per day, average consumption, each person uses the equivalent of a minimum water requirement for 40 people (Worldwatch 2004). In this desert and water-stressed environment, the Environmental Showcase Home (ESH) stands out as an example of building for and not against the climate.

The house was devised as a demonstration building showing what can be done in terms of minimising energy consumption, reducing water use, and selecting environmentally sound materials. The technologies and materials displayed are all easily available and the design of the 245m^2 house with four bedrooms, three bathrooms and outdoor pool, while appearing luxurious and inevitably using more resources than a smaller dwelling, is in line with the typical local specification, and is therefore able to demonstrate to the public and local builders that building sustainability does not have to compromise the accustomed way of life.

On the left is the garage used to display materials and information on the building, and on right is the house, with clerestory lights shaded by fabric sails.

The ESH addressed the use of energy by implementing a wide selection of measures that would not normally all be used in one single building, but demonstrate to the visitor what can be done. Its extensive use of recycled materials and its approach to reducing the use of water can be replicated wholesale in other buildings (see 6.1.6). In respect of water use, the indoor water needs are 43 per cent lower than those of a conventional Phoenix house: 520 litres per day versus 960 litres per day, or 130 litres per person based on four people living in the house. To achieve this, a number of approaches were taken. First, water needs were minimised by installing water-efficient appliances everywhere, including spray taps, low flush WCs, a front-loading washing machine, which saves water and energy compared to a top-loading one, and a water-efficient dishwasher, which uses 50 per cent less water than normal ones.

Second, the landscaping, which is the major reason for excessive use of water in such an arid environment, was planned to minimise the need for watering. The lawn area was reduced and plants that thrive in the desert were selected from an approved list issued by the Arizona Department of Water Resources, including native desert plants and a selection of imported drought-resistant species. Many of the plants are at home in the Sonoran Desert, including palo verde, mesquite, sweet acacia, desert ironwood and cacti such as saguaro, ocotillo, barrel and opuntia. Shrubs include Texas sage, cassia brittlebush, creosote, red sage, desert spoon, red yucca and agave.

Third, some of the water needed for watering the garden was taken from alternative sources to mains water, by collecting greywater and rainwater (see Chapter 6.2). Greywater is collected from the basins, showers, baths and washing machine and filtered and stored in an above-ground tank and rainwater is collected from the roofs and stored underground. This water is then used to irrigate the garden.

A sub-surface irrigation system ensures that the water is used where it is needed, that is at the plants' roots, without any waste and reducing evaporative losses. The irrigation system can be programmed as required and the plants were effectively weaned off watering over a period of five years. The result is an attractive low maintenance garden with low environmental impact and the house and garden together use 55 per cent less water than equivalent homes in the area.

The success of the house can also be measured by the fact that, by 2000, 30,000 people had visited the house and learnt about designing for sustainable energy, water and material use. Builders have used the technologies advertised by the house in new houses in the area, fulfilling the original ambition of the house.

Drought-resistant plants were selected.

Rainwater is collected in the gutter and directed to an underground tank along the chains among the planting.

The living room is flooded with natural light.

The greywater tank is located outside the utility room.

Cacti in pots and chimes made with reclaimed electricity connectors decorate the garden.

6.1.6 Sustainable design features

Community and culture
The house has been used as an educational facility for the ASU College of Architecture and Environmental Design to demonstrate good practice. It has also been used as a college laboratory to monitor the building and test ideas.

Health
Zero VOC interior paints and formaldehyde-free panels were used. Less than 25 per cent of the house has carpet, which was not fixed with adhesive.

Materials
The kitchen incorporates recycling and composting bins, reducing the waste to 25 per cent of typical amounts. The building materials used include: certified wood products, HCFC-free insulation, recycled plastic lumber, recycled rubber floor mats, carpet made of recycled plastic bottles, 70 per cent recycled content metal roofing, recycled biocomposite panels, bathroom floor and wall tiles made with 70 per cent recycled car windshield glass, and kitchen floor tiles made with 3 times recycled marble chips. Fly ash replaces 25 per cent of cement in all the concrete and cement products. Internal steel stud partitions are recyclable and avoid the use of solid timber.
Construction waste was minimised by maximising recycling of disgarded material and designing to standard dimensions.

Energy
Protection from the heat is the most important issue in the Phoenix climate. The building is oriented east–west minimising the façade size and openings with its plan's long axis east–west, preventing the low sun from penetrating the building. The overall glazed area has been reduced to 17 per cent of the floor area from the typical 23-35 per cent. The walls – concrete sandwich blocks infilled with polyurethane insulation – provide thermal mass and insulation. The timber ceilings and walls are insulated with cellulose fibre insulation, the slab has perimeter insulation and windows and doors are thermally broken with insulated sections.

Building fabric U-values:
Block walls – 0.23 W/m²K (R24)
Timber walls – 0.27 W/m²K (R21)
Roof – 0.15 W/m²K (R38)

The building is narrow, enabling good cross-ventilation and passive stack ventilation through high level windows protected from the sun by external fabric sails.
All rooms have daylight from two sides – electrical lights are not necessary anywhere in the house during daylight hours. A heat pump provides heating and cooling with excess in the summer used to heat water for domestic use. A solar panel provides the remaining hot water requirements (2,000 kWh). Six unglazed solar collectors provide hot water for the pool. A 24-PV panel array generates a 2.2 kW (peak) of electricity. Energy bills are estimated at $30 per month.

Water
See main text.

6.2 Alternative Water Sources

6.2.1 Water terminology

Terminology varies from one English-speaking country to another. In the US, the term greywater is sometimes used to describe wastewater, including that from the WCs.

6.2.2 The quality of recycled water

There are three main issues affecting quality of rainwater and greywater:

Aesthetic water quality
This is primarily a psychological issue, which depends on people's views and habits.

Microbiological water quality
This causes the most concern due to the possibility of recycled water containing pathogens, however, to date there are no reported cases of people becoming ill due to contact with recycled water. Rainwater is less contaminated than greywater, and while basic precautions should nonetheless be taken, there is no need for disinfection for use to flush WCs. Disinfection is recommended for greywater.

Chemical and physical quality
Chemical and physical pollution can also be of concern. Suspended particles may cause wear of pumps and valves. The PH of the water can affect components and the effect of disinfectants. Metals contained in recycled water may compromise its use for drinking and irrigation.

(Leggett *et al.* 2001)

6.2.3 Treating drinking water

(For sewage treatment see Chapter 6.3.)

In the UK the Environment Agency is responsible for maintaining the water quality of watercourses and the Drinking Water Inspectorate enforces the standards for drinking water set out in the Water Supply (Water Quality) Regulations 2001. These regulations set out classes of water cleanliness.

Class A is potable water and is required for kitchen sinks, showers, baths, cooling towers, farms and dairies.

Class B is required for laundry, surface cleaning materials, washbasins (WRAS 1999b).

Water from watercourses is extracted for distribution and consumption and has to be treated to achieve appropriate levels of cleanliness.

As rainwater either seeps through the ground to aquifers or flows into rivers, it is cleaned through biological action and filtration respectively. However, because of increasing

In developed countries potable water is generally used for all building-related uses regardless of whether such standards of cleanliness are necessary. Greywater and rainwater are alternative water sources that can be used for non-potable uses and, if treated appropriately, rainwater can also be used for drinking. Using alternative sources of water collected on the site reduces the need for the extraction, treatment, and distribution of fresh mains water, reducing pressure on freshwater sources and energy use.

Greywater

Waste water from typical buildings includes greywater and blackwater. Greywater is the wastewater from basins, sinks, baths and showers and blackwater is waste water from WCs and urinals (see 6.2.1). Greywater that has been cleaned by removing particles, disinfecting it, and possibly improving its appearance, can be reused for watering the garden, flushing WCs and washing laundry: this can save up to 40 per cent of water needs. The treatment of blackwater is more complex and discussed in Chapter 6.3. Some recommendations for the use of greywater include not using greywater with sprinklers, on acid-loving plants, on plants that are eaten raw, or on seedlings. The use of aggressive chemicals that might end up in the greywater should also be avoided.

There are a number of different systems for greywater reuse. A basic system operates by collecting water from showers, baths, and basins, but not sinks, through separate drainage pipes. The water is filtered and stored in a 120-litre underground tank, which includes an overflow to the mains sewer and an access hatch. The water is then pumped to a 60-litre header tank, when required, and treated with bromine or chlorine. The header tank has a mains connection to top up the tank if necessary. From the header tank the water is gravity fed to the WCs. Variations on this simple system are available and apart from avoiding disposing of harsh household chemicals in the basins, the system does not affect how people live.

This basic system can be expanded to include the reuse of kitchen wastewater, but in this case it requires more extensive treatment. Greywater from kitchen sinks, which contains oil, fat and food matter, is more contaminated than water from basins, baths and showers, which tend to contain only hair, skin, detergent and soap. More extensive systems are more akin to a reedbed treatment system (see Chapter 6.3).

Increasingly sophisticated greywater systems are coming on the market, as with a new package system, consisting of three chambers, with a cleaning capacity of 2400 litres per day. This system, which can be extended to increase treatment capacity, is designed to be installed indoors and is 600 (D) x 1350 (W) x 1880 (H) millimetres. The greywater is filtered before entering the first chamber and then dirt particles are decomposed through biological action in the first and second chamber. The third chamber incorporates a UV light lamp to disinfect the water, allowing it to be stored for longer periods. The clean water is then pumped to the point of use. The almost fully automated system flushes the filter clean into the mains sewer at regular intervals, and the sediment at the bottom of the two cleaning chambers is periodically drained into the sewers. This low maintenance system should appeal to those interested in a fix and forget solution.

Rainwater versus greywater

Despite its potential, greywater recycling is not as popular as rainwater recycling. This has perhaps to do with the more onerous requirements for cleaning greywater compared to rainwater. In fact, in many areas of Australia and other countries rainwater can be drunk untreated and it does not present a health risk.

In the UK, untreated rainwater is mainly collected for external uses such as in the garden or for cleaning cars. The simplest systems are rainwater butts, which can be freestanding or fixed to the wall and have a typical capacity of 100-200 litres. A tap at the bottom of the butt allows water to be extracted. If rainwater is filtered it can also be used to flush WCs or for laundry and can be used for hand washing (see Phillip Merrill Environment Center case study, p.268). Rainwater, as opposed to greywater, can be purified sufficiently to achieve potable standards (see Autonomous House case study, p.270).

A disadvantage of rainwater recycling is that the sewage volume is not reduced, compared to greywater recycling which reduces sewage volumes by the amounts of waste waster recycled. Another disadvantage of rainwater is its irregular occurrence, which necessitates large storage containers if rainwater is to be the only source of water. In domestic situations, greywater systems have the advantage over rainwater systems of benefiting from a balance between available water from basins, etc. (26 per cent) and water needed to flush WCs (31 per cent). A house of four could efficiently use a greywater system with a tank of 120 litres and expect to save 25-30 per cent of the water. This does not apply to commercial premises, where the amount of water required to flush WCs and urinals is usually double that collected from basins. In commercial premises, particularly where there are a low number of occupants in a building with a large area of roof, rainwater collection may be more appropriate. Furthermore, rainwater collection in commercial premises can be cost-effective, with payback periods of as little as two years, owing to over 50 per cent of the water needs being for low quality water, which can be satisfied by rainwater.

At the moment, installing water collection and recycling systems is often difficult to justify on financial grounds alone. The payback period for a greywater system is in excess of 20 years, with some estimates suggesting as much as 100 years (Hyde 2004), while some systems components have a life of only 15 years. Rainwater systems fare slightly better, providing potential savings of 50 per cent over yearly costs for mains supplied water (Leggett *et al.* 2001). This situation is changing as water charges increase steadily in Europe (in the UK 30 per cent increases in water charges are expected in the next four years (Gow 2004)), and while water recycling may already now be financially viable in remote non-connected locations, as prices rise it will become increasingly viable everywhere.

pollution, this treatment is, in certain areas, becoming less effective.

To achieve drinking quality water municipal treatment plants treat both ground and surface water and the treatment depends on the source of water, whereby groundwater is generally cleaner than surface water. Domestic-scale treatment systems tend to collect rainwater.

The first stage for treating surface water is to filter it and remove leaves, twigs and other floating material. Groundwater does not need this treatment; domestic-scale rainwater treatment systems do.

The second stage aims to remove fine floating particles that cloud the water. This can be done by coagulation and flocculation, where positively charged ions attract the largely negatively charged floating particles, which can then be filtered or settled out. Alternatively, these floating particles can be removed by slow or accelerated filtration through layers of progressively fine sand, whereby the slow filtration provides additional biological treatment of the water, while the fast filtration provides only mechanical filtering. Sand filtration is generally used on small domestic rainwater treatment systems.

The third stage aims to inactivate bacteria, spores, viruses and other pathogens that render the water unsafe to drink. This can be done by adding chlorine, chlorine dioxide or chloramines, which all produce a residual disinfectant that continues to be active throughout the distribution process up to the point of use, but have the disadvantage of producing by-products thought to be harmful to health. Alternative disinfectants include ozone, which does not produce a residual disinfectant and produces harmful-to-health by-products (bromine, formaldehyde and acetaldehyde), or UV light, which disinfects water by preventing pathogens from reproducing and does not have by-products, but does not produce residual disinfection, requiring its almost immediate use. UV disinfection is used in domestic applications and increasingly used in public applications, often combined with small amounts of chlorine to provide residual disinfection.

Case study: Rainwater for general needs

Millennium Green
Collingham, UK

Client: Gusto Construction
Main contractor: Gusto Construction
Completed: 1999

All houses have solar panels. Also visible on the roof is a light pipe that transfers light several metres into windowless parts of the building.

A shared green space provides a safe haven for the local fauna as well as absorbing stormwater run-off and minimising impact on the local storm sewer.

Collingham is a small village, between Newark and Lincoln in Nottinghamshire, and the location of the Millennium Green, one of the first commercial housing developments in the UK to address environmental issues, by building energy- and water-efficient houses at market prices. It is also an example of how demonstration and experimental green projects such as Hockerton Housing (see Chapters 1.4, 5.3 and 6.3) and the Autonomous House (see p.270), both located in Nottinghamshire, can act as inspiration and educational tools for others; in this case Stephen Wright, Gusto's chief executive, who in 1998 bought the 1.5-hectare Collingham site and decided to develop sustainable housing that would be commercially viable.

The housing development consists of 24 detached or linked houses. The appearance is traditional and in line with market expectations, but the building performance is superior to standard speculative housing designs. Walls are traditional cavity wall construction, but with a 150mm cavity filled with insulation. Traditional clay tile roofs are supported on engineered I beams and insulated with recycled cellulose insulation. Every aspect of the building performance has been considered and a resource-efficient solution implemented. The overall strategy is of insulating well and building airtight, then providing a portion of the energy through alternative sources such as the solar hot water panels installed on all units.

The same thinking went into reducing water use, whereby the first step was to install aerated taps and shower heads. Further to that, Gusto decided to make use of rainwater. They started by trying existing rainwater recycling systems and were not satisfied with the results. Rather than give up on the idea, Gusto developed a new system, which was then fitted to all houses as standard. The rainwater is used for flushing WCs, external use and for washing machines, and the mains water consumption has been reduced by 50 per cent.

The Gusto system, called Freerain, consists of a tank, a self-cleaning in-tank filter, a submersible pump and connecting pipework and controls. The tanks, made of recycled polyethylene, come in three standard sizes (3,500-, 4,700-, 6,500-litre), but can be linked together where greater capacity is required, such as in commercial installations. Rainwater tanks should be protected from sunlight that would otherwise support algae growth. At the Millennium Green, the tanks are placed underground, where they are protected from sunlight, but the system can also be installed in basements or other similar locations. The tanks generally do not, as some systems require, need to be surrounded in concrete to prevent uplift from rising groundwater.

Rainwater is collected from the roofs and directed through a rainwater downpipe into the tank and passes through a filter, which removes leaves and other debris. The water is then pumped as required to the appliances or external taps. The tank has an overflow to either a soakaway or the mains drain. The tank is expected to overflow a minimum of three times per year and should be sized to allow for that. This overflowing mechanism automatically cleans the filter. An access hatch at the top of the tank provides additional maintenance access.

See also: solar thermal 1 **Chapter 5.3**

View of the cul-de-sac of traditional-looking houses with advanced performance.

The tank has a mains water inlet to top it up in periods without rain. An electronically operated sensor switches automatically to mains water when the rainwater level is low. A monitor alerts of any operational problems but, otherwise, minimal maintenance is required. It is the potential of a system that can be installed and virtually forgotten, that makes this and other similar systems so attractive.

At the Millennium Green all the additional sustainable initiatives, including the rainwater recycling, added an extra 10 per cent to the total development costs. The additional costs were met by the developer, but as the buying public begins to appreciate the benefits of living in a healthy natural environment and the importance of protecting it, an extra 10 per cent on a buying price, particularly in affluent areas, will seem a small price to pay.

6.2.4 Sustainable design features

Site and ecology
A serviced office was built on site providing residents with on-site working facilities. The houses also have ISDN compatible telephone and internet connections.

Community and culture
Gusto construction is one of the first construction companies in the UK to become accredited with the Environmental Management System ISO 14001. The company has a policy of investing in staff training and development, and has a high staff retention rate. The increasingly experienced staff have improved the quality of the building work.
The developer remains active on the site asking for feedback from residents at annual meetings.
Residents' training in the use of the water and energy systems occurs when the residents move into their new home.

Health
The ventilation strategies provide good indoor air quality. Pollen filters have been introduced as standard on MVHR. All ground floors are wheelchair accessible.

Materials
Recycled cellulose insulation was installed in the roof. Gusto operates a waste management system and segregates site waste for recycling.
Domestic recycling facilities are located in the garages.

Energy
Building fabric U-values:
Walls – 0.20 W/m² K (R28)
Floors – 0.15 W/m²K (R38)
Roof – 0.15 W/m²K (R38)
Windows – 1.60 W/m²K (0.28Btu/ft²h°F)

Solar water heating provides hot water with a back-up of a gas condensing boiler. Heating controls and thermostatic radiator valves ensure efficient operation.
The houses were tested for air infiltration and achieved an air change rate of three air changes per hour at 50 pascals. Mechanical ventilation with heat recovery, operating at 70 per cent efficiency, provides fresh air while reducing ventilation losses in some of the houses, while others operate with passive stack ventilation in bathrooms and kitchens.
All houses were fitted out with compact fluorescent lighting and have a central light switch by the entrance door.
The houses achieve maximum ratings of SAP100, NHER10 and BREEAM Excellent.

Water
See main text.

Case study: Rainwater for washbasins

Phillip Merrill Environmental Center
Annapolis, Maryland, US

Client: Chesapeake Bay Foundation
Architect : SmithGroup Inc.
Civil engineer: Greenman-Pedersen
Structural engineer: Shermo Engineering Inc
Services engineer: SmithGroup Inc
Main contractor: Clark Construction
Completed: 2000

Smaller tanks collect rainwater from secondary roofs and release it slowly into the ground.

The Merrill Centrer is designed to be passive solar, uses energy-efficient appliances and renewable energy systems as well as being virtually water self-sufficient.

The Phillip Merrill Environmental Center is situated on Chesapeake Bay south of Annapolis. The building houses the Chesapeake Bay Foundation, a 35-year old organisation with more than 115,000 members, whose mission is to restore and protect the bay's ecosystem and resources, and promote environmental education. Chesapeake Bay, an estuarine system, is an ecosystem threatened by habitat destruction and increasing pollution of the water, including sediment, nutrients and toxic substances, which also affect fish stocks. According to the Foundation, the bay has already lost 60 per cent of its wetlands, 50 per cent of its forests, 90 per cent of its underwater grasses and 98 per cent of its oysters. The predicted 20 per cent increase in the local population in the next 25 years will result in an urbanisation of the watershed area and more polluted water draining into the bay.

The Foundation is working to improve the water quality and the productivity of the watershed. Some of the Foundation's activities include lobbying state and federal officials, filing lawsuits, oyster farming, planting underwater grasses, restoring riparian buffers, volunteer training in environmental issues and environmentally educating decision-makers in the area. The site which houses the Philip Merrill Environmental Center is one of the Foundation's restoration projects. With their new headquarters building the Foundation wanted to set an example for the future development of the watershed area, showing how to build in a way that minimises the building's impact on the environment.

The 3000m² two-storey building, located on a 12.5-hectare site, is designed to be environmentally sustainable. The building is sited following the Maryland Smart Growth Criteria, a set of sustainable development guidelines promoted by the Foundation, which advocate effective use of land and urban regeneration in order to protect natural environments. It is designed to be energy-efficient, provide a healthy interior environment and make use of sustainable materials and, perhaps most importantly, considering the aims of the Foundation, it is virtually water-autonomous.

In offices, the use of water is distributed differently than in homes, where showering and bathing account for a large percentage of water use. In offices, flushing WCs and urinals account by far for the majority of water used. The Merrill Center, which is occupied by approximately 100 people, dramatically reduces water requirements by using waterless composting toilets. Over a period of three years composting toilets convert human waste into compost, which is used as landscaping fertiliser. All appliances are water-efficient, including automatic taps and spray shower heads. Native species, acclimatised to local rainfall patterns, were planted in the surrounding site. These straightforward measures reduce the water consumption by 90 per cent compared to other similar buildings, to less than 900 litres (200 gallons) per day.

Having reduced the water use to a minimum, the next approach to reducing the building's water-related impact was to make use of rainwater, instead of well water, for general needs. The kitchen sink and the showers are the only source of potable mains water. The mono-pitch metal roof directs rainwater towards the front of the building where it is collected in a gutter and passed through a filter before being stored in three main cistern tanks. The water is then passed through a sand filter and chlorinated. Chlorination was required by the local health authority. The purified water is then distributed into the building and used for hand washing, washing equipment, cleaning, laundry, irrigation and fire suppression. To prevent accidental ingestion, signs advising users not to drink the water are located above the washbasins.

With thousands of members and volunteers using and visiting the building and its toilets annually, the use of rainwater and the composting toilets not only saves water and reduces sewage, but helps overcome prejudices by demonstrating how sustainable solutions are as easy to use and attractive as non-sustainable ones.

The three large rainwater tanks are located on the roof over the ground-floor offices to the left of the entrance.

The entrance elevation on the north side of the building. The natural landscape around the demolished club house was left practically untouched.

The washbasins have a warning sign alerting users to the non-potable nature of the rainwater.

The instructions above the composting toilets tell the user to add some wood shavings after each use.

6.2.5 Sustainable design features

Site and ecology
The building was built on the footprint of the old Bay Ridge Inn pool and pool house, minimising development on previously undeveloped greenfield sites. The total impervious areas were reduced by locating some of the car park below the building supported on piers. Only eight trees were cut down and 130 were planted. The whole site will be restored, in time, reinstating wetland, planting native trees, shrubs and underwater grasses and creating an oyster reef.

Community and culture
The design of the building is reminiscent of local architecture along the shoreline. The centre, with its conference hall, operates as a focal point for the environmental community.

Health
The work spaces are in close contact with the natural environment outside. Excellent natural light creates a stimulating environment. All paints are low VOC and timber panels have been left untreated.

Materials
The amount of material used to build was minimised by exposing the structure and avoiding unnecessary design features.
Renewable materials, such as cork and bamboo flooring, were used, as were materials made from waste products such as parallel strand lumber beams made of small timber sections. The roof and cladding are made of galvanised recycled steel. Rebar in concrete structure is made of 90 per cent recycled steel. The shading trellis is made of timber recycled from old pickle barrels. Ceiling tiles are made of 78 per cent recycled mineral wool and cellulose fibre.
All timber came from FSC-certified forests or sustainably managed forests.
More than 50 per cent of materials came from a 300-mile radius.

Energy
The PV array and a solar panel, which heats the filtered rainwater for hand washing, both help to reduce the amount of fossil fuel used to power the building.
Fabric U-values:
Roof – U-value 0.19 W/m²C (R30)
Wall panels – U-value 0.24 W/m²C (R23.5)
See also Chapter 5.2.

Water
See main text. The car parking drains water potentially containing oils and petrol into a bioremediation natural planted filtration system. The water then percolates into natural wetlands for more filtering.

See also: efficient and reduced vehicle use **Chapter 1.2**

See also: fine-tuning buildings **Chapter 5.2**

Case study: Rainwater for drinking

The Autonomous House
Southwell, Nottinghamshire, UK

Client: Brenda and Robert Vale
Architect: Brenda and Robert Vale
Main contractor: Nick Martin
Completed: 1993

6.2.6 Calculating rainwater collection

To calculate the amount of rainwater that can be collected from a roof it is necessary to know the footprint of the building and the annual rainfall of the area measured in millimetres of rain per year.

It is usual to assume that one can collect 80 per cent of the rainwater that falls on the roof. To calculate the amount of rainwater that can be collected the following calculation can be used:

Footprint of roof x rainfall per annum x 0.8

In the case of the Autonomous House the area of the roof was 140 square metres and the rainfall was 600 millimetres per year. The total amount of rainfall which could be collected was therefore 67,200 litres per year. This is equivalent to 184 litres per day. Comparing it to the average UK use of water of 145 litres per person per day this would not be enough to satisfy the needs of four people. However, by using composting toilets and by adopting a water-conscious approach, the consumption was reduced to only 35 litres per person. The total water use of the Autonomous House, with a family of four, was therefore 140 litres per day, which could easily be covered by the water collected.

The tank should be sized to contain the water for a four-week period without rain.

The Autonomous House, located in the small town of Southwell in Nottinghamshire, was designed to demonstrate that building a house completely autonomous from mains connections for power, water and sewerage was not only possible, but also fundable through traditional mortgage arrangements and buildable by traditional builders with primarily traditional building methods and skills. The resulting four-bedroom, 255m^2 house, including 66m^2 of uninhabitable basement, a 28m^2 conservatory and a 7m^2 porch, respects the urban grain and architectural language of the conservation area in which it is situated, while minimising energy and water use.

The building strategy to minimise the use of energy was to first eliminate heating and reduce other energy needs, and then provide the energy required through renewable technologies (see also Passivhaus standards, 5.1.1). A comfortable internal environment is maintained by passive means. Above ground, the external wall comprises a cavity wall construction with 250 millimetres of insulation. The insulation minimises heat losses while the airtight construction minimises ventilation losses. The internal leaf of the cavity wall, the concrete floors and the block partition walls provide thermal mass that absorbs internal and solar heat gains and obviates the need for space heating. A large conservatory, which is oriented west rather than the ideal south due to site planning issues, preheats the fresh air and provides a buffer to the main building. A 4.5 kW wood-burning stove acts as a back-up and focal point in the hall. Ventilation is provided by through-the-wall MVHR in the bathrooms and kitchen, and trickle vents in the living spaces. The bedrooms are located on the ground floor and the living rooms and kitchen on the first floor, following the logic that heat rises and bedrooms do not need to be as warm as living rooms, in the event only a 1°C difference was measured. Hot water is provided by a solar panel and all electricity requirements are covered by a grid-connected PV array installed on a pergola in the garden.

In terms of water use and disposal, the house is also autonomous. All water needs, including drinking water, are covered by rainwater collected from the roof of the house. To achieve water autonomy the first step was to reduce water needs. Waterless composting toilets were installed, which save over 30 per cent of water needs and also meant no blackwater was produced in the house. The greywater produced is filtered and drained in a soakaway in the garden. The second step was to collect rainwater as an alternative to mains water.

In the UK, local authorities do not generally grant permission for the use of rainwater for drinking or even washing purposes without additional purification, even thought its quality may achieve drinking standards. Elsewhere, such as in certain parts of Australia and New Zealand, rainwater can be used untreated or after simple filtration or minimal disinfection. Potential contaminants of rainwater are bird and animal waste on the surface from which the rainwater is collected, and airborne pollutants, particularly in urban areas. These contaminants can be diverted from a collection system by using an attachment that discharges the initial rainwater containing the majority of contaminants.

At the Autonomous House all the rainwater is collected from the clay tile and glass roof into a copper gutter. The smoother the collection surfaces are, the fewer contaminants are trapped and any that are can be washed off with the rainwater. Copper was chosen for its slightly disinfectant effect. The rainwater is then drained through a downpipe that discharges over a standard gully, which filters leaves and other large particles, and is covered with a copper sheathing to stop any contamination of its surface. The water is collected in 19 1,500-litre recycled orange juice tanks connected in parallel and series and located in the basement. The tanks are filled simultaneously and have an overflow to a soakaway in the garden.

The stored water is then pumped through a sand filter under the conservatory and then into another tank which stores the clean water. The sand filter removes suspended particles. Layers of increasingly fine sand are used to filter different-sized particles. On top of the sand an active layer of organic and inorganic particles called the 'Schmutzdecke', 'dirt cover' develops naturally. This layer helps break down the organic particles contained in the water. Below this layer, there is a layer of microorganisms that feed on organic contaminants. The Schmutzdecke has to be removed when it gets too thick; this is done by replacing the top layer of sand.

The storage tank for the filtered water is another recycled orange juice tank: it holds enough water for two weeks of use and enables the filter bed to be drained when the Schmutzdecke needs to be replaced or other maintenance becomes necessary.

The filtered water is then pumped from the 1,500-litre tank to a 250-litre header tank on a platform above the kitchen. A battery-operated 12-volt pump, activated by the lowering of ballcocks in the clean water storage tank as the water level drops, is used to pump water to the header tank as well as directly to the kitchen tap. The water for the kitchen tap is forced through a carbon core ceramic filter candle under the sink. This filter purifies the water to drinking standards and has to be brushed clean every other week, but because of the purity of the rainwater lasted two years rather than the typical six months. One of the two bathrooms also has a drinking tap, which is fed by gravity from the header tank and where the water is purified using the same type of carbon filter system used in the kitchen. The second bathroom relies on a jug of drinking water for teeth cleaning.

The cost of the system was partially offset by not needing to connect to the mains. The system works very well and even during the 1996 drought, the tanks of the house dropped by only 30 per cent.

The admirable low water use of approximately 35 litres per day per person has been achieved through changes in attitude rather than through technological means. However, since the architects and owners moved to New Zealand, the house has been occupied by three different tenants, all of whom benefited from a problem-free operation of the water system, suggesting that such achievements could be for everyone.

6.2.7 Sustainable design features

Site and ecology
The planting on the street side was maintained and provides a screen to the street.

Health
Carpets are not fitted and rugs are used in seating areas. This minimises the accumulation of dust and the potential for dust mites and other allergens.
All paints used are organic.

Materials
Materials were chosen from local sources where possible.

Energy
Building fabric U-values:
Walls – 0.14 W/m²K (R41))
Cellar floor – 0.25 W/m²K(R25)
Roof – 0.07 W/m²K(R81)
Glazing ave. – 0.85 W/m²K (0.15 Btu/ft²h°F)
Rooflights – 1.60 W/m²K (0.28 Btu/ft²h°F)

Space heating was measured to be 22 kWh/m²a
Windows are triple glazed and the rooflights are double glazed.
Through the wall 13-watt MVHR in the kitchen and bathrooms minimises ventilation losses.
Low energy light fittings are fitted everywhere and an energy-efficient fridge was installed.
Electrical needs are covered by a grid connected 2.16kW PV array.

Water
The main water saving is through the installation of composting toilets. The two ground-floor bathrooms are built back to back and two toilets are linked to one Clivus Multidrum composting tank located in the basement. See main text.

The traditional-looking building fits into the conservation area.

6.3 Reducing the Use of Mains Drains

6.3.1 Sustainable Urban Drainage (SUD) initiatives

In Atlanta 20 per cent of the trees were removed for development, which resulted in increased stormwater of 150 million cubic metres. To build sufficient containment for this amount of water would have cost $2 billion. The alternative to replant trees not only was far cheaper, but also enhanced the local environment.
(Wilson 2002)

Berlin has spent DM30 million over 12 years to replace concrete urban surfaces with planted surfaces to increase the natural water absorbance ability.
(Beatley 2000)

6.3.2 Options for reducing the use of mains drainage systems

- Integrate a SUD system, including:
  - maximising absorbent and planted areas
  - creating water catchment areas such as swales, ponds and lakes
- Collect and recycle rainwater within buildings or for irrigation
- On-site greywater treatment, options include:
  - indoor recycling systems
  - external planted treatment systems
  - soakaways and leachfields
  - treatment with blackwater
- On-site blackwater treatment, options include:
  - composting toilets
  - urine-separating toilets
  - package treatment plants
  - Living Machines
  - septic, settlement or filtration tanks plus secondary and tertiary treatment
  - primary treatment plus reedbeds, leachfields or secondary filtration

Reducing the use of the mains storm drains and the sewers by providing on-site systems to clean and drain or reuse rain-, grey- and blackwater can help to reduce the occurrence of sewage and stormwater pollution incidents; it can reduce the planned discharge of partially treated sewage effluent or polluted stormwater into watercourses; it can reduce the energy required to transfer and treat the waste water; and can contribute to replenishing groundwater sources. Of the three main approaches to reduce the use of mains drains, the simplest, when considering the technical and legal complexities, is to minimise stormwater run-off. On-site disposal of greywater also requires only limited expert support, while the treatment of blackwater on site is the most technically and legally demanding intervention.

Sustainable Urban Drainage (SUD)

The ground, whether it is soil, sand, clay or other material, acts as a water filter and, as rainwater percolates through various strata, it is partially cleaned. How clean the water gets depends on the pollution levels and the ground material: for example, clay and sand act as an excellent mechanical filter, while soil harbours microorganisms that break down organic compounds, providing biological treatment of the water. The potential for this natural cleaning mechanism is vastly reduced in urban environments where largely paved areas create impervious surfaces, directing rainwater to storm sewers rather than into the ground. This not only puts pressure on the use of the storm sewers, increasing occurrences of polluted overflows as described in the main introduction to this chapter, but also reduces the amount of water recharging local aquifers.

To reverse this effect, an approach known as Sustainable Urban Drainage (SUD) can be implemented, whereby the external works are designed to retain and drain rainwater on site. Impervious areas are minimised and permeable paving, gravel and planted areas maximised; balancing ponds, soakaways, swales and wetlands hold rainwater before slowly discharging it to the ground; rainwater harvesting can be used to divert rainwater from the sewers and, if used for irrigation, the rainwater will later return to the ground.

Reducing impervious surfaces also helps to reduce the occurrence of flooding in urban areas. Furthermore, as mentioned in the introduction to this chapter, urban stormwater can be polluted with toxic metals, pesticides, oils, animal waste and sediments. In a rainstorm, the first 6–15 millimetres of rain has been found to wash off approximately 80 per cent of the pollutants (EA 2004). By collecting this polluted rainwater in landscaped and other water-absorbent areas, it is not discharged through the stormwater sewer into the watercourses and does not need to be cleaned at a wastewater treatment plant, but can be treated as it percolates through the ground.

The technologies to retain and filter stormwater on site are becoming more common. Underground retention tanks, extra deep paving (see solarCity case study, p.276) and porous paving are all designed to create SUD systems. As well as the practical advantages of reduced flooding and pollution, increasing landscaped areas enhances the aesthetics of the urban environment and improves air quality.

Greywater and blackwater treatment

In addition to reducing the rainwater discharge into the sewers, reducing grey- and blackwater discharge is also beneficial and possible by recycling greywater and by treating grey- and blackwater on site. On-site small-scale and large-scale municipal sewage treatment (blackwater treatment) both involve similar processes, whereby the organic constituents of sewage are transformed into inorganic mineral form. The on-site treatment of greywater can be achieved by using methods similar to those used in the last stages of sewage treatment.

There are four main stages in large-scale sewage treatment and three at a smaller scale. The first preliminary stage filters large elements through a 25-50-millimetre filter gauge and is employed only in large-scale systems. This is followed by the primary treatment where solids settle at bottom of the treatment tank forming a sludge or float on the surface of the effluent, allowing them to be separated from the relatively clean water in between, which then goes through the secondary treatment. In small-sized systems the separation of solids from liquid effluent takes place in a septic, settlement or filtration tank. The sludge that is separated at this stage is treated separately (see 6.3.4).

The secondary treatment stage is a primarily biological treatment, but also allows further sludge to separate out. The liquid is cleaned by micro-organisms in the tank that feed on the organic material and the resulting liquid is increasingly clear. In small -scale treatment systems this stage can take place in a planted environment where the necessary micro-organisms live around the roots of the plants, in specially designed tanks which support micro-organism growth on a biofilm or, alternatively, in the ground, where further filtration takes place as well as biological treatment by micro-organisms in the soil. Some of the technologies appropriate for this secondary treatment can be used to treat greywater.

The final and tertiary treatment of the water is undertaken with UV light, which disinfects the water by breaking down the DNA of the viruses and bacteria, preventing them from reproducing, or through microfiltration, where water is passed through ultra-fine filters that prevent micro-organisms and bacteria getting through. In small-scale systems ultra-fine filters are commonly used, but may not be necessary if the secondary treatment is effective enough (see Hockerton Housing case study, p.278), and the use of UV light or other disinfection tends to be applied only if the water is to be reused within a building (see Living Machine case study, p.282).

Local treatment can be superior to centralised systems. While some UK water companies apply high treatment standards, which include tertiary treatment, many only apply secondary treatment. Small-scale system can more easily control the content of the waste water and reduce persistent chemical pollutants. As with SUD systems, on-site treatment, such as reedbeds, can create attractive and healthy natural environments.

6.3.3 Reduction of faecal coliform bacteria resulting from sewage treatments

	Faecal coliform bacteria per 100 ml of water (SAS 2004)
Raw sewage contains	10,000,000
Primary treated effluent	1,000,000
Secondary treated effluent	10,000
Tertiary treated effluent	35

6.3.4 Sludge treatment and use

Sewage sludge, resulting from the first stages of sewage treatment, can be further treated and then used as an agricultural and forestry fertiliser, used as land reclamation material, or disposed of through incineration or landfill. Beneficial uses are more economically and environmentally advantageous.

The possible treatments of sludge include: dewatering through filtering, centrifugation or evaporation; anaerobic digestion; and aerobic digestion.

Case study: Sustainable drainage

Thurgoona Campus
Charles Sturt University, Albury,
New South Wales, Australia

Project details, Chapter 4.4, p.177

The double-storey rainwater collection tanks have to be strapped back to the building structure.

One of the teaching blocks. Two-storey rainwater tanks are located on both sides of the staff room on the first floor and an undercroft on the ground floor.

Thurgoona Campus, which houses over 600 students and staff in energy-efficient rammed earth buildings, is entirely independent from the mains sewer. Located in a dry climate, the wish to be independent from mains sewers was primarily about saving water, rather than about reducing pressure on the sewer system.

The campus benefits from an award-winning water management system devised to minimise the use of mains water and avoid the use of the mains sewer system. Mains water use is restricted to drinking and personal hygiene purposes, and rainwater is used for irrigation and laundry. The use of waterless composting toilets throughout obviates the need for water to flush WCs as well as a system to treat blackwater. The only wastewater on site is greywater, which is treated and recycled for irrigation.

Rainwater is collected from the hard and soft landscaping and from all roofs. Rainwater collected from the roofs is used for laundry in the student accommodation and for the building's cooling system. Rainwater collected from the grounds and treated greywater is used for irrigation.

Each building has at least one large single- or double-storey rainwater collection tank. The rainwater needs minimal cleaning before use for laundry. In other areas of Australia rainwater is considered appropriate for drinking and personal hygiene, but here the authorities did not allow such uses for fear of possible litigation.

Rainwater from the grounds is collected and transferred through the site in swales and open waterways. The water follows the slight slope of the site to reach the wetlands, where it is filtered through sand and soil and where bacteria supported by the plants' roots treat it biologically. The filtered and treated water is transferred back uphill to a reservoir using a solar pump and energy from a windmill. The reservoir can hold enough water to irrigate the campus throughout the dry summer months. The water is regularly released into the system of wetlands to maintain the system.

The greywater from basins, sinks and showers is treated in a separate reedbed system.

The wetlands where the rainwater is treated are hardly recognisable after an extremely hot summer.

Swales and open waterways direct the rainwater to the wetlands.

The reservoir is hidden behind the mound. The fencing is to prevent unauthorised access the site.

Waterways crossing the roads direct the collected rainwater and create a traffic calming device.

View through the planted corridor between teaching blocks. Planted areas help reduce the stormwater run-off and swales direct the water into purification wetlands.

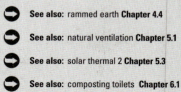

See also: rammed earth **Chapter 4.4**

See also: natural ventilation **Chapter 5.1**

See also: solar thermal 2 **Chapter 5.3**

See also: composting toilets **Chapter 6.1**

Case study: Sustainable urban drainage

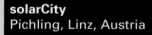

solarCity
Pichling, Linz, Austria

Project details, Chapter 1.1, p.20

The solarCity development in the Pichling area of Linz, with 1,317 housing units and a commercial and community centre, covers an area of 32.5 hectare. The development was conceived as a model of sustainable development and as such addresses issues of water use and drainage as part of a comprehensive strategy for sustainable design.

Rainwater run-off is minimised by extensive use of porous ground surfaces. Apart from the main road through the development, there are very few roads. These are used primarily to access the largely underground car parks to the housing units. This leaves much of the space between the housing blocks free from traffic and able to be planted. Pathways run parallel to the housing block, providing access to the front doors, and the planted ground acts as a water retention area. Swales are formed to collect and hold excess water from heavy rainfall. Rainwater from the roofs is collected and channelled to the planted areas surrounding the housing units rather than being discharged into the drains.

The outdoor car parking is paved with special pavers designed to maximise water retention. The 300-millimetre deep hollow concrete paving stones are set on a bed of gravel and sand and filled with sand and earth to support grass growing through the paving. The above average depth of the pavers and the sand work not only to absorb the rainwater, but also to filter any oil and other pollutants from the cars.

300mm deep hollow concrete paving on gravel and sand with grass growing through it absorbs the rainwater and filters any pollutants from the cars.

The car parking next to the community and commercial centre paved with special grass pavers (Community and commercial centre by architects Auer+Weber+Partner).

Access to the homes is via a footpath within a planted area between the housing units (Housing by architects Richard Rogers Partnership).

Rainwater channel beside a pathway discharging onto a grassed area..

Access to the communal green space via a little bridge over the water swales.

Rainwater from the roof is directed to a paved channel and transferred to grassed areas (Housing by architects Herzog+Partner).

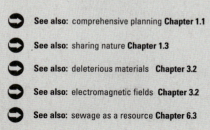

See also: comprehensive planning **Chapter 1.1**

See also: sharing nature **Chapter 1.3**

See also: deleterious materials **Chapter 3.2**

See also: electromagnetic fields **Chapter 3.2**

See also: sewage as a resource **Chapter 6.3**

Case study: Greywater treatment

The Robert A. Macoskey Center is part of Slippery Rock University and, while primarily involved in educational activities, it also uses its buildings, site and farm as a testing laboratory. It is in this role that the centre operates a small-scale wetland greywater treatment system. The system is part of a Pennsylvania Department of Environment Protection study to ascertain the potential for widespread use of on-site greywater treatment systems. The interest in natural water treatment systems is partially fuelled by the need for technology that does not rely on electricity, so as to be acceptable to the local Amish community. The local area has soil that is inappropriate for the use of leachfields or similar ground percolation systems (see 6.3.5) and the installation of a small wetland could allow local disposal of greywater.

The system tested collects water from all uses except the toilet, which is a waterless composting toilet. The greywater is transferred to a septic tank where any solids are settled out. The septic tank is expected to be emptied every 14 years. The overflow from the septic tank discharges into an underground tank with bentonite clay which provides a fine filtering medium. The discharge then passes into a second tank with gravel where it percolates into the ground.

The system is being tested by monitoring the quality of water in four points of the system and preliminary results are promising. In terms of space use the system is quite efficient and simple enough to be easily installed by non-expert workers.

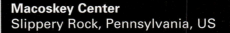

Macoskey Center
Slippery Rock, Pennsylvania, US

Project details, Chapter 4.6, p.196

The Macoskey Center houses a number of ecological-friendly building materials and technologies.

The second barn also collects rainwater in two rainwater butts.

The septic tank access hatches.

The barn collects and stores rainwater in an elevated rainwater tank.

The greywater treatment system is underground, with only the testing tubes and the septic tank hatches visible.

See also: composting **Chapter 4.6**

Case study: Secondary treatment with reedbeds

Hockerton Housing Project
Hockerton, Southwell, UK

Project details, Chapter 1.4, p.46

The reedbed is at the west end of the lake, the reeds are the light plants just before the water.

The water reservoir.

Reeds surround the edges of the lake and the shallower edges harbour a variety of plants and animals, while the lake is also enjoyed for boating and swimming.

The Hockerton Housing Project development of five earth-covered terraced houses on the edge of Hockerton village aims to have an autonomous existence. This is achieved by minimising energy requirements and generating enough green energy on site to cover them, collecting enough rainwater to serve all the residents' water needs, and treating all wastewater on site. The method used to treat the wastewater combines the use of a septic tank and reedbeds.

The Hockerton reedbeds are integrated in an artificial lake that also provides the houses with a recreational facility and fish-farming opportunity and enhances the natural environment and biodiversity. The lake is 120 metres long and 30 metres wide and holds approximately 3,000 cubic metres of water. The level is kept constant by adjusting the amount of water overflowing into a secondary pond through a sluice. The lake is 2.2 metres deep in the middle and has shallow edges to support a variety of plants and animals. It was formed by machine puddling a layer of clay, creating a sealed enclosure for the water. It was filled with rainwater over a two-year period, and is now filled with rainwater and with treated wastewater from the houses.

All the wastewater, including black- and greywater, from the houses is transferred to a communal septic tank for a five- to ten-day period where the solids are separated through settlement. The liquid is then passed through the reedbed treatment area, a process that takes an estimated three months. The reedbed is planned in a spiral with the inlet at the centre to maximise the length of the treatment circuit before the water passes through a gabion wall made of 30–60mm blocks of limestone and planted with irises, which separates the treatment area from the main part of the lake. Three different species of reeds are planted (typha, phragmytes and iris) in different areas and supply oxygen to the bacteria living around their roots, which digest the pathogens in the effluent as it slowly passes through.

The reedbed system cleans the water to a similar standard as that treated in a typical mechanical treatment plant and the lake water has met European Union bathing quality standards when tested. Consequently the lake is used as a recreation facility for boating and swimming.

The 190m² of treatment area easily copes with the wastewater from the current 17 residents plus visitors, but is expected to cope with up to 40 residents. The reedbeds need minimal maintenance, mainly consisting of clearing small saplings on the bank. The reed can be cropped and used as animal fodder or mulch. The septic tank is checked quarterly and, if necessary, some of the surface crust removed and composted on site.

The reedbed system is the final part of a comprehensive water management stratergy to achieve self-sufficiency in water use and disposal. While the reedbeds deal with the water disposal, two other systems are used to collect water. Water for non-potable uses, such as bathing, clothes washing and flushing WCs, is collected from throughout the site, including from the access road and from the fields, and directed through swales to a sump. From there the water is pumped to a reservoir holding 150 cubic metres of water (25m long and 2m deep), which was formed by lining an area behind an earth bund made with excavation material from the lake. The stored water is then passed through a sand filler and gravity fed into the houses. Water use is reduced by the use of low flush WCs and aerated taps and shower heads.

Water for potable uses is collected from the conservatory roof via copper pipes and stored in a 16-cubic metre tank. The water is passed through a 5mm string filter to remove small particles and a carbon filter to remove dissolved chemicals then purified with an ultraviolet light treatment to kill bacteria and viruses before being transferred to the drinking water taps of the house. Typical levels of faecal coliform bacteria after treatment are 0–10 coliforms/100ml in the non-potable water and 0 in the potable water.

The three systems have proved to work very effectively together. While Hockerton is a rural site, such systems are not restricted to rural locations. Reedbeds, with their potential for creating havens for wildlife and being linked to leisure uses, could be an ideal way to introduce the much needed natural environments in cities.

Reeds surround the reservoir of water collected for the whole site.

View of the lake from the bermed roof of the houses. A new office building and garages can be seen at the edge of the lake.

The water from the reservoir is passed through sand filters before being fed into the houses

6.3.5 Primary treatment with septic tanks

As at Hockerton, primary treatment for sewage can be provided by a septic tank. The aim is to separate the solid waste from the water, which is then cleaned biologically.

Septic tanks can have one or two chambers, both doing the same thing. The size of the septic tank has to be large enough to hold the waste water for approximately one day. At Hockerton the septic tank has a 10m-cubic metre capacity. The sewage enters the tank and most of the solids, including 30-50 per cent of the organic matter, settle to the bottom or float to the top of the tank, leaving relatively clean liquid in the middle. This liquid is pushed out of the tank as more sewage enters the tank. The floating crust material and the sludge have to be emptied every six months to six years, and can be composted locally. At Hockerton the tank is emptied as required.

Alternatives to septic tanks for the provision of primary treatment are settlement tanks and filtering chambers. Settlement tanks are similar to septic tanks, but retain the discharge for less time, need to be emptied more often and are suitable for larger populations. Filtering chambers separate the solids from the liquid effluent by filtering sewage mechanically. This can be done by passing sewage through a filter made of organic material such as tree bark suspended on a heavy duty net and resting on gravel to provide drainage.

Septic tanks can be used in conjunction with leachfields, which consist of a series of underground perforated pipes, set in a filtering medium such as sand, through which the septic tank discharge is passed. The discharge percolates through the pipes and into the ground where it is treated through the ground's filtering mechanism and the biological activity of microorganisms in the soil. The leachfields provide a secondary treatment which is provided by the reedbeds at Hockerton.

6.3.6 Water use at Hockerton

Approximately 1 cubic metre of water per day is used for normal use by all the members, including 5 litres per person per day of drinking water.

Water use at Hockerton is minimised through the following water-saving devices:

– low flush WCs (2-4 litres)

– flow restrictors in shower heads

– showers in preference to baths

– using water from the lake for gardening and occasionally for car washing

➔ See also: producing food on site **Chapter 1.4**

➔ See also: wind energy 1, 2 **Chapter 5.3**

Case study: Hybrid toilets

Piney Lakes Environment Centre
Melville, West Australia

Client: City of Melville
Architect and Project Managers: Ecotect Architects ®*
Services engineer: BCA
Structural engineer: Van Der Meer Engineering
Electricity load analysis: Murdoch University (RISE)
Contractor: Consortium Builders
Completed: 2001

*The Ecotect trademark isused under licence from Dr. Marsh of Square One Research P/L www.ecotect.com

Rainwater is pumped from the main tank to header tanks by means of a solar-powered pump

The Piney Lakes Environment Centre in Melville is a centre for education about the environment. It is linked to the Piney Lakes Reserve, a natural reserve of bushland and wetlands which includes Piney Lakes. The Environment Centre was conceived as a model for an autonomous education building and displays to the visitors the technologies used to create a building independent from mains electricity, water and sewer connections.

To power the building a collection of technologies was used, including wind and solar power, which provides approximately 2 kW average output with a 6 kW peak electricity output (see 6.3.7). As for the water supply, rainwater is collected from the roof and stored in a 60,000-litre tank at ground level and then pumped to smaller tanks above the building, where it is filtered and disinfected with UV light before entering the building. The purified rainwater is used for all purposes, and boiled if used for drinking. The building demonstrates two waterless toilet types together with waterless urinals. All these systems help minimise the need for water and avoid the need for a sewer connection. The hybrid toilet system is of particular interest to the visitors as its operation can be seen clearly in the basement.

Hybrid toilet systems operate partly like a mechanically operated package sewage treatment unit and partly like a septic tank. They provide primary and secondary treatment in two chambers and discharge treated effluent either to the ground or to a holding tank. This effluent is cleaner than that from septic tanks, but the system does not rely on electrically operated mechanical systems typical of many small sewage treatment package units. The standard hybrid toilet is a waterless toilet with a specially designed toilet pan to avoid soiling. A microflush version, which flushes 300 millilitres of water per use has also been developed. At the Piney Lakes Centre the two chambers or tanks are located in the basement on a concrete slab, but in different situations the tanks can be partially sunk underground.

The system operates by providing primary treatment similar to that of a septic tank in the first chamber and secondary treatment in the second chamber. Waste enters the first tank, which is full of water and ventilated through a vent pipe by means of a fan, which can be PV operated. Faecal matter and paper are partially dissolved in the water and decomposed through anaerobic bacterial action, reducing the mass to 5 per cent of its original volume. The non-digested matter settles at the bottom of the tank forming a layer of sludge. The sludge volume continues to be reduced through digestion, but very slowly and over a period of 4-7 years it will have accumulated to such an extent as to reduce the holding capacity of the tank and will have to be emptied. The anaerobic digestion of the bottom sludge will produce gases including mainly methane and CO_2, with small traces of hydrogen, hydrogen sulphide, ammonia and nitrogen, which are discharged through a vent. These gases will cause some of the sludge to rise and to prevent it from entering the second tank a separating chamber is introduced to intercept any solids. The waste can be held in the first tank for 83 days or more depending on the use of the system.

As more waste enters the first tank, water is displaced and pushed through the separating chamber and into the second tank. A maze of plastic piping and baffles in the second tank ensures maximum contact of the water with a biofilm on the surface of the plastic. The biofilm degrades the organic material in the effluent through anaerobic, aerobic and facultative treatment. The effluent moves slowly through the tank, a process that can take up to 135 days. The resulting effluent, which digests up to 99 per cent of the pathogens, is clean enough to be discharged to the ground through pipes similar to those used with leachfields (see 6.3.5), but if ground conditions are inappropriate, it can be transferred to a holding tank.

A veranda protects the entrance from the sun, while high-level windows let in light deep in the building. Rammed limestone walls and reclaimed light poles make up the structure.

View of the ground-installed photovoltaic array with the Environment Centre behind.

The tanks can be seen in the basement where there are also panels with information on the hybrid toilet system.

The solar hot water panels are located on the roof and the PV on the 'power tower'.

6.3.7 Sustainable design features

Site and ecology
The centre is part of a nature reserve.

Community and culture
The centre benefits from strong community support and received funding from local groups. The community took part in design consultation process.

Health
Paints and finishes have been minimised and natural finishes preferred. PVC was avoided.

Materials
The walls are made of rammed limestone. Recycled lighting poles were used as part of the building structure.

Energy
The building uses passive solar design methods to make use of solar gains in winter. The north elevation is glazed to take advantage of the low morning sun to warm up the offices. Later in the day and in the summer extensive overhangs protect the building from excessive heat gains.

The rammed limestone walls provide thermal mass, as does the earth berm on two sides of the building. The roof is covered with corrugated metal over an insulated sandwich panel and separated by a ventilation gap.

Hot water is supplied by solar thermal panels on the roof. Solar air heaters provide space heating and 3 kW PVs provide electricity. One PV installation on top of the 'power tower' tracks the sun, while a larger array is installed on the ground near the building. All street and car park lights have integrated PV panels and batteries to power the lights. A 5-kW wind turbine has also been installed and a 110-volt, 600-amp/hr battery bank stores the power from both wind and solar sources. A vegetable oil generator provides back-up power when necessary.

Night ventilation is activated by means of a building management system (BMS) and makes use of the diurnal temperature changes to cool the building in summer.

Water
See main text.

See also: demonstration buildings **Chapter 2.5**

Case study: Living Machine

Adam Joseph Lewis Center, Oberlin College
Oberlin, Ohio, US

Project details, Chapter 3.2, p.116

The Living Machine is situated in the small block on the right, which also includes the lecture hall, and is linked to the main teaching building.

Plastic trays suspend the plants on the surface of the effluent treatment tanks.

An inspection chamber is set in the 1-metre thick layer of planted gravel.

The top of the tanks is at table-height level, facilitating monitoring and maintenance.

The Living Machine is a water treatment system developed by John Todd that can provide primary, secondary and tertiary treatment to blackwater, greywater and industrial effluent. The Living Machine combines traditional and natural wastewater treatment systems. These systems are carefully designed, combining the appropriate technology with living organisms, such as micro-organisms, algae, snails, fish and planting, including flowers and trees, and can be adjusted as required to achieve virtually zero contaminants in the treated water. The design of the systems is tailored to the different types of waste, ranging from sewage to chemical waste, and have been sized to treat from 1,400 litres to 3.4 million litres per day.

At Adam Joseph Lewis Center, grey- and blackwater from the WCs is flushed to an underground septic tank where solids settle at the bottom of the tank and are anaerobically digested. The effluent resulting from this primary treatment is transferred to a second aerated tank, where aerobic digestion takes place. From here the effluent is pumped to three planted tanks in a greenhouse. These tanks contain plastic trays fixed near the surface of the water, on which plants are supported with their plant roots dangling in the water. Most of the plants are tropical, with some native plants. The roots provide an appropriate environment for waste-digesting microbial growth. As the water passes through these tanks it is biologically treated, after which it is transferred to a clarifier that filters and retains the microbes and reintroduces them into the planted tanks. From the clarifier the water is passed through a perforated pipe on the east end of the greenhouse. The perforated pipe is located in the 1m deep planted gravel mass that surrounds the tanks. The water passes from the east to the west side of the greenhouse through the gravel and the roots of the plants and is further cleaned. The final stage of the purification process involves passing the water though an ultraviolet disinfection unit, before it is used to flush urinals and WCs once again. The system can process up to 11,000 litres of grey- and blackwater per day. All of the water used in the building, is cleaned via the Living Machine. Of the water used in the building 80 per cent is used to flush WCs and all that comes from Living Machine.

This closed loop system requires monitoring and maintaining, for example, the plants need to be renewed every four years and the septic tank needs emptying every three. However, these requirements have been integrated within the teaching programme of the college. Students monitor the quality of the purified water testing for acidity, dissolved oxygen and suspended solids, as well as testing the microbes in the planted tanks to ensure that the correct mixture of microbes is present. The system has attracted the attention of students from outside the environmental studies course and is successfully working to raise awareness of environmental issues in general in addition to water-related problems and solutions.

See also: avoiding chemical and biological disease agents **Chapter 3.2**

Case study: Sewage as a resource

Human waste contains valuable nutrients such as nitrates, potash and phosphates. Making use of these nutrients as a natural fertiliser contributes to closing the nutrient cycle of the land. On a large scale, city sewage systems can dry and granulate sewage, making it appropriate for use as a fertiliser. Bristol-based Wessex Water operates a sewage recycling plant to treat and dry the sewage for the more than half a million inhabitants of the Bristol area (Girardet 1999b). On a small scale, composting toilets create a safe manure that can be applied to soil.

On a medium scale, an experimental system has been installed in 106 houses and the school in the solarCity in Linz. The system collects urine and faeces separately and uses them as fertilisers in the nearby farms.

The system involves the use of urine-separating toilets. The toilets, which look identical to standard toilets, have to be used sitting down. The weight of the user operates a valve that diverts the urine to a collection tank in the basement of the building. When the user stands up, the valve closes. A dual flush mechanism allows the user to flush up to 4–6 litres or as little as 1 litre, depending on requirements. The soil waste is flushed through a separate pipe to a settlement tank. Here the solids are separated from the water, which is transferred to a plant-based treatment area, before being discharged into the nearby river.

The urine is collected by the local farmers as soon as the tanks are full. Urine contains 70–80 per cent of the nitrates and 30–50 per cent of the phosphates disposed of by the human body and is sterile and therefore relatively safe to handle. Diluted with five parts of water, it can be used on plants and has a similar fertilising value to pig manure, but is more easily assimilated by the plants.

The decomposed solid waste is also used by the farmers, thus reducing the amount of synthetic fertilisers used and the need for central sewage treatment.

solarCity School
Pichling, Linz, Austria

Architects: Michael Loudon
Drainage technology: Linz AG Abwasser
Development company: Universale Bau AG, Bank Austria, CA
Completed: 2003

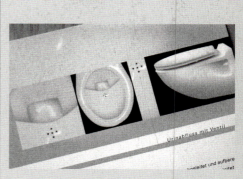

Internal view of school.

Extract from brochure describing the operation of the urine separating toilet.

External view of school with its sun-shaded extensive glazed passive solar façade.

See also: comprehensive planning **Chapter 1.1**

See also: sharing nature **Chapter 1.3**

See also: deleterious materials **Chapter 3.2**

See also: electromagnetic fields **Chapter 3.2**

See also: sustainable urban drainage **Chapter 6.3**

Postscript, Appendices
& Bibliography

Postscript

> The first step towards reducing our ecological impact is to recognise that the
> environmental crisis is less an environmental and technical problem than it is
> a behavioural and social one. It can therefore be resolved only with the help
> of behavioural and social solutions.
>
> Our Ecological Footprint, Wackernagel and Rees 1996

Researching this book I came across many extraordinary individuals, who are dedicated to improving people's lives while protecting the environment. They are the pioneers of our communities, and they are open to accepting both the responsibility and the challenge of promoting change. Gradually more and more of the population is following their lead, even if at a distance.

In order to develop a more sustainable world, change is essential, but people are generally reluctant to embrace it. It is disruptive and its outcomes are uncertain. Sometimes, perhaps, the change required seems so huge, and the outcomes so alien, that we subconsciously decide to ignore it. Resistance to it is particularly strong when it is perceived to put our quality of life at risk. As mentioned in the Introduction, attaining a more sustainable society will require a significant shift in our social values.

Our society generally values individuals for their social status and personal wealth, often made evident by overt consumption. In a sustainable society, the value of individuals might be measured by their contribution to society, rather than by how much they can extract from it. Making money may become a by-product of running a successful business and providing employment to local people, instead of its focus. To achieve such a society, the goals and expectations of many individuals would have to adapt significantly. Yet research into happiness encouragingly suggests that people are subconsciously and increasingly consciously striving for a life determined by social values that bring happiness without relying on economic wealth and excessive consumption (Layard 2005). People need to be educated about the advantages of a society that focuses on human relationships, the community and environment rather than competitive consumerism.

However, social change driven by education requires time, and the current shift towards a more sustainable society is occurring at a slower rate than the environmental degradation. The process of social transformation must occur faster and on a much larger scale, if we are to slow down, let alone halt, the environmental degradation that is already occurring.

As unpalatable as it may appear to some, legislative and financial measures are the only way to provide for relatively expedient change. This assertion is supported by historic evidence. In the building industry alone, legislation was necessary to outlaw ozone-depleting substances, introduce improvements in energy efficiency, and ban the use of toxic materials. Financial pressure has also been effective in encouraging environmental improvements. For instance, the oil price increases of the 1970s triggered a phase, albeit short-lived, of designing for energy efficiency. Currently, legislation and financial incentives are being introduced to counteract global warming. The European Union, for instance, has started carbon emissions trading and in the UK the thermal standards for buildings are being improved for the second time in only a few years. However, these initiatives are unlikely to be sufficient to achieve the reductions recommended by the scientific community. Moreover, a system to hold individuals directly accountable remains absent.

A compulsory individual scheme is key to achieving the environmental improvements needed. It would not only accelerate the speed of change, but also be an effective means of educating the general population. Too often, well-meaning voluntary initiatives, such as the widespread community recycling schemes, are simply ignored. On the other hand, initiatives that carry legal consequences, such as that against drink driving, both educate and induce individuals to act responsibly. In many European countries, within a few decades, drink driving went from being a minor offence, to being socially unacceptable and providing grounds for manslaughter convictions. We are seeing similar changes with respect to smoking. The difference between drink driving or smoking and global warming, is that the impacts of global warming appear unrelated, often being displaced in time and location from their causes. Many people have personal knowledge of the effects of drink driving and smoking. The effects of global warming, on the other hand, are impersonal, complex and not easily visualised. Society needs to be made aware of its global impacts.

The challenge is to create a legislative and financial system that holds individuals personally responsible for their environmental impacts. The ecological footprint (see p.12) would form a comprehensive base for calculating an individual's impact, but the system is very complex. A promising system, in terms of relevance and implementation possibilities, is one developed in the UK that focuses on global warming and works by allocating individual CO_2 quotas to all adults.

The Domestic Tradeable Quotas (DTQ) scheme developed by David Fleming and researchers at the Tyndall Centre for Climate Change Research, based in the UK, aims to make individuals accountable for their personal production of CO_2. The scheme would set a cap on the amount of CO_2 that UK households could emit each year. The annual budget would be shared equally among the adult population, which would also be issued with a CO_2 swipe card to keep track of each individual's personal carbon account. Unused credits would be traded for money through a national database, while individuals who run out of credits would have to purchase more, subject to availability. As the total budget would be capped, the total emissions could only drop and the concept would be to slowly reduce the cap to eventually achieve a safe level of carbon emissions (Anderson and Starkey 2004).

Because the issue of sustainability will only become more critical to life on Earth, it is likely that a system of personal accounting will have to be instituted. As with income tax, there will always be those who fight it or avoid it; a fact that does not put into question the strength of the system. Personal allocations would have to be calculated on the basis of all humans sharing the Earth equally. This would provide people in developing countries with scope and financial assistance to improve their quality of life, and help to create a more equitable and sustainable global society.

In such a scenario, built environment professionals would help individuals achieve reductions in their ecological footprints and carbon emissions, as well as help to improve their quality of life. The nature of the architectural work may change too, placing more emphasis on refurbishing existing buildings, urban improvements, landscaping and ecological product design.

To implement personal accounting systems and more stringent environmental legislation, the political environment has to be conducive to such interventions. Effecting change from the bottom up may be too slow, but the top-down approach also depends heavily on popular support. Without an educated electorate, radical top-down legislative changes will be politically unsustainable. However the change is needed to create more a sustainable society is effected, people play a fundamental role in the process; their education, therefore, remains a key element in the puzzle of sustainable development.

Maps	Projects	Information included in chapter(s) – project details in chapter listed in bold text	Compact city centre living	Reduced car dependency	Enhancing flora and fauna	Local food production	Community participation	Affordable living	Promoting training/employment	Enhancing community facilities	Actively promoting sustainability	Indoor air pollutants avoided	Zero potential toxins, e.g. PVC	EMF considered	Focus on accessibility	Restorative environment	Design for longevity and flexibility
3	21st Century Homes	3.3						•					•		•		•
4	Akademie Mont-Cenis	3.3/**5.3**					•		•	•						•	•
2	Argonne Center	**1.4**/2.5	•	•	•	•	•					•				•	
3	Barling Court	2.2	•	•				•									•
3	BCZEB	5.3		•	•					•	•	•				•	•
3	BedZED	4.5	•	•	•			•		•	•						•
3	BRE Building 16	5.0/4.2									•	•					•
3	Buoy Wharf	2.3	•					•	•								•
3	Carlisle Lane Housing	3.2	•	•				•									•
3	Chorlton Park	5.1			•			•								•	•
1	College Library SCU	5.1								•							•
4	Design Centre, Linz	3.1								•		•					•
3	Dyfi Eco Park	3.1/5.1/5.2			•				•			•					
3	Eden bus shelter	4.4										•	•				
1	Ellenbrook	2.5		•			•	•		•	•					•	
2	Environmental Discovery Center	4.1		•						•	•					•	
2	Environmental Showcase Home	6.1		•							•	•					
3	Fairfield Housing	2.1/3.2		•			•	•	•	•		•	•		•		
3	Gallions Ecopark	4.6	•	•			•										
4	Glashaus	2.4/3.2	•	•	•		•		•	•		•				•	
3	Glencoe Visitors Centre	4.1								•						•	•
3	Goethean Science Centre	2.1/3.4			•	•	•		•	•		•	•		•	•	
3	Greenwich Sainsbury's	5.2			•					•	•						•
2	Hidden Villa	5.3			•	•	•		•							•	
3	Hockerton Housing	**1.4**/5.3/6.3			•	•	•	•	•	•		•	•			•	
4	IGA Westpark	2.4		•	•						•					•	
3	Integer House	4.1/4.6									•	•			•		•
2	Lewis Center	3.2/6.3			•	•	•		•	•	•	•			•	•	•
3	London Fields Housing	1.2/**2.2**	•	•		•	•	•	•	•							•
2	Loudoun EcoVillage	1.3/3.4			•	•	•			•		•					•
1	Lyola Pavillions	1.3			•												•
2	Macoskey Center	4.6/6.3			•	•	•		•	•	•					•	•
3	Mile End Park	1.3		•	•		•			•					•	•	•
3	Millennium Green	5.3/**6.2**			•		•		•	•	•	•					•
4	Petuel Ring	1.2		•	•						•					•	
2	Phillip Merrill Center	1.2/5.2/**6.2**		•	•		•		•	•	•	•					•
2	Phoenix Central Library	5.1									•						•
1	Pinakarri Cohousing	**2.2**/2.3/5.1	•	•	•		•		•	•		•			•	•	•
1	Piney Lakes	6.3			•		•			•	•						
3	Powergen HQ	4.5			•											•	•
3	Queens Building	5.1	•	•						•	•	•					•
2	Resourceful Building	4.6	•					•				•					•
3	Robin Hood Chase	2.3/**2.4**					•		•	•		•					
4	RWE	5.1			•					•						•	•
2	Sanders Eco-Renovation	4.2						•								•	•
1	Sandy Information Centre	1.3			•					•					•		
4	Schreiber House	5.2			•	•					•	•				•	•
3	Slateford Green	1.2/3.3	•	•	•			•								•	•
4	solarCity Linz	1.1/1.3/3.2/6.3	•	•	•		•	•	•	•		•	•	•	•	•	
4	Solar Fabrik	5.3			•					•	•	•					•
4	Solarhaus Freiburg	5.1			•						•	•					•
4	Solarsiedlung	5.3	•	•	•			•		•		•	•				•
3	The Autonomous House	6.2				•						•					•
3	The Point	1.1/1.2	•	•			•			•							•
1	Thurgoona Campus	**4.4**/5.1/5.3/6.1/6.3		•					•	•		•				•	•
1	Uluru Kata Tjuta Centre	2.1			•		•		•	•		•					
4	Vaubon Freiburg	1.2	•	•			•			•		•					•
3	Weald & Downlands	4.3					•		•	•	•	•					•
3	Winter Gardens	2.4			•					•					•	•	•
3	York Road Housing	2.2						•				•			•	•	

Projects	Use of waste materials	Use of renewable/certified materials	Use of low manufacturing impact materials	Waste minimisation in construction	Waste minimisation in use	Minimise heat loss and passive heating	Passive/natural ventilation and cooling	Maximum natural light provision	Energy-efficient services and equipment	Performance assessment or monitoring	Renewable energy systems	Water-efficient appliances	Waterless toilets	Grey- or rainwater recycling	Rainwater collection for all uses	Alternative sewage system	SUD
21st Century Homes		•		•		•	•	•	•			•					
Akademie Mont-Cenis		•				•	•	•	•			•					•
Argonne Center	•	•	•			•	•	•	•		•	•					
Barling Court				•		•	•		•								
BCZEB	•	•		•	•	•	•	•	•	•	•	•					•
BedZED		•		•		•	•	•	•	•	•	•		•		•	•
BRE Building 16	•	•	•	•	•	•	•	•	•	•	•	•					•
Buoy Wharf	•			•			•										
Carlisle Lane Housing		•	•	•		•	•					•					
Chorlton Park		•	•			•	•	•									•
College Library SCU						•		•				•					
Design Centre Linz							•	•				•					•
Dyfi Eco Park	•	•	•			•	•	•	•	•		•					•
Eden bus shelter	•	•	•				•	•	•								
Ellenbrook		•		•		•	•										•
Environmental Discovery Center		•				•	•	•	•		•						
Environmental Showcase Home	•	•				•	•	•	•			•		•			
Fairfield Housing	•	•				•	•	•	•								
Gallions Ecopark		•			•	•	•	•	•	•	•	•		•			
Glashaus						•	•	•				•					
Glencoe Visitors Centre		•	•			•	•	•	•			•				•	•
Goethean Science Centre		•	•	•		•	•	•	•		•	•	•				•
Greenwich Sainsbury's	•				•	•	•	•	•	•	•	•					
Hidden Villa		•	•			•	•	•	•		•						
Hockerton Housing		•	•			•	•	•	•			•		•	•	•	•
IGA Westpark																	•
Integer House	•	•		•	•	•	•	•	•	•	•	•		•			•
Lewis Center	•	•				•	•	•	•	•	•	•				•	•
London Fields Housing	•	•				•	•	•	•			•					
Loudoun EcoVillage	•	•	•	•	•	•	•	•	•		•	•				•	•
Lyola Pavilions		•						•	•				•				
Macoskey Center	•	•				•	•	•	•		•	•	•			•	•
Mile End Park						•	•	•	•								•
Millennium Green						•	•	•	•	•	•			•			•
Petuel Ring																	
Phillip Merrill Center	•	•	•	•	•	•	•	•	•		•	•	•	•			•
Phoenix Central Library								•									
Pinakarri Cohousing	•				•	•	•	•	•	•							•
Piney Lakes	•	•	•			•	•	•	•	•		•		•	•		
Powergen HQ						•	•	•	•								•
Queens Building						•	•	•	•	•		•					•
Resourceful Building	•	•		•		•	•	•									
Robin Hood Chase	•	•	•			•	•	•	•			•		•			
RWE						•	•	•	•	•	•						•
Sanders Eco-Renovation		•				•		•									
Sandy Information Centre							•	•				•					•
Schreiber House	•	•		•	•	•	•	•	•			•					•
Slateford Green	•	•				•	•	•	•			•					•
solarCity Linz		•	•		•	•	•	•	•		•	•				•	•
Solar Fabrik						•	•	•	•		•	•	•				•
Solarhaus Freiburg						•	•	•	•	•	•	•					•
Solarsiedlung		•		•	•	•	•	•	•		•						•
The Autonomous House					•	•	•	•	•	•			•		•	•	
The Point						•	•	•	•	•		•					
Thurgoona Campus	•			•	•	•	•	•	•	•			•	•		•	•
Uluru Kata Tjuta Centre		•	•					•	•						•		•
Vaubon Freiburg																	•
Weald & Downlands	•	•	•	•	•	•	•	•									•
Winter Gardens		•				•	•	•									
York Road Housing						•	•	•	•			•					•

Locations, latitudes and solar irradiation (KWh/m²/year)

Map 1 – Australia

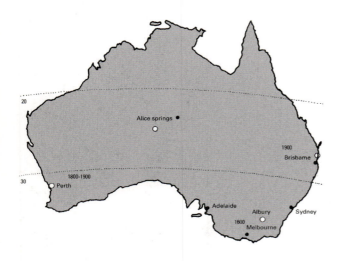

Map 2 – United States

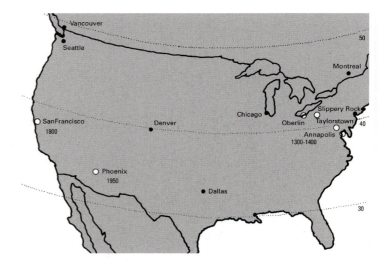

Map 3 – United Kingdom

Map 4 – Central Europe

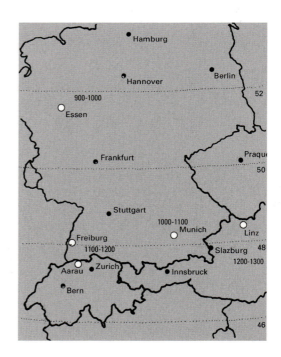

AVERAGE TEMPERATURES AND PRECIPITATION DATA (www.weatherbase.com, *www.metoffice.gov.uk/climate/uk/average/)

Climate	Weather station	Case study		Yearly average temperature °C	Yearly average high °C	Yearly average low °C	Average January temperature °C	Average January high °C	Average January low °C	Average July temperature °C	Average July high °C	Average July low °C	Average yearly precipitation mm	Mean January precipitation mm	Mean July precipitation mm
Temperate (maritime) – No Dry Season, Cool Summer	Fort William	Glencoe Centre		8	11	6	4	6	2	15	17	12	1930	220	120
	Perth UK	Fairfield Perth		8	12	4	3	6	0	15	20	10	780	60	70
	Edinburgh	Slateford Green / Pishwanton Gridshell		8	11	5	3	6	0	15	18	10	660	50	60
	Manchester	Chorlton Park / Winter Gardens		10	12	6	4	6	1	16	19	12	900	70	80
	Lincoln	Gusto / Hockerton Housing / Robin Hood Chase / The Autonomous House		9	13	5	2	5	0	16	21	11	590	50	60
	Rugby	Queens Building		9	12	6	2	5	0	14	18	11	620	60	50
	Coventry	Powergen HQ		9	12	5	3	6	1	16	12	11	670	50	50
	Aberystwyth,	CAT Visitors BLD		9				5		15			1010	95	74
	Cambridge	Dyfi Eco Park / Ionica HQ		9	13	5	2	5	0	15	20	11	530	50	50
	London	Alyesbury / BedZED / Carlisle Lane / Sainsbury's / London Fields / BCZEB	Barling Court / Buoy Wharf / Gallion / Integer / Mile End	10	13	5	3	6	1	16	21	11	750	70	40
	Bristol	The Point		11	13	8	5	7	3	18	21	14	719*	70*	47*
	Portsmouth	Weald & Downlands		10	13	7	5	7	2	17	20	13	790*	81*	47*
	Plymouth	Eden bus shelter		11	13	8	6	8	4	16	19	13	960	100	60
Temperate (continental) – No Dry Season, Cool Summer	Essen	Akademie Mont-Cenis / Glashaus / RWE		10	12	6	2	3	0	17	21	13	910	70	90
	Munich	IGA Westpark / Petuel Ring		8	12	3	-1	2	-4	17	22	12	920	40	120
	Freiburg	Solarhaus Freiburg / Solar Fabrik / Solarsiedlung / Vauban		9	13	6	1	3	-1	18	24	13	880	40	100
	Linz	Design Centre / SolarCity		8	12	5	-1	1	-3	18	23	13	860	50	110
	Zurich	Schreiber House		9	12	6	0	2	-1	18	22	14	1070	60	120
Temperate – No Dry Season, Warm/Hot Summer	Slippery Rock	Macoskey Center		8	15	2	-4	0	-9	20	27	13	1010	60	100
	Oberlin	Lewis Center		9	15	2	-5	0	-10	21	28	14	890	40	90
	Arlington	Loudoun EcoVillage		14	19	9	2	6	-2	26	31	21	990	70	100
	Annapolis	Phillip Merrill Center		13	19	8	1	5	-4	25	30	19	1060	80	90
Temperate – Summer Dry and Cool	San Francisco	Argonne Center / Hidden Villa / Resourceful Building / Sanders Eco-Renovation		13	17	10	10	13	7	15	18	12	510	100	
Dry climates – hot and very dry	Phoenix	Phoenix Ecohouse / Phoenix Library / Refurbished House		22	30	15	12	18	5	33	40	26	190	20	20
	Alice Springs	Uluru		21	28	13	28	36	21	11	19	3	270	30	10
Temperate – Summer Dry and Warm/Hot	Perth	Ellenbrook / Pinakarra / Piney Lakes		18	23	11	24	31	16	12	17	7	800	8	160
Temperate – No Dry Season, Warm/Hot Summer	Brisbane	Lyola / College Library, Sunshine Coast University / Sandy Information Centre		20	25	15	25	28	21	15	20	9	1190	160	60
	Albury	Thurgoona Campus		15	21	8	22	30	14	7	12	2	740	40	100

Bibliography

Addis, B., Talbot, R. (2001) *Sustainable Construction Procurement: A Guide to Delivering Environmentally Responsible Projects*, CIRIA C571, London: Construction Industry Research and Information Association

Addis, W., Schouten, J. (2004) *Principles of Design for Deconstruction to Facilitate Reuse and Recycling*, London: Construction Industry Research and Information Association

Addison, J. (1990) 'Asbestos', in *Building and Health: The Rosehaugh Guide*, London: RIBA Publications

Anderson, J., Shiers, D.E., Sinclair, M. (2002) *The Green Guide to Specification: An Environmental Profiling System for Building Materials and Components*, Oxford; Malden, MA: Blackwell Science

Anderson, K., Starkey, R. (2004) *Domestic Tradable Quotas: A Policy Instrument for the Reduction of Greenhouse Gas Emissions*, UMIST: Tyndall Centre for Climate Change Research

Arnold, D. (2004) 'Airy offices create 15% work boost', *Building Design*, 16 July 2004

Asthma UK (2004) *Asthma Fact File: The Asthma Audit*, London: Asthma UK

Attfield, R. (1999) *The Ethics of the Global Environment*, Edinburgh: Edinburgh University Press

Baker, N. (2001) 'Designing for comfort: Recognising the adaptive urge', Keynote presentation, *Cooling Frontiers Symposium*, College of Architecture and Environmental design, Arizona State University, Tempe, AZ, 4–7 October 2001

Baker, N., Steemers, K. (2000) *Energy and Environment in Architecture*, London: E&FN Spon

Barnes, M.A. (1994) 'A study of the process of emotional healing in outdoor spaces and the concomitant landscape design implications', Master of Landscape Architecture thesis, Berkeley: University of California, cited in Cooper Marcus, C., Barnes, M. (1999) *Healing Gardens: Therapeutic Benefits and Design Recommendations*, New York: John Wiley and Sons

Barton, H. *et al.* (1995) *Sustainable Settlements: A Guide for Planners, Designers and Developers*, University of the West of England and the Local Government Management Board

Barton, H. *et al.* (2002) *Shaping Neighbourhoods: A Guide for Health, Sustainability and Vitality*, London: E&FN Spon

Barton, H., Tsourou, C. (2000) *Healthy Urban Planning: A WHO Guide to Planning for People*, London: E&FN Spon

BCA (British Cement Association) (2001) *Ecoconcrete*, Crowthorne: British Cement Association

Beatley, T. (2000) *Green Urbanism: Learning from European Cities*, Washington, DC: Island Press

Bell, P.A. *et al.* (1978) *Environmental Psychology*, Philadelphia, PA: W.B. Saunders Company

Berge, B. (2000) *Ecology of Building Materials*, London: Architectural Press

BGW (2000) 'Bundeswasser und Gas' www.bgw.de

Bonnes, M., Secchiroli, G. (1995) *Environmental Psychology*, London: Sage Publications

Bordass, W. (1995) *Comfort, Control and Energy Efficiency in Offices*, BRE Information Paper IP3/95

Borer, P., Harris, C. (1998) *The Whole House Book*, Machynlleth: Centre for Alternative Technology

Bower, J. (2001) *The Healthy House: How to Buy One, How to Build One and How to Cure a Sick One*, Bloomington: The Healthy House Institute

BRE (2003) *Construction and Demolition Waste Report GBG 57 Part I and II*, Watford: Building Research Establishment

BRESCU (2000) *Energy Consumption Guide 19*, Watford: Building Research Establishment

Brophy, V. *et al.* (2000) *Sustainable Urban Design*, Dublin: Energy Research Group

Brundtland, G.H. *et al.* (1987) *Our Common Future*, Oxford: Oxford University Press

Burton, S (ed) (2001) *Energy Efficient Office Refurbishment*, London: James and James

Bush, B. (1997) *Ecology of a Changing Planet*, Englewood Cliffs, New Jersey: Prentice Hall

Butler, D., Davies, J.W. (2000) *Urban Drainage*, London: E&FN Spon

BWEA (The British Wind Energy Association) (2004) *Why Wind?* London: The British Wind Energy Association

Caborn, A. (2002) 'Could you feel at home with nowhere to park?', *The Observer*, 21 April 2002, p. 8

Chambers, N. *et al.* (2000) *Sharing Nature's Interest: Ecological Footprints as an Indicator of Sustainability*, London: Earthscan Publications Ltd.

CIBSE (1999) *Guide A: Environmental Design*, London: Chartered Institute of Building Services Engineers

CIRIA (1995) *Environmental Impact of Building and Construction Materials, Volume A – Summary, SP116*, London: Construction Industry Research Information Association

CIRIA (2000) *Sustainable Urban Drainage Systems: Design Manual for England and Wales*, CIRIA C522, London: Construction Industry Research Information Association

Clough, R., Martin, R. (1995) *Environmental Impact of Building and Construction Materials – Report 12 – Minerals*, London: CIRIA

Cooper Marcus, C., Barnes, M. (1999) *Healing Gardens: Therapeutic Benefits and Design Recommendations*, New York: John Wiley and Sons

Coventry, S. *et al.* (1999) *The Reclaimed and Recycled Construction Materials Handbook*, London: Construction Industry Research and Information Association

Coward, S.K.D. *et al.* (2001) *Indoor Air Quality in Homes in England*, BRE Report 433, Garston: CRC Ltd.

CPRE (Campaign to Protect Rural England) (2003) *Housing and Urban Sprawl*, London: CPRE

Crook, T. *et al.* (2002) *Planning Gain and Affordable Housing*, London: Joseph Rowntree Foundation

Crown (2003) *Energy White Paper. Our Energy Future, Creating a Low Carbon Economy*, Norwich: The Stationery Office

Crown (United Kingdom Government) (1998) *Our Healthier Nation: A Contract for Health*, Green Paper, London: HMSO

Crowther. D. (1994) 'Health considerations in house design', *PhD. thesis*, Cambridge University

Curwell, S. *et al.* (eds) (1990) *Buildings and Health: The Rosehaugh Guide*, London: RIBA Publications

Curwell, S. *et al.* (2002) *Materials: A Guide to the Selection of Environmentally Responsible Alternatives*, London: E&FN Spon

DaimlerChrysler (2004) 'DaimlerChrysler delivers the first fuel cell cars to customers in Berlin', Online: www.daimlerchrysler.com/projects

Daly, H. (1991) *Steady State Economics*, Washington, DC: Island Press, cited in Meadows *et al.* (1992) *Beyond The Limits*, London: Earthscan Publications Limited

Daly, H., Cobb, J. (1989) *For the Common Good*, London: Green Print

Day, C. (1990) *Places of the Soul : Architecture and Environmental Design as a Healing Art*, London: Aquarian